GARDNER'S *guide to*

colleges for **multimedia** & **animation** (4th Edition)

Garth Gardner, Ph.D.

GARTH GARDNER COMPANY

GGC publishing

Washington DC, USA · London, UK

Art Director: Nic Banks
Editorial: Chris Edwards

Editorial inquiries concerning this book
should be e-mailed to: info@ggcinc.com.
www.gogardner.com

Disclaimer
After publication of this manuscript,
changes may occur in the academic calendar,
admission and graduation requirements,
academic programs, course offerings,
regulations, staff, and tuition and fees. Such
changes administered by the individual
colleges and universities in this manuscript
should take precedence over this book. While
reasonable effort will be made to update
changes in subsequent editions, the reader
is encouraged to seek current information
from appropriate offices at the institute,
because responsibility for complying with all
applicable requirements ultimately rests with
the student or reader.

Although the author attempts to list the
courses in various academic departments,
course offerings may be limited by financial,
space, and staffing considerations, or may
otherwise be unavailable. Nothing in this
manuscript may be construed to promise
or guarantee registration in any course or
course of study (whether required or elective),
nor may anything be construed to promise
or guarantee acceptance into an academic
program.

GGC/Publishing is a department of, and
Gardner's Guide is a trademark of Garth
Gardner Company, Inc.

Library of Congress Cataloging-in-Publication Data

Gardner, Garth.
  Gardner's guide to colleges for multimedia and animation / Garth
Gardner.-- 4th ed.
    p. cm.
  Includes index.
  ISBN 1-58965-019-0 (pbk.)
  1. Computer graphics--Study and teaching (Higher)--United
States--Directories. 2. Computer graphics--Vocational guidance--United
States--Directories. 3. Universities and colleges--United
States--Directories. I. Title: Colleges for multimedia and animation. II.
Title.
  T385.G36 2004
  006.7'071'173--dc22
                              2004002908
Printed in Canada

Table of Contents

Acknowledgement

The author thanks the many people who have helped research, review, and design the materials in this current edition, including: Chris Edwards and Nic Banks. For shaping this project in the early editions, thanks to: Bonney Ford, Dexter Paul, Brenda Sanabria, Jim Hill, Dori Le Grand, Michelle Smilo, Kim Alexander, Debbie Young, Philip Gardner, Della Capers, Nic Banks, Tomoko Miki, Dr. Noel Mayo, and Prof. Gregory P. Garvey. In addition, I thank all the associates of GGC Publishing for their invaluable help and support.

About the Author

Garth Gardner, Ph.D. is a former professor of animation and multimedia. He has taught and lectured at several universities including The Ohio State University, William Paterson University, University of California Los Angeles, Fashion Institute of Technology, Florida A&M University, University of Southern California, Xavier University, and George Mason University. Dr. Gardner has spoken at numerous high schools and is the author of several books on the subject of computer graphics and animation. He is a graduate of San Francisco State University and The Ohio State University.

About this Book

Introduction

This book is written for the high school student, graduating senior, and college graduate who wishes to begin to pursue an academic career in the field of Computer Graphics and Animation. In short, it is written for the person who dreams of joining the ranks of an elite group of creative artists and scientists that are in the business of creating visual effects for feature films, experimental art, or television commercials. It is often difficult for beginners in this field to determine the academic path necessary to become a computer artist, scientist, or animator. These fields are still fairly new and most colleges have only recently begun to offer courses and degree programs in this area.

Gardner's Guide is designed to assist prospective students to locate a college, university, or institute that offers high- to low-end Computer Graphics through an Art or Science academic curriculum. This book will help students interested in Computer Graphics to answer the following questions:

What colleges and universities offer degree programs in Computer Graphics and Animation in the U.S?

Through which academic programs or departments are the degrees offered?

Who is the contact person?

What financial aid options are available through the department or school?

How many students are in the program or school?

What does the school cost for residents or non-residents of the state?

This guide is the first step to answering these questions and many others. The guide is designed to be used to quickly reference information on colleges that offer degree programs in Computer Graphics and Animation. Students are also advised to enlist the service of an academic guidance counselor to assist them in the process of selecting a college or university.

Computer Art Versus Computer Science Programs

Perhaps you are already aware of the differences between a degree in Computer Graphics from an Art School or Department versus a degree in Computer Graphics from a Science or Engineering Department; however, it is important to shed some light on this distinction. This book addresses, and combines two large groups of academic disciplines: Computer Graphics-Art Programs and Computer Graphics-Science Programs.

Computer Graphics-Art Programs profile the schools that offer a course or a degree program in Computer Graphics through their fine art- or design-related department. These degree programs may include, but are not limited to, the following emphasized areas: Multimedia, Graphic Design, Digital Photography, 3D Modeling and Animation, Web Design, and Interface Design. These programs usually emphasize the aesthetics of the art, and provide technical training on computer graphics software packages. In the Computer-Art program, computer training is the necessary means to achieve the art or design. The Artist is viewed as an end user of the computer, using the hardware and software to visualize his concepts. The artist is not limited being an end user. Often an Art major may choose to take electives in the Science area to enhance his knowledge of the computer operating system.

Computer Graphics Art majors may enroll in such science-based courses as C Programming, IRIX and UNIX.

Computer Graphics-Science Programs profile the schools whose computer science or engineering departments offer exemplary programs in Computer Science, with an emphasis in Computer Graphics. In addition, the science programs may also offer the following areas of emphasis: Virtual Reality, 3D Modeling, Animation, Advanced Visualization, and Medical Simulation. The science programs profiled in this book offer a computer science curriculum that teaches students how to program 2D and 3D computer graphics. The computer scientist is interested in creating new software or personalizing existing software, interfacing, or hardware that can be used to create or enhance a computer-generated image.

Training Versus Education in the Computer Graphics Field

Perhaps one of the most important issues for a student entering an academic Computer Graphics program is the issue of training versus education. Before enrolling in an academic program, the student should realize that this distinction is made in most academic programs. For example, a student who has graduated from a four-year college experience may go back to school to be trained on the latest Computer Graphics tools. On the other hand, a recent high-school graduate may seek an education in the discipline. Training is more direct and focused. The trained student will be able to operate a specific software, hardware etc.; however, the trained individual often needs to be retrained as the software or hardware is upgraded. In the Computer Art discipline a trained individual may understand the computer rather than the

art and aesthetics; they are technically proficient. An education is more general, not specific to any one hardware or software; rather, it is often more theoretical.

Profiled Categories

The schools that are profiled in this book offer programs or courses in Computer Graphics, Animation, or Multimedia at the graduate or undergraduate level. The schools are listed alphabetically by the name of the institution and are categorized alphabetically by geographic location. For each profiled school, the following facts are presented: Degrees Offered; Curricular; Facilities; Student Body; Faculty Profile; Deadlines and Financial Aid; Admission Requirement; Expenses, and Contact Person.

In some cases, the author has chosen to include relevant historical or other facts that may interest the prospective student. This information is included in the category named: Additional Information.

Financial Aid

Financial aid is available in the forms of loans, grants and scholarships. Financial aid is available to both undergraduate and graduate students. To apply for financial aid, a student must submit a Free Application for Federal Student Aid Programs. This form is available through the prospective school's financial aid office, or from a high school guidance counselor's office. Graduate students may apply in a similar manner for federal aid, however, graduate assistantships are available at most universities. Graduate assistantships give graduate students the opportunity to teach at the university or assist with research in return for a tuition waiver and a monthly stipend. Graduate students interested in these forms of financial aid should contact the department directly or the graduate school at the university. A graduate student may also be eligible to receive fellowships.

International Students' Admissions

International students are usually required to submit official transcripts from all previous secondary and post-secondary education institutions. American schools usually request that the transcripts be submitted in the language of the home school, and should also be accompanied by a certified English translation, preferably obtained from the student's national consulate in the Department of Education.

Applicants from non-English-speaking countries must demonstrate proficiency in the English language by submitting the TOEFL (Test of English as a Foreign Language) scores, by successfully completing courses in English for foreign students at a college or university in the United States, or by completing such courses at a recognized English-language program in a foreign country. Substantiation of English-language proficiency must be submitted prior to enrollment at the college. A minimum score of 550 on the TOEFL is necessary for admission to most colleges or universities.

International students must complete the school's financial affidavit and have all signatures officially notarized, indicating that he/she has made satisfactory arrangements for financing all educational and living expenses while in the United States.

A Certificate of Eligibility (I-20) will be issued only after the admissions requirements have been fulfilled, the student has been granted written acceptance by the school, and payment of the one-time, non-refundable acceptance fee and tuition deposit have been received. To remain in compliance with immigration regulations, international students must be enrolled for a minimum of 12 semester hours or full-time.

International students are usually billed for tuition at least twice and as much as four times the rate of in-state resident tuition. For assistance with the admission process, international students should contact the international students' office at the prospective college or university.

Abbreviations

Degrees

A.A.	Associate of Arts
A.S.	Associate of Science
B.A.	Bachelor of Arts
B.F.A.	Bachelor of Fine Arts
B.M.A	Bachelor of Media Arts
B.S.	Bachelor of Science
B.S.Sc.	Bachelor of Science in Science
D.E.	Doctor of Engineering
M.A.	Master of Arts
M.B.A.	Master of Business Administration
M.Eng.	Master of Engineering
M.F.A.	Master of Fine Arts
M.M.A.	Master of Media Arts
M.S.	Master of Science
M.S.C.S.	Master of Science in Computer Science
Ph.D.	Doctor of Philosophy
Ph.D.C.E.	Doctor of Philosophy in Computer Engineering
Sc.D.	Doctor of Science

Others

ACT	American College Testing Assessment
AVL	Advanced Visualization Lab.
CG	Computer Graphics
CLEP	General Examination of the College Level Examination Program
FAFSA	Free Application for Federal Student Aid
F/X	Visual Effects
GED	General Education Diploma
GPA	Grade Point Average
GRA	Graduate Research Assistant
GRE	Graduate Record Examination
GTA	Graduate Teaching Assistant
NSF	National Science Foundation
OS	Operating Systems
PC	Personal Computer
SAT	Scholastic Aptitude Test
SGI	Silicon Graphics Inc.
VR	Virtual Reality
2D	Two Dimension
3D	Three Dimension

Alabama

John C. Calhoun Community College

F/X Degrees Offered
A.A. through the Division of Fine Arts. Computer Graphics/Electric Imaging. Option II of Graphic Design Association of Applied Science degree.

Curricular
3D Modeling and Rendering; 2D Computer Animation; Multimedia/Interactive; Digital Painting/Drawing; Image Processing; Digital Video.

Facilities
Software used: Photoshop; Director; Illustrator; Freehand; PageMaker; QuarkXPress.

Student Body
Sixty undergraduate students are computer graphics majors. A total of 8,000 students attend the college.

Deadlines and Financial Aid
Various fellowships and traditional state, federal and city aid are available to students. Contact the Financial Aid Office for details on obtaining financial assistance at the college.

Admission Requirements
Application and fee, transcripts, and SAT or ACT scores.

Expenses
Tuition is $1,560 per semester.

Contact
P.O. Box 2216, Decatur, AL 35609. Telephone: 256-306-2500. Fax: 256-306-2885.

URL: Contact person: Dr. Arthur Bond. http://www.calhoun.cc.al.us./programs/.

University of Alabama at Birmingham

F/X Degrees Offered
The Computer and Information Sciences Department offers programs of study and research leading to the M.S. and Ph.D. degrees in computer and information sciences. Fields of specialization that reflect the interests of the faculty include computer graphics and vision, object-oriented distributed computing, artificial intelligence, and knowledge discovery and data mining.
The Ph. D. program usually requires a minimum of four years of study and research beyond the bachelor's degree. A minimum of one academic year of full-time residence is required. The M. S. program consists of 36 hours and can be completed in four semesters by students entering with no background deficiencies.

Curricular
Principles of Artificial Intelligence; Computer Graphics I and II; Image Processing; Modeling and Simulation I and II; Artificial Intelligence Seminar; Topics in Computer Graphics; Web-based technologies.

Facilities
Undergraduate students have access to a variety of computing resources including computing laboratories equipped with Microsoft Windows based workstations, Sun Solaris workstations and specialized laboratories for networking and telecommunication instruction using LINUX/Intel workstations. Additionally, students may apply for access to the various assets of the Alabama Supercomputer Center. In support of the doctoral

program and research the department sponsors research seminars, which involve guest lecturers and local graduate students and faculty who discuss research activities at the frontiers of the field. These seminars are open to all students in the department and undergraduate students may receive credit for attending.

Student Body
Total student enrollment exceeds 19,000.

Faculty Profile
There are 24 faculty members teaching in the Department of Computer and Information Science.

Deadlines and Financial Aid
The three main sources of aid available to UAB students are (a) appointments as a fellow or assistant, (b) awards from the individual graduate programs, and (c) federal aid programs administered by the Office of Student Financial Aid. Financial aid is also available in the form of Graduate Assistantships (GA's), Research Assistantships (RA's), and Minimum Duties Assistantships (MDA's). There are no forms to fill out for requesting financial aid. Most students are successful in obtaining assistantships or on-campus employment during their first year of study. The cost of living in Birmingham is less than average for most metropolitan areas. For Fall, ALL application materials (M.S. and Ph.D. programs) must be received by July 1. For Spring, ALL application materials (M.S. program only) must be received by September 1.

Admission Requirements
Undergraduates must submit an application form and processing fee, a complete set of official transcripts, admission test scores, and evaluation forms, a total of three are needed. Graduate students must submit an application and fee, GRE, transcripts, and letters of recommendation.

Expenses
Estimated tuition is $2,067 per semester for residents and $5,647 for non-residents.

Contact
Campbell Hall, Room 115-A, 1300 University Blvd., Birmingham, AL 35294-1170. Telephone: 205-934-2213 or 800-421-8743. Contact person: Tony Skjellum, Ph.D, Professor and Chair, UAB Department of Computer and Information Sciences. Email: tony@cis.uab.edu. URL: http://www.uab.edu/.

University of Alabama at Huntsville

F/X Degrees Offered
Computer Science Department. B.S., M.S., and Ph.D. Degrees. The Computer Science Department now offers a Master of Science in Software Engineering Degree.

Curricular
3D Modeling and Rendering; Introduction to Computer Graphics; Advanced Computer Graphics; Principles of Graphical User Interface Design; Computer Processing of Digital Images; Computer Geometry Modeling; Software Engineering.

Facilities
The department currently has two categories of computer systems: UNIX and Windows 2000/XP. This includes a network of Sun Sparc stations, a network of Silicon Graphics workstations, and a network of PCs. Along with access to a Cray at the nearby State of Alabama Supercomputing Center. The Linux software includes: Ascent Logic RDD-100-R4.1.1; GhostView 1.5; ImageMagick Tools; Khoros 2.2; LaTex 2e; and Sun Java Developers Kit 1.2.1. The Windows software includes: Borland

Turbo C++ 3.0; PV-WAVE Version 6.02; Rational Rose Enterprise Suite; and Sun Java Developers Kit 1.4.1. The computer lab also includes: (12) Digital Circuit Simulator/Tester and (12) IDL 800 Digital Labs Experimentational Bread Boards. The campus fiber backbone facilitates access to World Wide Web. The department has a microcomputing laboratory for instruction in logic design and computer architecture.

Student Body
There are 275 undergraduates and 160 graduate students in the department (50 Ph.D., 110 M.S.). Total enrollment of 6,800 students on campus.

Faculty Profile
There are 30 faculty members in the Computer Science Department.

Deadlines and Financial Aid
Various fellowships and traditional state, federal and city aid are available to students. Contact the Financial Aid Office for details on obtaining financial assistance at the university. Graduate Ph.D. admission requests are considered in January for August admission. Master's students should also apply in January for admission in August, although master's admissions are considered throughout the year. Early applicants have a greater chance of being awarded financial assistance.

Admission Requirements
Undergraduate students must submit an application and fee, SAT or ACT, and high school transcripts. Graduate students must submit an application and fee, GRE scores, transcripts, and letters of recommendation.

Expenses
Tuition for residents is $1,808 per year and $3,793 per year for non-residents.

Contact
Computer Science Department, Huntsville, AL 35899. Telephone: 256-824-5178 or 800-UAH-CALL (in local area). Fax: 256-824-5093 or 256-824-6290. Contact person: Dr. Heggere S. Ranganath, Chair. Email: info@cs.uah.edu. URL: http://www.uah.edu/.

Additional Information
The department has active research programs in a number of areas, including scientific visualization, computer graphics, parallel computing, computer vision, image processing, data mining, and large image database query.

University of Montevallo

F/X Degrees Offered
B.F.A. in Art with a focus in Graphic Design. There are six different studio concentrations: ceramics, drawing, graphic design, painting, photography, printmaking, and sculpture.

Curricular
The College of Fine Arts prepares students as visual artists, performers, musicians, arts educators, and communication specialists. The College provides instruction, performance opportunities and cultural events essential to the liberal arts education. Graphic Design courses including Introduction to Computer Graphics and Advanced Computer Graphics. Multimedia and Web Design Courses are among the offerings. And new as of the fall of 2003 is a digital media arts minor. Course choices range broadly across the fields of computer graphics, digital video, web design, digital audio, and music technology.

Facilities
Advanced Macintosh laboratory for graphic design students. Color printers, Scanners, Digital Cameras.

Software for creating animation and multimedia and graphic design projects.

Student Body
There are 200 Students in the Department.

Faculty Profile
There are ten faculty members in the Department of Art.

Deadlines and Financial Aid
Applications for admission should be submitted as soon as possible after September 1 of the candidate's senior year in high school. Various forms of financial aid are available including federal and state aid, grants, loans, and work-study arrangements. To be considered for financial aid students must file a FAFSA.

Admission Requirements
Application and fee, high school transcripts, SAT or ACT.

Expenses
Tuition for residents is $1,620 per year and $3,240 per year for non-residents.

Contact
Office of Admissions, Palmer Hall, Station 6030, University of Montevallo, Montevallo, AL 35115-6000. Telephone: 205-665-6030 or 800-292-4349. Fax: 205-665-6383. Contact: Dean Ken Procter. URL: http://www.montevallo.edu/.

Alaska

University of Alaska at Anchorage

F/X Degrees Offered
B.A., B.S. in Computer Science, B.F.A. in Art.

Curricular
Courses in Computer Science: Design and Analysis; Computer Modeling and Simulation; Computer Graphics; The Department of Art: Graphic Design; Advanced Graphic Design; Computer Art.

Facilities
Macintosh laboratory; UNIX workstations.

Student Body
Total enrollment at the university is 15,200 undergraduate students.

Deadlines and Financial Aid
Various fellowships and traditional state, federal and city aid are available to students.

Admission Requirements
Undergraduate applications for admission will be processed when the following materials have been received: official transcripts from all colleges and universities previously attended, and either the ACT, SAT or the ASSET test.

Expenses
Lower-division tuition for undergraduates (Course Numbers 050-299) is $82 per credit hour for residents, and $256 per credit hour for non-residents. Upper-division undergraduates (Course Numbers 300-499) is $93 per credit hour for residents, and $267 per credit hour for non-residents.

Contact
Admissions, 3211 Providence Dr., Anchorage, AK 99508. Telephone: 907-786-1800. URL: http://www.uaa.alaska.edu/.

Arizona

Arizona State University

F/X Degrees Offered
B.F.A. and M.F.A. with an emphasis in Intermedia Arts. Areas include Video Art, Performance Art, Installation Art, Audio Art, Mixed Media, and Digital Media.

Curricular
Courses in Computer Art and Computer Animation; Computer Imaging; Video Art. The intermedia program includes everything from installation and mixed media, to digital audio, video, animation, compositing and rapid prototyping.

Facilities
Computer graphics laboratories are generally microcomputer-based with a variety of software and peripherals for animation, video, interactive media, and high-end SGI animation workstations. Among the special facilities available to students are a digital video lab and two stereo-modeling facilities called PRISM (Partnership for Research in Stereo Modeling) labs. In the 3-D animation and compositing lab, students create fine arts animations and use sophisticated compositing software to combine 3-D animation with video and audio they have created in the animation classes.

Students also can broaden their experience and exposure in the field by participating in the TeleSculpture Conference held at ASU each fall, or attending and volunteering at Siggraph, the world's largest conference dedicated to computer graphics and interactive techniques.

Student Body
There are 960 students in the School of Art.

Faculty Profile
There are 58 faculty members teaching in the School of Art, 10 teach in the Intermedia area.

Deadlines and Financial Aid
Various types of undergraduate and graduate assistance are available, including scholarships, fellowships and awards. Graduate students can also find employment through teaching assistantships. Submit all application materials by November 1 and receive notification by December 1. Submit materials by December 1 and receive notification by Jan. 15. Applications received after December 1st may take longer to process.

Admission Requirements
To be eligible for admission to ASU, you must have graduated or will be graduating from a recognized high school with satisfactory scholarship defined as meeting both general aptitude and competency requirements. Arizona Residents must meet any one of the following aptitude requirements: Class Rank: Top Quarter; Composite Score: ACT 22 or SAT 1040; GPA (4.0 = A): 3.0. High school GPA will be calculated on courses that meet competencies only. Arizona residents who do not meet the requirements described above but rank in the second quarter of their graduating class or have a cumulative GPA of 2.5-2.99 (4.0 = A) may be admitted with conditions. Non-residents must meet any one of the following and the Competency Requirements: Class Rank: Top Quarter; Composite Score: ACT 24 or SAT 1110; GPA (4.0 = A): 3.0. Nonresidents who believe they have a strong high school background and who rank in the second quarter of their graduating classes or who have a GPA of 2.5-2.99 (4.0=A) will be considered on individual merit. To be eligible for admission to graduate studies, you must have the following: U.S. bachelor's degree or the equivalent from a regionally accredited institution. (A bachelor's degree in the U.S. is a four-year degree that follows twelve years of primary and secondary school work.) Equivalent

to a (B) average for your major program of study (in the last 60 semester hours or 90 quarter hours of undergraduate course work). If you do not meet the minimum GPA, your application may still be considered although the degree program office may require additional supporting documents. Qualifications as specified by your degree program (for example: tests, portfolios, letters of recommendation, etc.)

Expenses
Annual tuition for residents is $3,593 and non-residents pay $9,412.

Contact
Undergraduate or Graduate Advisor, Studio Art, Herberger School of Art, Arizona State University, P.O. Box 871505, Tempe, AZ 85287-1505. Telephone: 480-965-8521. Fax: 480-965-3468. URL: http://art.asu.edu.

Collins College

F/X Degrees Offered
Career areas include Visual Communication, Graphic Design, Multimedia, Web Page Design, Computer Graphics, Animation, Computer Network Technology, Game Design, and Media Arts; Film and HDTV and Motion Graphics and Visual FX. Degrees include: A.A. and B.A. in Visual Communication; B.A. in Animation; A.A. and B.A. in Media Arts; B.A. in Game Design.

Curricular
Motion Graphics and Visual FX combines live action footage, animated clips, photography, type, graphic elements and audio to produce a seamless integration of elements into effective commercial presentations. Graduates of this program qualify for entry-level employment in broadcast graphics and cable television production, visual effects

companies and entertainment graphics companies (motion pictures, television, video, animation), post production/editing companies, industrial video and film companies and companies specializing in Webcasting. This program is designed to prepare graduates for entry-level positions as motion graphics and visual effects technicians. Film and HDTV utilizes cinematography and digital film imaging to produce a demo reel. Students integrate text, graphic elements and action on the screen to convey a message or provide entertainment in the film or HDTV environment. Graduates of this program qualify for entry-level employment in the broadcast and cable television and film industry working on movies and television shows or in corporate production and post-production houses. This program is designed to prepare graduates for entry-level positions as HDTV videographers or film and HDTV production technicians.

Facilities
The library supports the educational needs of the student body by providing a place where students can find up-to-date information on current issues in graphic design, animation, computer network administration, e-commerce, programming and general education. The library contains numerous collections including a reference section, periodical collection, fiction and non-fiction collections, videos, CD-ROM products and equipment. Computers, Internet access, printers and a photocopier are available for student's use.

Student Body
There are 5,500 students enrolled. Many classes are seminars and small discussion groups.

Faculty Profile
Six faculty members teach at the Center for Advanced Digital Applications.

Deadlines and Financial Aid

Financial Aid is a process that many of our students utilize. Every student needs a plan for paying for their education. While some pay by cash, many students use financial aid to help with their college costs. Our friendly Financial Aid staff is available to assist you through the financial aid application process. We are committed to helping every student, whether applying for financial aid or paying by cash, in completing their financial aid plan. We've helped many students just like you. Financial Aid is available for those who qualify. Most student financial aid is provided in the form of grants through federal and state funded programs.

Admission Requirements

Students should apply for admission as soon as possible in order to be officially accepted for a specific program and starting date. To apply, students should complete the Application Form and bring it to the school or call for a priority appointment to visit the school and receive a tour of its facilities. All applicants are required to complete a personal interview with an admissions representative. Parents and spouses are encouraged to attend. This interview process helps determine the applicants interest and eligibility. Once an applicant has completed and submitted the Application and Enrollment Agreement, the school reviews the information and informs the applicant of its decision. If an applicant is not accepted, all fees paid to the school are refunded. Individuals may apply up to one year in advance of a scheduled class start. The following items must be completed at the time of application: attestation of graduation from high school or equivalency; request for high school or GED transcript (and college transcripts, where applicable); application/enrollment agreement (if applicant is under 18 years of age it must be signed by parent or guardian); financial aid forms (if applicant wishes to apply for financial aid); payment of application fee (non-refundable unless applicant is denied admission); letter of intent. The school reserves the right to reject applicants if the items listed above are not successfully completed.

Expenses

Tuition is $996 per semester for residents and $1,338 for non-residents.

Contact

Collins College, 1140 South Priest Drive, Tempe, AZ 85281. Telephone: 1-800-876-7070. URL: http://www.collinscollege.edu

Additional Information

Collins College was formerly known as Al Collins Graphic Design School. Prior to 1997, Al Collins Graphic Design School emphasized programs in the Visual Communication fields of study, such as graphic design, and computer graphics. Since 1997, additional programs have been implemented in the areas of visual communication, animation, personal computer/network technology, media arts (digital video, television & cinema production, film & HDTV, motion graphics & visual FX) and game design.

Northern Arizona University

F/X Degrees Offered

The College of Fine Arst offers a Computer Art program that emphasizes Digital Imaging, 2D Animation, Multimedia, and Interactivity.

Curricular

2D Computer Animation; Multimedia/Interactive; High-level Programming; Digital Painting/Drawing; Image Processing.

Facilities

Hardware: 16 Macintosh station laboratory. Software: Adobe Photoshop; Macromedia Director; Fractal; Design Painter; QuarkXPress; Illustrator.

Student Body

There are 50 undergraduate students in the computer graphics area.

Faculty Profile

There are 25 faculty members teaching in the department.

Deadlines and Financial Aid

Two broad categories of financial assistance are available to graduate students at NAU. The first is awarded on the basis of academic merit or the ability to perform specific services. The second is based on demonstrated financial need. Students may apply for the following types of aid: graduate assistantships; graduate scholarships; need-based assistance; additional kinds of assistance, including benefits for veterans. Undergraduates: application deadlines for each semester are indicated below. All students are encouraged to apply as soon as possible. Prospective freshmen should apply in fall of their senior year. Transfer students may apply for any semester with two semesters of course work outstanding. Fall application priority date is March 1st; spring application priority date is December 1st; summer application deadline is May 15th.

Admission Requirements

Undergraduates: a signed and completed admission application; an official copy of high school transcript; scores from either the SAT or the ACT. Arizona residents will be offered admission if they meet the following: 3.0 or higher GPA (on a 4.0 scale), or 22 ACT or 1040 SAT composite score, or top 25 percent class rank and have no deficiencies in the required course requirements. Arizona residents may be admitted if they meet the following: 2.5-2.99 GPA (on a 4.0 scale), or top 50 percent class rank top 25 percent class rank and have no more than one deficiency in any two subjects in the course requirements. Students with a combination math/science deficiency are not admissible. Conditionally admitted students may be required to participate in academic assistance programs. Nonresident students will be offered admission if they meet the following: 3.0 or higher GPA (on a 4.0 scale), or 24 ACT or 1110 SAT composite score, or top 25 percent class rank and have no deficiencies in required course requirements. Nonresident students may be offered admission based on individual circumstances and/or space availability if they meet the following: 2.50-2.99 GPA (on a 4.0 scale), or top 50 percent class rank top 25 percent class rank and have no more than one deficiency in any two subjects in course requirements. Students with a combination math/science deficiency are not admissible. Conditionally admitted students may be required to participate in academic assistance programs. Graduate students should contact the Graduate Office.

Expenses

Tuition for 12 credit hours is $12,028 for non-residents; residents pay $3,508 for 12 credit hours.

Contact

NAU, S. San Francisco St., Flagstaff, AZ 86011-6020. Telephone: 928-523-4612 or 888-667-3628. Fax: 928-523-5511. Contact person: Romanna J. Flores. E-mail: rjf@nauvax.ucc.nau.edu. URL: http://www.nau.edu.

Additional Information

The Computer Art program supports the creative process from inception to presentation. Its goal is to nurture the lifelong process of personal and artistic development. Students from various departments fulfill degree requirements by combining a major with an art and technology emphasis. Students analyze historical perspectives and contemporary public policy issues concerning art and technology. Student work is disseminated in an international environment through broadcasting, print publication, and electronic distribution.

Phoenix College

F/X Degrees Offered
B.F.A. in Graphic Design through the Department of Art.

Curricular
Introduction to Computer Graphic Art; 2D Computer Design; 3D Computer Design; Computer Art; Electronic Publishing Design; Electronic Presentation Design; Multi-presentation Graphics; Computer Animation.

Facilities
Macintosh systems; Accel-A-Writer Laser Printer; Apple LaserWriter IINTX printer; Hewlett Packard Paint Jet color printer; Tektonix Phaser PX color printer; Howtek Personal color scanner; HP Scanjet Plus b/w scanner; Bravo computer slide maker; RasterOPs 32-bit video card for video in- and output.

Student Body
There are 200 undergraduate students in the department; 60 Graphic Design majors.

Faculty Profile
23 faculty members teach in the art department.

Deadlines and Financial Aid
The Financial Aid program at Phoenix College is designed to provide financial assistance to eligible students from federal, state, institutional, and private funding sources. The program also provides information to families about sources of funding, application procedures, and advice on financial and budgeting issues. Financial assistance may be provided in the form of loans, grants, scholarship, and employment offered singularly or in some combination, depending upon the level of financial need, and various eligibility criteria. Phoenix College subscribes to the National Association of Student Financial Aid Administration Standards of Good Practice, and maintains membership in the national, regional, and state financial aid professional associations.

Federal, state and private aid are available. For details contact the Financial Aid Office.

Admission Requirements
Undergraduates: an application and fee, official transcripts, SAT or ACT scores, and portfolio.

Expenses
Tuition is charged per academic credit hour and will be different according to residency classification. Fees may vary according to course. For Maricopa County Resident it is $51 per credit hour; Out-of-County Unclassified is $76 per credit hour (Students enrolling for 1-6 semester credit hours); Out-of-County $210 per credit hour (Students enrolling for 7 or more semester credit hours); Out-of-State Unclassified $76 per credit hour; (Students, including F-1 students, enrolling for 1-6 semester credit hours); and Out-of-State $216 per credit hour(Students, including F-1 students, enrolling for 7 or more semester credit hours).

Contact
Department of Art, Phoenix College, 1202 W. Thomas Rd., Phoenix, AZ 85013. Telephone: 602-285-7282. Fax: 602-285-7700. Contact person: Cathy Taylor. E-mail: Cathy.Taylor@pcmail.maricopa.edu. URL: http://www.pc.maricopa.edu/.

University of Advancing Technology

F/X Degrees Offered
A.A. and B.A. in Multimedia/Digital Animation and Production; B.A. in Multimedia/Virtual Reality; Bachelor of Applied Science in CAD Technology within Virtual Reality.

Curricular

Life Drawing; 2D Design; Word, Excel, PowerPoint and Access; Computer Typography and Layout Design; 2D Computer Graphics Tools; Keys to Success; Design Aesthetics and Color Theory; Animation Theory; Internet; 3D Animation and Rendering Tools; Cinematography; Computer Programming Concepts; Visual Basic Programming; Aesthetic Principles of Interface Design; Portfolio Development; Visual Basic II - Graphical Programming; Character Modeling for Animation; Authoring Environments: Authorware; Object Oriented Programming; Writing for Multimedia Applications; Legal Aspects of Electronic Media; UNIX; Issues in VR/Professional Practice; Environment Construction; JAVA; Virtual Reality Systems; VRML; Multimedia Internship.

Facilities

The University invested a great deal of time researching current trends in the field of digital video production, studios, and sound recording/editing technologies before constructing the the facilities which now includes a Digital Studio. The University has also established the Computer Reality Center, an application development research division. The Center hires students for modeling, animation, programming, and Web page development positions to assist in the production of industry contracts. There are three media stations set up in the Student Commons for video editing projects. The specifications for each station are: Media 100 V20-DV Power Grade machines; PIII 600 mHz Intel processor; 36 GB video array (two striped 18 GB hard drives); and iFinish (Media 100's proprietary software). There are two Microteck large format scanners (tabloid or 11"x17" in size); 2 Canon A1 Digital Cameras that can be checked out from the library; 3 Zr-10 cameras (1-chip miniDV cameras); 2 Canon GL1 cameras (3 chip miniDV cameras); 1 Canon XL-1 miniDV camera with a

telephoto and wide-angle detachable lenses (a 3 chip camera). The school also offers a wide variety of up-to-date software.

Student Body

There are 850 total enrollment at the university.

Faculty Profile

There are more than sixty full-time faculty teaching at the university.

Deadlines and Financial Aid

The University offers the following to qualified students: Federal Pell Grant, Federal Supplemental Opportunity Grant (FSEOG), Federal Work-Study, and Stafford/Ford Federal Direct Loans. Loans from the William D. Ford Federal Direct Loan Program equate to standards of the lender-based Federal Family Education Loan Program (FFELP), formerly known as the Guaranteed Student Loan Program. Contact the Student Financial Services Office for more information.

Admission Requirements

The University welcomes all applicants who display a passion for the application of technology. All applicants must have a high school diploma or hold the educational equivalent. Applicants under the age of 18 must have a legal guardian sign all admission agreements and a financial responsibility statement. The following is required: Grade Point Average: A cumulative high school grade point average of 2.5 meets the requirement for admission in place of ACT or SAT scores; GED: A minimum score of 500 is required and meets the requirement for admission in place of ACT or SAT scores; ACT: An ACT minimum score of 21 meets the requirement for admission in place of cumulative high school GPA of 2.5 or a SAT score; SAT: SAT minimum score of 500 in the Verbal and 520 in the Math or a combined minimum total of 1020 points or higher meets the requirement for admission in place of cumulative high school GPA of 2.5 or an ACT score;

College Credits: Successful completion of 15.0 credits, (2.0 CGPA or better) from an accredited institution meets the requirement for admission in place of cumulative high school GPA of 2.5, ACT or GED average scores. Military Service: Four years of satisfactory military service.

Expenses

Beginning in January 2004, the undergraduate tuition rate will be $375 per credit hour. 2003 tuition for the graduate program is $426 per credit hour. Beginning January 2004, the graduate tuition rate will be $455 per credit hour. For students enrolling after September 15, 2003, undergraduate tuition is $6,800 per full time semester (12 credits or higher) with no tuition increase prior to January 2005. Semesters exceeding 18 credit hours will require academic approval. Graduate tuition is $4,125 per semester (6 credits or higher) with no tuition increase prior to January 2005.

Contact

University of Advancing Technology. 2625 W. Baseline Rd., Tempe, AZ 85283-1042. Telephone: 602-383-8228 Fax: 602-383-8222 or 800-658-5744. Contact person: Dominic Pistillo, president. Email: studentservices@uat.edu.
URL: http://www.uat.edu/.

Additional Information

The University of Advancing Technology (UAT) started out in 1983 as a computer-aided design (CAD) systems consulting company and high-end computer manufacturer. Since then, UAT has evolved into a nationally recognized leader in technology education. UAT has evolved from a computer training school into an accredited senior-level college hat provides training and education in multimedia, animation, interactive media, Internet technologies, computer programming, network engineering, Internet administration, software engineering, computer aided design, animation and game design. The University offers accredited associate's, bachelor's and graduate degrees. The Professional Development Center offers corporate tech training, certification, and continuing education in these same areas as well.

Arkansas

Arkansas State University

F/X Degrees Offered
B.S., M.S. in Computer Science.

Curricular
Computer Graphics I and II; Software Engineering I and II; UNIX Systems Programming; Analysis of Algorithms; Compilers; Image Processing; UNIX Network Programming; Artificial Intelligence.

Facilities
Windows network; Pentium systems; inkjet printers; video projector used for classes. UNIX systems; Pentium systems running LINUX Student access from PC laboratory. Other facilities--DEC 5500 running ULTRIX; PC laboratory; Netware network; 25 Macintosh systems; three laser printers; one line printer; one scanner. Software includes: LispWorks; Mathematica; Microsoft Visual C++; Microsoft J++; Microsoft Office 2000; Minitab statistical package; Dr Scheme; Spimsal assembly; language simulator; Squeak; and SWI-Prolog. ASU is rated as one of the top 50 *Most Wired* campuses by Yahoo.

Student Body
There are 10,000 students.

Faculty Profile
A 24:1 student-to-faculty ratio.

Deadlines and Financial Aid
Several types of aid are available, including: grants; need-based financial aid that does not have to be repaid; loans; scholarships; college work-study; need-based employment opportunities.

Admission Requirements
Application and fee, transcripts, and SAT or ACT. Graduate students are advised to contact the Graduate Office.

Expenses
Tuition is $1,092 for resident undergraduates: non-residents should expect to add $2,796 in addition to the tuition charged to residents; graduates: $1,380 for residents, and non-residents pay $3,468.

Contact
Admissions, Arkansas State University, P.O. Box 1630, State University, AR 72467. Telephone: 870-972-3090 or 800-643-0080.
URL: http://www.cas.astate.edu/.

Arkansas Tech University

F/X Degrees Offered
B.S., M.S. in Computer and Information Science.

Curricular
Computer and Information Science courses include: Computer-Aided Design Graphics; Advanced Computer-Aided Design Graphics; Presentation Graphics; Applied Computer Graphics; Computer Graphics.

Facilities
Computer laboratory for students in the department.

Student Body
There are 197 students in the department.

Faculty Profile
There is a student-faculty ratio of 18 to 1.

Deadlines and Financial Aid
Financial assistance consists of scholarships, grants, loans, and part-time employment, which may be offered singularly or in various combinations

depending upon the degree of need. Contact the Student Aid Office for details.

Admission Requirements

Application and fee, SAT or ACT, high school transcripts. Every student must file an initial application for admission and submit proof of immunization for measles, mumps, and rubella (students attending part time or born before January 1, 1957, are not required to submit immunization records).

Expenses

Tuition is estimated at $1,656 per semester for residents and $3,312 for non-resident students.

Contact

Arkansas Tech University, Corley Building, Room 262, Russellville, AR 72801. Telephone: 501-968-0663 or 800-582-6953 in Arkansas. Contact person: Ronald Robinson, Department Head. URL: http://www.atu.edu/.

Harding University

F/X Degrees Offered

Art Department offers a B.F.A. in Graphic Design.

Curricular

Computer Graphic Design; Drawing; and Beginning and Advanced Graphic Design courses that use computer technology to solve design problems.

Facilities

Computer Graphics laboratory:15 Macintosh computers; laser printers; flatbed scanners; digital camera; color laser printer. Software includes multimedia and graphic design packages.

Student Body

There are 70 Graphic Design majors.

Faculty Profile

Three Graphic Design professors.

Deadlines and Financial Aid

Deadline for Art Department scholarship applications is April 15. Portfolio submission is necessary for art scholarship application. Financial aid is available to most Harding students in the form of scholarships, government grants, loans, work-study programs and vocational rehabilitation programs.

Admission Requirements

General application fee, high school transcript with overall 3.0 GPA, and ACT or SAT scores.

Expenses

Annual tuition is $10,120. Graduate is $5,832.

Contact

Art and Design Department. Box 12253, Searcy, AR 72149-0001. Telephone: 501-279-4000. Fax: 501-279-4717. Contact person: Dr. John Keller, chair. E-mail: jkeller@harding.edu. URL: http://www.harding. edu.

California

Academy of Art College

F/X Degrees Offered
A.A., M.F.A. and B.F.A. in Motion Picture and Video, Graphic Design, and Computer Art.

Curricular
Students can enroll in different core courses on the Macintosh, PC or Silicon Graphics workstation, including: Introduction to the Computer; Computer Graphics; Computerized Paint Systems; Computer Illustration; Electronically Enhanced Photo; Computers for Textiles; Introduction to Animation; Storyboard: Digital Media and Video; Digital Media: Interface design; Introduction to Gaming; Digital Reproduction Techniques; Desktop Design; Game Design and Construction; Computer Rendering and Animation; Digital Portfolio; The Digital Production Studio; SGI Paint and Image Processing; 3D Modeling and Animation (Maya or Softimage); Visual Effects for Film and TV; Character Animation; 2D Animation for Digital Media; Digital Imaging.

Facilities
The Academy of Art College's campus is truly in the heart of the city with more than 20 facilities including 10 student housing dormitories and apartment buildings. A convenient campus shuttle bus system transports students between Academy buildings. Every department has been provided ample labs with industry-standard technology. The 180 New Montgomery Street building houses a Mac lab with over 300 computers, an SGI lab with 100 SGI workstations, and an audio/visual and motion picture lab that includes a newly purchased AVID 8000 edit suite and a fully automated library. There are more than 60 SGIs, in addition to Macintosh and PC. Software includes Photoshop, Maya, Softimage. The Film Department offers the latest in creative technology, including Arriflex SR-1 cameras and Sony S-VHS master editing suites. 340 Macintoshes including 100 G3, Strata 3D, FormZ, Director. There are 180 workstations available 18 hours daily. Various multimedia and animation workstations for creating high-end 3D and 2D computer animation.

Student Body
There are 6,600 students attending the college; 2,500 computer art students.

Faculty Profile
Most faculty members are half-time instructors and professionals in their field.

Deadlines and Financial Aid
Rolling admission.

Admission Requirements
Application and fee, statement of intent, resume, two letters of recommendation, portfolio and transcripts.

Expenses
Tuition is approximately $550 per credit for full-time undergraduate students, and $600 per credit for graduate students.

Contact
Academy of Art College, 79 New Montgomery St.4th Floor, San Francisco, CA 94105. Telephone: 415-274-2219 or 1-800-544-ARTS, ext 2219. Fax: 415-263-3130. Email: admissions@academyart.edu. URL: http://www.academyart.edu/.

Antelope Valley College

F/X Degrees Offered
A.A. degrees in Computer Graphics, Computer Imaging, and Electronic Presentation. Certificates in

Computer Graphics, Digital Imaging, and Electronic Presentation.

Curricular

Courses within the Art Department are directed toward individuals developing artistically through enhanced comprehension, skills acquisition and personal enjoyment of art works. Art history, art appreciation, drawing, illustration, painting, ceramics and sculpture are among the courses offered. Art courses provide a solid foundation for those moving into computer graphics, multimedia and are transferable to four-year institutions.

Facilities

A graphics laboratory is equipped with 12 Macintosh workstations; dye-sub printer; inkjet printer; laser printers; high-resolution flatbed scanner; digital cameras; film and video editing and production equipment.

Student Body

Size of graduating class averages 1,937.

Faculty Profile

Total full-time undergraduate faculty: 101; total part-time undergraduate faculty: 270.

Deadlines and Financial Aid

Financial aid is available from various sources such as federal and state programs, community organizations, and individual donors. Aid can be awarded in the form of grants, loans, college work-study employment, scholarships, or a combination of these. Students seeking financial aid are required to file an FAFSA and provide income verification. Applicants must be enrolled in 6 or more units. Forms and applications are available in the College Financial Aid Office.

Admission Requirements

Application and fee, and high school transcript.

Expenses

Tuition for residents at $4,617 per year and $7,374 per year for non-residents.
Estimated tuition is $12 per credit for in-state students, and $142 for out-of-state students.

Contact

Admission Office, 3041 W. Ave. K, Lancaster, CA 93536-5426. Telephone: 661-722-6300. Email: info@avc.edu.
URL: http://www.avc.edu/.

Art Center College of Design

F/X Degrees Offered

B.F.A. and M.F.A. in Film, Illustrations, Graphic Design, Industrial Design Photographer. M.S. degree in Computer Graphics that allows students to conduct research in the field of Interactive Media, Multimedia and Interface Design. B.S. in Product Design and Transportation Design.

Curricular

Computer Graphics; Introduction to Computer-Based Design; Digital Design: Elements and Processes; Computer Graphics Workshop; Sound for Digital Media; Interactive Media; 3D Modeling; 3D Animation; Softimage; Advanced 3D Model.

Facilities

The General Motors Computer Graphics Laboratories occupy 11,000 square feet in a newly designed wing of the campus. The equipment includes: 62 workstations: 31 Octanes, 31 SGI/NT 320s. Software includes: Alias Wavefront Studio, Alias Wavefront Maya, Alias Wavefront Composer, Alias Wavefront Studio Paint, Active Worlds, Adobe Acrobat, Adobe After Effects, Adobe Illustrator, Adobe Photoshop, Adobe Premiere, Adobe Type

Manager, Alias Wavefront Studio, Kinetix 3D Studio Max, Macromedia Director, Macromedia Dreamweaver, Macromedia Flash, Macromedia Freehand, Maya Fushion lite, Maya Unlimited, Microsoft Powerpoint, Paintshop Pro, Paraform, Quicktime, Solidworks SGI/NT Peripherals include: 31 21-inch SGI monitors, 31 Zip drives, 10 Jaz drives, 1 HP 5000 laser printer. Apple Macintosh Workstations include: 140 G4/500s, G4/450s, G3/300s, G3/266s. Design Software includes: Adobe Acrobat, Adobe Acrobat Distiller, Adobe Go Live, Adobe Indesign, Adobe Ilustrator, Adobe Image Ready, Adobe After Effects, Adobe Pagcmaker, Adobe Photoshop, Adobe Premiere, Adobe Streamline, Apple Final Cut Pro, Ashlar Vellum 3D, BBEdit, Claris Works, Cult Effects, Electic Image, Equilibrium Debabilizer Pro, Fetch, Form ZJS RR, Meta Creations Design Expression, Meta Creations Poser, Meta Creations Ray Dream Studio, Meta Creations Painter, Meta Creations Painter 3D, Meta Creations Bryce, Macromedia Director, Macromedia Dreamweaver, Macromedia Flash, Macromedia Freehand, Macromedia Fontographer, Macromedia Fireworks, Macromedia SoundEdit 16, Media Cleaner Pro, Media 100 5.0, Microsoft Office 98, Net Objects Fusion, Puffin Commotion, QuarkXpress, Quicktime VR Authoring, Strata Media Paint, Strata Studio Pro Periphcrals include: 140 Zip drives, 4 CD recording drives, 21 color flat-bed scanners, 16 laser printers, 45 Jaz drives, 5 35mm slide scanners, 5 4x5 slide scanners, 100 Wacom tablets, 4 color laser printers. Digital Video Editing Stations include: 9 Media 100 stations, 9 External Array 100 gigs, 9 Mackie Mixers, 4 Sony BetaCams, 12 Sony Trinitron monitors, 12 SVHS decks, 1 Sony Hi 8 deck, 10 Final Cut Pro Stations, 10 SVHS decks, 10 Sony Trinitron monitors, 3 DV decks. Animation projects can be completed using a professional animation crane as well as fully equipped computer animation capabilities. Two screening rooms seat 450 and 80.

Student Body

Total enrollment exceeds 1,400.

Faculty Profile

There are 60 full-time, and 235 part-time faculty members teaching at the college.

Deadlines and Financial Aid

Students applying for financial aid and scholarships must submit all application and financial aid materials by the following deadlines: summer term, February 1; fall term, March 1; spring term, Sept. 15; graduate students: applications are accepted on a rolling admissions basis, with consideration given as long as room remains in a class.

Admission Requirements

Admission to Art Center is based on a strong portfolio and sound academic record in high school or college. The following is required: a fully completed application for admission, application fee, official high school and college transcripts, SAT or ACT for students currently enrolled in high school, compact portfolio of original work, minimum of 12 and maximum of 20 original samples, including work related to an applicant's proposed major. Portfolios submitted for advanced standing should consist of 20 or more samples representing work completed in the major area. A slides-only portfolio is not acceptable. Slides or photographs of 3D or oversized pieces are acceptable but do not replace the required original works. Sketchbooks may also be included. Graduate students: a completed application for admission, application fee, official transcripts from all colleges attended, portfolio demonstrating a focused body of work, letter of intent, short resume; candidates must have earned a bachelor's degree.

Expenses

Undergraduates pay $11,074 per semester. Graduates pay $11,704 per semester.

Contact

Art Center of Design, 1700 Lida St., Pasadena, CA 91103. Telephone: 626-396-2373. Fax: 626-405 9104. URL: http://www.artcenter.edu/.

Additional Information

In the college's General Motors Computer Graphics Laboratories, facilities are available on campus for students to explore interactive multimedia and photo-realistic 3D environments.

California Institute of Technology

F/X Degrees Offered

B.S. and M.S. in Computer Science.

Curricular

Various courses in advanced scientific visualization.

Facilities

More than 1,000 computers are on campus. An estimated 400 computers are attached to computers available for undergraduate use, of which 100 are in the Computer Science Department. There is a Hewlett Packard laboratory, known as *HPug*, which is run by undergraduates. This laboratory is adjacent to a Macintosh laboratory, a Sun laboratory, and PC/Windows stations. Color printers and scanners are also available for student use. In certain academic divisions, students can access Silicon Graphics computers. It is even possible to apply for special access to the Parallel Supercomputing Facility on campus. All student houses have their own network (10 Base-T Ethernet) ports in every room. The Center for Advanced Computing Research: a 256-node SPP-2000; a 512-node Paragon; the 512-node Intel Touchstone Delta; a 12-node IBM SP2; a 30 TB IBM tape robot with HPSS.

Student Body

Total student body: 900 undergraduates and 1,000 graduate students.

Faculty Profile

There are 1,033 faculty members in residence. This includes 281 professorial faculty, 194 research faculty (including 104 research fellows), 140 visiting faculty, 82 emeriti faculty, 290 post-doctoral scholars, and 46 other faculty members.

Deadlines and Financial Aid

All early admissions application materials must be submitted to the Caltech Office of Undergraduate Admissions by November 1. Last year, roughly two-thirds of the undergraduate student body received some assistance through the Caltech Financial Aid Office. This office administers and coordinates federal, state, private and institutional funds for grants and scholarships.

Admission Requirements

Undergraduates: students must submit an application and fee, transcripts, and SAT or ACT scores. Graduate students: must submit an application and fee, the GRE test scores, letters of recommendation, and transcripts.

Expenses

Estimated tuition is $21,000 per year for undergraduates, and $23,000 for graduate students. Undergrads are required to live on campus for the first year.

Contact

California Institute of Technology, Pasadena, CA 91125. Telephone: 626-395-6811. Fax: 626-795-1547. URL: http://www.caltech.edu/.

California Institute of the Arts

F/X Degrees Offered

The School of Art offers undergraduate and graduate programs in the areas of Art, Graphic Design, and Photography and Media, as well as a graduate Integrated Media Program. The undergraduate programs lead to a Bachelor of Fine Arts (BFA) degree and the graduate programs to a Master of Fine Arts (MFA) degree.

Curricular

The school offers: Computer Animation 3D; Computer Animation and Music; Beginning Computer Animation; Character Animation; Experimental Animation courses. Coursework for these programs is drawn from more than 80 classes offered by the School of Art each semester. BFA students are further required to take general education courses in the School of Critical Studies while MFA students in the Integrated Media Program must enroll in Integrated Media (IM) classes every semester. School of Art students also take advantage of numerous elective courses throughout CalArts-in the schools of Critical Studies, Dance, Film/Video, Music and Theater.

Facilities

The School of Art's production facilities integrate both traditional and new technologies to encourage creativity across a wide variety of artmaking métiers. Lab directors, aided by student staff, are available to provide instruction and guidance to ensure that all facilities are used effectively and safely. All labs directly support the curricula offered by the School of Art. Beginning undergraduate students in the programs in Art and Photography and Media share studios. MFA students and most upper-level undergraduates in these programs are assigned individual studios. Graphic Design students are assigned individual desks and work spaces in a shared studio environment. Most studios are spacious and receive natural light. All studios are available to students around the clock during the academic year. The MacLab is used for creating digital and print-based work, including drawing, painting, photo manipulation, editorial design, type design, 3-D rendering, motion graphics, sound design and Web, CD and DVD authoring. The lab is equipped with Macintosh workstations with high-speed Internet connections, black-and-white high-resolution printers, video projectors, flatbed and slide scanners, digital still and digital video cameras and CD and DVD burners. Two adjunct labs support the MacLab: Pre-Press offers fee-based large-format printing while the MotionLab provides digital editing and DVD authoring facilities as well as digital video cameras for check-out.

Student Body

There are 1,200 students attending the institute and approximately 110 in the Art Program.

Faculty Profile

There are over 40 faculty members teaching at the California Institute of the Arts with a Student/faculty ratio of 7:1.

Deadlines and Financial Aid

Due to the limited funds available in some programs, it is important for students to meet the financial aid deadline of March 3. Financial aid is available in the form of Grants, Pell Grants, SEOF Grants, CRL A and F. A portfolio is required. Label everything you submit with your name, the date completed, dimensions and medium; and indicate the top of each slide. Include a typed list with this information and descriptions of your individual pieces which will add to the faculty's understanding of the work. Send slides in a round 80-capacity carousel; do not send 140-capacity carousels. Slides in slide sheets will not be reviewed. Be sure to preview your carousel before sending it. Make sure that all slides are oriented correctly and indicate the top right of each slide. If you submit videocassettes or films, indicate the running time of each piece. All films should be head out. If possible, transfer Super-8mm to videocassette. Do not submit unmounted or unsleeved photographic prints. All websites should be submitted on CD; do not merely supply us with a URL. Digital portfolios should be set at screen resolution.

Admission Requirements
Admissions decisions are made by a faculty committee comprised of instructors in the applicants chosen Program. Admission requirements include application and fee, transcripts, personal statement, artistic evaluation, and portfolio.

Expenses
Annual tuition is $22,190 for full-time students.

Contact
California Institute of the Arts, 24700 McBean Parkway, Valencia, CA 91355. Telephone: 661-255-1050. Fax: 661-254-8352. General Contact: 800-545-2787. Contact person: Tracy Weed, Admissions Department.
URL: http://www.calarts.edu/.

Additional Information
California Institute of the Arts was incorporated in 1961 through the vision and generosity of Walt and Roy O. Disney, and Lulu May Voln Hagen, and through the merger of two professional schools: the Los Angeles Conservatory of Music, founded in 1993, and Chouinard Art Institute, founded in 1921.

California State University, Northridge

F/X Degrees Offered
The CSUN Department of Art, Video/Film Art area of concentration is a comprehensive art program leading to a B.A., M.A. and M.F.A. degrees.

Curricular
Video/Film Art Area of Concentration: Courses--Introduction to Video/Film Art; Computer Animation; Digital Technologies in Art; Advanced Video/Film Art; Advanced Studies in Video/Film Art; Studio Problems in Video/Film Art; Advanced Studio Problems in Video/Film Art; Introduction to Visual Technology; Animation I and II; Computer Graphics.

Facilities
Adobe Illustrator, Adobe Photoshop, various Web design software programs. Various film and video production tools.

Deadlines and Financial Aid
Federal Stafford Loan, Parent Loan for Undergraduate Students (PLUS), Short-term Loan, Lender Links; Federal Pell Grant, Supplemental Educational Opportunity Grant (SEOG), Cal Grant, State University Grant (SUG), Educational Opportunity Grant (EOP); The Federal Work-Study Program; University Scholarships, Northridge Presidential Scholarships, and a free scholarship search service (FASTWEB). The priority deadline filing date for the upcoming academic year at CSUN is March 2.

Admission Requirements
First-time freshman admisssion requirements are: high school graduate; qualifiable eligibility index; completed with grades of C or better in each of the courses in the comprehensive pattern of college preparatory subject requirements. Courses must be completed prior to the first enrollment in

the California State University. Eligibility Index: the eligibility index is the combination of your high school GPA and your test score on either the ACT or the SAT I. Your GPA is based on grades earned during your final three years of high school (excluding physical education and military science), and bonus points for each 'C' or better in approved honors courses. Graduate Admission: applicants who are meeting University requirements for admission and desiring admission to a master's program will be reviewed in the appropriate department. The department will determine whether or not the student meets requirements for admission to its program. Some departments may require a departmental application. Those students who meet departmental and university requirements will be admitted as either Conditionally Classified or Classified graduate students. In order to be admitted to California State University, Northridge in a master's program, students must meet the following requirements: have a baccalaureate degree from an accredited university or college; have been in good standing at the last institute attended; have at least a 2.5 GPA in the last 60 semester/90 quarter units attempted, independent of when the baccalaureate was granted; the entire semester or quarter in which the 60-90 units began will be used in this calculation. Lower-division courses or courses taken in extension (except in concurrent enrollment at CSUN in the upper division) after obtaining the bachelor's degree will be excluded from the calculation; submit departmental application as required; submit all required applications, transcripts, test scores, and supporting information as required by Admissions and Records, and the Department.

Expenses
Undergraduate tuition is $1,222 per year for in-state residents, and an additional $282 per unit for out-of-state residents. Graduate tuition is $1,327 per year

for in-state residents, and an additional $282 per unit for out-of-state residents.

Contact
Admissions and Records, California State University, Northridge 18111 Nordhoff St., Northridge, CA 91330-8207. Telephone: 818-677-2242. Fax: 818-677-3766. Contact person: Julia Schlosser. Email: julia.schlosser@csun.edu.
URL: http://www.csun.edu/digitalart/.

California State University, San Bernardino

F/X Degrees Offered
B.S., M.S.,and Ph.D. in Computer Science.

Curricular
Advanced Visualization and Computer Graphics courses.

Facilities
Department facilities--hardware: five computer labs with more than 120 PCs. Sun Sparc Classics. Software systems and languages: Ada; C; C++; Pascal; Lisp; Prolog; Samlltalk; X-Windows; Fortran; HTML; TCI/TK; Rational Rose/C++; Mosaic; Netscape; Lynx; Emacs; Showcase; Java.

Student Body
There are 200 students in the department.

Faculty Profile
There are 14 full-time faculty members in the art department.

Deadlines and Financial Aid
Graduate teaching assistantships are available through the department. These assistantships offer students a stipend of $1,335.

Admission Requirements

Application and fee, GRE score, three letters of recommendation, a statement of purpose, a baccalaureate degree in Computer Science or a related field, and completion of three preparatory courses.

Expenses

Tuition for up to six credits for in-state residents is $616.50. Full-time students pay $902.50. Out-of-state students pay the in-state tuition plus an extra $188 per unit.

Contact

Department of Computer Science, California State University, San Bernardino, CA 92407. Telephone: 909-880-5330. Contact person: Dr. Arturo I. Concepcion, graduate coordinator. E-mail: concep@csci.csusb.edu.
URL: http://www.csci.csusb.edu/.

California State University, Stanislaus

F/X Degrees Offered

B.S. in Computer Science.

Curricular

Systems Analyst/Programmer, System/Network Administrator, graduate work in Computer Science, Software Engineering. Courses include 3D Modeling and Rendering; High-level Programming; Computer Graphics I and II. The computer graphics courses are part of a CSAB-accredited general undergraduate program in Computer Science.

Facilities

The Computer Graphics program uses a mixture of Sun Sparc 2; Generic 486; NeXT; Macintosh platforms. C Programming is used to create images.

Student Body

There are 100 undergraduate students.
Faculty
There are five faculty members in the Computer Science Department.

Deadlines and Financial Aid

Various fellowships, and traditional state, federal and city aid are available to students. Contact the Financial Aid Office for details on obtaining financial assistance at the university.

Admission Requirements

Application and fee, transcripts, SAT scores. You may fill out a CSU Mentor electronic form or the printable PDF Version (2004-2005 Application) of the application for admission. Or, contact the office for more specific details on the admission process.

Expenses

Full-time students pay $1,141 and out-of-state students pay the in-state tuition plus an extra $288 per unit. Full-time graduate students pay $1,237.

Contact

801 W. Monte Vista Ave., Turlock, CA 95382. Telephone: 209-667-3531. Fax: 209-664-7113. Contact person: Thomas J. Carter, Chair. E-mail: CJorritsma@csustan.edu.
URL: http://www.cs.csustan.edu/.

Chapman University

F/X Degrees Offered

B.F.A. in Film and Television, Emphasis in Film and Television Production; M.A. in Film Studies; M.F.A. in Film and Television Production.

Curricular

Introduction to Visual Storytelling; Film and Television Workshop; Computer Graphics I and II; Introduction to Video Engineering; Animation

Workshop; Introduction to Multi-Image; Entertainment Arts Forum; Editing I and II; Location Filmmaking; Film Production; Non-Linear Editing; Advanced Film Production.

Facilities
Computer Graphics Macintosh laboratory; Film production equipment and multimedia stations for the production of Graphic Design and Animation. DEC Micro VAX II; DEC workstations.

Student Body
Orange campus enrolls 2,100 undergraduates and 1,100 graduate students; academic centers enroll 6,500; 160 full-time students in the department.

Faculty Profile
The student/faculty ratio at the school is 14:1.

Deadlines and Financial Aid
More than 60 percent of students receive some sort of financial aid. To receive primary consideration for housing and financial aid, apply for admission by March 1st for the fall term and November 1 for the spring term. If applying after these dates, the student receives full consideration for admission, but no guarantee is given regarding availability of housing and financial aid. Financial need is determined by taking into account such things as earnings, expenses, assets, and the number of children. The financial aid package created may be in the form of scholarships, grants, loans, part-time employment or some combination.

Admission Requirements
Undergraduate students must complete the application for undergraduate admission and return it to the Admission Office with the fee; have the high school send an official transcript to the Admission Office, send transcripts of any college-credit courses; have the ACT, SAT or CLEP scores sent to Chapman University. Graduate students should contact the Graduate Admissions Office for details on the application process.

Expenses
Tuition is $21,656 per year for undergraduates and $570 per credit for graduate students.

Contact
333 N. Glassell St., Orange, CA 92666. Telephone: 714-744-7018. Contact person: Prof. Maureen Furniss. Telephone: 714-997-2400. URL: http://www.chapman.edu.

Additional Information
The Bachelor of Fine Arts programs in Broadcast Journalism and Film and Television Production are production-oriented, giving students the opportunity to produce their own programs while they also study how to tell a story visually, and how to develop those stories using the conventions of film and television. These preprofessional degrees are designed to prepare students for specific career paths in film, television and radio.

City College of San Francisco

F/X Degrees Offered
A.A. degree and Certificate of Completion in the CCSF Film Department.

Curricular
Basic Film Production; Lighting; Beginning Film Editing; Advanced Film Editing; Directing; Motion Picture Special Effects; Film/Video Work Experience; Film Production Laboratory. Graphic design courses include Industrial Design, Art and Photography.

Facilities
For film animation, optical printing, and rotoscoping.

Student Body

An estimated 30,000 students are enrolled in the college.

Faculty Profile

Fourteen faculty members teach in the Film Department.

Deadlines and Financial Aid

Various forms of state and federal aid are available to students. Rolling admission.

Admission Requirements

Application and fee, transcripts, GED or high school diploma.

Expenses

Tuition is $18 per credit for in-state residents, and $162 per unit for out-of-state students. International students pay $171 per unit.

Contact

City College of San Francisco, School of Liberal Arts, 50 Phelan Ave., San Francisco, CA 94112. Telephone: 415-239-3127. Fax: 415-452-5110. Contact person: Bruce Smith, Dean.
URL: http://www.ccsf.edu/.

Additional Information

This two-year program is geared towards training students in all aspects of motion picture production, in preparation for independent filmmaking, employment in the professional motion picture industry, or pursuit of a four-year/graduate film program.

Cogswell Polytechnical College

F/X Degrees Offered

B.A. in Computer and Video Imaging; B.A. in Computer and Video Imaging; B.A. in Digital Motion Picture; B.A. in Digital Audio Technology; B.A. in Software Engineering; B.A. in Digital Arts Engineering.

Curricular

Principles of Graphic Design; 3D Viewing; Storyboarding; 2D Animation; Midi Fundamentals; 3D Animation; Audio Recording; CG Character Animation; Video Post-Production; Peripheral Devices; Computer Imaging Concepts; Scriptwriting.

Facilities

Includes PC workshops with digitizing tablets; CD-ROM; RGB/NTSC monitors; capture boards; scanner; camera; video printers; film recorder. Eight Silicon Graphic workstations, and a DAT. PC software includes AutoCAD; 3D Studio; Animator Pro from Auto desk; Crystal/Topas from Crystal Graphics; Fractal Designer Painter; Adobe Photoshop. SGI workstation software includes Maya and Eclipse; Pandemonium. Facilities also include 24-, 16- and 8-track recording studios, using MIDI and digital audio systems for synchronous tape, digital recording, and audio for video post-production. Individual classroom MIDI stations and sound design laboratories are also available.

Student Body

Total student enrollment is 350.

Faculty Profile

A total of 15 full-time faculty and 45 adjunct faculty teach at the college. Three full-time faculty and several adjunct faculty teach in the area of Visual Effects. Class sizes range from 10 to 20 students for lecture and laboratory sessions.

Deadlines and Financial Aid

Federal Pell Grant, Federal Supplemental Educational Opportunity Grant, Federal Work-Study, Federal Perkins Loan Program, Federal Family Educational Loan Program, Cal Grant A and B (California residents only), Title 38 (Veterans

Benefits). Cal Grant Deadline: March 2nd for the following fall. Applicants are urged to apply for Fall: June 1, 2002; Spring: October 1, 2002; Summer: February 1, 2003.

Admission Requirements
Admission decisions are based on a careful evaluation of the applicant's academic record, test scores, written application, and essay. Although applications for admission are accepted at any time, the deadline is normally 12 weeks prior to the beginning of the trimester for which the student is applying. Admitted students may begin either full-time or part-time study during the fall, spring, or summer trimesters. Although applications for admission are accepted at any time, the deadline is normally four weeks prior to the beginning of the trimester for which the student is applying. Admitted students may begin either full-time or part-time study during the fall, spring or summer trimesters. Satisfactory completion of two years of mathematics (including algebra and geometry); one year of science; three of years English; high school GPA of 2.5.; placement tests in mathematics and English prior to enrolling in classes; three pieces of original artwork (drawings, paintings, slides, floppy, VHS) and two letters of recommendation from current teachers and/or counselors. The portfolio must contain slides or photos of at least seven original drawings and/or paintings. In addition, you may include photos or slides of sculpture, printouts or computer created images, and/or video tape. All portfolio material must be contained in a hardcover 1" or 1.5" three-ring binder. Requirements for transfer students are different.

Expenses
Full-time resident tuition is $4,800 per trimester of 12-16 credit hours, or $400 per credit.

Undergraduate Contact
Admissions Office, Cogswell Polytechnical College, 1175 Bordeaux Dr., Sunnyvale, CA 94089. Telephone: 408-541-0100 or 800-COGSWELL. Fax: 408-747-0764 E-mail: info@cogswell.edu. URL: http://www.cogswell.edu/.

Additional Information
Computer and Video Imaging teaches fundamental and advanced concepts in such areas as Illustration, Graphic Design, 2D and 3D Animation, Scriptwriting, Storyboarding, Authoring, Video Production, and Sound Design. Students will be challenged with a variety of computer graphics and animation styles currently used in the film and broadcast industries.

College of the Canyons

F/X Degrees Offered
Degree programs in Computer Science, Graphic Design, and Animation.

Curricular
The curriculum in Animation Production and Computer Animation provides a foundation in art and design, as well as courses in current technology. All students are required to complete short films in order to understand story concepts and post-production. Students are expected to take an active role in classroom critiques, providing stimulating discussions. Guest speakers are invited from the industry, and students are encouraged to seek out internships. Through individual attention and encouragement, students gain valuable skills and produce a professional portfolio. Classes include: Introduction to Animation; Story Development and Storyboarding; Animation Production; Advanced Animation; Animation Portfolio; Drawing I, II, and III; and Introduction to Digital Media.

Facilities

Facilities include a computer lab equipped with Gateway P3 computers and a drawn animation lab. Software includes 3-D Studio Max, Maya, Flash, Premiere, DigiCel, Photoshop, and Sound Forge. Other equipment includes lunchbox pencil test systems on carts, mini DV camcorder, and DAT audio recorder.

Student Body

There are approximately 12,000 students attending the school.

Faculty Profile

Class sizes are small.

Deadlines and Financial Aid

Financial aid is available in the form of grants, loans, and scholarships. Aid is based on need, although most students qualify for at least some.

Admission Requirements

First-time students must submit a completed application for undergraduate admission, application fee, either SAT or ACT scores, and an official copy of their high school transcript.

Expenses

Tuition for residents is $18 per credit hour and $148 per credit hour for non-residents.

Contact

Department Animation, College of the Canyons, Santa Clarita, CA 91355. Telephone: 661-362-5039. Fax: 661-259-8302. Contact: Sheila M. Sofian, Chair. Email: sheila.sofian@canyons.edu. URL: http://www.coc.cc.ca.us/

Additional Information

Media Arts at College of the Canyons is divided into three programs: Animation, Design Arts and Technology and Radio Television Film. Design Arts and Technology is further divided into two areas of focus: Multimedia and Graphic Design. Each program offers unique course work tailored to the demands of their respective industries. Recognizing that each of the areas of study require similar skills and that many students may cross over from one field to another, it makes sense to have information pertinent to all fields located on one common website. Moreover, a common website broadens students' awareness of all the exciting fields within media arts and may facilitate the development of new relationships between students from potentially isolated areas of study.

Ex'pression Center for New Media

F/X Degrees Offered

Associate and Bachelor of Applied Science Degrees in Sounds Arts, Digital Visual Media, and Digital Graphic Design. Fourteen-month total immersion programs.

Curricular

Courses are offered in the Basics of Computers, Fine Arts, 2D and 3D Graphics and Animation, Fundamentals of Sound and Audio Acoustics, Analog Consoles and Tape Machines, Microphones, MIDI, Music Theory, the Newest Digital Workstations and Consoles in the audio industry today. Digital Graphic Design area offers courses in Formal Graphic Design Principles, Color Theory, Typography, Branding, Print Design, Animation Principals, Motion Graphics, User Interface Design, and Digital Video Skills. Other courses in posters, CD covers, brochures, interactive kiosks, websites with Flash, TV commercials, and short films. The Expression Digital Visual Media Program is designed to enhance the student's knowledge and skills through an intensive series of courses that cover a wide spectrum of digital visual media including 3D modeling and animation; compositing; digital film and video effects; creating graphics for the Internet; and more. Students gain experiential knowledge through extensive lab time using multiple hardware platforms. A one-to-one (student-to-machine) lab ratio allows students to individually explore the intricacies of a wide variety of graphics software. Students create a series of projects throughout the program in addition to a final project specially developed to demonstrate their knowledge and abilities to potential employers.

Facilities
Meyer Hall is where students record live concerts and use Vicon 8 motion capture to animate the 3D characters they create. Apple G4 Lab fully equipped for graphic design, video and 3D programs. The latest computing from Apple and Dell, large hard drives and RAM. Every classroom is wired for sound with projection from any source. Software includes: Kaydara Filmbox; Adobe After Effects; Adobe Photoshop; Adobe Illustrator; Adobe Premiere; Final Cut Pro; Deep Paint 3D; Quark; Macromedia Flash; Macromedia Dreamweaver; Microsoft Office.

Student Body
There are 30 students per graduation class.

Faculty Profile
There are 27 faculty members teaching the program.

Deadlines and Financial Aid
Expression Center offers four annual Eckart Wintzen scholarships that are earmarked for three different local high schools. There are also loan options as well as many student loan options.

Admission Requirements
Submit an application with the fee; 30 students are accepted every two months; Entrance Interview. Portfolio is optional at this point.

Expenses
Tuition for all three programs (Digital Graphic Design, Digital Visual Media and Sound Arts) ranges from $37,450 to $42,450 depending on the number of General Education credits completed.

Contact
6601 Shellmound St., Emeryville, CA 94608. Telephone: 877-833-8800 or 510-654-2934. Contact person: Andrew Britt, Director. E-mail: data@xnewmedia.com. URL: http://www.xnewmedia.com/.

Foothill College

F/X Degrees Offered
A.A. in Art, Communication with a focus in Graphic Design; A.S. in Computer Science; A.A. in Graphic Design and Computer Graphics; A.S. in Interactive and Multimedia Technologies; A.A. in Photography and Digital Imaging.

Curricular
Art: Introduction to Computer Graphics; Illustration with the Macintosh. Communication: Introduction to Computer Graphics; Introduction to Graphic Design; Introduction to QuarkXPress; Introduction to Adobe Illustrator; Introduction to Fractal Design Painter; Graphics Design and Layout on the Computer; Introduction to Photoshop; Advanced Photoshop. Interactive and Multimedia-- Multimedia and Digital Video Basics; 3D Modeling and Animation for Multimedia; Using the Internet; World Wide Web and Electronic Publishing. Computer Science--UNIX System Administration; UNIX Shell Programming; Computer Graphics Programming.

Facilities
Several Macintosh laboratories with such software programs as Fractal Design Painter, QuarkXPress,

Adobe Illustrator, Photoshop, and several others. Software includes DreamWeaver; Extreme 3D; Final Cut Pro; and many more up-to-date titles.

Student Body
Total enrollment: 19,000.

Faculty Profile
There are 500 faculty members teaching at the college.

Deadlines and Financial Aid
Various forms of financial aid are available to students including state and federal aid, and scholarships. Applicants must file FAFSA form with the Office of Financial Aid.

Admission Requirements
GED or high school transcripts, application and fee.

Expenses
Tuition is $12 per credit for residents and $111 per credit for non-residents.

Contact
Foothill College, Admission Office, 12345 El Monte Rd., Los Altos Hills, CA 94022-4599. Telephone: 650-949-7777. Fax: 650-949-7048 Email: ctis@fga.fhda.edu.
URL: http://www.foothill.fhda.edu/index.shtml

Humboldt State University

F/X Degrees Offered
B.A. in Studio Art with an emphasis in Graphic Design/Computer Graphics.

Curricular
Courses in Macintosh Literacy for the 21st Century; Digital Expression; Advanced Digital Expression; Alternative Photography; Digital Imaging.

Facilities
Macintosh workstations with such software programs as Fractal Design Painter; QuarkXPress; Adobe Illustrator; Photoshop; and Web Design software.

Student Body
There are 350 Graphic Design majors; 7,500 total enrollment.

Faculty Profile
Three faculty members teach courses in computer graphics.

Deadlines and Financial Aid
Various forms of financial aid are available to students including state and federal aid, work study, and scholarships. Applicants must file FAFSA form with the Office of Financial Aid.

Admission Requirements
GED or high school transcripts, application and fee. You must have a qualifiable eligibility index.

Expenses
Tuition for residents is $13,708 per year for full-time students. Non-residents pay $13,708 per year plus $282 per credit hour. Graduate tuition per year is $13,274.

Contact
Graphic Design Department, HSU, Arcata, CA 95521-8299. Telephone: 707-826-5811. Fax: 707-826-6190. Contact person: Prof. Mark Isaacson.
URL: http://www.humboldt.edu/.

Modesto Junior College

F/X Degrees Offered
The Computer Graphic Applications Associate Degree A.S. and Certificate programs lead to four application options: Business Desktop Publishing;

Micro Computer Graphics; World Wide Web and Multimedia Publishing; and 2D/3D Animation and Illustration.

Curricular
3D Modeling and Rendering; 3D Computer Animation; 2D Computer Animation; Multimedia/Interactive; High-level Programming; Low-level Programming; Digital Painting/Drawing; Image Proccssing; Virtual Reality; Digital Video; Stereo Imaging; Micro Computer Graphics; Computer Illustration Software; Image Manipulation Software; Publishing on the World Wide Web; Introduction to 3D Modeling.

Facilities
Teaching laboratory of 24 PC-based systems; open laboratory of 24 PC-based systems; Macintosh laboratory.

Student Body
There are 600 undergraduate students.

Deadlines and Financial Aid
Grants and scholarships are available. Deadline: circa August 13th for the fall semester.

Admission Requirements
Application, open admissions.

Expenses
Tuition is $18 per unit for residents. Out-of-state tuition is $118 per unit.

Contact
435 College Ave., Modesto, CA 95350. Telephone: 209-575-6081. Fax: 209-575-6086.
URL: http://mjc.yosemite.cc.ca.us/.

Mount San Antonio College

F/X Degrees Offered
The Computer Graphic Applications Associate Degree A.A. with a forcus in Computer Art and Animation.

Curricular
Graphic Design, 3D Animaton, Multimedia courses.

Facilities
Labs are equipped to teach 3D computer animation.

Student Body
Approximately 45,000 students attent the college.

Deadlines and Financial Aid
Grants and scholarships are available. Deadline: circa August 13th for the fall semester.

Admission Requirements
Application, open admissions.

Expenses
Tuition is $11 per unit for in-state residents. Out-of-state tuition is $154 per unit.

Contact
1100 N. Grand Ave., Walnut CA 91789. Telephone: 909-594-5611 ext. 4570. Fax: 909-468-3993. Contact person: Dr. Stephen Runnebohm, Dean, Humanities and Social Sciences.
URL: http://www.mtsac.edu/.

Orange Coast College

F/X Degrees Offered
Certificates in Digital Media through the Fine Arts Department.

Curricular
Introduction to Computer Graphics; Images and Illustration for Computer Graphics; Photography

and Computer Graphics I and II; Interactive Multimedia; Image Processing for Digital Video; 2D Animation; 3D Animation; Portfolio Development; Introduction to Digital Photography; Lettering and Computer Typography; Computer Art Production; Computer Advertising Design and Copywriting.

Facilities

There are 30 high-end Macintosh workstations; laser printers; scanners; film recording camera; CD writer; Internet access.

Student Body

Approximately 350-400 students in the Department.

Faculty Profile

There are 13 faculty members teaching courses in the area of Computer Graphics.

Deadlines and Financial Aid

Contact the Admissions Office, Rm. 109, 2701 Fairview Rd., Box 5005, Costa Mesa, CA 92628. Telephone: 714-432-5072.

Admission Requirements

File application form, high school graduate-entrance requirement, transcripts required.

Expenses

Tuition is $18 per unit for in-state residents, and $168 per unit for out-of-state students.

Contact

Electronic Media Department, 2701 Fairview Rd., Box 5005, Costa Mesa, CA 92628. Telephone: 714-432-5171. Fax: 714-432-5075. Contact person: Lisa Bloomfield, Chair. Email: lbloomfield@occ.cccd.edu. URL: http://www.occ.cccd.edu/.

Otis College of Art and Design

F/X Degrees Offered

Certificate in Computer Graphics; B.F.A. in Graphic Design; Digital Media/Toy Design.

Curricular

Introduction to the Macintosh; Adobe Photoshop; Computer Graphics for Computer and Textiles; Introduction to Multimedia; Introduction to Macromedia Director Adobe Illustrator; Digital Media Arts Lab; Mac Lab in Motion Graphics; Digital Media Arts Lab; Special Effects; Character Animation; Computer Modeling and Animation; Advanced 3D Animation.

Facilities

Hardware: NT workstation, Macintosh computers, flatbed color scanners, CD-ROM burners; one Sanyo VHS video deck. Software: Adobe Photoshop; Sound Edit; Adobe PageMaker; Macromedia Freehand; Adobe Illustrator; Broderbund KidPix; Altsys Fontographer; Macromedia Director; AutoDesSys FormZ; Adobe Premiere; Fractal Design Painter; Strata Studio Pro; Macromedia Swivel 3D; Pixel Paint Professional; QuarkXPress; Microsoft Word; Morph; Kai's Power Tools.

Student Body

Approximately 800 students are enrolled in the college.

Faculty Profile

There are 236 faculty teaching at the college; approximately 200 are part-time.

Deadlines and Financial Aid

Financial aid is available only to fully Matriculated (degree-seeking) students meeting a minimum class load (6 or more credit units per semester) who show financial need. For information, please contact the

Financial Aid Office at 213-251-0542. The academic Management Services payment plan is designed to help students divide educational expenses into convenient monthly payments. This is the only payment plan offered at Otis. There are no interest charges. AMS offers a 12, 11, or 10 month payment beginning May 1 for the Fall/Spring enrollment period.

Admission Requirements

Application and fee, high school transcripts, portfolio, essay, and recommendations. Each Applicant is required to present a portfolio of his or her work for review. The portfolio should demonstrate the prospective student's strengths, individual growth and interests. The final portfolio should reflect the applicant's best examples in observational drawing, color, composition and concept. A Minimum of Twelve and a maximum of twenty pieces should be submitted. Each applicant is required to submit a one page typed writing sample on one of the following topics. 1. Focus on a specific moment or event that was influential in your life. 2. Describe what your life as an artist or designer will be like after you graduate from Otis.

Expenses

Tuition is $22,820 per year for full-time students.

Contact

Otis College of Art And Design, 9045 Lincoln Boulevard, Los Angeles, CA 90045. Telephone: 800-527-OTIS or 310-665-6984. Fax: 310-665-6821. Email: otisinfo@otis.edu. Contact person: Harry Mott, Chair.
URL: http://www.otis.edu/.

Platt College

F/X Degrees Offered

B.A. in Media Arts. A.A. degree in Graphic Design, Multimedia Design, Animation, and Digital Video Production.

Curricular

Vocational-oriented training in Graphic Design with an emphasis on Computer Graphics and Multimedia. 3D Modeling and Rendering; 3D Computer Animation; 2D Computer Animation; Multimedia/Interactive; Web site design; Digital Video, and more.

Facilities

11 Student workstations equipped with Pentium 4 2.0Ghz processors, fully networked and running Windows 2000 Professional. Each machine is configured with 512Mb of RAM, video card with at least 32Mb memory, CDRW, Zip drive, 19" monitor. Each machine is online with T1 internet access. For classroom instruction, the instructor's monitor is shown on a large projection screen. 18 student workstations equipped with dual 600Mhz or faster Pentium III processors, fully networked and running Windows 2000 Professional. Each machine is configured with 1Gb of RAM, Nvidia GeForce 2 or 3 video card with at least 32Mb texture memory, CDRW, Zip drive, 19" or larger monitor, 9-17Gb SCSI system disk drive plus a 40Gb IDE data disk drive. Each machine is online with T1 internet access. For classroom instruction, the instructor's monitor is shown on a large projection screen. For shooting digital video to later integrate with 3D imagery, a stage with green chroma key walls and floor is always ready. Software includes: Adobe Photoshop, Illustrator, After Effects. Macromedia: Director, Flash, Dreamweaver, QuarkXpress, NewTek LightWave 3D, Final Cut Pro, Sonic Foundry: Acid, Sound Forge. Some of the systems include, but are not limited to: Dual 1.25Ghz PowerPC G4, 256K L2

cache & 2MB L3 cache/processor, 167Mhz System Bus, 512Mb PC2700 DDR SDRAM, 120Gb Ultra ATA drive, SuperDrive (DVD-R/CD-RW), ATI Radeon 9000 Pro, scanner, T1 internet access.

Student Body
Approximately 400 students attend the college.

Faculty Profile
Twelve faculty members teach in the department.

Deadlines and Financial Aid
Various fellowships and traditional state, federal, and city aid are available to students. Contact the Financial Aid Office for details on obtaining financial assistance at the college.

Admission Requirements
Application and fee, transcripts, SAT scores.

Expenses
Tuition ranges from $12,000 to $17,000 per degree program 11.5 months to 2.5 years.

Contact
6250 El Cajun Blvd., San Diego, CA 92115. Telephone: 800-255-0613 or 619-265-0107. Fax: 619-265-8655. Contact person: Gayle Paterson, Admissions Advisor. E-mail: info@platt.edu. URL: http://www.platt.edu/.

San Diego State University

F/X Degrees Offered
B.S. in Television, Film, and New Media Production (Liberal Arts and Science). M.A. in Television, Film, and New Media Production. M.F.A. in Graphic Design through the School of Art, Design, and Art History.

Curricular
Film and Television Cinematography; Art Direction for Television and Film; Production Design for Television and Film; Advanced Film and Video: Field Production; Advanced Film and Video: Studio Production; Animated Film Techniques; Advanced Creative Production; New Media Production; Technology and Mediated Interaction; Seminar in Criticism of Electronic Media and Cinema; Seminar in Media Message Design.

Facilities
Animation stands, and video and film production equipment. Extensive graphic design laboratory with Macintosh workstations.

Student Body
There are 22,590 undergraduate students, and 5,782 graduate students.

Faculty Profile
There are 31 full-time faculty members.

Deadlines and Financial Aid
Students will be admitted to the graduate program only in the fall semester, and applications must be received by the School of Communication by March 1. To be considered for financial aid, a FAFSA must be completed and mailed to the processing service listed on the form as soon as possible after Jan. 1 and before the CSU priority filing date of March 2. Graduate students are employed in the School of Communication in teaching, research and other areas. Graduate teaching associateships in communication are available to a limited number of qualified students. A limited number of graduate assistantships are also available in the School of Communication for those with academic or professional experience in various research and creative areas. Contact the graduate director or any of the graduate advisors for further information. Call 619-594-5450 for an application.

Admission Requirements
Applicants to the School of Art, Design and Art History must submit the Graduate Review

application and a portfolio by March 1st for the fall semester, and by Oct. 1 for the spring semester. Students applying for admission to the M.A. degree in Television, Film and New Media Production are evaluated according to the following criteria: undergraduate major or minor in radio and television, film or a related communication discipline; minimum overall undergraduate GPA of 2.8–3.0 in the last 60 semester units attempted as an undergraduate; acceptable GRE scores on the verbal and quantitative sections of the test; three letters of recommendation: at least one letter from an academic reference and at least one from a professor or professional acquainted with the applicant's creative activities; a personal statement of purpose that discusses the applicant's background, interests and abilities that apply to the desire for an advanced degree in telecommunications. Applicants must be prepared to submit a portfolio of previous creative activity. Health insurance is also mandatory.

Expenses
Residents pay $1,128 per term. Non-residents pay a $288 per semester unit in addition to the per unit resident's fee.

Contact
Department of Computer Science, 5500 Campanile Drive, San Diego, CA 92182-7720. Telephone: 619-594-6191. Fax: 619-594-6746. Contact person: Dr. Leland Beck. Email: beck@cs.sdsu.edu. URL: http://www.sdsu.edu/.

San Francisco Art Institute

F/X Degrees Offered
B.F.A. in Interdisciplinary Studies in Fine Art; M.F.A. in Digital Media.

Curricular
Training in various computer graphics applications. There are courses in Painting/Drawing, Photography, Printmaking, Filmmaking (Narrative, Documentary & Experimental Cinema), Interdisciplinary Arts, Digital Media, New Genres (Performance Art, Video, and Installation) and Sculpture/Ceramics.

Facilities
Hardware: 25 Macintosh workstations; APS DAT drive; Micronet CD-ROM burner; 25 Wacom drawing tablets and pens; Epson ES 1200 dpi flatbed scanners; Polaroid Sprint Scan film scanner; Polaroid HR 5000 film recorder; JVC VHS videotape decks; Epson stylus color printers; Apple LaserWriter 16/600 grayscale printers and a Hewlett Packard 560 color printer. Software: Adobe Premiere; Photoshop; Illustrator; Dimensions; Fractal Design Poser; Painter; Macromodel; Fontographer; Freehand; Sound Edit; Director; Ray Dream Designer; Microsoft Office; Quark and Hsc Vector Effects; Convolver; Kai's Power Tools and Kpt Bryce. The department also offers T1 access to the Internet from all CDM stations, and complete e-mail and World Wide Web services.

Student Body
Total student body: 662.

Faculty Profile
More than 60 faculty members plus visiting faculty teach at the institute.

Deadlines and Financial Aid
M.F.A. students must submit their application by February 15 for the fall, and November 1 for the spring. B.F.A. applications are reviewed on a continual basis through Sept. 1 for the fall, and Jan. 10 for the spring semester. The financial aid priority deadline is March 2. Financial aid awards are made on a rolling basis beginning April 1 of each year for the next summer, fall, and spring enrollment. CAL Grant applications must be submitted no later

than the March 2 deadline. Applicants filing early receive priority for available institutional aid; late applications will result in decreased aid.

Admission Requirements
Undergraduates: application and fee, statement of purpose, high school transcript, ACT or SAT scores, portfolio of 20 examples. An interview may be required. Graduate students: application and fee, two copies of the written statement of purpose, official transcripts, two copies of portfolio inventory.

Expenses
Tuition is $23,508 per year.

Contact
San Francisco Art Institute, 800 Chestnut St., San Francisco, CA 94133. Phone: 415-771-7020. E-mail: sfaiinfo@sfai.edu. Admission: 800-345-7324. URL: http://www.sfai.edu/.

San Francisco State University

F/X Degrees Offered
Department of Design and Industry offers a B.S. and M.A.; M.A. Department of Art offers an M.F.A. Computer Science offers B.S. and M.S. degrees. Cinema Department offers a B.A. and M.A. in Film Studies; Creativity and Art Education Area.

Curricular
The Art Department and Inter-Arts Center: various courses in Computer Art; Graphics Design; Conceptual Design; Advanced Computer Graphics and Animation. Courses in Interactive Media; Network-Based Art; Robotics; Digital Video; Cultural Theory. Cinema: courses in Film Production; Character Animation; Animation Production.

Facilities
Macintosh workstations, and SGIs; a DEC Alpha; 10 HP RISC workstations for the graphics class; two other computer laboratories; film production equipment. The John F. True 24-hour computing lab allows students to have access to computing resources with connectivity to the Internet and standard software applications. In total, over 1,500 PCs and Macintoshes are available to students, supported by the Division of Information Technology, the colleges and other departments at SFSU. Many are general purpose computing labs, offering standard software applications; others are specialty labs, with discipline-specific software. Over 300 dial-in modems provide remote access for the campus community. All classrooms, computer labs, and on-campus housing have high-speed network access. There are a number of computer workstations on campus designed to meet the needs of students with various kinds of disabilities. The Division of Information Technology offers free short courses and workshops throughout the year to faculty, staff and students on basic, intermediate and advanced skills in computers, from word processing and spreadsheets to graphics, databases and Web pages.

Student Body
Fifty undergraduates; six graduates/post doctoral students in the Computer Graphics area. Computer Science: a total of 300 undergraduates and graduate students in the department. More than 30,000 students are enrolled in the university.

Deadlines and Financial Aid
M.F.A. deadline: middle of February each year. B.A. is always open. The student must file the FAFSA by March 2nd prior to the upcoming academic year to be considered for all types of financial aid. If the student misses the March 2nd priority deadline, s/he may still file the FAFSA, but will be considered for remaining available funds only, usually limited

to Pell Grants and student loans. Undergraduate admissions for the fall semester are closed as of April 1st for resident students. All applications must be received by this date.

Admission Requirements

Undergraduates: must file a complete undergraduate application as described in the undergraduate admission booklet, and a non-refundable, application fee, submit the SAT or ACT. Graduate students: receive from and file an application to the Graduate Division; obtain a university Bulletin from the bookstore; review the Bulletin for university requirements and to determine if there are supplemental departmental admission and application requirements; contact the department and submit any additional materials requested. Attain Classified Graduate Standing by consulting the major department regarding any test scores (e.g., GMAT, GRE, etc.) that may be required.

Expenses

Tuition is $1,023 per semester for undergraduate residents; non-resident students pay $288 per academic unit plus resident fees.

Contact

1600 Holloway Ave., San Francisco, CA 94132. Telephone: 415-338-2291 or 415-338-2176. Fax: 415-338-6537. Contact person: Stephen Wilson, Department of Art. E-mail: swilson@sfsu.edu. URL: http://www.sfsu.edu/

San Jose State University

F/X Degrees Offered

B.A. Computer in Fine Art. An interdisciplinary undergraduate degree program requiring inter-departmental and university study. M.A. Multimedia Computing in the Arts. M.F.A. Computers in Fine Art. B.F.A. in Graphic Design and Animation.

Curricular

Introduction to Computers in Art; Computer Graphics and Animation; Seminar in Computer Graphics; Graduate Tutorials in Computer Graphics 6; Introduction to Computers in Art. Electives: Computer Graphics and Animation; Advanced Computer Projects in Art; Computer Graphics for Designers; Applications of Computers to Design; Advanced Electronic Music; Television Production; Computers and Intelligence; Computer Applications Seminar; Instructional Interactive Video.

Facilities

Computer Animation and Digital Video: SGIs; Maya; Multiform; Softimage; Integrated Video; Xaos Tools; Ridge 32 Raster Technology; Targa PC with TIPS; RIO; UNICAD; Macintosh workstations with Director; Adobe Premiere; Renderman; Bellum; Infinite-D; StrataVision; MiniCAD; Broadcast Video Editing Suite and Patch Bay with MII; 3/4-inch Hi8 mm; S-VHS; RasterOps Video Expander; Silicon Graphics Video Framer. Multimedia and Interactivity: IBM P52 Audio Visual Capture system with Toolbook; Plus Storyboard Live; Linkway; Digital Video Interactive; MIDI Sampler; Synthesizer; Interface; Panasonic Videodisc Recorder and Player System; Image Database with Image ASX; Shoebox; Embark; Radiant CNX. Image Processing: Macintoshes with Photoshop; Beachtron Painter; Nixon slide and negative scanner; color flatbed scanners; RGB; Hi8 mm and S-VHS cameras; Matrix film recorder; Targa workstations with TIPS; Lumena; PCs with Corel Draw; Photoshop. Virtual Reality: Pentium workstations; 3D sound; Polhemus Isotrak ll; Eye Beam Headmount Display. Telecommunications and Networking: Small-room video conferencing system; desktop video conferencing for both Macintosh and PC with shared whiteboard; Timbuktu; Person-to-Person; Envision; connections to campus fiber-optic backbone and Internet; Sun Sparc and 3/280 Server workstation servers; World Wide Web; Mosaic Server with CADRE homepage.

Student Body
Total students in the School of Art: 1,320.

Faculty Profile
Ten faculty members and one technical staff person are associated with the Computer in Arts and Design Research and Education (CADRE) Institute.

Deadlines and Financial Aid
Fall semester deadline: November 1, spring semester deadline: April 1.

Admission Requirements
Complete application; portfolio review; may include examples of digital imaging (slides or disk); computer animation; video or interactive multimedia; statement of objectives; coursework plan; indicate completed courses (with semester) which fulfill requirements of the major.

Expenses
Resident tuition is $1,023 per semester; non-residents pay an estimated $1,023 per semester plus the $282 -out-of-state fee per credit.

Contact
Computers in Fine Art: Computers in Art, School of Art and Design, San Jose State University, One Washington Square, San Jose, CA 95129-0089. Contact person: Professor Joel Slayton, Director, CADRE Institute. Telephone: 408-924-4368. E-mail: slayton@sjsuvm1.sjsu.edu. URL: http://www.sjsu.edu/.

Additional Information
The CADRE Institute of the School of Art and Design at San Jose State University is an interdisciplinary academic program dedicated to Experimental Applications of Computer Graphics, Interactive Multimedia and Electro-Acoustics. CADRE faculty and students are actively engaged in research, testing and exploration of new computer-based media in the visual arts, design, sound, installation, performance and education. The CADRE Institute offers advanced instruction in each of these areas as well as specialized undergraduate and graduate programs. The Electronic Acoustic Studio, a sister program in the Music Department, provides for study in digital composition and performance. Additional adjunct programs in Theater Arts, Engineering and Computer Science provide opportunities for interdisciplinary study. The School of Art and Design offers professional programs in Pictorial and Spatial Art, Photography, Graphic Design, Illustration, Interior Design, Industrial Design, Art Education, and Art History. Industry Sponsors: corporations involved in sponsored project support and in providing facilities include: Apple Computer, Asanti Technologies, Caliber Tech Inc., Compression Laboratories Inc., E-mu Systems, Ford Motor Company, IBM, OpCode, Pacific Bell, RasterOps Inc., Riverview Systems Group, Panasonic Corp., Silicon Graphics Inc., Software Systems Inc., Sun Micro Systems, and VideoMedia Inc., Conferences.

Santa Monica College, Academy of Entertainment & Technology

F/X Degrees Offered
A.A. through the Santa Monica College, Two-year Certificate Program in Computer Animation or Interactive Media through the Academy of Entertainment & Technology.

Curricular
Courses in Computer Graphics, Animation, Modeling, Graphic Design, Web Design, and Interactive Multimedia.

Facilities
Macintosh workstations, PCs and SGIs. Software includes Deamweaver, Flash, Photoshop, Director, 3D Studio Max, Maya and other multimedia and design packages. The academy also has the following equipment available: Unix web server for student sites, ProTools 24|Mix stations, Windows and Macintosh classrooms with 24 student workstations and instructor video projection. Computers are also available in Student Services for word processing, internet access, and e-mail. The computer lab has 80 mac/pc computers, a CD burner, color laser printer, scanners, and a network rendering queue.

Student Body
There are 24 students per course. Total enrollment: 800 students.

Faculty Profile
Eight full-time faculty members teach at the academy; several part-time and adjunct faculty.

Deadlines and Financial Aid
Various forms of state and federal aid are available to students. Rolling admission at Santa Monica College. The Academy of Entertainment & Technology has a fall and spring deadline.

Admission Requirements
Application and fee, transcripts, SAT, portfolio. Courses in the Animation program requires passing a portfolio course (ET50a) or submitting a portfolio in lieu of the class. Passing of ET50a or a substituting a portfolio requires a submission consisting of traditional art work demonstrating drawing, color, composition and concept, and a facile ability with a pencil.

Expenses
The Academy programs operate within the California Community College system. Enrollment fees for Academy classes are the same as for all other classes at Santa Monica College: California residents pay $11 per unit, plus nominal student activity fees and materials fees. Non-resident tuition ranges from $125 - 140 per unit.

Contact
Academy of Entertainment & Technology, 1660 Stewart St., Santa Monica, CA 90404. Telephone: 310-434-3700. Fax: 310-434-3768. Contact person: Lydia Casillas, Academic Counselor. Email: casillas_lydia@smc.edu.
URL: http://academy.smc.edu/.

Stanford University

F/X Degrees Offered
M.S., M.S.C.S. and Ph.D. with a concentration in Computer Graphics.

Curricular
Courses in Computer Graphics, Artificial Intelligence, and various courses in Advanced Scientific Visualization.

Facilities
Computer Science Department Computer Facilities (CSD-CF) provides UNIX, PC and Mac administration for the Computer Science Department administration and for a number of research groups within the department. Department hardware includes: Xenon, a Sun-4/670 with four CPUs, the primary student machine; Radon, an HP 9000-755 computer for student use; various medium to large UNIX machines; hundreds of workstations and X-terminals from Sun Microsystems, Digital Equipment Corporation, Hewlett Packard, SGIs, IBM and NCD.

Student Body
The department has approximately 160 doctoral students and 350 master's students. The university enrolls 14,000 students.

Faculty Profile

There are 42 faculty members teaching in the department; 1,300 faculty members teach at the university.

Deadlines and Financial Aid

All incoming Ph.D. students are supported by a departmental assistantship or by fellowship. Assistantship holders receive a stipend plus a nine-unit tuition credit each quarter. If there is an insufficient number of Ph.D. students to staff teaching and research assistantships, then such positions are offered to qualified students in the M.S.C.S. program. Applications and all supporting documentation for admission to the Ph.D. and the M.S.C.S. programs must be received before Jan. 1. Financial aid information for Ph.D. students will be made available upon the students' acceptance.

Admission Requirements

Application and fee, transcripts, references and GRE. Information on admission can be found in the Guide to Graduate Admissions. The primary criterion for admission to Stanford is academic excellence, and the most important single credential is the high school transcript. While the majority of thestrongest candidates have an unweighted GPA between 3.6 and 4.0 as well as SAT I verbal and math scores of at least 650 each, there are no minimum figures set for grade point average, test scores, or rank in class.

Expenses

Tuition is $1,199 per unit.

Contact

Computer Science Department, 353 Serra Mall, Stanford University, Stanford CA 94305-9025. Telephone: 650-723-2273. Fax: 650-725-7411. Contact: Professor Hector Garcia-Molina, Chair. E-mail: admissions@cs.stanford.edu. URL: http://www.stanford.edu/.

Additional Information

Founded in 1965, the Computer Science Department is a center for research and education at the graduate level. Students admitted to the Ph.D. program usually combine course work and participation in a research group during their first year, and devote themselves entirely to research thereafter. Students must pass the comprehensive examinations that test the breadth of their computer science knowledge, and a qualifying examination in their specialty area.

University of California at Berkeley

F/X Degrees Offered

B.S., M.S. and Ph.D. in Computer Science through the Berkeley Computer Graphics Laboratory. Multimedia Interface Graphics.

Curricular

Advanced Computer Graphics; Animation; Scientific Visualization.

Facilities

The Computer Graphics laboratory includes Macintosh computers with various software programs; VAX; Tektronix; Sun workstations; IBM; Lyon Lamb; various film and video output equipment.

Student Body

There are 21,500 undergraduates, and 9,500 graduate students attending the university. There are 500 students in the computer science program.

Faculty Profile

There are 147 faculty members in the computer science department.

Deadlines and Financial Aid

Various forms of federal and state aid are available. Students may receive aid in the form of direct loans, Perkins loans, fellowships and scholarships. Undergraduate deadline: November 1-30 for the following fall semester.

Admission Requirements

Undergraduates: SAT I and II, satisfy the university's A-F requirements; application and fee. Graduate students: student deadline for fall semester is Jan. 5.

Expenses

Resident tuition for undergraduate and graduate students is $2,926.96 per year; non-residents pay $10,033.95 per year.

Contact

UC Berkeley, Computer Science, 387 Soda Hall #1776, Berkeley, CA 94720. Telephone: 510-642-6000 or 510-642-3068.
URL: http://www.berkeley.edu/.

Additional Information

Berkeley's Department of Electrical Engineering and Computer Sciences (EECS) offers one of the most comprehensive research and instructional programs in this field anywhere in the world. Berkeley EECS has a particular strength in large interdisciplinary real-world system projects that bring to bear core technologies seamlessly across electrical engineering and computer science.

University of California at Davis

F/X Degrees Offered

The Computer Science Department offers A.B. and M.F.A. degrees.

Curricular

Multimedia; Interactive; Digital Painting/Drawing; Image Processing; Virtual Reality; Digital Video. The CSE and CS majors include theory, software and hardware and in addition the CSE major includes electronics.

Facilities

Students have access to a wide variety of research and instructional resources, including numerous workstations and general purpose processors. These resources include: over 100 workstations of Sun, SGI, and DEC, which support student and faculty research; over 100 computers, consisting of HP, DEC, SGI, and Sun workstations, as well as PC's and Mac's, all supporting instructional activities; access to a variety of parallel and supercomputer systems at the Lawrence Livermore National Laboratory and the San Diego Super Computer Center. Other facilities include the Computer Engineering Research Laboratory; Computer Engineering Workstation Laboratory; Departmental Computing Facilities and Services; Digital Communications Research Laboratory; Digital Design Laboratories; Digital Signal Processing and Communications Laboratory; High Power Microwave Generation Laboratory; Opto-Electronics Facility; Micro-fabrication Facility; Microwave and Antenna Research Laboratory; Solid-State Circuits Research Laboratory; Systems, Control and Robotics Laboratory; Center for Image Processing and Integrated Computing.

Student Body

There are 300 undergraduates, and 15 graduate students are in the department.

Faculty Profile

Eleven faculty members teach in the department.

Deadlines and Financial Aid

Graduate students seeking assistantship for fall admission: February 1. More than $2,000,000 is awarded from more than 150 scholarship funds to approximately 1,500 students. Selection is based on academic performance and promise of future achievement; an essay and a letter of recommendation are required. Admissions contact person: Veronica L. Cohen.

Admission Requirements
Graduate applicants must submit an application and fee, department application form, GRE scores, and three or more letters of recommendation. Undergraduate students must submit an application and fee, SAT or ACT, and transcript.

Expenses
Undergraduate resident tuition is $6,437.50 per year for full-time, and $20,647.50 per year for non-resident full-time students. Graduate residents pay $7,062.50 year, and non-resident tuition is $19,552.50. Graduate tuition can be reduced under certain circumstances.

Contact
Art Department, UC Davis, Davis, CA 95616. Telephone: 530-752-0105. Fax: 530-752-0795. Contact person: Josie Valdez, Undergraduate Advisor. Email: valdez@cs.ucdavis.edu. URL: http://www.ucdavis.edu/.

University of California at Los Angeles

F/X Degrees Offered
School of Theater, Film and Television. B.A. in Motion Picture/Television; an M.F.A. in four distinct professional areas: Production/Directing, Screen Writing, the Producers Program, and Animation; M.F.A. and Ph.D. degrees in Critical Studies. Architecture and Urban Design Department: M.Arch I, M.Arch II, M.A., Ph.D. degrees. Visualization Center Earth And Space Sciences Department: concentrations in: (1) Animation, (2) Digital Imaging, (3) Desktop Publishing and (4) Interactive-Multimedia Design.

Curricular
Screen Writing Fundamentals; Screen Writing Fundamentals Workshop; Film Production; Film Post-Production; Television and Video Production; Film Production Workshop; Television Production Workshop; Writing the Short Screenplay; Directing the Actor for the Camera; Animation Design; Writing for Animation; Animation Workshop; Advanced Animation Workshop; Computer Animation in Film and Video.
Architecture and Urban Design Department Curriculum: 3D Modeling and Rendering; 3D Computer Animation; 2D Computer Animation; Multimedia/Interactive; High-Level Programming; Digital Painting/Drawing; Image Processing; Virtual Reality; Digital Video. Sciences Department Classes: 3D Modeling and Rendering; 3D Computer Animation; 2D Computer Animation; Digital Painting/Drawing; Image Processing; Volume Visualization; Digital Video.

Facilities
Three motion sound stages; one completely equipped animation laboratory; one scoring stage; one re-recording stage; three film-editing rooms; mixing rooms; viewing rooms; negative cutting rooms. Television facilities include three TV studios; one Master Control room; five video viewing rooms; two time-code rooms; 20 video-editing rooms; one fully equipped remote van. Architecture and Urban Design Department Facilities: SGI Onyx/IR; Multiple SGI Indigo II/Impact/Extremes; Multiple Suns; Multiple Intel Pentiums. Visualization Center: equipped with a non-linear computer-based editing system; new in/output devices and a faster network that will be made up of a variety of platforms, including SGIs, Suns, Macintoshes and PCs. Software includes: Maya; Autodesk3D; Premiere; AfterEFX;

Pandemonium ; AVS (Advanced Visual Systems); IDL; Mathematica; Maple; Matlab (MathWorks).

Student Body
Architecture Department: 250 graduate students. Visualization Center: 20 undergraduates; 61 graduates/post-doctoral; 35 others (includes extension students, staff). Students Profile: estimated total enrollment by area: B.A., 70; M.F.A. Production/Directing, 83; M.F.A. Screen Writing, 50; M.F.A. Producers Program, 27; M.F.A. Animation, 27; M.A., 26; Ph.D., 29.

Deadlines and Financial Aid
The postmark deadline for filing the undergraduate application is November 30. The deadline for receipt of the Supporting Materials (the written portfolio) is the last Friday in January. Graduate applications are available beginning in August. The postmark deadline for filing the graduate application is November 1.

Admission Requirements
Production/Directing: an acceptable bachelor's degree in any area. Supporting Materials: a statement of purpose; three letters of recommendation; a two-three-page description of a film or television project that might be undertaken during graduate residence at UCLA. Animation: an acceptable bachelor's degree in any area; a statement of purpose; three letters of recommendation; a description of an animation project, preferably in storyboard form, that might be undertaken during graduate residence at UCLA. Other creative work may be submitted.

Expenses
Estimated undergraduate tuition for three quarters on campus is $5,819.52 for residents and $20,029.52 for non-residents. Graduate fees are $6,317.50 for residents and $18,807.50 for non-residents.

Contact
Student Services, Department of Film and Television, UCLA, Box 951622, Los Angeles, CA 90095-1622. Telephone: 310-825-5761. Architecture and Urban Design Contact: Architecture and Urban Design Department 317 Perloff Hall, UCLA, L.A., CA 90095-1467. Telephone: 310-825-7857. Fax: 310-825-8959. Contact person: Bill Jepson, Director of Computing. E-mail: bill@ucla.edu. Visualization Center, Earth And Space Sciences Department Contact: Earth And Space Sciences Department, UCLA, Geology Building, B707, Los Angeles, CA 90095. Telephone: 310-206-2140. Fax: 310-825-2779. Contact person: Bruce McCrimmon.
URL: http://www.ucla.edu/.

Additional Information
The M.F.A. in Animation is a three-year program that trains and supports the student of animation in defining and developing his or her own style and philosophy as an animator. The basic philosophy of UCLA's Animation Workshop is one person, one film; each filmmaker has complete control over his or her film's content, ideas, viewpoint, style, purpose, audience, form, process and value.
The Visualization Center Earth And Space Sciences Department's primary function is to introduce students and faculty to the use of computer visualization, image processing, and animation software, and to encourage them to use such software in their future work.

University of California at Los Angeles, Extension

F/X Degrees Offered
Certificate Program in Computer Graphics has four specialized areas: Desktop Publishing, Animation, Digital Imaging, and Interactive Multimedia Design.

Curricular

Desktop Publishing: study graphic design and page layout using such software as QuarkXPress, PageMaker, Photoshop and Illustrator, which allow students to combine images in the creation of professional-looking documents. Animation: students learn the fundamentals of both 2D and 3D computer animation using such software as Macromedia Director, Form-Z and Electric Image. Digital Imaging: allows students to explore graphic design and image editing using such software as Photoshop, Painter, Illustrator and Freehand. Interactive Multimedia Design: create interactive media by combining text, still images, animation, sound and video using such software as Apple Media Tool, Premiere, After Effects and Macromedia Director. UNIX Operating System and Applications: Introduction to C Programming Language; Introduction to UNIX; Advanced C Programming Techniques. Graphics Programming and Multimedia: 3D Graphics Programming Techniques Rendering; 3D Graphics Programming Techniques: Interactive Games and Multimedia; A Multimedia Workshop: CD-ROM Productions and Windows; Fundamentals of Interactive Multimedia; Introduction to Creating Digital Effects: An Intensive Silicon Graphics Workshop; 2D Paint and Imaging Techniques Using Parallax Matador; Digital Technologies; 3D Animation, Modeling, and CAD Tools; 3D Animation Using Wavefront Explore; Non-Linear Video Editing with Avid Media Suite Pro; 2D Imaging and Special Effects Using Elastic Reality. Computer Modeling Animation and CAD: Introduction to Character Animation Using Animation Master Version 3; Fundamentals of AutoCAD: A Workshop; Fundamentals of 3D Studio: A Workshop; Intermediate 3D Studio: Project Workshop; Film Recording and Frame-By-Frame Video Animation.

Facilities

Equipment for creating 2D and 3D computer animation, video, film and effects.

Student Body

There are 110,000 students annually.

Faculty Profile

Part-time instructors hired to teach a designed course.

Deadlines and Financial Aid

Extension Grants: a very limited number of Extension Grants are available each quarter for students who establish a financial need. Up to 90 percent of $300 in enrollment fees can be waived under this program in no more than one limited-enrollment course and no more than two courses per quarter total. Application packets will be available November 15 in the UCLA Extension Financial Aid Office and must be returned at or before 5 p.m., December 1, to be considered for the winter quarter. Federal Loan and Grant Programs: you may be eligible for Federal Pell Grants and low-interest Federal Stafford Loans if you are enrolled in qualified UCLA Extension certificate programs.

Admission Requirements

Complete application.

Expenses

Varies depending on course.

Contact

UCLA Extension, Computer Graphics Program, P.O. Box 24901, Los Angeles, CA 90024-090. Contact person: Lynn Murphy. Telephone: 310-206-1422. URL: http://www.research.ucla.edu/media.htm.

University of California at San Diego

F/X Degrees Offered

Visual Arts Department: B.F.A. and M.F.A. Fine Arts program with Computer Arts area. Emphasis on Interactive Media including Installation, Web and Virtual Reality. Computer Science: B.S. and M.S. in Advanced Visualization for Science and Mechanical Engineering.

Curricular

Undergraduates: Studio Video; Introduction to Filmmaking; Scripting and Editing Strategies; Sound And Lighting Techniques; Advanced Editing; Advanced Filmmaking Strategies; Animation; Advanced Camera Techniques; 3D Modeling and Rendering; 3D Computer Animation; 2D Computer Animation; Multimedia/Interactive; High-Level Programming; Low-Level Programming; Image Processing; Virtual Reality; Digital Video; Installation; Robotics. Science Curricular: 3D Modeling And Rendering; 3D Computer Animation; High-Level Programming; Virtual Reality; Volume Visualization; Stereo Imaging.

Facilities

Hardware: Seven SGI Indigo workstations; SGI workstations; one SGI Crimson server; Macintosh imaging stations; Macintosh scanning station; two Postscript printers; Sony 3 CCD camera; Phillips projector; one Polaroid film recorder; one Sony 3/4-inch deck; one Sony Hi-Fi VHS deck. Software: Interactive Effects Amazon Paint; Maya; Island Paint; Island Draw; Island Write. Five film-editing rooms: two with six-plate flatbeds, two with four-plate flatbeds, one with two-plate flatbeds; black and white 16 mm film processing; one Model J 16 mm contact printer; one computer-controlled optical printer with 16 mm camera and both 16 mm and 35 mm projector movements; one Acme 16 mm animation camera and stand; one 16 mm and 35 mm rotoscope; one Steenbeck 16 mm six-plate flatbed editor; one 3/4-inch Hi8 video editing suite; one 3/4-inch post-production A/B-roll editing suite with Video toaster; two screening rooms with 16 mm, Super 8 and video equipment: one CP 16-sync camera with Nagra field recorder; one Sony DXC 3000 camera with 6800 3/4-inch field deck; one four-track portable cassette recorder; one Super-8 camera; Super-8 and 16 mm projection equipment; location lighting equipment; two Arion slide dissolve units; Steddicam Junior and various tripods; 12 SGI Workstations, 12 Macintoshes; dye-sub printing, 3/4-inch video in and out; Media 100 editor; Maya, Photoshop; Director; Premiere; and additional facilities available through the Science Department. SDSC operates powerful high-end computing resources led by NPACI's Blue Horizon, a 1,152-processor IBM SP capable of 1.7 trillion calculations per second. With 6 petabytes of archival tape storage, 500 terabytes of online disk storage, and teraflops of computing power, SDSC expertise is backed by large-scale knowledge management resources.
In April 2004, SDSC will deploy DataStar, a 7.9 teraflops supercomputer with total shared memory of 3.2 terabytes. DataStar will be among the 20 top supercomputers in the world and targeted at large-scale, data intensive scientific research applications.

Student Body

One hundred undergraduates and 20 graduate students in the Department of Art. Four undergraduates and two graduate students of the Computer Graphics area in the Computer Science Department.

Faculty Profile

Thrity full-time faculty members teach in the Visual Arts Department.

Admission Requirements

Undergraduates application and fee, letters of recommendation, transcript, ACT or SAT, portfolio (if art student). Graduate students should contact the Graduate Office for requirements.

Deadlines and Financial Aid

Various forms of federal and state aid are available. Students may receive aid in the form of loans, grants or scholarships. February 1 deadline for M.F.A. program. The Triton Registration Installment Program (TRIP) may be used for payment of fees. The TRIP is a monthly payment option that can be used as an alternative method of financing registration fees and nonresident tuition over a short period of time. Please contact Student Business Services for more information.

Expenses

Estimated tuition for undergraduate residents of California is $13,055 and $13,070 for non-residents.

Contact

9500 Gilman Dr., La Jolla, CA 92093-0327. Telephone: 858-534-5000. Fax: 858-534-8651. Contact person: Mike Bailey. E-mail: mjb@sdsc.edu. URL: http://www.ucsd.edu/.

Additional Information

Media Major: This major is designed for students who want to become creative videomakers, filmmakers and photographers. It combines the hands-on experience of making art with practical and theoretical criticism, provides historical, social and esthetic backgrounds for the understanding of modern media, and emphasizes creativity, versatility and intelligence over technical specialization. The program prepares students to go on to more specialized graduate programs in the media arts, to seek careers in commercial film, television or photography, or to develop as independent artists.

University of California at Santa Barbara

F/X Degrees Offered

Department of Computer Science offers a B.S. and M.S. in Computer Science. Department of Art Film Studies offers a B.A. and M.F.A. in Computer Imaging; Intermedia; Video and Film.

Curricular

Computer Science: Introduction to Computer Programming; Introduction to C and UNIX; C and UNIX; Computer Graphics; Introduction to Computer Vision; Artificial Intelligence; Computer Graphics; Pattern Recognition; Program Verification; Computer Architecture; Algorithms and Complexity; Mathematical Theory of Computation; Semantic Models; Software Systems; General Computer Systems Modeling and Analysis; Scientific Computation. ArtProject Development for the Short Film; Film Technology; 16 mm Production; 16 mm Crew Production; Animation; Special Topics in Film Production.

Facilities

Computer Science: The facilities for Computer Science are based on a client/server architecture with two file server machines. Workstations throughout the department access files on these servers via a TCP/IP-based network. The client/server architecture allows the department to have the computing power of many machines, while still conserving disk space and easily maintaining a standard set of files and programs. Other facilities include a Computer Science Instructional Laboratory:38 Pentium computers running Sun's Solaris operating system are available 18 hours a day for completing homework, for study and for communicating with fellow students. Consultants are available in the afternoon and evening hours to help new users make their way around the system;

a high-speed duplexing laser printer. Graduate Student Laboratory: PCs and Macintoshes.; a high-speed duplexing laser printer serves the graduate students' printing needs; Meiko Parallel Processing Facility: a Meiko CS-2 MPP system, consisting of Sparc Viking nodes; eight of the 64 nodes are configured for I/O, each with a 1GB disk. This parallel processor is used for experimental computer science and applications research in high-performance computation, as well as instruction. Research Laboratories: all of the department's research groups have acquired their own laboratory facilities. Laboratories contain primarily Sun Sparc stations, but also include Macintosh, SGIs and Pentium-based computers. Laboratories also house special networking and other equipment suited to their research task. Graduate students often spend more time in these laboratories than they do in the common laboratory, GSL. Art: the advanced program is based on the interdisciplinary, collaborative work with the College of Engineering and is supported by software from Maya. Experimenting with on-line networks, animation, and computer-driven objects with installations and performances, in a teamwork production atmosphere, is strongly stressed.

Student Body
There are 250 undergraduates and 100 graduate students in the Computer Science Department; more than 17,000 students attend the university.

Faculty Profile
Twenty faculty members in the Computer Science Department, 12 faculty members in Film Studies, and 22 faculty members in the Fine Arts program.

Deadlines and Financial Aid
Application deadline is Jan. 15 of every year for all departments and programs. UCSB provides three main types of support for graduate students: fellowship or merit-based support; academic apprentice positions; need-based support, which is offered through the Financial Aid Office. All domestic graduate students at UCSB are required to file the FAFSA by the March 2 deadline to be considered for most student aid. Admission Quarter and Priority Filing Period are as follows: fall (Sept.-December), November 1-30; winter (Jan.-Mach), July 1-31; spring (April-June), Oct. 1-31. Aid is awarded on the basis of financial need as well as scholastic merit. Financial aid is generally given in the form of a package of aid consisting of scholarship, grant, loan and work-study funds. Roughly 55 percent of UCSB students receive some form of financial aid.

Admission Requirements
Application and fee, transcripts, SAT or ACT. Graduate students must submit an application and fee, transcripts, and GRE scores.

Expenses
Undergraduate and graduate tuition is $4,600 per year for residents and $14,000 for non-residents.

Contact
Computer Science Department, University of California, Santa Barbara, CA 93106. Telephone: 805-893-4321.
URL: http://www.ucsb.edu/.

University of San Francisco

F/X Degrees Offered
Computer Science Department. An undergraduate degree (B.S. in Computer Science) emphasizing software engineering, with attention paid to graphical user interfaces. A master's degree (M.S. in Com puter Science) in Software Engineering, which requires a sequence of three SE courses and a choice of emphasis in Computer Graphics or Networks.

Curricular

3D Modeling and Rendering; 3D Computer Animation; 2D Computer Animation; Multimedia/Interactive; High-Level Programming; Low-Level Programming; GUI-by-demo systems; X and Windows Programming; options for Parallel Processing.

Facilities

Hardware: PC workstations; Macintoshes. Additional hardware available for research: Suns; double Pentium; nCube/32. All hardware is fully networked. Also available: color scanner, 1200 dpi color printer, high-resolution color X-terminals. Software: POV-Ray; Rayshade; X/Motif; research interface design tools and builders; graphics APIs; HyperGraph used as text in senior course; Visual C++ required in several courses.

Student Body

One hundred undergraduates and 40 graduate students in the department.

Faculty Profile

Nine full-time and three part-time faculty in the department.

Deadlines and Financial Aid

Undergraduates:rolling admissions plan; priority deadline for fall term is preceding February 15, and for the spring term, preceding December15. For application materials, contact the Office of Admissions, or phone 800-CALL-USF (outside California) or 415-422-6563 (in California). Graduate: rolling admissions plan; deadline for consideration for Merit Scholarships starting in the fall term is preceding July 1; deadline for consideration for Merit Scholarships starting in the spring term is preceding December 1.

Admission Requirements

Undergraduates: application and fee, SAT or ACT, letters of recommendation, high school transcripts.

Graduate students: GRE score, transcripts, application and fee, two letters of recommendation; contact the Graduate Office for details.

Expenses

Undergraduate tuition is $830 per credit. Graduate tuition is $880 per unit.

Contact

University of San Francisco, 2130 Fulton St., San Francisco, CA 94117-1080. Telephone: 415-422-6342. Fax: 415-422-2995. Contact person: Benjamin Wells. E-mail: wells@usfca.edu. URL: http://www.usfca.edu/.

University of Southern California

F/X Degrees Offered

M.F.A. Film, Video and Computer Animation through the School of Cinema-Television.

Curricular

Undergraduates: Introduction to Cinema; Fundamentals of Film; Motion Picture Camera; Motion Picture Editing; Directing for Television; Makeup for Motion Pictures; Introduction to Special Effects in Cinema; Animation Theory and Techniques; Introduction to Computer Animation. Graduate: Creative Cinema; Production I; Production II; Understanding the Process of Filmmaking; Special Effects in Cinema; Intermediate Graphics; Intermediate Electronic Imaging; Intermediate Computer Animation; Introduction to Film, Video and Computer Animation; Production III; Animation Production I; Animation Production II; Animation Production III; Planning the Advanced Production; Advanced Directing; Advanced Production Design; Advanced Editing; Advanced

Cinematography; Advanced Producing; Advanced Graphics.

Facilities
Software: Maya; Softimage; Ultimatte; Parallax; Side Effects; Xaos; Pixibox; Storagetech. Hardware: VFX; SCH; RFX; SGI.

Student Body
More than 25,000 students are enrolled in the university.

Faculty Profile
Thirty-one full-time faculty, more than 50 adjunct, more than 60 lecturers, more than 10 emeritus professors, and research associates work at the School of Cinema and Television.

Deadlines and Financial Aid
February 15 for the fall semester. There is no spring admission to the Animation Program. Undergraduate students may apply for financial aid from the School of Cinema-Television after completing their junior year as Cinema-Television major's; graduate students may apply for financial aid after one academic year. Financial aid is awarded in the form of scholarships, assistantships and hourly employment. Teaching assistantships are available to graduate students only. Jobs available through the school include projectionist, messenger, stockroom attendant, and production and clerical assistants. All restricted financial aid is intended only for Cinema-Television students who have been enrolled at USC at least two full semesters. Application for aid may be made during a student's second semester in residence; however, awards are usually not made until the semester following application. More than 21 scholarships are available exclusively to Cinema-Television students.

Admission Requirements
Undergraduates: application and fee, high school transcripts, portfolio, SAT or ACT scores. Graduate

students: USC Graduate Application; transcripts (from all colleges attended); GRE scores (and TOEFL if required). USC Office of Graduate Admission: 213-740-1111. Send to the CNTV Office of Student Affairs: (213-740-2911) a photocopy of USC application, Personal Statement, VHS portfolio samples, resume, three letters of recommendation. Minor Program: departmental application, academic records, personal statement, portfolio list and letters of recommendation.

Expenses
Students in the School of Cinema-Television pay an estimated tuition of $26,000 per year.

Contact
Cinema-Television Office of Student Affairs, University Park, Los Angeles, CA 90089-2211. Telephone: 213-740-2911 or 213-740-1111. URL: http://www.usc.edu/.

Additional Information
M.F.A.: The M.F.A. degree in Film, Video and Computer Animation is a two-year (four-semester) graduate program designed for students who have clearly identified animation as their primary interest in film and television. The program integrates both classical and computer animation and prepares students to work in both areas. Graduates are expected to have a comprehensive knowledge of animation from conception through realization; an understanding of the history of the medium and its aesthetics; the fundamentals of computer technology, animation software, and the elements of film, video, and interactive technology. Admission is once a year in the fall; there are no spring admissions. Approximately 20 students will be enrolled in each incoming class. In addition to practical production, the program will also provide field-work experience and industry residencies to facilitate the student's transition into the profession.

Colorado

Colorado State University

F/X Degrees Offered
B.A., M.S., Ph.D. in Computer Science.

Curricular
Courses in Computer Graphics.

Facilities
Hardware: HP/DEC/Sun systems; graphics laboratory (5); HP arch. laboratory; AT&T Networks laboratory; IBM AI laboratory; Sequent; other Sun/HP/DEC workstations. University facilities--Hardware: Large UNIX systems; graphics/visualization laboratory. Software systems and languages: UNIX; C; Pascal; Fortran; C++; many applications.

Student Body
There are 350 students in the department, 70 of which are graduate students; 16,500 students attend the university.

Faculty Profile
Twenty full-time faculty members in the department.

Deadlines and Financial Aid
Colorado State operates on rolling admissions. Graduate assistantships are available to students in the Science Department. Assistantships range from fellowships of $2,500 per year to teaching and research assistantship stipends of $1,100 per month. Admissions Applications Deadlines: six months prior to start of term. Assistantship application deadline: April 1 and November 1.

Admission Requirements
Application and fee, transcripts and GRE score.

Expenses
Tuition is $3,745 per year for residents and $14,217 per year for non-residents.

Contact
CSU, Computer Science Department, Fort Collins, CO 80523-1873. Telephone: 970-491-5792. Fax: 970-491-2466. E-mail: csdept@cs.colostate.edu. URL: http://www.cs.colostate.edu/.

Colorado Institute of Art

F/X Degrees Offered
Associate of Applied Science in Media Arts and Animation; Music Video Business; Multimedia; Visual Communication. B.A. of Applied Science in Computer Animation.

Curricular
Animation Courses--Audio/Video Technology; Animation/Typography Design; Computer Paint; Image Manipulation; Animation for Multimedia; Basic CAD and 3D Modeling; Computers in Animation; Animation for Interactive Games; Desktop Video; Computer Graphics; Advanced 3D Modeling/Animation; Networking Techniques. Video Production Courses--Advanced Lighting; Business Management for Film/Video; Directing; Electronics for Video; Film/Video Technology; Introduction to Editing; Lighting for TV; Multi-Camera Video Era Field Production; Non-Linear Editing; Post-Production; Principles of Digital Video System; Teleconferencing; Video Computer Communications.

Facilities
Macintosh and PC workstations for creating animation, multimedia and graphic design.

Student Body
There are 300 students in the area of Media Arts and Animation.

Faculty Profile

There are 25 faculty teach in the area of communication; 15 faculty teach in the area of Music and Video Business.

Deadline and Financial Aid

A number of full tuition merit scholarships to graduating high school seniors. Contact the Admissions Office for details. Scholarships cover tuition only. Students attending the Institute on scholarships must attain at least a 2.5 cumulative GPA in order to retain eligibility. Full-time students who receive federal or state-sponsored financial assistance must maintain satisfactory academic progress for financial assistance eligibility.

Admission Requirements

Acceptance is based on the following conditions: an official, final high school transcript displaying a graduation date and a cumulative GPA of at least 2.0, or a high school transcript displaying a cumulative GPA of 2.0 through the junior year for students who apply before high school completion. An official high school transcript is required following the completion of the senior year and subsequent graduation; in the event an official high school transcript is unavailable, an official college transcript displaying the name of the high school attended and date of graduation must be submitted. College courses must display a cumulative GPA of at least 2.0. Each individual who seeks admission to The Art Institute of Colorado will be interviewed either in person or by telephone by an Assistant Director of Admissions.

Expenses

All programs are $342 per credit.

Contact

200 E. Ninth Ave., Denver, CO 80209. Telephone: 800-275-2420. Fax: 303-860-8520. Contact person: Rhonda Sekich.
URL: http://www.aic.artinstitutes.edu/.

Additional Information

The programs prepare students for entry-level jobs in their fields. Intensive 24-month programs are offered in Visual Communications, Music and Video Business, and Industrial Design Technology. Interior Design has a 27-month program, while Animation Multimedia is 18 months long. All programs are offered on a year-round basis.

Colorado Technical University

F/X Degrees Offered

B.S., M.S. and D.C.S. in Computer Science.

Curricular

Interactive Interface Design and various other courses in Advanced Computer Graphics, and Software Engineering for Computer Science majors.

Facilities

UNIX workstations; IBMs; five Pentium laboratories.

Student Body

Total student enrollment is 1,800.

Faculty Profile

Student-to-faculty ratio is 15:1

Deadlines and Financial Aid

Various forms of federal and state aid are available. Students may receive aid in the form of loans, grants or scholarships.

Admission Requirements

Admissions requirements for all programs include a high school diploma or GED, a personal interview with the school, and in certain programs successful performance on one or more entrance assessments.

Expenses

Tuition is $155 per credit hour for undergraduates; $250 per credit for master's students; $350 per credit for doctoral students.

Contact

Admissions, 4435 N. Chestnut St., Colorado Springs, CO 80907-3896. Telephone: 719-598-0200. URL: http://www.ctu-coloradosprings.com/

University of Colorado at Boulder

F/X Degrees Offered

B.A., B.F.A. and M.F.A. in Photography and Media Arts; Electronic Media through the Department of Art. M.S. and Ph.D. in Computer Science.

Curricular

Advanced Computer Imaging; Beginning Video Production; Intermediate Video Production; Advanced Video Production; Intermediate Screen Printing; Basic Photography; Computer Imaging; Electronic Arts Survey; History of Media Arts.

Facilities

A partial list of facilities in the various research laboratories include: SUN and Solbourne workstations; DEC MIPS and Alpha workstations; Mac workstations with Symbolics boards (AI labs); HP PA-RISC workstations; NCD X-Terminals; DEC Sable multiprocessors; DEC Alpha/PC cycle farm. Equipment also includes video production, film and computer graphics facilities. Software systems and languages include: C, C++; Fortran; ML; Lisp; Matlab; Mathematica; SPEC benchmarks; PerfectClub; OSF/1; DEC UNIX; SunOS; PVM; MPI.

Student Body

An estimated 23,000 students attend the university; an estimated 800 are in the Department of Art.

Faculty Profile

Five faculty members teach courses in the area of electronic media; 28 faculty members teach in the Department of Art.

Deadlines and Financial Aid

General admissions deadlines for the fall semester in February or March. Contact the school for more specific deadlines.

Admission Requirements

Graduate students: contact the specific department for information about its graduate programs and requirements; file a formal application for admission with that department; supply requested information such as transcripts, recommendations, deposit fees or test scores; submit a financial aid form to the Office of Financial Aid; GRE scores. All application materials MUST be postmarked by Jan. 15. Applications received after the deadline, or incomplete applications, will not be considered and will be returned. The Department of Fine Arts admits students for the fall semester only.

Expenses

Tuition is $1,596 per semester for undergraduate in-state residents and $9,754 for out-of-state residents.

Contact

University of Colorado at Boulder, Office of Admissions, Campus Box 30, Boulder, CO 80309-0030. Telephone: 303-492-6301. Contact person: David Smith. Email: David.Smith@Colorado.edu. URL: http://www.colorado.edu/.

Additional Information

The department has also maintained an extensive Visiting Artist Program since 1972. Artists of major national and international status are in residence on the Boulder Campus for short periods of time. These artists present a public lecture as well as a seminar and individual student critiques. Approximately 14 artists visit the department during the academic year. Interdisciplinary Arts is a new area of the department, which will emphasize skills in the Media of Video, Computer Graphics, Performance Art, Installations and so forth. Resident faculty skilled in these areas will assist students from both a conceptual and technical point of view.

University of Colorado at Colorado Springs

F/X Degrees Offered
Computer Science Department. Both the graduate (M.S.) and the undergraduate (B.A.) programs are offered. Ph.D. in Electrical Engineering and Computer Science.

Curricular
3D Modeling and Fendering; 3D Computer Animation; Computer Graphics Animation and Scientific Visualization Techniques; Geometric Modeling; Computer Graphics; Topics in Computer Graphics; Virtual Reality and Computer-Human Interaction.

Facilities
Software Development Laboratory contains more than 40 microcomputer workstations. Software Engineering Laboratory (SEL) contains six DEC station workstations and four Sun 3 X-terminals. The Computer Science Advanced Computing Laboratory contains three DEC station workstations, three Silicon Graphics workstations and two Alpha DEC station workstations. This laboratory supports research in artificial intelligence, databases and graphics. The CAD/Graphics Laboratory contains a network of two Sun workstations, four NCD X-terminals and three multimedia PCs.

Student Body
One hundred undergraduates in the B.S.; 100 graduates in M.S.; five students are enrolled in the Ph.D. program.

Faculty Profile
Fourteen faculty members teach in the Computer Science Department.

Deadlines and Financial Aid
Graduate assistantships available for Ph.D. students for a stipend of $12,000. Admissions application deadline: July 1. Assistantship application deadline: February 15.

Admission Requirements
Application and fee, transcripts and GRE scores.

Expenses
Tuition is $1,813.60 per semester for undergraduate residents, and $6,845.60 per semester for undergraduate non-residents. Graduate residents pay $183-277 per credit hour, and non-residents pay $511-824 per hours.

Contact
P.O. Box 7150, Colorado Springs, CO 80933-7150. Telephone: 719-262-3493. Fax: 719-262-3369. Contact person: Dr. Marijke Augusteijn, Chair. E-mail: mfa@antero.uccs.edu. URL: http://www.uccs.edu/.

University of Denver

F/X Degrees Offered
B.F.A. and B.A. in Graphic Communication; B.S. in Computer Science.

Curricular
Graphic Communications Design: Introduction to the Macintosh; Intermediate Computer Graphics; Illustration and Graphic Design;

Creative Team Projects; Symbol and Graphic Communication Design. Computer Science: Introduction to Computer Graphics; Advanced Computer Graphics; Special Topics in Graphics. The computer science programs include both flexible and structured degrees for undergraduate and graduate students. The school emphasizes current technology and instruction from nationally recognized faculty, reinforced by well-equipped laboratories and research, and interdisciplinary study in small classes.

Facilities

Macintosh laboratory with several software packages including Adobe's Illustrator and Photoshop; Aldus Freehand; QuarkXPress; PageMaker; laser and lintronic printers; Microtek scanner; color QMS output devices.

Student Body

Ten thousand students are enrolled in the university.

Faculty Profile

There are 389 full-time faculty, 386 adjunct faculty and 19 part-time faculty.

Deadlines and Financial Aid

The University of Denver offers both merit-based and need-based financial assistance to students. Students may receive assistance from DU, state or federal sources. More than 50 percent of the students receive some form of scholarship or financial aid. For best consideration, students must file the FAFSA by February 15.

Admission Requirements

Application and fee, ACT or SAT, transcripts, teacher recommendation and school counselor report.

Expenses

Tuition is $24,264 per year for full-time students.

Contact

Department of Computer Science, University of Denver, 2360 S. Gaylord St., Denver, CO 80208-0183. Phone: 303-871-2453. Fax: 303-871-3010. Email: info@cs.du.edu.
URL: http://www.cs.du.edu/.

University of Northern Colorado

F/X Degrees Offered

Department of Visual Arts offers a B.A. in Art.

Curricular

Classes are offered in three directions: Computer Graphics, Computer Art and Computer Art Graphics for Art Educators. 3D Modeling And Rendering; 2D Computer Animation; Multimedia/Interactive; Digital Painting/Drawing; Image Processing; Computer Graphics for Art Education.

Facilities

IBM Pentium laboratory; Macintosh laboratory. Software: Super Paint; Deneba Artworks; Painter; QuarkXPress; Illustrator; Freehand; Brush-strokes; Morph; Premiere; Director; Swivel Pro; Photoshop; HP color scanners.

Student Body

Four hundred undergraduates and 15 graduate students in the department (interdisciplinary Computer Science and Journalism). Total of 10,000 at the University.

Faculty Profile

One faculty member teaches Computer Graphics courses.

Deadlines and Financial Aid

Various fellowships and traditional state, federal and city aid are available to students. Contact the

Financial Aid Office for details on obtaining financial assistance at the university.

Admission Requirements
Application and fee, transcript, SAT or ACT scores.

Expenses
Tuition is $3,241.74 per year for residents, and $12,367.74 for non-resident students.

Contact
University of Northern Colorado, Greeley, CO 80639. Telephone: 970-351-2143 ext. 2426. Fax: 970-351-2299. Contact person: Anna Ursyn. E-mail: aursyn@ GoldnG8.UnivNorthCo.edu.
URL: http://arts.unco.edu/pva/default.html/.

University of Southern Colorado

F/X Degrees Offered
Department of Art. B.A., B.S. and B.F.A. with an emphasis in computer imaging and computer animation as part of the art major. Animation is PC-based, Graphic Design series is Macintosh-based, both with internships, PBS TV station on campus. A major in Mass Communications leads to degrees of bachelor of arts (B.A.) and bachelor of science (B.S.).

Curricular
3D Modeling and Rendering; 3D Computer Animation; 2D Computer Animation; Digital Painting/Drawing; Image Processing, Digital Video. Communication Courses--Media and Society; Advanced Desktop Publishing; Media and Human Relations; Introduction to Television Production; Media Laboratory; Direct Advertising; Introduction to Interactive Media; Advanced Television Production; Advanced Media Laboratory.

Facilities
PCs and Macintosh workstations; 3D Studio Max, Director and Photoshop.

Student Body
One hundred undergraduate students; 4,000 students attend the University.

Faculty Profile
Seven full-time faculty, artist-in-residence, and visiting artist program.

Deadlines and Financial Aid
There are several Scholarships and Grants and other forms of aid that help students pay for their USC education. The deadline for the spring semester is November 17; for the summer, April 26; and for the fall semester, July 26.

Admission Requirements
A completed USC application for admission; an application fee (non-refundable), an official transcript of high school records sent directly to USC from the high school, and scores from either the ACT or the SAT.

Expenses
Tuition is $28,692 per year for undergraduates and $32,784 for graduates.

Contact
University of Southern Colorado, Pueblo, CO 81001-4901. Telephone: 719-549-2816 or 800-USC-GROW. Fax: 719-549-2120. E-mail: croque@usc.edu. URL: http://www.usc.edu/.

Connecticut

Connecticut College

F/X Degrees Offered
B.A. in Art. Certificate in Arts and Technology.

Curricular
Center for Arts and Technology allows students to take classes outside of the major in Computer Graphics, Virtual Reality and Multimedia.

Facilities
The Center for Arts and Technology is equipped to offer various courses in Advanced 3D Computer Graphics and Animation.

Student Body
There are 1,700 students in the college.

Faculty Profile
Student-to-faculty ratio is 11:1.

Deadlines and Financial Aid
Sixty percent of all students at the college receive financial aid on need basis only. No merit-based scholarships are available. The Connecticut College Math and Computer Science Scholarship Program (CC-MACSS) is designed to supplement the education of students majoring in math or computer science through extensive support services and programs which increase knowledge and skills.

Admission Requirements
Application, 3 SAT II or ACT scores, transcripts, letters of recommendation, essay and fee.

Expenses
Tuition is $37,900 per year.

Contact
Connecticut College, 270 Mohegan Avenue, New London, CT 06320-4196. Telephone: 860-439-2200. Fax: 860-439-4301. Co-Directors David Smalley and Noel Zahler of the Center for Arts and Technology. URL: http://www.conncoll.edu/.

Yale University

F/X Degrees Offered
B.F.A. and M.F.A. in Art through the School of Art.

Curricular
Graphic Design; Web Design courses; Videomaking; Multimedia Design; Drawing; Painting; and Photography.

Facilities
The faculty, researchers, and students in the Department of Computer Science have access to a wide variety of ever-changing state-of-the-art computing resources, ranging from laptops, conventional PC's and scientific workstations to high-powered compute-servers and workstation clusters used as parallel computers. All of the computer systems are interconnected by a switched Ethernet local network, which is connected to the Internet via fiber optic technology to the campus backbone. Also recently installed is a wireless network permitting instant laptop access to the Internet anywhere in the building, and ultimately anywhere on campus. All four faculty, Ph.D. students, and researchers are equipped with an advanced-technology PC running some variant of the Linux or Windows operating systems. The computing needs of undergraduate and master's students are met through the Zoo, an educational laboratory with approximately 40 dual-processor Linux workstations which allow for remote as well as on-site access. Individual research groups have additional

specialized equipment for robotics, computer vision, parallel computing, networking, and other research efforts. There are a number of parallel and distributed computing testbeds, including a Silicon Graphics Origin 2000, a DEC Alphaserver 4100, and an IBM Beowolf cluster of twelve Netfinity 4000R processors. Students in computer science, both graduate and undergraduate, have liberal access to all of these facilities. In this way students play a vital role in contributing to our understanding of theoretical and experimental issues in computer science.

Student Body

There are 5,150 undergraduate students and 5,500 graduate students enrolled in the university.

Deadlines and Financial Aid

Last year 45 percent of the undergraduate class was granted financial aid. Various forms of aid are available including federal grants, scholarships and fellowships.

Admission Requirements

SAT II or ACT, application and fee, two essays, three letters of recommendation. Graduate students should contact the graduate school.

Expenses

Tuition is $21,600 per year for undergraduates.

Contact

Yale University, School of Art, New Haven, CT 06520. Telephone: 203-432-4771. Fax: 203-432-9392. URL: http://www.yale.edu/.

Delaware

University of Delaware

F/X Degrees Offered
B.A., M.S., and Ph.D. in Computer Science.

Curricular
Courses offered in Computer Graphics and Advanced Visualization.

Facilities
Department facilities--Hardware: Sun workstations; several Sun file servers; DEC Alphas; SGIs. Software systems and languages: UNIX; C; C++; Lisp; Scheme; Linda. University facilities--Hardware: 375 PCs; 180 Macintoshes; 58 Sun workstations; 100 X-terminals; several Sun Sparc 2000 file servers; SGI Power Challenge; Cray super computer. Software systems and languages: UNIX; DOS; Macintosh OS.

Student Body
There are 85 graduate students in the department; 14,500 undergraduates; 3,364 graduate students are enrolled in the university.

Faculty Profile
Sixteen faculty members are in the department.

Deadlines and Financial Aid
The University of Delaware awards more than $90 million annually in aid that comes in the from of grants, scholarships, and loans. There is no set of numbers (SAT scores, GPA, class rank) that will guarantee a scholarship or scholarship amount. Admissions application deadline: November 1 for spring, July 1 for fall.

Admission Requirements
GRE scores, application and fee, transcripts. Contact the Graduate Office for details on the admission procedures.

Expenses
Undergraduate tuition is $12,616 per year for residents and non-residents pay $22,146 per year.

Contact
103 Smith Hall, Newark, DE 19716. Telephone: 302-831-2713. Fax: 302-831-8458. Contact person: Professor Caviness. E-mail: caviness@cis.udel.edu. URL: http://www.cis.udel.edu/.

Florida

Full Sail

F/X Degrees Offered
Specialized Associate Degrees in Film and Video Production, and Digital Media. Degrees also offered in Computer Animation; Computer Graphics and Special Effects; Computers in Digital Media; Digital Media Assembly; Virtual Reality; Advanced Tapeless, Game Design; Traditional Animation.

Curricular
Film and Video Production--Introduction to Media Arts; Sound for Motion Pictures and Television; Video Production; Creative Writing; Set Design; Construction and Special Effects; Lighting for Film and Video; Film Production; Make-up and Special Effects; Film History; Post-Production; Film Project; Digital Audio Workstations; Entertainment Business. Digital Media--Introduction to Media Arts; Business of Living; Sound for Motion Pictures and Television; Video Production; Creative Writing; Computer Graphics and Special Effects; Design and Art Theory; Digital Audio Workstations; Computers in Digital Media; Virtual Reality; Computer Animation; Digital Media Assembly; Post-Production; Entertainment Business. Computer Animation-- Principles of Animation; Managing the Animation Project; 2D Animation; 3D Modeling Basics; Curves and Surfaces; Lighting and Effects; 3D Animation Creation; Keyframe Animation; Camera Animation; Inverse Kinematics; Dynamics; Rendering. Computer Graphics--Computer Graphics Tools; Design and Color; Layout and Composition; Digital Imaging and Manipulation; Special Effects Tools; 3D Modeling; Introduction to Animation and Computer Graphics Project. Computers in Digital Media Assembly--Script and Storyboard Preparation for Interactive Media; Interface Design and Structure; Assembly with Authoring Programs; Desktop Video Manipulation; Digital Sound for Multimedia; Final Post-Production; Mastering to CD Format. Virtual Reality--Concepts in Virtual Reality; Virtual Reality Hardware Controls; Software for Authoring Virtual Reality Projects; Virtual Reality Project Design; Mastering to Media; Virtual Project Management; Virtual Reality Applications and Uses. Advanced Tapeless--File Management Skills; Introduction to FM Synthesis; Advanced Timbre Patching Methods; Advanced Editing; Advanced Sequencing Methods; Advanced Studio Interfacing; Advanced Tapeless Project.

Facilities
Avid online digital video editing suite, in line with current industry standards, which include broadcast quality, and utilizes Pro Tools digital audio. A second Avid is utilized in another video suite; Newtek Video Toaster 4000 suites are utilized in the creation of online graphics in 2D and 3D. Each suite utilizes a Newtek Toaster 4000 computer graphics composer workstation. The SGI laboratory features a combination of advanced systems. The IBM/PVS Supercomputer server suite hosts the IBM/pvs (power visualization system) server and a Supercomputer. The central processing unit for a number of digital media laboratories, the IBM/pvs Supercomputer server is equipped with MPEG compression software and digital video editing software. A Macintosh laboratory features 18 Macintosh computers; one host computer and an instructor computer for lecture support. Peripherals include color scanners; Wacom tablets; Quicktake digital cameras; dye-sub/wax thermal color printers and S-video decks. All laboratories are networked together and have Internet access. Fargo dye-sub/ wax thermal color printer. Software includes: Adobe Photoshop; Illustrator; Premier; Streamline; After Effects; Macromedia Director; Animation Director;

Animation Master; KPT Power Tools; Flash; Dreamweaver; Fractal Design Painter; and Digital Box Office software.

Student Body

More than 3,100 students are enrolled in the school.

Deadlines and Financial Aid

Eligibility for federal financial aid programs requires that a student be a U.S. citizen or eligible non-citizen. To qualify for financial aid, a student must be enrolled in one of the specialized associate degree programs. Those seeking financial assistance are required to complete an application for federal aid. Appropriate applications and additional information can be obtained through the Financial Aid Office. Upon request, students may receive an estimate of what financial aid they qualify for prior to submitting an enrollment application.

Admission Requirements

Application must be completed, including a $150 application fee. To reserve a seat, a $500 enrollment deposit plus $300 for each additional degree must be sent. A copy of your high school diploma or GED (with transcripts if available) must also be sent prior to start date.

Expenses

Tuition varies depending on your choice of programs, on the number of Full Sail degrees you take, and on your previous college and/or work experience. 10- to 14-month degree programs are estimated at $31,575.

Contact

3300 University Blvd., Winter Park, FL 32792. Telephone: 407-679-6333 or 800-226-7625. Fax 407-678-0070.
URL: http://www.fullsail.com/.

International Fine Arts College

F/X Degrees Offered

B.F.A. and M.F.A. in Computer Animation, Film, Graphic Design, Interior Design, Photography and Visual Arts.

Curricular

Classes for teaching 3D Modeling, Animation, Movie Special Effects, Video Games, Cartoon Animation and 3D Graphics for Television.

Facilities

Computer Animation student equipment includes 20 Integraph Windows NT workstations, 63 SGI workstations, more than 60 Macintoshes, three Avid Express stations, 13 Media 100 editors. The resources available to Graphic Design students include the Macintosh computer laboratories with the latest versions of professional desktop publishing software. Also at the students' disposal are b/w laser printers, color flatbed and slide scanners, and dye-sublimation color printing stations, which produce photographic quality prints. Through elective courses, students have opportunities to develop skills in a variety of traditional media including painting, illustration and drawing. Film students have access to professional cameras, lighting and audio equipment to Media 100 and AVID film editing stations; IFAC provides students with state-of-the-art, industry-standard equipment, computers, and software to develop each student's movie-making skills in the challenging, high-tech area. The department is equipped with all the gear that students need: Bolex cameras (including: Arri 16 bl, Arri 16 sr and digital video cameras), complete lighting packages (with HMI and kinoflo lights), camera dollies, and more than a dozen Media 100 and Avid editing suites.

Student Body

Total enrollment of 1,200 students, with an average of 20 per class.

Deadlines and Financial Aid

Rolling admissions. Students are admitted year-round. Those seeking financial assistance are required to complete an application for federal aid. Appropriate applications and additional information can be obtained through the Financial Aid Office. Upon request, students may receive an estimate of what financial aid they qualify for prior to submitting an enrollment application.

Admission Requirements

Application and fee; high school transcripts. Graduate students must contact the school directly.

Expenses

Cost is $319 per credit for students in the Computer Graphics area.

Contact

Computer Animation, 1737 N. Bayshore Dr., Miami, FL 33132. Telephone: 305-995-5000 or 800-225-9023. Fax: 305-374-5933.
URL: http://www.ifac.edu/.

Miami-Dade Community College

F/X Degrees Offered

School of Film and Video. A.A. degree in Film.

Curricular

Four-course sequence of Computer Graphics/Animation for Film Production and TV Broadcast students. (Also has fine arts courses, graphics arts CG courses, architecture and engineering CAD.) 3D Modeling; 3D Computer Animation; 2D Computer Animation; Multimedia/Interactive.

Facilities

Macintosh laboratory using Illustrator, Photoshop, Premiere; Amiga/Newtek Toaster Laboratory using Lightwave 3D.

Student Body

There are 300 undergraduates and 50 industry professionals.

Faculty Profile

Twelve faculty members teach in the area of technology.

Deadlines and Financial Aid

Various fellowships and traditional state, federal and city aid are available to students. Contact the Financial Aid Office for details on obtaining financial assistance at the college.

Admission Requirements

Application. Open admission.

Expenses

Tuition is $41.25 per credit for residents and $139 per credit for non-residents.

Contact

11380 N.W. 27th Ave., Miami, FL 33167. Telephone: 305-237-7077. Fax: 305-237-1367.
URL: http://www.mdcc.edu/college_wide/.

Ringling School of Art and Design

F/X Degrees Offered

B.F.A. in Computer Animation, Fine Arts, Digital Imaging, and Graphic Design.

Curricular

Traditional Animation I, II; Computer Animation I, II; Storyboard Process; Special Topics in Computer Animation or B/W Photography; Video Production;

UNIX Scripting; Advanced Computer Animation; Professional Presentation; Graphic Design I; Introduction to Interactive Design.

Facilities
SGI workstations; Macintosh computers. Software: Maya; Softimage. Video facilities--BetacamSP editing suite; Abekas A66; S-VHS; MII; 3/4-inch U-Matic; Video Toaster; digital audio suite. Computer classroom facilities--Macintosh computers; flatbed scanning stations; video capture station; instructor projection stations; Hewlett Packard and LaserWriter printers. Software: Adobe Illustrator; Adobe Photoshop; Aldus Freehand; Aldus PageMaker; Fractal Design Painter; Macromedia Director; QuarkXPress; Suitcase; Screenplay; Sound Edit; Studio Pro.

Student Body
There are 140 undergraduate students in the department.

Faculty Profile
More than seven faculty members teach courses in the area of Computer Animation, and six teach in the area of Graphic Design.

Deadlines and Financial Aid
More than 70 percent of Ringling students receive some form of financial aid each year. Financial aid is available in the form of grants, scholarships, loans and student employment. Most financial aid is awarded to students based on demonstrated financial need, which is determined by completing the FAFSA. Applicants who want to be considered for all types of financial assistance administered through the Office of Financial Aid must complete the following requirements: apply for admission to the school, (a financial aid packet will be mailed to you upon receipt of your application for admission), complete the necessary financial applications by the priority deadline of March 1; financial aid award letters will be mailed as soon as the financial aid

application process is complete. The award letter must be either accepted or rejected, signed and returned in a timely manner.

Admission Requirements
Application form and fee, official transcript, portfolio, two letters of recommendation, SAT or ACT.

Expenses
Tuition is $9,430 per semester.

Contact
Office of Admissions, Ringling School of Art and Design, 2700 N. Tamiami Trail, Sarasota, FL 34234-5895. Telephone: 941-351-5100 or 800-255-7695. Fax: 941-359-7517.
URL: http://www.rsad.edu/.

Additional Information
Computer animation majors focus on becoming computer graphics animators. They have the opportunity to study with faculty who are established leaders in the field. Although much of the studio curriculum includes interaction with the computer, the basis of all courses is in traditional conceptual development and the use of drawing as a tool for communication. Every project begins with sketches on paper. Students develop concrete drawings, storyboards and visual planning notes before they begin working with the computer.

University of Central Florida

F/X Degrees Offered
B.A. degree in Motion Picture Technology. The program is a liberal arts-based set of educational experiences leading to mainstream and independent filmmaking, animation, and future industry developments. Film major with concentration in Animation or Production/Screen Writing.

Curricular

Production/Screen Writing: concentration on producing, directing and screen writing, production management, design, film history, criticism and theory are also a part of this track. Courses include: Introduction to Screen Writing; Introduction to Film Production; Documentary Film; History of the Motion Picture; Film Theory; Colloquium; Film Directing; Production Management; Intermediate Film Production; Intermediate Screen Writing; Advanced Scriptwriting; Scriptwriting Workshop; Advanced Film Production; Film Production Workshop; Cinema-tography; Motion Picture Genre/Aesthetics. Animation: concentration on cel- and computer-generated motion picture and video animation planning, scripting, storyboarding, design and drawing, and filming/taping. Film majors adopting this track will enroll in animation courses, but the track will also require enrollment in Screen Writing and, at least, Beginning 16 mm Filmmaking and Documentary Video. Art direction and film history, criticism and theory will also be a part of this track. Introduction to Screen Writing; Introduction to Film Production; Introduction to Cel Animation; Introduction to Computer Animation; Intermediate Film Production; Intermediate Cel Animation; History of the Motion Picture; History of Animated Films; Advanced Computer Animation; Computer Animation Workshop; Advanced Cel Animation; Cel Animation Workshop; Animation Workshop.

Facilities

High-end computer animation and traditional animation facilities. Computer laboratories include Macintosh, PC, Amiga and SGI workstations.

Student Body

The UCF Motion Picture Division accepts approximately 30 students each academic year.

Faculty Profile

Seven Motion Picture faculty members.

Deadlines and Financial Aid

Grants, loans and work-study.

Admission Requirements

An overall 3.0 (on a 4.0 scale) GPA and a minimum of 45 hours of previous college work, a written essay, a full transcript of all grades in all previous college-level work, and evaluation of other materials, such as a portfolio, when possible. Applications and/or portfolios must be submitted after Sept. 15, but before Jan. 15. Applications received during this open application period are for admission consideration only for the program beginning in the fall.

Expenses

Tuition is approximately $94.42 per credit for residents and $462.02 for non-residents.

Contact

CREAT Digital Media Program - University of Central Florida Orlando Tech Center, Building 500 Orlando, FL 32816. Phone: 407-823-6100 Fax: 407-823-6103. Contact person: Dr. Michael Moshell, Professor, Digital Media and Computer Science, and Director of CREAT Digital Media Program. Email: j.m.moshell@dm.ucf.edu. URL: http://www.dm.ucf.edu/.

Additional Information

The Film Program's specific courses combine instructions in the history, theory and criticism of motion pictures with intensive class work in the hands-on aspects of writing and making films and videos. Cooperative opportunities to work with the growing Orlando film industry (Disney/ MGM, Universal, Century III, Nickelodeon and many others) are an integral part of the UCF film experience. Experts from the professional film and animation industries come to campus to present lectures, demonstrations of new techniques and technologies, workshops and courses. Field trips to the local studios and location shoots are scheduled. The motion picture business in Orlando represents the largest private-sector investment in permanent production facilities outside of New York and Los Angeles. The university has a center for research in computer graphic visual simulation.

University of Florida

F/X Degrees Offered
M.F.A. degree in Art with concentrations in Electronic Intermedia and Multimedia; M.Eng. through the Department of Computer and Information Sciences and Engineering; B.F.A. in Visual Art with a concentration in Electronic Media through the College of Art. B.S. in Digital Arts and Sciences; M.S. in Digital Arts and Sciences; Combined B.S. and M.S. in Digital Arts and Sciences.

Curricular
Digital Art Studio: Bit-Mapped and Object-oriented Graphics; 3D Modeling; Computer Animation; Hypermedia and Interactivity; Image Processing. Advanced Studies I-IV. Engineering courses include--Computer Vision; Computer Graphics; Visual Modeling; Advanced Concepts in Computer Simulation. Undergraduate courses include--Digital Art Studio; Advanced Video Studio; Advanced Computer Graphics. B.S.--Computational Structures in Computer Graphics; Introduction to Computer Vision; Systems Simulation; Digital World Production Studio; Computer Art: Animation & Interactivity; Computer Art: Montage; Video Art: Montage. M.S.--Computer Vision; Computer Graphics; Computer Simulation Concepts; Visual Modeling; Advanced Concepts in Computer Simulation; Artificial Intelligence Concepts; Dig.

World Inst. Grad. Prod. Thesis; Elec. Music Comp.--Digital I; Elec. Music Comp.--Digital II.

Facilities
Hardware: PCs and vector facilities; operating system includes MVS/ESA with JES2 and VM/ESA; IBM high-end workstations. The operating system is UNIX computing; IBM mainframe accounts; mainframe printing; supercomputing access and the use of interactive terminals, and microcomputer classrooms. Some laboratories are equipped with Apple Macintosh, IBM and IBM-compatible microcomputers. Computer Science Department--Hardware: MasPar MP2; several HP workstations; IBM RTs and PS2s; SGI 3D workstations; nCube 64-node MIMD computer. Software systems and languages: UNIX; C++; C; Pascal; Fortran; APL; Lisp; Dylon; Prolog; 3DSMAX; Char; Studio; Houdini; SimStudio; Lightscape; CosmoWorlds; VRCreator.

Student Body
An estimated 39,000 students attend the university.

Faculty Profile
Thirty full-time faculty teach in the department.

Deadlines and Financial Aid
Grants, loans, work-study and other types of financial aid are available.

Admission Requirements
Applicants must submit GRE scores, graduate application, transcript and a portfolio for admission consideration. A minimum of three years residency is normally required for studio majors culminating with an M.F.A. exhibition. M.S. admission requirement: Intro to Computer Science; Discreet Structures; Computer Organization; Data & Algorithm Structures; Operating Systems.

Expenses
Undergraduate tuition is $92.68 per credit for residents and $291 for $460.28 non-residents.

Contact

School of Art and Art History, College of Fine Arts, University of Florida. P.O. Box 115801, 101 Fine Arts Building C, Gainesville, FL 32611-5801. Telephone: 352-392-0201. Fax: 352-392-8453. URL: http://www.arts.ufl.edu/ART/.

University of South Florida

F/X Degrees Offered

The major concentrations available to B.A.-seeking students are: Electronic Intermedia (Computer Images); Photography; Cinematography; Studio Art and other fine-arts courses. B.F.A. in Studio Art. Major concentrations available to M.F.A students are: Drawing; Computer Imaging and Film. Students who wish to work with more than one media, or in a combination of media, are encouraged to do so.

Curricular

Introduction to Computer Images; Advanced Computer Images; Computer Animation; Beginning-Advanced Film; Beginning-Advanced Electronic Media.

Facilities

Macintosh workstations are in the Department of Art. Central site computing equipment includes IBMs, and laser and impact printers, providing MVSVM operating system environments, UNIX platform, and large NT and NetWare file and print servers. PC workstations terminals; microcomputers; printers and other associated equipment.

Student Body

Two hundred students in the department, 50 in the Computer Graphics area.

Faculty Profile

Approximately 18 full-time faculty, 23 faculty members in the Fine Arts Department, one full- and one part-time faculty member teach in the area of Computer Graphics.

Admission Requirements

Undergraduates: applicants must submit an SUS Application for admission, a non-refundable application fee, an official high school transcript, official GED scores if applicable, SAT or ACT scores, and a TOEFL score if applicable. A freshman may elect to enter the College of Fine Arts as a major in one of the four departments as early as his/her initial entry into the university provided he/she has successfully completed an audition or portfolio review in the appropriate department or school. Graduate students: in addition to the portfolio, applicants to the M.F.A. degree program are required to submit a statement of intent, which indicates their aims and goals as a graduate student at USF, and three letters of recommendation.

Deadlines and Financial Aid

Grants, scholarships, low-interest loans and federal work-study are all available. Students may apply for most financial aid by submitting the FAFSA. Graduate students: assistantships are awarded by the individual departments of each college. Contact the graduate program director or department chair for more information.

Expenses

Tuition is $1,163.40 per semester for residents and $5,574.72 for non-residents.

Contact

University of South Florida, College of Visual and Performing Arts, 4202 E. Fowler Ave., FAH 110, Tampa, FL 33620. Telephone: 813-974-1748. Fax: 813-974-9226. Contact person: Bruce Marsh. URL: http://www.arts.usf.edu/.

Valencia Community College

F/X Degrees Offered
Department of Graphics Technology. A.A. in Graphic Design.

Curricular
3D Modeling and Rendering; 3D Computer Animation; 2D Computer Animation; Multimedia/Interactive; Digital Painting/Drawing; Image Processing. Computer Animation I and II.

Facilities
Amigas; Macintoshes; Fiery printer; Strata Studio Pro software.

Student Body
Approximately 60,000.

Deadlines and Financial Aid
More than one-third of Valencia's students qualify for, and receive, financial aid.

Admission Requirements
Students must submit an application, fee and transcript; SAT or ACT score may be required.

Expenses
Tuition is $57.62 per credit for residents and $216.46 non-residents.

Contact
P.O. Box 3028, Orlando, Florida 32802-3028.
Telephone: 407-299-5000.
URL: http://valencia.cc.fl.us/.

Additional Information
The Graphic Design Technology program is designed to prepare students for employment as designers, commercial artists and computer graphic designers. Digital Pre-Publishing Technology prepares students for employment in areas of computerized layout, prepress production, and entry-level multimedia graphics.

Georgia

Dalton State College

F/X Degrees Offered
A.A. programs in Computer Science and Drafting and Design. Certificate programs also available.

Curricular
3D Modeling and Rendering; 3D Computer Animation; 2D Computer Animation; Digital Painting/Drawing; Image Processing.

Facilities
Software used: AutoCAD RIZ; AutoSurf-Designer; AutoArch; Microstation V5; 3D Studio; Animator Pro. Several computer labs available.

Student Body
Approximately eight to 15 students in the Computer Graphics area.

Faculty Profile
One professor teaches Computer Graphics.

Deadlines and Financial Aid
Financial aid at Dalton State College consists of grants, campus employment, loans, and a variety of scholarships. DSC SCHOLARSHIPS provide funds to students who demonstrate academic excellence and/ or financial need. These scholarships are awarded by the Dalton State College Scholarship Committee for one academic year. The DSC Scholarship Application and Financial Aid Application are required. All scholarship applications are available upon request from the Financial Aid Office.

Admission Requirements
Application and fee, transcripts, and ACT or SAT scores.

Expenses
Tuition is $697-$1,023 per semester for residents. Non-resident tuition is $2,223-$3,921 per semester.

Contact
213 N. College Dr., Dalton, GA 30720. Telephone: 706-272-4434. Fax: 706-272-4563. URL: http://www.daltonstate.edu/.

Emory University

F/X Degrees Offered
B.A., M.S., and Ph.D. through the Department of Mathematics and Computer Science.

Curricular
Courses in Computer Graphics through the Science Curriculum.

Facilities
The Math/CS Computing Lab comprises two spaces: an open lab and a teaching lab. Each space houses 32 SUN workstations running Solaris, SUN's version of a UNIX operating system. This setup is designed to allow students to work in a modern computing environment that is similiar to many computing research and development facilities found in academic and industrial environments. Software systems and languages: Solaris; C; C++; Fortran; Pascal; Java; Tcl; Perl; Matlab; Mathematica. University facilities--Hardware: Sparc Center 1000 timesharing cluster; Macintosh and PC laboratories.

Student Body
Fifteen graduate students in the department.

Faculty Profile
Six faculty members in the department.

Deadlines and Financial Aid
Some need-based aid is gift aid (grants), some you must earn (Federal Work-Study), and some is in the

form of educational loans. Admissions application deadline: March 1. Assistantship application deadline: March 1.

Admission Requirements
Application and fee, transcripts, GRE scores, and three letters of recommendation.

Expenses
Tuition is $13,800 per semester.

Contact
Emory University, Department of Mathematics and Computer Science, Suite W401, 400 Dowman Drive, Atlanta, Georgia 30322. Telephone: 404-727-7580. Fax: 404-727-5611. Contact person: Ron Gould, Professor. E-mail: rg@mathcs.emory.edu. URL: http://www.mathcs.emory.edu/.

Georgia Institute of Technology

F/X Degrees Offered
M.S. and Ph.D. in Computer Science through the College of Computing-Graphics Visualization Center. Master's in Architecture and Industrial Design.

Curricular
3D Modeling and Rendering; 3D Computer Animation; 2D Computer Animation; Multimedia/ Interactive; Digital Painting/Drawing; Image Processing; Virtual Reality; Digital Video; Stereo Imaging. Modeling & Rendering with Maya.

Facilities
The Graphics Visualization Center engages in collaborative research including areas such as visualization, animation, VR, design, collaboration, usability, multimedia, cognition, digital culture, Internet tools, education and computing

environments. Two courses are offered using the College of Computing lab with SGI systems.

Student Body
There are 400 undergraduates and 200 graduate students in the department. A total of 30 students are enrolled in the two Architecture and Industrial Design courses.

Faculty Profile
Forty-six faculty are affiliated with the Graphics Visualization Center.

Deadlines and Financial Aid
Georgia Tech offers three different processes to apply for financial aid, depending on the type(s) of aid desired. These processes are the same when you renew your aid, which must be done every year by May 1 (returning students and graduate students). The priority deadline for all incoming freshmen is March 1. The majority of funds offered by Georgia Tech carry a need-based selection criteria, including federally funded educational loans (i.e. Stafford Loan) and grants (i.e. Pell Grant) for both students and parents.

Admission Requirements
M.S. program: application, three recommendation letters (forms are mailed), a personal biography (forms are mailed), scores from the GRE. The General Exam scores should be in the 80 percentile range or higher in all three areas. The Computer Science subject exam scores should be in the 75 percentile range or higher.

Expenses
Tuition is $12,726 per year for residents, and $24,652 per semester for non-residents.

Contact
801 Atlantic Drive Atlanta, GA 30332-0280 Telephone: 404-894-3152. Fax: 404-894-9846. Contact person: Joan Morton. E-mail:

joan@cc.gatech.edu.
URL: http://www.gatech.edu/.

Georgia State University

F/X Degrees Offered
Hypermedia and Visualization Laboratory. B.S. and M.S. through the Department of Mathematics and Computer Science.

Curricular
3D Modeling and Rendering; 3D Computer Animation; 2D Computer Animation; Multimedia/Interactive; Digital Painting/Drawing; Image Processing; Digital Video.

Facilities
Departmental computing facilities for research and instruction include a departmental network of PCs and UNIX workstations and a 16-processor Origin 2000 supercomputer. The department operates five laboratories, including one with ATM switches for network research and another for hypermedia and visualization research. University-wide, a four-processor Silicon Graphics Power Challenge L provides support for research and instructional use. More than 100 network file servers provide access to centrally supplied software, support e-mail (GroupWise), and provide services to more than 4,000 microcomputer workstations, including more than 450 workstations in open and instructional labs. The University operates a Digital Arts and Entertainment Laboratory, with state-of-the-art Kodak equipment and a four-processor Onyx machine. The University is one of a few selected to participate in the Internet2 project.

Student Body
There are 400 undergraduates and 60 graduate students.

Faculty Profile
Sixty faculty members in the Computer Science and Mathematics Department.

Deadlines and Financial Aid
Includes scholarships, grants, loans and employment. Recipients are selected on the basis of demonstrated financial need and academic achievement. Information concerning application for financial assistance is available from the Office of Student Financial Aid. Application packets for the school year are available after Jan. 1. All documents required for admission to Georgia State must be received by the following application deadlines: for winter quarter, application must be received by November 1; for spring, February 1; for summer, April 15; for fall, May 1. Graduate students may qualify for a graduate research assistantship. GRA stipend is estimated to be $600 per quarter.

Admission Requirements
Freshman applicants must submit an official high school transcript and standardized test (SAT or ACT) report; a completed application form accompanied by a $25 non-refundable application fee is required of all applicants.

Expenses
Tuition for residents is $1,604 per semester and $6,416 per semester for non-residents.

Contact
College of Arts and Sciences, Georgia State University, P.O. Box 4038. Atlanta, GA 30302-4038. Telephone: 404-651-2294. Fax: 404-651-1542. Contact person: G. Scott Owen. E-mail: sowen@gsu.edu.
URL: http://www.cs.gsu.edu/.

Savannah College of Art and Design

F/X Degrees Offered
B.F.A., M.F.A. and M.A. in Computer Art and Video. Other Degrees offered: Photography; Sequential Art; Graphic Design; Industrial Design.

Curricular
Computer Art:Introduction to Computer; Advanced Computer Literacy; Introduction to Video; Introduction to Graphic Design; Introduction to Animation; Electronic Painting; Desktop Publishing; 2D Computer Animation; Introduction to Programming; Intermediate Programming; 3D Modeling and Animation; Advanced Animation Studio; Post-Production for Computer Art; Multimedia and Interactivity; 3D Computer Concepts I; Computer Art and Video Post-Production. Video:Introduction to Computers; Introduction to Video; Lighting; Pre-Production; Field Production Techniques; Post-Production; Multi-camera Production; Sound Design; Directing the Documentary; Advanced Video; Senior Project; Graduate Field Production; Video in Society; Graduate Sound Design; Graduate Post-Production; Interactive Video Production; Writing for Television; Advanced Production Technologies.

Facilities
Macintosh; IBM-compatible; Amiga and Silicon Graphics laboratories. Software includes a full range of Graphic Design on the Macintosh, and Maya and Softimage on the SGI Platform; video equipment; voice-over studio; video wall digital audio system; Tascam Midi studio; studio and field DAT recorder; Video Toaster with vending stations; single-frame controller; generator; studio; Panther Dolly. Two SGI laboratories with a total of 21 computers and an image-$14 server; Wavefront TAV; Kinamation; Dynamation; 3D Design with MetaBalls; Paint; Video Composer Professional; Explorer; Softimage; Xaos Tools; C with OpenGL library; two PC laboratories with a total of 25 computers; Autodesk 3D Studio; Crystal Topaz; Macromedia Director; Adobe Premiere; Lumena, Tips, Fractal Design Painter; Pro HiJaak; 14 Wacom Tablets; five Macintosh laboratories with a total of 80 computers; four Color One scanners and seven laser printers; MacFormZ; Photoshop; Fractal Painter; Dabbler; Director; QuarkXPress; Freehand; Illustrator; PageMaker; CodeWarrior IDE C/C++; Claris Works; MacWrite. All laboratories fully networked. Other equipment includes:18 Amiga; two Toasters; Imagine 3.0; Deluxe Paint; DigiPaint; Pixel Pro; Vista Pro; AdPro; also Amiga-based DPS Digital Disk Recorder; Management Graphics Solitaire Film 4k Recorder; Tektronics Phaser III Color Laser Printer; S-VHS cuts-only suite; Flyer AV Roll non-linear editing system; Macintosh-based midi sequencer; Hi8 editing suite; and 3/4 SP deck.

Student Body
There are 377 undergraduates and 70 graduate students in the department. Total student body is 5,500.

Faculty Profile
Fifteen faculty members in the department. Ratio of 20-1 student to faculty.

Deadlines and Financial Aid
Students are not eligible to receive awarded financial aid until the term begins for which they are enrolled. Aid is applied to the student's account at the end of the drop/add week each term, based upon enrollment level as follows: Georgia S.I.G. (full award for full-time enrollment only); Federal S.E.O.F. (full award for full-time or three-quarter-time); Federal Pell Grant (full award for full-time, partial award for three-quarter-time); Georgia T.E.G. and Georgia Hope Grant (full award for full-time enrollment only; applied during the fourth week of each term).

Admission Requirement
Undergraduates: application for admission, non-refundable application fee, official transcript from last high school attended showing all four years of the student's grades, official report of SAT or ACT scores, three letters of recommendation (see application form for procedure), portfolio presentation and interview encouraged but not required. Graduate students: application for admission, non-refundable application fee (the application form and application fee may be submitted prior to submission of the portfolio), official transcript from each college attended; applicants must hold a bachelor's degree from an accredited college or university or should anticipate completion of a bachelor's degree before the anticipated enrollment date, three letters of recommendation (see application form for procedure), statement of purpose detailing academic and professional goals, personal interview (may be waived because of distance), portfolio of studio work.

Expenses
Tuition is $19,035 per year.

Contact
Computer Art Department, The Savannah College of Art and Design, 342 Bull St., P.O. Box 3146, Savannah, Georgia 31402. Telephone: 800-869-SCAD or 912-525-6352. Fax: 912-525-4852. Contact person: Larry Valestine, chair.
URL: http://www.scad.edu/.

Additional Information
The computer art program of The Savannah College of Art and Design offers B.F.A., M.F.A. and M.A. degrees, which prepare students to produce professional work for business and media employers, and which teach skills and concepts needed for using the computer in new and innovative ways as the field develops. Students have the opportunity to learn software such as Wavefront and Softimage, as well as four different platforms (Macintosh, IBM-compatible, Amiga and Silicon Graphics workstations) in state-of-the-art facilities. The curriculum is varied, emphasizing not only animation, but also video editing, multimedia and graphic design principles, which enhance careers in computer presentation. The graduate program enables students to expand their technical skills with challenging projects in exploratory, up-to-date idioms of computer art and to develop analytical and critical skills. The curriculum is also enhanced by an active program of visiting professionals.

University of Georgia

F/X Degrees Offered
B.F.A. and M.F.A. through the School of Art. M.S. and Ph.D. in Computer Science Department.

Curricular
3D Modeling and Rendering; 3D Computer Animation; 2D Computer Animation; Multimedia/Interactive; Digital Painting/Drawing; Image Processing; Virtual Reality; Digital Video; Stereo Imaging.

Facilities
Hardware: Macintosh; Silicon Graphics. Software: Stratavision; Sketch; Infini-D; Maya; Showcase; Mosaic; Debabelizer; Apple Media toolkit. Computer Science Department facilities--Hardware: numerous Sun workstations; PCs; Macintoshes; MasPar; Hypercube. Software systems and languages: C++; C; Pascal; Fortran; Smalltalk; ML; DBMSS; Maple; Mathematica; MatLab.

Student Body
There are 900 undergraduates and 150 graduate students in the Department of Art.

Faculty Profile
There are 53 faculty in the Arts, and 15 faculty members in the Computer Science Department. Total enrollment: 31,288

Deadlines and Financial Aid
There are several scholarships available at the school in addition to federal aid. Deadline: Applications must be postmarked no later than February 1 of the high school graduating year. Students should submit the following: 10 slides of their work, a one-page statement about their reasons for wanting to be an art student, two letters of recommendation from art teachers, high school records and SAT scores. The application should also include the student's name, address, school and city. Only the slides will be returned to the student. Graduate assistantships are available through the Department of Computer Science, ranging from Graduate teaching assistantships to graduate research assistantships.

Admission Requirements
Admission standards for the Lamar Dodd School of Art may vary from those set by other schools and departments within the Franklin College of Arts and Sciences. For final degrees in studio art (BFA and AB Studio Art), acceptance into the Lamar Dodd School of Art is contingent on both overall GPA and a portfolio review.

Expenses
Tuition is $1,709 per semester for Georgia residents taking 12 or more hours, and $5,657 per semester for non-residents taking 12 or more hours.

Contact
University of Georgia, 101 Visual Arts, Athens, GA 30602. Telephone: 706-542-1511. Fax: 706-542-0226. Contact person: Jane Sanders, Business Manager. E-mail: jsanders@uga.edu. URL: http://www.visart.uga.edu/.

Additional Information
The University of Georgia offers undergraduate degree programs in the studio discipline, art education, and art history. A number of graduate programs are also available, and the curricula are enriched through broadly based studies in the liberal arts made available by the College of Arts and Sciences.

Hawaii

University of Hawaii at Manoa

F/X Degrees Offered
B.F.A. and M.F.A. in Expanded Arts, Computer Science, and Graphics Design.

Curricular
Design Studio I, II and III. Various courses are offered through the Expanded Arts Program. The curriculum includes an introduction to the use of all Design Laboratory equipment.

Facilities
The Design Laboratory includes: computer graphics systems (Macintosh computers, hard drives, large screen monitors, b/w and color scanners, laser printers, color printers and appropriate drawing, typographic, authoring and illustration software); graphic arts equipment (a copy camera, P.M.T. processors, ultraviolet vacuum exposure unit, darkroom facilities that can accommodate up to 20x24 lithographic film development, an enlarging/reducing photocopier, 35 mm copy stand and lights). The Electronic Arts Laboratory integrates both analog and digital devices that generate, modulate, record and project sonic and visual information. Students are encouraged to produce traditional forms of electronic music, video, 2D and 3D animation, and experimental combinations of these forms. The laboratory is online and the potential use of the Internet as an effective art medium is studied. Multimedia workstations include PCs; Macintoshes and Amigas, and are interfaced with an assortment of Hi8 and S-VHS video decks; a digital sound synthesizer; scanners; printers; a video projector; digital and analog cameras; and an Amiga-based video Toaster workstation.

Student Body
There are 20,000 students enrolled in the university.

Faculty Profile
Five faculty members teach in the Graphic Design area; two faculty members teach in the Expanded Art Program.

Deadlines and Financial Aid
Scholarships, grants, loans and employment are available. Financial aid application packets are available at the office. Although the priority deadline for applications is March 1 for the following academic year, applications will be processed on a first-come, first-served basis until funds run out. Graduate students: teaching assistantships are also available. Graduate assistants can receive an initial stipend is $12,820 (nine-month appointment) or $14,830 (11-month appointment). Graduate assistants are awarded tuition waivers, but they are not exempt from the general fees, special course fees listed in the catalog, and the Graduate Student Organization fee. Applications should be sent to the chair of the appropriate department before February 1. Each application must be accompanied by three letters of recommendation from former professors or employers.

Admission Requirements
Undergraduates: students seeking admission to candidacy for the B.F.A. must pass a portfolio review. Freshman applicants must submit an application, official SAT-I or ACT scores, high school transcripts and recommendations from school officials. Applicants taking the high school GED test must submit GED results in addition to high school transcripts. Graduate students: applicants for the M.F.A. must present evidence of a B.F.A. or a B.A. Applicants with non-traditionally graded undergraduate or graduate transcripts must submit

GRE scores and course performance report forms if these transcripts contain 25 percent or more of the applicant's credit hours; portfolio and three letters of recommendation.

Expenses
Tuition is $1,656 per semester for residents $4,896 for non-residents.

Contact
Art Department, 1680 East-West Road, Honolulu, HI 96822. Telephone: 808-956-7420. Fax: 808-956-3548. URL: http://www.hawaii.edu/.

Additional Information
The Expanded Arts Program allows students to explore the relationships between art, culture and technology within an intermedia environment. The format of the Expanded Arts Program emphasizes theory, and frames the practice of making art within historical and cultural critique, and a regional context. Some courses address visual language systems and creative processes. Students engage in projects in combined 2D, 3D and time-based media, which question and seek to understand the role of the artist and the function of art in today's world. Other courses focus on new technology and practice. The Graphic Design Program has the largest number of majors in the Art Department. Fifteen to 20 students graduate with a B.F.A. in the area of Graphic Design each year.

Idaho

Boise State University

F/X Degrees Offered
B.S. and M.S. in Computer Science through the Department of Mathematics and Computer Science. B.A. in Art.

Curricular
Introduction to Computer Graphics.

Facilities
There are seven College of Engineering computer lab/classrooms designed to provide the specialized support needed by Engineering students. These labs are in addition to the University open computer lab located in ET 239 and ET 212. The College's Information Technology department supports these labs and consists of 5 full time System Administrators who are responsible for the support and installation of hardware and software for each lab. Instructors can fill out the software request form and submit it to the IT department if the software they need in a lab is currently not an available option.

Student Body
There are 75 students in the Department, 10 take the CG course every other year.

Faculty Profile
10 faculty members teach in the department.

Deadlines and Financial Aid
Financial aid is available through the university in the form of federal grants, loans, and scholarships.

Admission Requirements
Application and fee, transcript, SAT or ACT, and GRE if applying to the M.S. program.

Expenses
Tuiition is $3,251 per year residents and $9,971 per year non-residents. Health insurance is mandatory.

Contact
Mathematics and Computer Science, 1910 University Dr., Boise, ID 83725. Telephone: 208-426-5640. Fax: 208-426-426-2470. Contact: Tim Anderson, Email: tim@cs.boisestate.edu.
URL: http://www.boisestate.edu/.

University of Idaho

F/X Degrees Offered
B.A. and B.F.A. in the Art and Architectural Department. B.S., Ph.D., in Computer Science and Computer Engineering.

Curricular
Graphics design courses in the Art Department.

Facilities
The computer science department is running HP/UX version 10.20, Windows, Macintosh, IBM and SGI workstations. As well as several up-to-date computer programs.

Student Body
There are 10,000 students in the university.

Faculty Profile
Student-faculty ratio in the major: 18:1.

Deadlines and Financial Aid
Students applying for any type of need-based financial aid must have a processed FAFSA on file with the UI Financial Aid Services Office. This form may be completed any time during the academic year using either the paper application or the online form. However, for priority consideration, FAFSA must be in the hands of the processor by February 15. Scholarships are also available.

Admission Requirements

SAT or ACT, high school transcripts, application and fee.

Expenses

Tuition is $3,348 per year for residents and $10,740 per year for non-residents.

Contact

University of Idaho, Admission, P.O. Box 444253, Moscow, ID 83843-4199. Telephone 208-885-6111. 800-88-UIDAHO. Fax: 208-885-4477. Email: cs@cs.uidaho.edu.
URL: http://www.uidaho.edu/.

Illinois

Columbia College Chicago

F/X Degrees Offered
Film Department offers an M.F.A. in Film and Video and Photography. The Art Department offers a B.A. in Art with a focus in Computer Graphics, Graphic Design.

Curricular
Film Video--Directing the Dramatic Film; Video Production I; Editing for Film and Video; Animation I, II and III; Optical Printing; Composition and Optic; Production Manager/Film Producer Video Editing; Advanced Animation Techniques I; Rotoscope; Advanced Animation Techniques: 3D Animation; Drawing for Animation I and II; Image and Story; History of Video Art; Computer Animation I.

Facilities
Includes an animation studio with a computer-enhanced Oxberry animation camera; a rotoscope and optical printers; a sound studio suitable for recording; transferring and mixing in 16 mm; editing suites offering Steenbeck flatbeds and 3/4-inch video units. 14 SGI workstations. High-end software includes Maya and Softimage.

Student Body
More than 6,500 students attend the college; 1,200 art students; 1,600 film students.

Faculty Profile
Thirteen faculty members in the Film and Video Graduate Program, 18 faculty members in the area of Arts, Entertainment and Media Management Programs.

Admission Requirements
A completed graduate application; application fee; a self-assessment in essay form, approximately three to five pages; official transcripts from each college or university; three letters of recommendation. Deadline and Financial Aid Arts, Entertainment and Media Management, fall admission deadline is Aug. 15; spring deadline is March 15, Arts Entertainment and Media Management, December 29; Film and Video: no spring admission. Federal Student Aid deadline is Jan. 1 to June 30. Federal, and state aid are available including work-study and Illinois Monetary Award Program.

Expenses
Tuition is $7,440 per semester. Additional fees apply to film production, ranging in cost from $8,000 to $20,000.

Contact
Columbia College Chicago, 600 S. Michigan Ave., Chicago, IL 60605-1996. Telephone: 312-663-1600. Fax: 312-986-1091. Email: sfs@colum.edu. URL: http://www.colum.edu/.

Additional Information
The M.F.A. program in Film and Video prepares for professional careers in film and video production, college teaching, theatrical and non-theatrical fiction film, documentary film and video, animation, and independent filmmaking.

DePaul University

F/X Degrees Offered
B.S. in Computer Science with a minor in Computer Graphics through the school of Computer Science, Telecommunication and Information systems.

Curricular

For Computer Graphics minor: Introduction to Structured Programming Using C; Principles of Computer Science I; Principles of Computer Science II; Computer Graphics I; Survey of Computer Graphics; Independent Study.

Facilities

The configuration includes a Harris Nighthawk and several Sun Sparc centers for student use; access to IBM PC laboratories and Macintosh laboratories at the Loop and Lincoln Park campuses. There are numerous dial-up phone numbers available for off-campus work. Permanent student Internet access accounts are available along with dial-in SLIP connections. The school operates specialized laboratories for artificial intelligence, computer vision and graphics, software engineering, telecommunications, local area networks and computer telephony. One laboratory allows students to explore specialized software. The laboratories include both PCs and UNIX workstations. The school also operates an IBM ES9000/9221.

Student Body

There are 10,100 students are enrolled in the university.

Faculty Profile

There are 49 faculty members in the department.

Deadlines and Financial Aid

Nearly 65 percent of all undergraduates receive some form of financial aid. One or more types of financial assistance are usually combined in a package to meet individual needs. This package can include grants, federal loans, and scholarships.

Admission Requirements

The school recommends you apply by February 1st for Priority/Regular admission or by November 15 for Early Action Program admission. Applications are considered on a space available basis until August 15 by rolling notification. Either the SAT or ACT is required. Complete and return the application for admission and the fee and submit official transcripts from all colleges attended.

Expenses

Tuition is $18,750 per academic year.

Contact

Office of Admission, DePaul University, 1E. Boulevard, Chicago, IL 60604. Telephone: 312-362-8300 or 800-4DEPAUL.
URL: http://www.depaul.edu/.

Lewis University

F/X Degrees Offered

B.A. in Radio and Television Broadcasting. B.A. in Art and Computer Graphic Design.

Curricular

Various courses in production of Television Graphics including Videotape Editing and Special Topics in Media. As well as drawing, software, and art history courses.

Facilities

Equipped with state-of-the-art 3D digital video effects, 3D animation, digital non-linear editing, and digital audio production. Majors also train on multi-format AB-roll editing, including VHS; S-VHS; 3/4 U-Matic; Beta Cam; and Beta Cam-SP. Art--Macintosh computer laboratory.

Student Body

There are 4,350 students attending the university.

Faculty Profile

Student-to-teacher ratio: 16:1.

Deadlines and Financial Aid

Combination of scholarships, grants, loans, and employment are available to students. The Office of

Financial Aid administers programs in cooperation with federal, state and private agencies, as well as funds provided through the university. Funding may be based on financial need or may be based on academic, athletic, or fine-arts merit.

Admission Requirements
Application and fee, ACT or SAT, high school transcript.

Expenses
Tuition is $7,975 per semester.

Contact
Lewis University, A Christian Brothers University, Route 53, Romeoville, IL 60446. Telephone: 800-897-9000 or 815-836-5250.
URL: http://www.lewisu.edu/

Additional Information
Lewis was founded in 1932 as a technical school. It became Lewis College in 1960, and has grown into a co-education university which was incorporated in 1973. Since 1960, Lewis has been sponsored by the Christian Brothers, a Roman Catholic teaching order.

Northern Illinois University

F/X Degrees Offered
B.F.A. in Studio Art with a concentration in Design. B.A. in Arts Education.

Curricular
Courses include--Fundamentals of Electronic Media; Study in Motion Graphics; Fundamentals of Computer Graphics; Computer Graphics; Intermedia Arts; Video Art; Media Graphics; Time Arts; Sculpting.

Facilities
Macintosh hardware and software for creating animation and computer-based designs. Photoshop; Illustrator; Director; 3D Studio Max.

Student Body
There are 23,000 students attending the university.

Faculty Profile
There are 53 faculty members teaching in the Department of Art; four faculty in the Time Arts Area.

Deadlines and Financial Aid
All application material for admission must be completed by December 1 for the spring semester, May 1 for the summer semester, and July 15 for the fall semester. The Student Financial Aid Office is responsible for administering and coordinating aid from federal, state, private and university sources. Scholarships, grants, loans and employment are available to approved students.

Admission Requirements
Application and fee, ACT score, high school transcripts.

Expenses
Tuition is $1,692.72 per semester for residents and $3,385.44 for non-residents.

Contact
Office of Admissions, Williston Hall 101, Northern Illinois University, DeKalb, IL 60115. Telephone: 815-753-7856.
URL: http://www.niu.edu/.

Additional Information
The School of Art, with a faculty of more than 60 artists, designers, and scholars, and an enrollment of more than 800 undergraduate and 130 graduate students, is a comprehensive public university art schools in the United States, with a nationally established reputation in a number of field.

The long-standing quality of the School of Art's programs, its affiliation with a major university, its location near the population centers of northern Illinois, and the competitiveness of its educational costs make Northern's program in the visual arts one of the best education values for art students. Faculty and students who work and study in the visual arts at Northern are responsible for its excellent reputation, having received awards and honors in both artistic and academic fields. Graduates from the School of Art are sought by employers ranging from large and small businesses, to public school systems throughout Illinois, to colleges and universities, as well as museums and galleries.

Northwestern University

F/X Degrees Offered
B.S., M.A., M.F.A. and Ph.D. degrees in Media Studies through the Department of Radio/TV/Film. Certificates available through The Center for Art and Technology.

Curricular
3D Modeling and Rendering; 3D Computer Animation; 2D Computer Animation; Multimedia/Interactive; Digital Painting/Drawing; Digital Video; Media Constructing; and Directing.

Facilities
Four SGIs with Softimage; one UNIX Web server. University facilities--Macintosh-based laboratories with extensive peripherals; non-linear editing facilities. Network access to national Supercomputer centers is available to support research projects and instruction. Accounts are granted at National Science Foundation (NSF) Supercomputer centers through a review process, and link more than 100 department computers, of which 50 are located in the department's four computer laboratories.

The computer graphics undergraduate laboratory contains specialized RISC workstations and input/output devices to support computer-aided design, geographical information systems, facility management and visualization software.

Student Body
There are 300 undergraduates and 50 graduate students.

Faculty Profile
Fourteen full-time faculty members teach in the Department of Radio/TV/Film, along with several professional part-time faculty.

Deadlines and Financial Aid
Northwestern University offers financial assistance to its students on the basis of need and not on the basis of merit. Applicants who wish to be considered for fellowships and scholarships must apply by Jan. 15 of the academic year preceding that for which financial aid is requested. Undergraduates must submit an application for admissions before June 2 for the fall quarter, November 1 for the winter, February 1 for the spring, and May 1 for the summer. Financial Aid applications are due by February 15. The Graduate School provides fellowships and scholarships; departments or programs determine the fellowship and scholarship awards, and also recommend the awarding of teaching assistantships. Principal investigators and/or departments award research assistantships. Graduate students seeking loans must make application to a financial aid officer in the Graduate School.

Admission Requirements
Undergraduates must submit application and fee, ACT or SAT I, and high school transcript or college if transferring. Contact the Undergraduate Admissions Office for details on the application process. Prospective graduate students should contact the graduate office for details on the application process.

Expenses
Tuition is $25,677 per year for full-time students.

Contact
1905 N. Sheridan Rd., Evanston, IL 60201. Telephone: 847-491-7315. Fax: 847-467-2389. Contact person: Professor Larry Lichty, Department of Radio/TV/Film. Email: lichty@northwestern.edu. URL: http://www.northwestern.edu/.

Additional Information
Northwestern University's Department of Radio/TV/Film offers both undergraduate and graduate degrees in media studies in a liberal arts environment. In addition to 2D and 3D computer animation and interactive multimedia, students are encouraged to study a wide range of subjects in the production, history, theory, policy and industry practice of the media arts.

Saint Xavier University

F/X Degrees Offered
B.A. in Art through the Department of Art. B.A. in Computer Science.

Curricular
Computer Graphics; Photo-Image Manipulation; Typography; Drawing; Printmaking; and several Design courses.

Facilities
Macintosh and PC computer graphics laboratories that include all basic graphics and web design applications.

Student Body
5,200 total student enrollment.

Faculty Profile
Student-to-faculty ratio is 16:1.

Deadlines and Financial Aid
Various forms of aid are available to students. These include, but are not limited to, federal aid, loans and scholarships. There are also several state programs available.

Admission Requirements
Completed application files are reviewed by the Admission Committee and admitted students are notified of a decision within two weeks. Students must submit the following: a completed application, application fee, an official high school transcript or GED score report, a recommendation from the high school guidance counselor, and ACT or SAT score report. Applications for admission are processed throughout the year.

Expenses
Tuition is $16,500 per year or $550 per credit hour.

Contact
3700 W. 103, Chicago, IL 60647. Telephone: 773-298-3080 or 800-GO2-XAVU. Fax: 773-779-9061. Contact person: Jayne Hileman. E-mail: hileman@sxu.edu. URL: http://www.sxu.edu/.

School of the Art Institute of Chicago

F/X Degrees Offered
M.F.A. in Art and Technology, Filmmaking, Fine Arts, Video, Photography and Visual Communication. B.F.A. and M.F.A. applicants who wish to combine two or more of the following areas: electronics, performance, sound, art and technology, or video, should apply for admission through the Time Arts Program rather than through a single department. Time Arts is a collaborative, interdisciplinary program composed of film,

holography, performance, sound, art and technology, and video.

Curricular

Art and Technology Studies: Computer Imaging I; Systems and Processes I; 2D Computer Animation; Kinetics; Electronics; Beginning Holography; Computer Imaging II; Advanced Computer Projects; Introduction to 3D Computer Animation; Experimental Computer Programming; Digital Techniques for Kinetics; Electronic Theory; Interactive Multimedia; Interactive Media for Performance; Multimedia Installations; Telecommunication Art; Intermediate/Advanced Holography; Computer Holography; Kinetics and Electronics; Desktop Publishing for Artists; Digital Video; Advanced 3D Animation I, II; Advanced Computer Animation: Summer Studio; Robotics I: Actions; Robotics II: Awareness; Advanced Art and Tech Projects. Filmmaking--Workshop: 16 mm Creative Filmmaking; Film I: Introductory Production; Documentary Filmmaking; Film II: Intermediate Production; Alternative Techniques in Animation; Drawing for Animation; Animation I; 8 mm Filmmaking; Multilevel Animation; Film III: Advanced Production; Film Editing; 3D and Puppet Animation; Animation II; Drama and Film; Experimental Film Narrative; Image Making-The World of Do-it-Yourself Image Making; Advanced Cinema Projects. Video: Image Processing I; Basic Video: Production II; Computer Video; Advanced Video Production Seminar; Video Computer Synthesis; Videotape Editing; New Documentary Forms; Electronic Field Production; Video Diary/ Sketchbook; Advanced Computer Video; Video Installation; Video Strategies.

Facilities

Macintosh computers; Amiga computers; IBMs and IBM-compatible computers with Lumena software; SGI computers; Softimage software; video digitizes; color scanners; film and video recorders;

keyboards with MIDI interfaces; holography and computer holography studios; electronics workshop for kinetic sculptures and interactive installations. Cameras: NPR; CP; Bolexes; 58s; Tripods. Recorders: Nagras, Sony TCDM5s, editing equipment; five flatbed editing machines. Three optical printers: two J-Ks and one Oxberry 1500; Bell and Howell contact printer, Model C; Oxberry animation stand; Sound mixing and transfer facilities. Computer laboratory with 10 Macintosh computers; color and b/w printers; slide scanner; flatbed scanner. Video recording equipment: 3/4-inch to 3/4-inch video editing; wave-form monitor; 8-channel mixer; Yamaha SPX-90 special effects generator; 4-track cassette deck; half-track reel-to-reel tape deck; 3/4-inch and VHS deck with monitor; audio mixer, eight-inch, two out. Slide projector; 16 mm Pageant film projector; video-8 camera; light kit; Sony field recorder; video effects generator; time base corrector. Two large-scale video synthesis systems; Fairlight computer-video instrument; Beta I, High-8, and 3/4-inch editing systems; portable recording systems; studio VCRs; color special-effects generator; three Macintosh II computers; A/B-roll editing; individual studios.

Student Body

There are 18 graduate students in the Computer Graphics area; 1,900 undergraduates and 500 graduate students attend the institute.

Faculty Profile

Twelve faculty members in Arts and Technology; 13 faculty members in Filmmaking, and 15 in the Video Department.

Deadlines and Financial Aid

For applicants wishing to enroll in September, the process can begin as early as the preceding December when a packet of information that includes the FAFSA, the application for institutional aid, and a calendar of important dates will be available from the school. To ensure priority consideration, the needs analysis document and institutional aid application must be filed by March 1. The needs analysis document can be filed as early as January.

Admission Requirements
Application for admission is open to high school graduates, students who have successfully completed the General Educational Development (GED) requirements, and transfer students from accredited colleges and universities. The following are required: a completed application form and application fee, a portfolio of works, a statement of purpose, as explained in the application form instructions, official transcripts from each school previously attended, and three letters of recommendation.

Expenses
Tuition is $710 per credit hour.

Contact
The School of the Art Institute of Chicago, Office of Admissions, 37 S. Wabash Ave., Chicago, IL 60603-3103. Telephone: 312-899-5100. Fax: 312-899-1840. E-mail: arted@artic.edu. URL: http://www.artic.edu/saic/.

University of Chicago

F/X Degrees Offered
B.A., M.S., and Ph.D. in Computer Science.

Curricular
Internet services; JAVA; simulation; Computer programming; Computer Graphics.

Facilities
Department facilities--Hardware: 75 Suns; 50 Macintoshes. University facilities--Hardware: 4K Macintoshes; 6K PCs; 2,000 UNIX workstations. In addition to general University computing facilities,

Undergraduate Computing Laboratory includes three-dozen Macintosh computers and a dozen Sun Sparc and SGI workstations with extensive peripherals and software. The University provides each student with high-speed internet in their rooms, as well as state-of-the-art computing clusters and e-mail stations all across campus.

Student Body
Total enrollment of 9,639 students; 100 science students in the department.

Faculty Profile
Thirteen full-time faculty members teach in the Computer Science Department.

Deadlines and Financial Aid
All accepted students who demonstrate financial need receive adequate financial aid. Approximately two-thirds of all students in the College receive aid. Aid is usually in a combination of scholarships, loans and campus employment. There are several deadlines to remember. Early Action is for candidates who would like an admission decision in mid-December and a provisional financial aid assessment by early January. Candidates must complete their applications by November 1 and may apply to other schools if they wish. In other words, Chicago's early action program is non-binding; admitted students need not reply to the offer of admission until May 1. International students may only choose Early Action if they are not applying for financial aid. Regular Notification is for candidates who would like an admission and financial aid decision by early April. Candidates must complete their applications by January 1 and must reply to the offer of admission by May 1. Fellowships and other various forms of graduate assistantships are also available to students.

Admission Requirements
Application and fee, transcripts, GRE scores, letters of recommendation.

Expenses

Tuition is $29,238 per year.

Contact

Department of Computer Science, The University of Chicago, 1116 E. 59th Street, Chicago, IL 60637. Telephone: 773-702-6144. Fax: 773-702-6144. Contact person: David B. MacQueen, Chair. E-mail: URL: http://www.uchicago.edu/.

University of Illinois at Chicago

F/X Degrees Offered

M.F.A. in Art; B.S., M.S. and Ph.D through the Computer Science Department.

Curricular

3D Modeling and Rendering; 3D Computer Animation; 2D Computer Animation; Multimedia/Interactive; High-Level Programming; Low-Level Programming; Digital Painting/Drawing; Image Processing; Virtual Reality; Volume Visualization; Digital Video; Stereo Imaging.

Facilities

EVL has multiple high-end Silicon Graphics Onyx Reality Engine systems used for Virtual Reality research, which are complemented by a dozen or so SGI Indy workstations and various Macintoshes, and older SGI workstations. EVL is a MetaCenter Regional Alliance member, which means it has access to supercomputers over the VBNS network. C and C++ programming languages are used with a suite of SGI packages like Inventor, Performer, Maya and Softimage.

Student Body

Fifty graduate students in the department.

Faculty Profile

Five faculty members teach at the laboratory.

Deadlines and Financial Aid

Various fellowships and traditional state, federal and city aid are available to students. Contact the Financial Aid Office for details on obtaining financial assistance at the university. Eight graduate assistantships are available each year in the department.

Admission Requirements

The UIC Office of Admissions and Records (OAR) is responsible for evaluating all undergraduate student applications, and your first step is to complete the UIC Undergradutate Application, select Engineering as your choice of programs. Students are required to submit application, fee, and transcripts.

Expenses

Tuition is $1,924 per semester for residents and $5,772 per semester for non-residents.

Contact

University of Illinois at Chicago, 851 S. Morgan St., Room 1120, Chicago, IL 60607-7053. Telephone: 312-996-3002. Fax: 312-413-7585. Contact person: Tom DeFanti. E-mail: tom@uic.edu. URL: http://www.uic.edu/.

Additional Information

The Electronic Visualization Laboratory (EVL) advances research in computer graphics and interactive techniques through its blend of engineering, science and art; students receive M.S., Ph.D. and M.F.A. degrees through the UIC Electrical Engineering and Computer Science department, and the UIC School of Art and Design. EVL's current research emphasis is Virtual Reality; however, faculty and students are also involved in a number of related cutting-edge problems: multimedia; scientific visualization; new methodologies for informal science and engineering education; paradigms for information display; algorithm optimization for parallel computing; sonification and abstract mathematical visualization. Most recently recognized for its work in Virtual Reality with the introduction of the CAVE virtual environment in 1992, EVL has a history of innovative contributions to the computer graphics field since its inception in 1973. EVL contains state-of-the-art graphics workstations and a video editing suite, plus access to the SGI Power Challenge Array and Convex Supercomputers at the National Center for Supercomputing Applications, and to the IBM SP-2 at Argonne National Laboratory.

University of Illinois at Springfield

F/X Degrees Offered
Computer Science Department. B.A. and M.A. in Computer Science.

Curricular
3D Modeling and Rendering; 3D Computer Animation; 2D Computer Animation; Multimedia/Interactive; High-Level Programming; Introduction to Graphics and a graduate-level course on Graphics; User Interface Design.

Facilities
Computing equipment available to students in the program includes PC-compatibles; Macintoshes; SGI; HPs and Sun workstations, all connected to a local network of 16 transputer parallel processors. Internet facilities are available through these platforms, and by modem connections. Macintosh laboratory.

Student Body
Sixty undergraduates and 80 graduate students in the department.

Faculty Profile
Five full-time faculty members in the department.

Deadlines and Financial Aid
Various fellowships and traditional state, federal and city aid are available to students. Contact the Financial Aid Office for details on obtaining financial assistance at the university.

Admission Requirements
Entrance requirements include two semesters of programming experience in a high-level language such as Pascal, C or Fortran. These courses may be taken at UIS, but will not be applied toward the 60 hours required for the degree. Required mathematics courses are two semesters of calculus, one semester of discrete math, and one semester of linear algebra. These courses may be taken at UIS and applied toward the required 12 hours of general electives. However, students are urged to complete these hours before entering the program.

Expenses
In-state tuition for Fall 2003 and Spring 2004 is $129.50 per credit hour for graduate students and $115 for undergraduates. For out-of-state residents, tuition is $345.00 per credit hour for undergraduates and $388.50 for graduates.

Contact
University of Illinois at Springfield, Springfield, IL 62794. Telephone: 217-206-7328 or 800-252-8533. Contact person: Scott Grissom. E-mail: grissom@uis.edu.
URL: http://www.uis.edu/.

Additional Information
Beginning with the Fall 2003 semester, the University of Illinois at Springfield will offer, completely online, six degree programs, an online minor and a graduate certificate program.

University of Illinois at Urbana-Champaign

F/X Degrees Offered
Department of Computer Science. B.S., M.S. and Ph.D. School of Art and Design offers a B.F.A. and M.F.A.

Curricular
Science Curricular: 3D Modeling and Rendering; 3D Computer Animation; 2D Computer Animation; Multimedia/Interactive; High-Level Programming; Low-Level Programming; Digital Painting/Drawing; Image Processing; Virtual Reality; Volume Visualization; Digital Video; Stereo Imaging. Art Curricular: Digital Imaging; Computer Techniques in Design; Computer Applications in Design I; Digital Photography; Video for Artists I and II; Computer Device Interfacing for Non-Computer Majors; Computer User Interfaces and Visualization for Non-Computer Majors; Computer Graphics; Advanced Topics in Computer Graphics.

Facilities
Graphics and Multimedia Laboratory: This laboratory contains special purpose PC's, workstations and A/V equipment for graphics, animation and multimedia development and production. Powerful graphics workstations by SGI and HP are complemented by powerful PC counterparts with Evans & Sutherland graphics cards, all supporting the real-time display of complex geometric models and scenes that can be recorded using an HP video server. These machines are also equipped with cameras and microphones, and are interconnected with a high-performance ATM network to support projects in multimedia and teleconferencing. Students have used this lab to create systems to support a client/server VCR, video conferencing, audio-on-demand and multimedia mail. Embedded and Real-Time Systems Laboratory: The research focus is secured, robust and flexible software architecture of networked intelligent devices. Students use design stations in the laboratory for dedicated or real-time computing applications. The lab includes PCs, micro-controllers, networks, and electro-mechanical devices such as an inverted pendulum and water-seesaws. In cooperation with the Department of Electrical and Computer Engineering, students also have access to a newly developed intelligent traffic control laboratory where they must efficiently navigate and negotiate computer controlled model cars through highways and crossroads. Software Design and Development Laboratory: This laboratory contains Sun SPARC Ultra workstations with a suite of software development tools. Students taking courses in advanced programming, operating systems, and software development use this lab extensively. The 1235 lab has 34 Sun Blade 1000's running Solaris 8. This lab is used for instructional purposes and student usage. It is equipped with one laser printer. The 1245 lab has 26 Sun Blade 1000's and Sun Ultra 10s running Solaris 8. The Sun Blade 1000's are equipped with the Sun Creator3D Series 3 Graphics Accelerator. The Sun Ultra 10s are equipped with cameras and have the Elite 3D frame buffer. The Ultra 10s are equipped for multimedia purposes but can be used for regular usage. This lab is equipped with one laser printer.

Student Body
Total enrollment is 36,400.

Faculty Profile
More than 45 faculty members in the School of Art and Design.

Deadlines and Financial Aid
Various types of financial aid are awarded on the basis of need, academic merit, or both. At Illinois, all students who qualify for need-based aid receive some type of assistance. There are two general

categories of financial aid: gift aid, which includes grants and scholarships; and self-help aid, which includes student loans and Federal Work-Study (part-time employment). Also, a limited number of merit-based scholarships are available through individual colleges and departments, and in most cases, you are automatically considered for these awards upon admission. Reserve Officers Training Corps (ROTC) scholarships are also available through the Army, Navy, and Air Force Departments. For full consideration for all sources of need-based financial aid that the Office of Student Financial Aid (OSFA) administers, complete a Free Application for Federal Student Aid (available via FAFSA-on-the-Web at www.fafsa.ed.gov, from your high school, or OSFA) and submit it to the federal processor by March 15. If you apply by March 15, OSFA will send you an estimated award letter in April reflecting the amount of aid you are likely to receive if you attend Illinois.

Admission Requirements
Freshman admission decisions are based on an evaluation of a variety of factors: High school; coursework requirements; ACT Composite score or SAT I total score; Cumulative High School Percentile Ranking (HSPR) at the end of the junior year; Personal Statement; Some curricula may require an audition, interview, portfolio, or Professional Interest Statement.

Expenses
Tuition is $14,410 per year for residents and $25,450 for non-residents.

Contact
1304 W. Springfield Ave., Urbana, IL 61801. Telephone: 217-333-6148. Fax: 217-333-3501. Contact person: Don Hearn. E-mail: hearn@cs.uiuc.edu.
URL: http://www.cs.uiuc.edu/.

Additional Information
Located in the adjoining cities on Champaign and Urbana approximately 140 miles south of Chicago, the University offers more than 4,000 courses every semester. About 80 percent of all class sections have fewer than 30 students; 46 percent have fewer than 20.

Western Illinois University

F/X Degrees Offered
B.S. and M.S. in Computer Science. Minor in Film.

Curricular
Graphical User Interface Programming; Internet; Computer Simulation; Computer Graphics I and II.

Facilities
Hardware includes access to the mainframe; IBMs; VAX minicomputers; several large IBM ATs and IBM-compatible PCs are available to students. Fine Art: film production and traditional animation equipment; various systems available through the Computer Science Department.

Student Body
There are 2,500 graduate students at the university.

Faculty Profile
Twelve faculty members are in the Science Department.

Deadlines and Financial Aid
Graduate assistantships are academic, merit-based award programs, which provide students with work opportunities in a job closely related to the academic field of study. Students with graduate assistantships will receive a stipend up to $4,560 per academic year and a waiver of tuition. Assistantship applications received prior to March 15 may be given priority consideration. Assistantships are available only to graduate students who have been accepted in degree

programs. Special programs for minority graduate students are also available. For these and any other assistantship programs, contact the Graduate and International Studies Office at 309-298-1806. Federal aid, scholarships and loans are also available; contact the Financial Aid Office.

Admission Requirements
Undergraduates should submit an application and fee, SAT or ACT score, and transcripts.

Expenses
Tuition is $3,915 for residents and $7,830 for non-residents.

Contact
Stipes Hall 101, Western Illinois University, 1 University Circle, Macomb, IL 61455-1390. Telephone: 309-278-298-2442. Fax: 309-298-1039. Email: D-Beveridge@wiu.edu. URL: http://www.wiu.edu/.

Indiana

Ball State University

F/X Degrees Offered
B.A. in Telecommunication through the College of Communication, Information and Media, minor in Film; B.F.A. in Art with a focus in Environmental/Exhibition Design; Graphic Design.

Curricular
Telecommunication courses: Electronic Media Revolution; Multimedia Design and Production; Organizational Video Production; Video Production; Single Camera Video Production; Advanced Video Production; Film Production; Video Graphics Technology. Art Courses: Introduction to Computers; Advanced Use of Computer in the Fine Arts; Computer Imaging.

Facilities
The advanced graphics labs are located in the Cooper Science Building. They are available to all Ball State students. They are managed by University Computing Services and are staffed during all business hours with students and staff to answer computing questions. The software and hardware are geared toward the production of video, audio, 3D and 2D graphics, web-interactivity, etc.

Student Body
There are 366 total in the Art student body.

Faculty Profile
Seventeen faculty members in the Telecommunication Department; 20 faculty members teach in the Department of Art.

Deadlines and Financial Aid
Application for admission to the University must be completed before March 1 for priority consideration for the fall semester; before December 1 for the spring semester; before April 1 for the summer semester and first summer term; and before May 1 for the second summer term. Applications may be submitted up to one year in advance. About two-thirds of all Ball State students receive some form of financial aid, including scholarships, grants, loans and student employment. To be considered for most financial aid programs, students must complete and submit the FAFSA form by March 1. For more information, contact the Office of Scholarships and Federal Aid at 800-227-4017.

Admission Requirements
Application and fee, official transcript or GED, and SAT or ACT score. Students applying to the Department of Art must submit a portfolio.

Expenses
Tuition is per year $5,532 for residents and $13,950 for non-residents.

Contact
Admission Office, Ball State University, Munie, IN 47306. Telephone: 765-285-5162 Fax: 765-285-6605. URL: http://www.bsu.edu/.

Indiana University

F/X Degrees Offered
B.A. in Comparative Literature with a concentration in Interrelationship of the Arts; B.A. in Film through the Film Studies Department; B.S. in Computer Science. B.F.A. in Studio Art with a concentration in Computer Art.

Curricular
Several theoretical film and art courses offered through the Comparative Literature Department. Film and cel animation production courses through the Film Studies Department. Computer Science

courses include Working the World Wide Web; User-Interface Programming; Mastering the World Wide Web; Interactive Graphics.

Facilities
The Information Technology Computing labs are distributed across the campus at Indiana State University (ISU). The Student Computing Complex (SCC) stands in the middle of 15 individual computing facilities. These facilities, with over 500 workstations, are connected through network services and are dedicated to academic endeavors. The labs are open to all Faculty, Staff and Students with valid ISU identification. Equipment includes Cel animation stand; film and video equipment for production and post-production; interactive media equipment; computer graphics laboratory.

Student Body
Total of 25,000 undergraduates, and 10,000 graduate students attend the university.

Faculty Profile
An average of 30 faculty members in each of the departments mentioned above.

Deadlines and Financial Aid
Students can obtain information about financial assistance through the Financial Aid Office, through the Student Employment Office, or through the schools and department. Deadline for admission is Jan. 15 for the fall semester, Sept. 1 for the spring, and Jan. 1 for the summer.

Admission Requirements
Freshmen are not admitted directly into a major. All freshmen are expected to meet the standards outlined in the freshman application materials. Students must submit an application for admission and fee, transcripts, and SAT or ACT.

Expenses
Tuition is $2,661 per semester for residents and $4,673 per semester for non-residents.

Contact
Admissions Office, Indiana University, 300 N. Jordan Ave., Bloomington, IN 47405. Telephone: 812-237-2121 or 800-742-0891. Fax: 812-237-8023. URL: http://www.indstate.edu/.

Purdue University

F/X Degrees Offered
The Department of Technical Graphics offers A.S., B.S. and M.S. degrees in Applied Computer Graphics Technology. After taking core graphics courses, students can specialize in three areas: Computer Illustration/Animation; Publishing Media; Engineering Design Graphics.

Curricular
3D Modeling and Rendering; 3D Computer Animation; 2D Computer Animation; Digital Painting/Drawing; Virtual Reality; Digital Video; CAD; Computer Gaming; Prepress Publishing.

Facilities
Two 23-station Macintosh laboratories; two 23-station Pentium multimedia laboratories; two 23-station laboratories; one applied research/development and instructional laboratory containing SGI; IBM; Pentiums; Macintoshes; digital video and VR equipment. Software: 3D Studio; 3D Studio Max; Adobe Freehand; Adobe Illustrator; Adobe PageMaker; Adobe Photoshop; Adobe Premier; Maya; Animator Pro; AutoCAD; AutoCAD Designer; BC Framer; Cadkey; DataCAD; EMT; Macromedia Director; Macromedia Authorware; Microsoft PowerPoint; Pro Engineer; QuarkXPress; SDRC IDEA's; Visual Basic. There are 6 Silicon Graphics workstations used for animation, 3D modeling, CAD, and rendering, and 8 high-end Windows NT workstations used for animation, digital video, multimedia production, web

development, and video editing. In addition there are a number of output devices for small and large high-resolution color prints.

Student Body
There are 325 undergraduates and 10 graduate students.

Faculty Profile
Eighteen faculty members teach in the department.

Deadlines and Financial Aid
Various fellowships and traditional state, federal and city aid are available to students. Contact the Financial Aid Office for details on obtaining financial assistance at the university.

Admission Requirements
Admission requirements depend on the Purdue school you wish to enter. For most programs, the required college grade point average (GPA) ranges from 2.5 to 3.0 on a 4.0 scale. Based on space availability, the GPA requirements could be raised or program could be closed without published notice. Undergraduate students must submit an application and fee, ACT or SAT scores, transcripts and a recommendation from a high school counselor or principal.

Expenses
Tuition is $5,860 per year for residents and $17,640 per year for non-residents.

Contact
1419 Knoy Hall, Room 363, West Lafayette, IN 47907-1419. Telephone: 765-494-7505. Fax: 765-494-9267. Contact person: Gary Bertoline. E-mail: grbertol@tech.purdue.edu.
URL: http://www.purdue.edu/.

Additional Information
Graduates of the program are employed as practitioners or managers in computer graphics-related fields, such as prepress publishing, marketing, computer gaming, interactive multimedia development, computer animation, CAD, VR, WWW page design, digital imaging, digital video, architectural illustration, and design/drafting.

Rose-Hulman Institute of Technology

F/X Degrees Offered
B.S. in Computer Science.

Curricular
3D Modeling and Rendering; High-Level Programming; Low-Level Programming; Fractals; Artificial Intelligence; Web Based Information Systems.

Facilities
The Sun Lab contains 24 Sun Workstations, including 12 new SunBlade 150s. There are 4 cubicals for Senior Projects, each with a dedicated Intel workstation configured for 'dual boot' (Linux or Windows XP). A dedicated Sun Ultra-10 workstations are also available. An HP LaserJet printer. An overhead projector and retractable screen. The new lab includes Warthog, Shadow, Skyhawk, and Spitfire and all Lab workstations have been upgraded to Solaris 9.

Student Body
There are 140 Computer Science majors. An average of 6,478 students enroll in the freshman class of the institute each year.

Faculty Profile
Eleven faculty members teach in the department.

Deadlines and Financial Aid
Various fellowships and traditional state, federal and city aid are available to students. Contact the

Financial Aid Office for details on obtaining financial assistance at the university.

Admission Requirements
Undergraduate students must submit the following: secondary school record, SAT or ACT tests, a recommendation from a high school counselor or principal, a personal interview if possible.

Expenses
Tuition is $24,700 per year.

Contact
5500 Wabash Ave., Terre Haute, IN 47803-3999. Telephone: 812-877-8429. Fax: 812-877-3198. Contact person: Dr. Cary Laxer. E-mail: laxer@cs.rose-hulman.edu. URL: http://www.rose-hulman.edu/.

Additional Information
Three courses in the computer graphics area are taught by the Computer Science department at Rose-Hulman. These courses cover 2D graphics, 3D graphics and fractals. Students are exposed to the fundamental algorithms, concepts and applications appropriate for each course. Numerous projects reinforce this material and allow the students to be creative in generating a wide variety of images.

Taylor University

F/X Degrees Offered
B.A. or B.S. in Computing and System Sciences. Available tracks in the CS major include Computer Graphics; Artificial Intelligence; Business Information Systems, and Scientific Computing. There is also a joint major with the Art Department, titled Computer Graphic Arts, that requires half of the major hours from Computer Science and half from Art.

Curricular
3D Modeling and Rendering; 3D Computer Animation; 2D Computer Animation; Multimedia/Interactive; High-Level Programming; Digital Painting/Drawing; Image Processing.

Facilities
One Sparc 20; four Sparcs; two DEC Alphas (OSF); four Pentium (linux); 15 Pentiums; Macintoshes; one CNAPS 512-node SIMD parallel processor; one Parsytec 8-node MIMD parallel processor. There are numerous labs, including an artificial intelligence lab and an IBM PC lab.

Student Body
There are 110 majors in the department.

Faculty Profile
Seven faculty members in the Computer Science Department.

Deadlines and Financial Aid
Various fellowships and traditional state, federal and city aid are available to students. Contact the Financial Aid Office for details on obtaining financial assistance at the university.

Admission Requirements
Submit an application and fee, transcript, and SAT or ACT scores.

Expenses
Tuition is $18,306 per year.

Contact
500 W. Reade Ave., Upland, IN 46989. Telephone: 765-998-5162. Fax: 765-998-4940. Contact person: Beth Holloway. Email: btholloway@tayloru.edu. URL: http://www.tayloru.edu/.

University of Indianapolis

Assistant Professor. Email: taugner@uindy.edu.
URL: http://art.uindy.edu/.

F/X Degrees Offered
B.A., B.S. and B.F.A. in Visual Communication.

Curricular
Various Computer Graphics and Desktop Publishing courses.

Facilities
Eighteen computer graphics laboratories with Macintosh workstations; Photoshop.

Student Body
There are 500 art students; 4,000 total enrollment at the university.

Admission Requirements
Application and fee, transcripts, diploma, and SAT or ACT scores.

Faculty Profile
Seven full-time faculty members.

Deadlines and Financial Aid
Pell Grant; Iowa Tuition Grant; Institutional Grants; Scholarships; Needs Perkins Loan; Stafford Loan. Students must apply for financial aid as soon as possible after Jan. 1 by filing a FAFSA with the Financial Aid Office.

Admission Requirements
High school diploma or GED with GPA of 2.3 minimum on a 4.0 scale, ACT score of 20 on the composition, or SAT of 840 Verbal/Math, application and fee, and a $100 non-refundable deposit.

Expenses
Tuition is $537 per course.

Contact
University of Indianapolis, 1400 East Hanna Avenue, Indianapolis, IN 46227-3697. Telephone: 563-788-3253 or 1-800-232-U of I (8634). Fax: 563-327-9615. Contact person: Julia Taugner, M.F.A.

Iowa

University of Northern Iowa

F/X Degrees Offered
B.A., B.S., M.A. and Doctor of Industrial Technology through the Department of Industrial Technology.

Curricular
Computer-Aided Design and Drafting; Construction Graphics; Graphics; Graphic Arts Technology; Desktop Composition; Computer Application in Industrial Technology.

Facilities
Equipment includes: 15 iMac 333Mhz, CD and zip drives, 100Mb Ethernet equipment, Mac OS 9.2, 6 Pentium III 800Mhz Dell Dimension workstations with floppy, zip, and CD drives, 100Mb Ethernet equipment, Debian Linux, Windows NT 4.0. These stations are for special purpose graduate/undergraduate software and research needs, and may not be scheduled for classroom instructional use, they are currently on 10Mb Ethernet links; 1 Networked HP Laser-jet IIIsi printer; 28 Pentium III 800Mhz Dell Dimension workstations with floppy, zip, and CD drives, 100 Mb Ethernet; Debian Linux; Windows NT 4.0, These stations are used for mainly for introductory classes but share the same capabilities as stations in Wright 339. 1 Networked HP 8150 printer. Total, there are four specialized area-specific laboratories with approximately 20 stations, each with different software. Specialized software includes: Splus, VB, Jgrasp, Grasp, Gnat, Cygwin, JDK, BlueJay

Student Body
There are 340 students in the department.

Faculty Profile
Five faculty members teach in the area of Computer Graphics.

Deadlines and Financial Aid
Various forms of federal, state and local aid are available in the forms of scholarships, grants and loans. Contact the Financial Aid Office for details.

Admission Requirements
Application and fee, high school transcript, ACT or SAT, rank of upper half of the high school class, meet the minimum high school core requirement. The criteria for admission requires evaluation of the student's portfolio, academic transcripts, standardized test scores, statement of purpose, letters of recommendation, and other indicators of potential success as a professional artist. Application forms are available from the KCAI Admissions Office.

Expenses
Tuition is $4,915.50 per year for residents and $9,833.90 for non-residents.

Contact
University of Northern Iowa, Department of Industrial Technology, Industrial Technology Center 25, Cedar Falls, IA 50614. Telephone: 319-273-2311. URL: http://www.uni.edu/.

Kansas

University of Kansas

F/X Degrees Offered
Electrical Engineering and Computer Science Department. B.S. for Computer Science, Computer Engineering and Electrical Engineering; M.S. and Ph.D. degrees in Computer Science; M.S., Ph.D. and D.E. degrees in Electrical Engineering.

Curricular
Undergraduates: broad-based introductory courses in Computer Graphics are offered. The target audience is primarily those wishing to pursue careers as system programmers and developers, either (i) using graphical tools such as OpenGL and OpenInventor to develop graphics applications, or (ii) developing implementations of common graphical algorithms such as those on which OpenGL depend. The department offers several courses at the graduate level dealing with topics such as Interactive Systems, Image Synthesis, Geometric Modeling and Image Processing. 3D Modeling and Rendering; 3D Computer Animation; 2D Computer Animation; Multimedia/Interactive; Image Processing; Volume Visualization.

Facilities
Department facilities--Hardware: 150 workstations, including 50 X-terminals, SGI stations, 10 Alphas, 6 DEC servers, two SGI Challenge servers, 2.4 Gbit MAGIC Network. Full range of software systems and languages.

Student Body
There are 256 undergraduates and 61 graduate students in the department. A total of 28,000 students attend the university.

Faculty Profile
Nineteen faculty members teach in the department. A total of 1,900 faculty members teach at the university.

Deadlines and Financial Aid
The application deadline for the School of Engineering is December 1 for early consideration for the following fall semester, and no later than February 1. Students may enter the School of Engineering as freshmen, but all admissions, both in-state and out-of-state, are on a selective basis. One-third of the freshman class receive financial aid. Applications and supporting materials should be received by February 1 for admission to the fall semester and Oct. 15 for admission to the spring semester for maximum opportunities for assistantships and scholarships. However, applications received after these dates are not excluded. Graduate students may apply for a graduate assistantship through the department. Annual stipend received by graduate assistants range from $10,500 to $11,000.

Admission Requirements
The application form should request admission to the School of Engineering, with a major in Electrical Engineering (major code 0438), Computer Engineering (major code 440) or Computer Science (major code 441). Applicants should have strong preparation in mathematics and science. Math ACT scores or college-level math course grades demonstrating this preparation are required.

Expenses
Tuition is $117.55 per credit for residents and $366.75 per credit for graduate students and non-residents.

Contact
1502 Iowa Street, Lawrence, KS 66045-7576. Telephone: 1-888-MT OREAD (Kansas only) or 785-

864-3911. E-mail: adm@ku.edu.
URL: http://www.ku.edu/.

Kentucky

University of Kentucky

F/X Degrees Offered
Art Department, Digital Media program. B.A., B.F.A., M.F.A.

Curricular
3D Modeling and Rendering; 3D Computer Animation; 2D Computer Animation; Multimedia/ Interactive; Digital Painting/Drawing; image Processing; Digital video; Stereo Imaging; Digital Photography; Telecommunications; Holography.

Facilities
The College of Fine Arts has two Macintosh laboratories with Macintoshes running many of the standard graphics and multimedia software (including Photoshop, FreeHand, Illustrator, Quark, Director and Sound Edit). Facilities also include video editing capabilities, as well as exhibition and screening spaces. Additional facilities, software and courses are available to students outside the College of Fine Arts.

Student Body
2,200 undergraduates students within the Art Department.

Faculty Profile
Twenty-four full-time faculty, four teaching in the digital media area.

Deadlines and Financial Aid
Various fellowships and traditional state, federal and city aid are available to students. Contact the Financial Aid Office for details on obtaining financial assistance at the university.

Admission Requirements
For admissions information contact the Undergraduate Admissions Office: 859-257-2000. Graduate School: 859-257-4613. Department of Art: 859-257-2727.

Expenses
Tuition is $2,273.25 per semester for residents $5,613.25 for non-residents.

Contact
207 Fine Arts Bldg., Lexington, KY 40506-0022. Telephone: 859-257-2727. Fax: 859-257-3042. Contact person: Robert Shay, Dean. Email: rshay@.uky.edu. URL: http://www.uky.edu/.

Louisiana

University of Southwestern Louisiana

F/X Degrees Offered
The Center for Advanced Computer Studies offers four graduate degrees: Doctor of Philosophy in Computer Engineering (Ph.D.C.E.); Doctor of Philosophy in Computer Science (Ph.D.C.S.); Master of Science in Computer Engineering (M.S.C.E.); Master of Science in Computer Science (M.S.C.S.).

Curricular
Courses in Visual/Image Computing and Computer Graphics; Artificial Intelligence; Introduction to Robotics; Animation; and others.

Facilities
There are several labs available to students. Windows NT Lab: The Windows NT includes one file server and 30+ client machines. This lab is configured to be usable for closed lab activities, i.e., activities in which the instructor and the students are engaged in collaborative problem solving and software development. In terms of software, in addition to the Windows NT operating system, the lab provides programming development environments such as Visual C/C++, Visual BASIC, Java, Franz LISP, and MS Access. It also provides support software such as MS Word, MS Excel, MS FrontPage, and other utilities. It is located in the Mezzanine floor of the Conference Center. Hours are posted outside the lab. SUN Ultra Workstations-SL Lab: The SL lab consists of a file server; a few clients assigned to faculty and support staff; and 31 clients for student use (s18.sl.louisiana.edu through s49.sl.louisiana.edu) located in the Stephens Hall Lab. The client machines are all Sun SS-5/170s, with 64 MB of memory, 2 GB of disk, and a 17" color monitor. All workstations run the Unix operating system. This lab is intended for general program development; it is available to CMPS students enrolled mainly in CMPS150, 260, and 261. It is located in the first floor of Stephen's Hall-across St. Mary's from the Conference Center. Lab hours are posted. SUN Ultra Workstations-UCS System: The UCS system is distributed in two lab locations: the Solarium Lab (first floor, Conference Center), and the Stephens Hall Lab (first floor, Stephens Hall). This system consists of a file server and 153 Ultra 5 workstations, each with 64 Mbytes of memory, 4 Gbytes of disk; a few of these are assigned to support staff, but most are available for student use. All workstations run the Unix operating system. Workstations located in the Conference Center are named d1.ucs.louisiana.edu through d116.ucs.louisiana.edu, and those in Stephens are named s4.ucs.louisiana.edu through s17.ucs.louisiana.edu and s50.ucs.louisiana.edu through s64.ucs.louisiana.edu. Both locations are open-access to all university students and can be used for general activities such as email and Internet browsing. They are also used for several CMPS classes. All faculty, staff, and students may obtain an account on the UCS system, which provides a variety of academic applications and a campus e-mail address.

Student Body
There are 170 students in the department; a total of 16,463 students attend the university.

Faculty Profile
Twenty faculty members in the department.

Deadlines and Financial Aid
Fellowships with stipends of $16,000 per year; research assistantships stipends of $12,000, and teaching assistantships of $5,000 to $8,000 per year. Admissions application deadline: April 1 for the

summer; May 1 for the fall; November 15 for the spring. Assistantship application deadline: March 1 for fall; November 1 for the spring. Financial Aid: Complete the FAFSA. Applications are available after Jan. 1 of each calendar year in the USL Financial Aid Office. Suggested application date for federal and state aid is March 1.

Admission Requirements
Application and fee, transcripts, and GRE scores.

Expenses
Tuition is $3,532.75 per semester for residents and $6,622.75 per semester for non-residents.

Contact
P.O. Box 41771, Lafayette, LA 70504. Telephone: 337-482-6147. Fax: 337-482-5791. Contact person: Dr. Magdy Bayoumi, Head. Email: admission@louisiana.edu/.
URL: http://www.louisiana.edu/Academic/Sciences/CMPS/.

Additional Information
USL has a long history of computer science education and, in fact, started the first chapter of the ACM (Association of Computing Machinery: a professional society for computer scientists) in 1961. Today the student ACM chapter is involved in social as well as educational activities.

Maine

University of Maine

F/X Degrees Offered
B.A., B.S. and M.S. in Computer Science.

Curricular
3D Modeling and Rendering; 3D Computer Animation; 2D Computer Animation; High-Level Programming.

Facilities
The Department of Computer Science has approximately 100 computer systems. The computers are connected to a state-of-the-art 10/100 Mbs switched network. The computing environment is primarily made up of Sun, SGI and Linux Unix systems along with a large number of Windows 95/98/NT systems and Macintosh systems. The department is connected to the campus via a gigabit link. The department maintains two PC labs for use by undergraduate and graduate CS students. They consist of 41 Pentium II and III class machines running Windows 9x connected to a Novell Netware 5.0 server. The department also maintains a Unix cluster available to all its undergraduate and graduate students. It contains four SGI Indigo's and one SGI Indigo2, four Sun Ultra 5's, and three Pentium II systems running Linux. These Unix boxes are connected to a Sun Ultra 1 server. Printing needs are accommodated by two HP 8000 DN high speed laser printers, and 2 OkiData dot matrix printers.

Student Body
There are 160 undergraduates and 15 graduate majors in the department.

Faculty Profile
Ten faculty members in the department.

Deadlines and Financial Aid
Various fellowships and traditional state, federal and city aid are available to students. Contact the Financial Aid Office for details on obtaining financial assistance at the university. Early Action Applicants: Oct. 1-November 30 for the fall semester admission. All Applicants: November 1 for the spring semester.

Admission Requirements
Completed application for undergraduate admission with the appropriate application fee, official high school transcript submitted to UMaine by the high school. Official SAT or ACT scores submitted to UMaine by the testing agency (first-year candidates only), high school guidance counselor recommendation (for current high school seniors only), official university/college transcripts submitted to UMaine by the post-secondary institution.

Expenses
Tuition is $4,710 for residents and $13,410 for non-residents.

Contact
Department of Computer Science, 237 Neville Hall, University of Maine, Orono, ME 04469-5752. Telephone: 207-581-3941. Fax: 207-581-4977. Email: Ellen_Johndro@umit.maine.edu. URL: http://www.umaine.edu/.

Maryland

Anne Arundel Community College

F/X Degrees Offered
A.A.S. in Media Production; Certificate in Graphics Design, Photography and Video through the Department of Communication Arts Tech. A.S. degree in Computer Science.

Curricular
Introduction to Graphic Arts; Introduction to Computer Graphics; Digital Imaging with Photoshop I and II; Layout and Design with Adobe Illustrator; Introduction to Desktop Publishing; Desktop Publishing with Quark XPress; Computer Graphics with Corel Draw; Advanced Graphics with Corel Draw; Desktop Video with Adobe Premiere; Introduction to Digital Multimedia Design; Animation; Web Design.

Facilities
Two IBM laboratories using IBM Pentiums; Macintosh laboratory using Umax S900 clones; 604E processors. Server; Raid; video suite; color laser and inkjet printers. CD and Iomega internal drives in each computer. Photoshop, Freehand, Lightwave and others. More than 20 systems in each lab.

Student Body
There are 200 students in the department.

Faculty Profile
Four full-time and eight to 12 adjunct faculty teach classes in the computer graphics areas.

Deadlines and Financial Aid
The school offers a Weinberg Merit Scholarship awarded to two full-time CAT majors each year, as well as numerous other financial aid options.

Admission Requirements
Application and fee. Contact the admissions office for details.

Expenses
Tuition is $66 for residents per semester $208 per semester for non-residents.

Contact
Comm. Arts Tech. Department, Anne Arundel Community College, 101 College Parkway, Arnold, MD 21012. Telephone: 410-777-2372. Contact person: Patricia Gregory, Chair. E-mail: pagregory@mail.aacc.cc.md.us.
URL: http://www.aacc.cc.md.us/.

Maryland Institute College of Art

F/X Degrees Offered
B.F.A. in Visual/Communication Graphic Design and Illustration; M.F.A. in Traditional Studio Forms of Art; M.F.A. in Digital Arts

Curricular
Visual Communication Design Co-op; Intermediate Computer Graphics; Advanced Computer Graphics; QuarkXPress; Meta-Media Computer Graphics; Imaging for Television; Drawing for Animation I, II; Imaging Technology; Illustrator; Photoshop; Hypercard; Painter; Macromind Director.

Facilities
Three computer graphics laboratories with Macintoshes; Epson color printers; laser printers; color scanner; Zip drives; Canon CJ-10 color copier.

Software: Adobe Photoshop; Premiere; Illustrator; Aldus Freehand; PageMaker; Macromedia Director; Fractal Design Painter; QuarkXPress; many other software programs for producing computer graphics on the Macintosh. Two labs for PCs and Macs.

Student Body
There are 877 undergraduate students and 90 graduate students attending the institute; 125 students in the Graphic Design and 100 students in the Illustration area.

Deadlines and Financial Aid
Fall term Sept. 1, begin application procedures. March 1, complete admission and financial aid application procedures. Mail to: Scholarship Coordinator Maryland Institute, College of Art. All materials must be received by February 1. Spring term starts June 1; begin application procedure December 15; complete admission and financial aid application procedures. The candidate reply date is two weeks after acceptance.

Admission Requirements
Scholarship application form, application for admission, transcripts, letters of recommendation, test scores and portfolio of artwork. The portfolio is the most meaningful indicator of serious artistic commitment, ability, and potential to succeed in MICA's rigorous studio environment. Your artwork reflects your visual sensitivity, your intellectual curiosity and creativity, your motivation and self-discipline, and your previous experience in the visual arts. The Admission Committee assesses the way you express your thoughts and ideas visually. Your previous training and technical abilities are also evaluated. Portfolios are evaluated on an individual basis, in the context of the specific educational background and experiences of each applicant.

Expenses
Tuition is $22,980 per year.

Contact
Office of Undergraduate Admission. 1300 Mount Royal Ave., Baltimore, MD 21217-4191. Telephone: 410-669-9200. Fax: 410-225 2384. URL: http://www.mica.edu/.

University of Maryland at College Park

F/X Degrees Offered
B.S., M.S. and Ph.D. in Computer Science with concentration areas in: Artificial Intelligence; Database; Numerical Analysis; Software Engineering; Systems and Theory of Computation.

Curricular
Among the 40-plus courses offered through the CIS Department at the undergraduate level are: Introduction to C Programming; Introduction to the UNIX Operating System; Internet and Other Networks; Introduction to Artificial Intelligence; Programming Robotics; Database Design; Image Processing; Human Factor in Computer and Information Systems; Special Problems in Computer Science. These courses are geared towards preparing students technically for the field of computer-generated effects. Research Activities--through the Advanced Visualization Laboratory (AVL), graduate students can actively pursues joint projects with researchers on campus and at neighboring institutions to develop visualization tools for their particular requirements. On these projects, the researchers use their grant funding to support collaborative efforts. These projects range from small efforts such as providing figures for masters and doctoral theses to supporting ongoing research programs.

Facilities

Visualization Software: AVS; AVS Express; Data Explorer; Precision Visualize Wave; IDL; Explorer; Maple Software; Mathematica. Color Imaging Facilities--SGAI Galileo 139 D9-GV-TWO video system; DiaQuest controller; Folsom Otto 9500 scan converter; Panasonic TQ-3031F video optical disk recorder; Panasonic LQ-3032T video optical disk player; Macintoshes; Panasonic AG-7750P single-frame S-VHS VCR; Panasonic Ag-W1 multi-format S-VHS VCR; Panasonic AG-1970-P editing S-VHS VCR; RGB video distribution and switching systems. Computing Facilities--SGIs; Sun Sparc station 10/30 with four Ross processors; Sun Sparc station and Sparc station IPX; Macintoshes.

Student Body

Approximately 24,400 undergraduates and 7,800 graduates students attend the university; 1,100 undergraduates and 235 graduate students are Computer Science majors.

Faculty Profile

More than 43 faculty members are in the Department of Computer Science.

Deadlines and Financial Aid

Undergraduates: many scholarships are available through the university, and others for advanced students are administered directly by the department. Additional funding may be obtained through student employment. A well-qualified student may be hired as part of a department laboratory staff, or by a professor to assist in research. Students can also participate in internship and cooperative education programs. The application deadline for fall semester admission is Jan. 15. The spring semester application deadline is Oct. 15, but spring semester admission is available only if you are already a student at the University of Maryland, College Park. Most financial aid consists of research assistantships, teaching assistantships,

or fellowships. Graduate students may qualify for graduate research assistantships, and fellowships are available through the department. These stipends range from $10,000 to $13,400 per year.

Admission Requirements

A completed application; two copies of transcripts for all previous academic study, GRE and Advanced GRE test scores (the scores must be less than two years old), recommendation letters from three individuals, a statement of Goals and Research Interests, form for Merit-based Financial Aid if you are requesting aid, and a check or money order in the amount of $40.

Expenses

Tuition for residents is $3,379.50 and $8,716.50 for non-residents.

Contact

Visualization and Presentation Lab, Building #224 (MS: OIT/VPL), University of Maryland College Park, MD 20742. Phone: Fax: 301-405-0720. E-mail: avl-request@avl.umd.ed. URL: http://www.umd.edu/.

Additional Information

The Advanced Visualization Laboratory (AVL) of the University of Maryland, College Park campus, was created in October 1991 to facilitate the use of state-of-the-art visualization techniques on campus. The complementary goals of the AVL are to meet the general graphic needs of the academic community by offering new user services, and to meet the specific needs of individual researchers by working with them to produce visualization tools. The AVL is an initiative of the Computer Science Center (CSC), which is responsible for academic computing support campus-wide.

University of Maryland Baltimore County

F/X Degrees Offered
B.F.A. in Visual Arts with concentrations in Film, Video/Film, Imaging and Digital Arts; M.F.A. in Imaging and Digital Arts. B.A. and M.S. also available in the Computer Science Department.

Curricular
The curricular combines aspects of a traditional graduate art programs with the new technologies and intermedia art making. The M.F.A. is a comprehensive 60-credit degree, of which half the credits are reserved for the students' own research work culminating in a thesis exhibition and written thesis. Twelve credits are reserved for thesis preparation and exhibition. The department considers it to be a three-year program. The first semester consists of a structured program that introduces students to the technical and conceptual areas of Imaging and Digital Arts. During the second semester the student's research is reviewed for advancement to candidacy. Courses and Seminar include: Introduction to Imaging and Digital Arts Seminar; History and Theory; Contemporary Art, Theory and Criticism; Imaging and Digital Studio; Advanced Imaging and Digital Studio. Undergraduate courses for Film, Film/Video, Imaging and Digital Arts emphasis include Film I and II; Introduction, Intermediate and Advanced Computer Art; Introduction, Intermediate and Advanced Video Art; Animation; Imaging Research Center Internship.

Facilities
The school maintains and operates over 20 computer labs at UMBC. Of these most are classroom labs with instructor units connected to a data projector. The majority of labs are currently running Windows 2000 and Linux in a dual-boot system but they also maintain Macintosh OSX (10) and SGI units as well. All the labs run the MS Office suite and web software as well as a wide range of department specific programs. Systems include: SGI laboratories; Maya certified training centers; private color and b/w dark rooms with 40-inch processors; 16 and 35 mm film production equipment; 16 and 35 mm aerial optical printer and animation stand; film-to-video transfer; 3/4-inch SP, S-VHS and Hi8 video production equipment; Video effect devices for image processing; private AB-roll computer-controlled video editing suites; private film editing suites; shooting studios; digital and analog sound studios. Recording Facilities-- non-linear digital video editing; lighting and grip equipment; computer animation output to 35 mm motion picture film, Beta, 3/4-inch SP and S-VHS. Twenty-one SGI workstations with Wavefront and Softimage. An advanced laboratory with several Sun workstations and SGI workstations. Another SGI laboratory houses more than 50 SGI workstations that are used by the Computer Science Department. Several Macintosh laboratories are available in the Art Department.

Student Body
Six to eight full-time students are accepted to the graduate program yearly; 100 undergaduate students in the area of Imaging and Digital Arts. Total of 10,500 students attend the university.

Faculty Profile
Fifty faculty teach in the department. Total of 1,500 faculty and staff.

Deadlines and Financial Aid
There are two application deadlines. The first is February 15 of each year for those applicants who would like to be considered for a Graduate Merit Fellowship and Scholarship Award. These scholarships cover most of the tuition expenses and provide a stipend for the first year of graduate

school. The second deadline is March 15 for all applicants. Departmental research assistantships, which include tuition remission, health benefits and stipend, are awarded at this time. All applicants are notified by April as to the Graduate School's decision. Undergraduates: UMBC assists students in meeting educational expenses by administering and coordinating a variety of federal, state and institutional student aid programs, including grants, scholarships, loans and paid employment. UMBC undergraduate students can apply to more than 17 grant programs, more than 15 UMBC Merit Scholarships, and more than 30 scholarships. Students must submit applications between Jan. 1 and February 1, but no later than March 1. Admission Requirement
Undergraduates: must submit an application for admission, official high school transcript and SAT or ACT scores, and a recommendation from high school principal or counselor. Graduate: application for Graduate School Admission, transcripts, portfolio and GRE scores.

Expenses
Tuition for resident is $7,388 per year and $14,240 for non-residents.

Contact
Imaging and Digital Arts. University of Maryland, Baltimore, 5401 Wilkens Ave., Baltimore, MD 21228-5398. Telephone: 410-455-2163. Fax: 410-455-1053. Contact person: Dan Bailey, Director. Email: bailey@umbc.edu.
URL: http://www.umbc.edu/.

Additional Information
The program integrates ideas and research with an interdisciplinary approach to the Imaging and Digital Arts of computer, video, film and photography. Students are challenged to foster an understanding of various media and are directed to think beyond the traditional boundaries of specialized technologies or methodologies. To support this program, UMBC has established an array of imaging equipment. Central to UMBC's facilities is the Imaging Research Center, known for experimental computer visualization and animation.

Massachusetts

Brandeis University

F/X Degrees Offered
Computer Science Department offers B.S., M.S. and Ph.D. degrees.

Curricular
Computer Graphics courses; Artificial Intelligence; and other related courses.

Facilities
Department facilities--Hardware: HPs; 25 UNIX workstations; two Symbolic Lisp Machines; 35 PC/Macintosh workstations; one Butterfly. Software systems and languages: UNIX; full range of languages. The lab contains top of the line Workstations, PCs and Macs (running various versions of Unix) which are upgraded on a three year rotation schedule. The lab is exclusively for the use of Computer Science students, faculty, and staff.

Student Body
Approximately 125 undergraduates and 35 graduate students are Computer Science majors; 2,900 undergraduates and 1,000 graduate students are enrolled in the university.

Faculty Profile
Fiftenn faculty members teach in the department. A total of 354 full-time faculty and 159 part-time faculty teach at the university.

Deadlines and Financial Aid
Need-based financial aid is a combination of loans, work and grant awards offered to students whose families demonstrate financial eligibility for assistance. Need-based aid is available from federal, state and private sources, including Brandeis University. Most students qualify for low-interest educational loans from the federal government. Many of these programs require no payment of principal or interest during college; however, as a loan, this funding source does require repayment. Graduate students: can obtain a teaching assistantship from the department. These assistantships provide students with a stipend of $11,500 per year. Admissions Applications Deadline is March 1.

Admission Requirements
Undergraduates must submit an application and fee, high school transcripts, and ACT or SAT scores. Graduate students: application and fee, transcripts and GRE scores.

Expenses
Tuition is $27,344 per year.

Contact
Computer Science Department, Volen Center Complex, Waltham, MA 02254. Telephone: 781-736-2701. Fax: 781-736-2741. Contact person: Richard Alterman, Professor. E-mail: alterman@cs.brandeis.edu.
URL: http://www.cs.brandeis.edu/cs/index.html.

Emerson College

Degrees Offered
B.A. and B.F.A. in Mass Communications with concentrations in Film, Television, Video Production; M.F.A. and M.A. in Mass Communication.

Curricular
The Film curriculum integrates theoretical and applied course work in film production, screen writing and film studies. Classes in film history and theory provide students with a perspective on film aesthetics and technology, the industry's growth, and its role in reflecting and shaping society.

Production work begins with Super 8/Hi8 mm, and moves into 16 mm with advanced exercises in color cinematography, lighting, sound and editing. Electives provide students with various options from animation to documentary. The B.F.A. intensive program requires students to produce a major film production project. The Video/Television concentration provides theory and hands-on experience to prepare you for TV station, cable, network and media-related careers. Students move through a three-course production sequence designed to advance their expertise and promote creativity, critical thinking and analysis. A capstone course enables selected students to complete major video projects from planning and writing through post-production and evaluation. Electives range from the impact of TV on children's behavior to space satellite communication and fiber optics. Film I, II, III; Animation I and Workshop; Introductory, Intermediate and Advanced Video Production.

Facilities

Video/TV facilities include two fully equipped production studios complete with professional-quality studio cameras, eight 3/4-inch U-Matic editing suites, an Avid digital non-linear media composer editing system, inter-format and Paltex computer-assisted video post-production suites, and field production units. Journalism students have access to a fully computerized classroom and a desktop publishing system. Film majors use a variety of 16 mm cameras (Arriflex, CP-16, Bolex, Bell and Howell, Canon), 8 mm and video cameras, and an Oxberry animation stand. Editing facilities include Steenbeck Editors, bench editing booths, printing and sound equipment, and a 25-person Super-8 editing room. Audio students utilize state-of-the-art studios complete with multitrack equipment, digital processing, recording and editing. Academic Computer Center: more than 60 PCs, including Macintosh, IBM and PC-compatibles, which run graphic design and desktop publishing software; two microcomputer systems are configured as graphics workstations with AutoCAD software; two microcomputers, a VAX 4500 and a microVAX 3400 with access to SPSS and Minitab statistical packages; full Internet access. Smaller satellite laboratories on campus include a Macintosh laboratory for journalism students, and a graphic design laboratory for students of advertising, public relations and political communication. Two Macintosh laboratories provide connections to the Internet; Avid non-linear digital and S-VHS editing systems.

Student Profile

More than 2,700 undergraduate students and 900 graduate students attend the college.

Faculty Profile

Thirteen faculty members in the Department of Mass Communications.

Deadlines and Financial Aid

Application deadlines for fall entrance: freshmen, early action is November 15; regular admission is February 1; transfer applicants, priority deadline is March 1. Application deadlines for spring entrance: freshmen, priority deadline is November 15; transfer applicants, priority deadline is November 15. The College provides extensive financial aid opportunities to students who qualify on the basis of need. Merit-based scholarships are available in the Visual Effects discipline. Trustee Scholarships are awarded annually to 45 of the most outstanding applicants to Emerson College. These awards accompany an invitation to join Emerson's Honors Program. Dean's Scholarships are awarded annually to approximately 75 applicants on the basis of superior academic, personal and extracurricular accomplishments. All applicants to the College are considered for this scholarship. All materials submitted for the standard application are reviewed.

Admission Requirements

Undergraduate admission: application and essay. Checklist: counselor recommendation and official high school transcript, academic teacher recommendation, scores on SAT or ACT, financial aid application.

Expenses

Tuition is $11,072 per semester for full-time students.

Contact

Office of Admission, 120 Boylston St., Boston, MA 02116. Telephone: 617-824-8500. Fax: 617-824-8609. E-mail: admission@emerson.edu. URL: http://www.emerson.edu/.

Hampshire College, Amherst

F/X Degrees Offered

B.A. degree in Computer Graphics, Film and Photography through the School of Humanities and Arts; B.A. in Multimedia.

Curricular

Hampshire has no set programs; its students use the full range of consortium offerings to design their own. Courses in Film/Video Workshop, Film Video Workshop II ; Film Video projects in the community; Film/Video Workshop III: Music Video and PSA; Interface Design.

Facilities

Macintosh graphics laboratory; video production facilities and traditional animation equipment. Multimedia lab with PCs and Macintoshes.

Student Body

More than 1,160 students attend the university.

Faculty Profile

Thirty-two faculty members teach in the School of Humanities and Arts.

Deadlines and Financial Aid

Film: complete all applications material by February 1. Hampshire's financial aid program consists of scholarships, grants, loans and work-study. Candidates must complete the Hampshire College Financial Aid Form (HCFA) as well as the standard Financial Aid Form (FAF). Early-decision candidates submitting applications for financial aid on time will receive notification of their tentative awards with the letter of admission. Application is due on November 15; notification mailed by December 15.

Admission Requirements

Basic Application (Part A); Activities Index (Part B); personal statement, analytic essay or academic paper; teacher recommendation; secondary school transcript.

Expenses

Tuition is $28,832 per year.

Contact

School of Humanities and Arts, Amherst, MA 01002. Telephone: 877-937-4267. Fax: 413-559-5631. Contact person: Steve Weisler, Director of Cognitive Science. URL: http://www.hampshire.edu/.

Harvard University

F/X Degrees Offered

B.A. in Visual and Environmental Studies with a concentration in Film and Video.

Curricular

Fundamentals of Filmmaking: Studio Course; Introduction to Small-Format Video: Studio Course; Film Animation: Studio Course; Intermediate

Filmmaking: Studio Course; Video Strategies: Seminar/Workshop; Intermediate Film Animation: Seminar.

Facilities

The Harvard Technology Showcase is an advanced multi-media facility offering state-of-the-art Power Macintosh and PC computing tools. The Showcase is available to FAS students and faculty wishing to explore multi-media and advanced technologies. The Showcase features equipment for scanning, video capture and editing, CD-ROM writing, and digital photography. There are also facilities such as a recording studio, darkrooms, graphic presses and an animation stand.

Student Body

There are 7,600 undergraduates and 12,000 graduate students enrolled in the university.

Faculty Profile

Approximately 26 faculty members teach in the Department of Visual and Environmental Studies.

Deadlines and Financial Aid

Various fellowships and traditional state, federal and city aid are available to students. Contact the Financial Aid Office for details on obtaining financial assistance at the university.

Admission Requirements

Admission to the VES Department requires a written application for committee evaluation, consisting of the Plan of Study and previous academic record. The committee also considers evaluations submitted by faculty pertaining to performance in their VES courses. For this reason, prospective applicants should take at least one of the two-digit studio courses offered by the department (such as VES 10ar, 15a, 20a, 30a, 40a, 50 or 70), with VES 10ar being especially recommended because of its focus on drawing. The number of concentrators is limited, and the criteria for acceptance include strong performance in at least one studio course and a record of honors grades. In order to become a VES concentrator, one should apply for admission to the department at the end of the freshman year, or, for transfers, as soon as possible after arriving.

Expenses

Estimated tuition cost is $22,694 per year.

Contact

Department of Visual and Environmental Studies, Harvard University, Carpenter Center, 24 Quincy St., Cambridge, MA 02138-3999. Telephone: 617-495-3216. Fax: 617-495-8197. Contact person: Kathleen Chaudhry.
URL: http://www.harvard.edu/.

Additional Information

The Visual and Environmental Studies Department was the result of merging the already existing Department of Architectural Sciences and an evolving program in visual arts, which drew upon filmmaking and teaching of film studies in the Department of Anthropology. Its symbolic and functional home is the Corbusier-designed Carpenter Center for the Visual Arts located next to the Fogg Museum and the Department of Fine Arts. The aim of the department is to achieve an understanding of the structure and meaning of the visual arts, and to build an environment through theoretical and practical explorations in areas that include painting, sculpture, design, film, video and photography. Programmatically, there are two major tracks or emphases within the field: Studio Arts, and Film and Video. The first includes drawing, painting, sculpture, photography, design and graphics; the second, cinema, animated film, and video. Concentrators are required to do some course work in both tracks, even if their interests center in only one, and to seek a balance between theoretical or historical courses and studios.

Massachusetts College of Art

F/X Degrees Offered
M.F.A. and B.F.A in Media and Performing Arts with concentrations in Filmmaking, Photography, Video and Studio for Interrelated Media; B.F.A with a concentration in Graphic Design. A certificate is also offered in design.

Curricular
Courses for Media and Performing Arts. Filmmaking: Introduction to Filmmaking; Filmmaking; Advanced Filmmaking; Experimental Animation; Professional Post-Production Techniques; Filmmaking Seminar; Non-Linear Editing: Film and Video. Video: Introduction to Video; Advanced Video; Installation of the Moving Image. Studio for Interrelated Media (S.I.M.): The Moving Body; People, Places, Things and Time; Light and Lighting; The Electronic Image; Computer Animation and Video; Media Internship; Studio for Interrelated Media; Computer-Controlled Media: Creative Robotics. Courses are also offered in World Wide Web home page authoring and design; Computer Arts Center. Media Arts: Computer; Introduction to CADD; Introduction to Computer Illustration; Introduction to Computer Graphics; Computer Design Applications; Introduction to 3D Computer Graphics; Photoshop; Introduction to Computer/Video Animation; Introduction to Multimedia; Computer/Video Animation Projects; 3D Computer Animation; Desktop Publishing; Quark Prepress; Advanced Macintosh; Design and Graphics Programming I; Computer Graphic Portfolio Projects; The Electronic Image; 2D Computer Animation and Video; Computer-Controlled Media: Creative Robotics; Interactive Multimedia; Computer Algebra.

Facilities
Mass Art currently has two Macintosh laboratories, primarily supporting courses in 2D and 3D design, using a variety of software for page layout; image manipulation; drawing; painting; 3D modeling. Software includes: QuarkXPress; Adobe Photoshop; Adobe Illustrator and Fractal Design Painter. A high-end laboratory for multimedia; CD-ROM authoring; electronic book production and CAD. Software includes Macromedia Director; Adobe Premiere; Macromedia Sound Edit; Avid Videoshop and Bentley Microstation. Facilities with half-inch S-VHS editing suites; 3D animation-to-video using 486 machines with PAR boards; computer device control and robotics.

Student Body
There are 1,300 undergraduates and 100 graduate students attending the college.

Faculty Profile
More than 16 faculty teach in the area of Media and Performing Arts.

Deadlines and Financial Aid
Assistantships: the college awards three types of assistantships to M.F.A. students: technical, administrative and teaching. All assistantships are assigned as either quarter, half or full assistantships; the award is based on the number of hours of work per week (2.5 to 10 hours). All assistantships are awarded by the Graduate Dean and are made according to student need and ability, as well as departmental needs and budgetary allotments. Most M.F.A. students will receive at least one assistantship for which they are qualified during their second year; however, there is no guarantee that a student will be awarded an assistantship.

Admission Requirements
Undergraduates should submit an application and fee, transcript, portfolio, statement of purpose, supporting material (optional) and interview

(optional). Priority deadline is March 1. Graduate: application and fee, transcript, portfolio, statement of purpose, resume, interview and letters of reference. Deadlines are March 15 for fall, and November 1 for spring matriculation.

Expenses
Undergraduate tuition is $200 per credit hour and graduate tuition is $600 per credit hour.

Contact
Admissions Office, 621 Huntington Ave., Boston, MA 02115. Telephone: 617-232-1555. Fax: 617-739-9744. URL: http://www.massart.edu/indexF1.html.

Additional Information
The Computer Arts Center is an interdisciplinary environment available to all departments for courses, workshops and independent projects. A sequence of courses providing intensive computer graphics training can be taken through both the Communication Design Department and the Studio for Interrelated Media. A student with a special interest in computer applications can work independently with a faculty advisor to plan and execute a thesis project or develop course work in the computer center. In addition, students who have performed well in their major area can apply for a supervised open major with an emphasis on computer applications.

Massachusetts Institute of Technology

F/X Degrees Offered
The Media Arts and Sciences program includes three levels of studies at MIT: a doctoral program, an M.S. program and an undergraduate major.

Curricular
News in the Future; Holography and 3D Imaging; Scene Representation; Interactive Cinema; Physics and Media; Personal Information Architecture; Structured Video; Hyperinstruments/Opera of the Future; Intelligent Graphics; Machine Understanding; Autonomous Agents; Society of Mind; School of the Future; Tools to Think With; Mid-Level Vision; High-Level Vision; Multi-Modal Interaction; Looking at People; Vision Texture; Speech; Music Cognition.

Student Body
There are 6,000 undergraduates and 6,000 graduate students attending the institute.

Faculty Profile
Nineteen full-time faculty members teach classes at the Media Laboratory.

Deadlines and Financial Aid
Financial support includes fellowships, traineeships, teaching and research assistantships, and loans. Many forms of support are granted for merit, while others are granted for financial need or for a combination of merit and need. The Institute's undergraduate financial aid program ensures that an MIT education is accessible to all qualified candidates regardless of their financial resources. MIT provides financial aid to meet the full cost of an MIT education, based on the calculated needs of the family. During 2001/2002, approximately 75 percent of all undergraduates received some type of financial assistance. The amount of financial aid for which an undergraduate is eligible is determined by the family's financial situation. Using information provided by the family on the Free Application for Federal Student Aid (FAFSA) form and the College Scholarship Service (CSS) PROFILE form, MIT establishes dollar amounts for the parents' and the student's contributions. In addition, all aid recipients are expected to meet a portion of their need

through a loan, part-time job, or both. This self-help component is set annually ($5,600 for 2002/2003). The balance is met with grants. This policy assures each student a reasonable loan, and provides an equitable distribution of grant funds. In 2001/2002, the average MIT scholarship awarded to students who were eligible for aid was $18,200.

Admission Requirements

Applicants to the graduate programs are expected to have demonstrated a substantial level of commitment and accomplishment in their area of concentration prior to application, with an emphasis on creative extensions of that domain. Because every area depends heavily on computational methods, familiarity with UNIX and modest proficiency in programming in C and LISP (or equivalence) are expected of all applicants. Many successful applicants have academic backgrounds that are variously described as unorthodox, innovative or self-generated. Their backgrounds are emphatically not narrowly technical, but instead anticipate the mix of disciplines found within the program; some of them come from art schools, some from engineering schools, and some from both or neither. Completed applications must be submitted in early January (the exact deadline is announced on each year's forms). The principal components of an application are: an academic transcript, the applicant's statement of objectives, and three letters of recommendation. GRE is not required. Some groups also require the submission of a portfolio of relevant work, and most of the other groups will accept such portfolios for consideration. Undergraduate students must contact the Admissions Office.

Expenses

Undergraduate and graduate tuition is $28,030 per year.

Contact

Program in Media Arts and Sciences, MIT, 20 Ames St., Room E15-226, Cambridge, MA 02139-4307. Telephone: 617-253-5114. Fax: 617-258-6264. Contact person: Ms. Linda Peterson, Degree Program Coordinator. E-mail: linda@media.mit.edu. URL: http://web.mit.edu/.

Additional Information

The activities of the Media Arts and Sciences Program and the Media Laboratory cluster into three sections: the Information and Entertainment Section, the Learning and Common Sense Section, and the Perceptual Computing Section. The Information and Entertainment Section operates at the juncture of expression and engineering. Research results include operas, digital video representations, 3D images, physical interfaces and newspapers. Entering students are generally schooled in at least one of the disciplines associated with the faculty within the section, but typically study in more than one area; research assistantships and thesis topics frequently grow to encompass the activities of more than one area to help refine views of the intersection of entertainment and information studies as a modern academic discipline. The Learning and Common Sense Section is concerned with basic ideas about thinking, learning and the nature of knowledge. In some projects, researchers create computer programs that learn in new ways, or represent knowledge in new ways. In other projects, researchers create computational tools and media that help people (particularly children) learn new things in new ways. The section's research diverges from traditional approaches in artificial intelligence (AI) in its emphasis on understanding ordinary activity. The group aims to develop programs with *common sense* capabilities with multiple representations of knowledge. There is also a strong emphasis on behavior-based approaches to AI, focusing particularly on the actions of (and interactions among) autonomous computational agents. In studying how people learn (and in creating new learning environments), the group embraces a constructionist approach based on the idea that people learn most effectively when they are actively engaged in designing and constructing personally meaningful things. In this work, researchers work closely with children and teachers at local schools and museums, with special emphasis on under-served communities. The Perceptual Computing Section research is concerned with the machine interpretation of sensory data primarily visual and auditory datafor the understanding of surrounding situations. At the Media Laboratory, the central goals of perceptual computing are to make machines smarter and more convenient for people to use. Researchers want computers to be able to accompany music, to participate in dialogs, and to see the world as computer users see it. The Perceptual Computing Section includes researchers studying vision, audition and methods to combine them. The vision research covers the spectrum from low-level to high-level, with emphasis on motion, texture, recognition and situation understanding. The auditory research covers music and speech, with emphasis on building interactive systems. The multimedia research combines eye and hand motion with speech to understand human dialog.

Montserrat College of Art

F/X Degrees Offered
Montserrat offers a Bachelor of Fine Arts Degree and a Diploma of the College with concentrations in Fine Arts, Graphic Design, Illustration, Painting + Drawing, Photography, Printmaking, and Sculpture. In addition, Montserrat offers a complementary program in Art Education.

Curricular
Computer Design I and II; Digital Photography; Computer Imaging; Web Authoring; Digital Photo/ Advanced Concepts; Computer Animation.

Facilities
At Montserrat, computers are located in most of the traditional studios side by side with easels, darkrooms, and printmaking presses. Three computer labs support numerous studio and liberal arts courses. Adjoining each of these labs is drawing, discussion, and critique space. Some of the most important work during class time takes place in these areas away from the computer monitor. Three workstations in the Senior Graphic Design Studio; Macintosh workstations in the Graphic Design Laboratory; Macintosh workstations in the Multimedia Digimaging Laboratory; open access to all systems when classes are not in session. Software includes: Adobe PhotoShop, Adobe Illustrator, Adobe Acrobat, Quark Xpress, Macromedia Director Studio, Macromedia Flash, Macromedia Dreamweaver, Maxon Cinema 4DXL, Final Cut Pro, BBEdit.

Student Body
Thirty students in the Graphic Design major.

Faculty Profile
Four faculty members.

Deadlines and Financial Aid
Rolling admission with a deadline of Aug. 1 for the fall, and December 1 for the spring. March 1 financial aid deadline for both semesters.

Admission Requirements
Application and fee, statement or essay, portfolio, two letters of recommendation, high school transcript, SAT or ACT scores, college transcript if transfer applicant. The portfolio is one of the most significant parts of your application. You will want to choose work that is current and exhibits your skill and originality.

Expenses

Tuition is $17,200 per year.

Contact

Montserrat College of Art, 23 Essex St., P.O. Box 26, Beverly, MA 01915. Telephone: 978-922-8222. Fax: 978-922-4268. Contact person: Diane Allenberg. URL: http://www.montserrat.edu/.

New England School of Arts and Design

F/X Degrees Offered

B.F.A. and Diploma in Graphic Design with Concentration in Broadcast, Design and Illustration.

Curricular

Computer Typography; Advanced Computer; 2D Animation; Principles of Animation; Computer Applications in Design; Art Direction for Photography; Electronic Illustration.

Facilities

Two Macintosh-based laboratories house. Two LaserWriter b/w printers; one Tektronix color printer; one b/w Abaton scanner; one Hewlett Packard color scanner; two CD-ROM players. Software available for use with the Macintosh computers falls into three basic categories paint and graphics programs that allow students to draw, paint and use color electronically (Adobe Illustrator, Aldus Freehand, Adobe Photoshop, SuperPaint); desktop publishing software, which gives the graphic designer electronic control of text, typography, layout and design (Adobe Photoshop, QuarkXPress, Aldus PageMaker); and presentation graphics, which can be used to create multimedia presentations (MacroMedia Director, Adobe Photoshop, Swivel 3D, Diva Videoshop).

Student Body

Approximately 150 students enrolled in day programs and between 250 and 300 in evening and summer classes. The average class size is approximately 12, with no studio allowed to exceed 25 students. Computer graphics classes involve no more than eight students, allowing each student access to a workstation both during and outside of class time.

Faculty Profile

Most of the approximately 65 current faculty members teach part-time while maintaining active involvement in their professions.

Deadlines and Financial Aid

Federal programs include grants, low interest loans, and employment programs. The Commonwealth of Massachusetts awards loans and grants to state residents who demonstrate financial need. The University and private agencies/organizations award scholarships, grants and loans to needy students. Financial aid awards are made to assist students in financing the cost of education when their personal and family resources are not sufficient. Hence, most funding is awarded on the basis of demonstrated need. Merit based funding is also available through selected programs.

Admission Requirements

Diploma all applicants to the New England School of Art and Design must be high school graduates or holders of a GED. Exceptions to this rule may be made in unusual circumstances at the discretion of the Admission Committee. Such applicants may only be admitted as Continuing Education students; however, they may apply at a later date for recognition as Diploma Candidates provided they have since earned a high school diploma or its equivalent; an application form, a non-refundable application fee, official transcripts of grades from high school as well as any colleges attended, and two letters of recommendation. Applicants to the B.F.A. program must also submit official SAT scores, informational interview and a portfolio.

Expenses
Tuition is $9,335 per semester.

Contact
The New England School of Art and Design at Suffolk University, 1st floor, Donahue Building, 41 Temple Street, Beacon Hill, Boston, MA 02114. Telephone: 617-573-8470. Fax: 617-720-3579. URL: http://www.suffolk.edu/nesad/.

Northeastern University

F/X Degrees Offered
Multimedia Studies Department. B.S. and B.A. in Media Studies. Department of Art offers B.A. and B.S. in Art with a concentration in Animation. College of Computer Science. B.S., M.S. and Ph.D. in traditional Computer Science.

Curricular
Art courses include 2D Computer Animation; Scriptwriting; Web Design; Graphic Design; 2D Computer Animation; Traditonal Animation; Multimedia/Interactive; Digital Painting/Drawing; Digital Video. Computer Science Courses: 3D Modeling and Rendering; 2D Computer Animation; Multimedia/Interactive; High-Level Programming; Low-Level Programming; Image processing; Virtual Reality; Diagram Understanding.

Facilities
Macintosh with hi-resolution monitors; laser printers; phase change color printer; film recorder; color scanners; CD-ROM players; Zip removable drives; Motion Capture System, PC Labs. Software: Maya, Adobe Illustrator; Adobe PhotoShop; Adobe Premiere; The Adobe Font Library; Aldus Persuasion; QuarkXPress; PosterWorks; MacroMedia Director; Netscape Navigator; Fractal Design Painter; Swivel 3D and many single-copy programs for individual projects including: Morph and Kai's Power Tools. Students also attend classes in, and use, the facilities of the department's Photo Laboratory, as well as the TV Training Studio, a new center for analog and digital video creation and editing. Facilities through the Science Department—UNIX laboratories are open to all students in the College of Computer Science. A large number of machines are available including Suns and various MIPS architecture. The Macintosh and PC laboratories are open to all students in the College of Computer Science. IBM-compatible laboratories are also available.

Student Body
There are 400 students in the department and 200 in the areas of Multimedia and Animation concentrations; 190 graduate students in the College of Computer Science.

Faculty Profile
Twenty-four full-time faculty members teach in the Department of Visual Arts. Two teach couses in Animation. Five teach courses in Media Studies.

Deadlines and Financial Aid
Northeastern University admits qualified freshmen and transfer students to all programs in September and January. In most programs, transfer students may also apply for entrance at the beginning of the March and June quarters. Admission is selective and priority is given to candidates who apply by March 1.

Admission Requirements
Decisions on admission are made as soon as all required credentials (including first marking-period senior grades and SAT or ACT test scores) have been submitted and reviewed. In all cases of acceptance, candidates must complete their senior year of high school. Applications, along with the initial payment

of one-third tuition plus the fee, are due: mid-September for the fall; mid-January for the winter; last week of March for the spring; mid-June for the summer.

Expenses
Tuition is $7,000-$8,415 per quarter for undergraduate students, and an estimated $575 per graduate-quarter hour of credit for all credit courses.

Contact
College of Computer and Information Science, Northeastern University, Cullinane Hall, 360 Huntington Avenue, Boston, Massachusetts 02115. Telephone: 617-373-2462. Fax: 617-373-5121. Contact person: Richard Rasala, Dean. E-mail: undergradschool@ccs.neu.edu. URL: http://www.ccs.neu.edu/.

Additional Information
Computer Graphics courses are available through the Art and Architecture Department, and the Computer Science Departments. The concentration is a preprofessional program in the study of visual language and communication, which emphasizes the breadth of vision that a liberal arts education offers. The studio curriculum balances creative exploration with the development of analytical and critical abilities, and integrates traditional instruction with approaches to design using digital tools. Students are encouraged to build on a basic foundation of color, structure, form, sequence and problem-solving while exploring a wide range of media and technology. The department believes that graphic designers should be familiar with past and contemporary design solutions. Students in the concentration are given a thorough grounding in the history of art and design. Students also gain 2D and 3D experience in media such as charcoal, paints, construction tools, photography, video and computer graphics.

University of Massachusetts at Amherst

F/X Degrees Offered
Department of Art. The Computer Arts Program offers B.F.A. and M.F.A. degrees. With an emphasis on Fine Arts, the department combines technical and aesthetic principles. Students pursue work in still imagery as well as time-based art. M.S. and Ph.D. in Computer Science.

Curricular
3D Modeling and Rendering; 3D Animation; 2D Computer Animation; Multimedia/Interactive; Digital Painting/Drawing; Image Processing; Digital Video.

Facilities
Amiga with Deluxe Paint, Imagine; Macintoshes with Photoshop, PageMaker, Infini-D, Director, etc.; SGIs with Maya. 3/4-inch and Hi8 video editing; sound editing; frame-by-frame recording and Hi8; film recorder, scanner, digitizer, etc.

Student Body
Thirty-nine undergraduates and six graduate students in the computer graphics area in the Department of Art; 90 students in other courses. Approximately 200 undergraduates and 150 graduate students in the Computer Science Department. A total enrollment of 17,000 undergraduates and 5,900 graduate students attend the university.

Faculty Profile
Forty-two faculty members teach in the Computer Science Department, and three faculty members teach in the Computer Art area in the Department of Art.

Deadlines and Financial Aid

The university offers the William D. Ford Direct Loan Program, which has replaced the Stafford Loan Program at UMASS. To apply for aid, complete the FAFSA or Renewal Application and mail it to the processing center by February 15 for priority consideration. Application deadline dates are February 1 for the fall semester and Oct. 15 for the spring. The Computer Science and Art Departments offer stipends for graduate assistantships, research assistantships, and fellowships. The average stipend awarded is $14,000 per year.

Admission Requirements

Undergraduate admissions: the most important criterion in the admissions decision is the high school academic record: quality and level of courses, GPA, class rank and grade trends. SAT or ACT scores are required. Achievement tests and letters of recommendation are not required but can strengthen an application. A personal statement, work experience, and extracurricular activities are also considered. Graduate admission: application and fee, personal statement, residency statement and transcripts.

Expenses

Tuition is $1,714 per year for residents and $9,756 per year for non-residents.

Contact

Fine Arts Center, U Mass, Amherst, MA 01003-4610. Telephone: 413-545-3640. Fax: 413-545-3929. Contact person: W. Bruce Croft. E-mail: admissions @cs.umass.edu.
URL: http://www.cs.umass.edu/.

University of Massachusetts at Boston

F/X Degrees Offered

B.A. and M.A. in Art.

Curricular

Studies in Film and Video; The Documentary Film; Film-Video I, II and III.

Facilities

Computer Graphics in video production; video production facilities. Facilities also include software such as Final Cut Pro, iMovie and SoundForge.

Student Body

There are 9,000 undergraduates and 3,000 graduate students enrolled in the university.

Faculty Profile

Nine full-time professors in the department.

Deadlines and Financial Aid

Various fellowships and traditional state, federal and city aid are available to students. Contact the Financial Aid Office for details on obtaining financial assistance at the university.

Admission Requirements

SAT or ACT scores, high school transcripts, application and fee.

Expenses

Tuition is $6,227 per year for residents and $16,887 for non-residents.

Contact

University of Massachusetts at Boston, 100 Morrissey Blvd., Boston, MA 02125-3393. Telephone: 617-287-5000. Fax: 617-287-5999.
URL: http://www.umb.edu/

University of Massachusetts at Lowell

F/X Degrees Offered
Computer Science Department offers programs leading to the B.S., M.S. and Sc.D. degrees. Strong emphasis on Computer Graphics, Data Visualization, Computer Human Interaction, and Multimedia.

Curricular
3D Modeling and Rendering; 3D Computer Animation; 2D Computer Animationn Multimedia; High-Level programming; Digital Painting; Image Processing; Virtual Reality; Volume Visualization; Digital Video.

Facilities
DECs, SGIs, Suns and PC laboratories. One Supercomputer. For CS public access, the department has a workstation laboratory consisting of 25 DEC stations, a public research annex with six workstations, and a PC laboratory with 28 stations. In addition, the department maintains three additional PC laboratories.

Student Body
There are 200 undergraduates and 100 graduate students in the department.

Faculty Profile
Fifteen full-time faculty members teach in the department.

Deadlines and Financial Aid
Various fellowships and traditional state, federal and city aid are available to students. Contact the Financial Aid Office for details on obtaining financial assistance at the university.

Admission Requirements
Graduating high school seniors and high school graduates who wish to be admitted to the university must comply with the following file an official application form with the University of Massachusetts at Lowell, request high school principals or guidance directors to forward to the Office of Admissions transcripts of high school grades including grade reports for at least the first quarter of the senior year, complete and file the College Board Student Descriptive Questionnaire, and arrange to take the College Entrance Examination Board SAT or ACT. Graduate Admission: application form, proof of residency form, letter of recommendation, residency status for tuition classification purposes.

Expenses
Tuition is $215 per credit hour.

Contact
University of Massachusetts at Lowell, One University Ave., Lowell, MA 01854. Telephone: 978-934-3620. Fax: 978-452-4298. Contact person: Georges Grinstein. E-mail: grinstein@cs.uml.edu. URL: http://www.uml.edu/.

Michigan

College for Creative Studies

F/X Degrees Offered
B.F.A. in Graphic Communication, Photography, Computer Graphics, and Fine Arts: Painting, Print Media, Sculpture.

Curricular
Computer Graphics courses are integrated into most departments. Photography: Animation; Computer Slide Multimedia; Video Production. Computer Technology: Digital Art; Digital Painting; Photo Illustration; Digital Multimedia; Advanced Digital Multimedia; Basic Computer Animation; Advanced Photo Illustration. Graphic Communication: Introduction to Computers; Introduction to Art Direction I and II; Computer Layout PageMaker; Video Computers; Digital Imaging Workshop Seminar.

Facilities
Students have access to three Macintosh facilities where software programs are available for creating page layout, illustration, animation and multimedia. Windows-based applications, CAD and rendering programs. Two Silicon Graphics facilities--14 SGI, one laboratory running Maya software and the other running CDRS. These laboratories are used to develop 3D design concepts, animation techniques, and high-end rendering. The Imaging Studio has high-end Macintosh-based workstations networking with a Silicon Graphics Cyclone/Canon CLC700 (CT) four-color process printer. Other services include color digital printouts, color laser copies, digital typesetting and photographic stats. The College's campus totals 10.5 acres, with approximately 232,000 square feet of instruction space. Providing top-notch facilities is a high priority at CCS. The new Walter B. Ford II Building is a state-of-the art facility for instruction in design. Wired with a single digital network to carry voice, data and video, it has high-tech flexible classrooms incorporating both traditional and computer workstations and a 250-seat auditorium equipped with the capacity to project digital images and sound. It also houses a clay modeling studio with a spray booth and custom-made tables and a rapid prototyping machine and provides space on all its floors for the exhibition of student work. The College's computer labs (which house over 380 workstations), wood shop, metal shop and foundry are open to students in every department and the art library is a superb resource. CCS is the only school in Michigan that has a hot glass studio and pours iron (in addition to bronze and aluminum).

Student Body
Total student body is 975.

Faculty Profile
Forty faculty members teach in the Graphic Communication Department.

Deadlines and Financial Aid
Students are encouraged to submit portfolios by March 1 for scholarship consideration. Merit awards range from $500 to a full year of tuition for a full-time student. Awards to part-time students are adjusted accordingly. Scholarship amounts are renewable for up to three additional years of continuous study based on academic, and artistic performance and review. The majority of the students enrolled at the college are eligible for some form of financial assistance through federal, state, college and private sources. All students interested in financial aid must complete the FAFSA before February 15 for high school seniors of Michigan, or March 15 if continuing or transfer students.

Admission Requirements

Application and fee, official high school transcript with a minimum of 2.5 or GED with 55 composite score, ACT or SAT, minimum 10-piece portfolio, personal interview, if within 250-mile radius, or phone interview. An acceptable portfolio is one that exhibits technical and conceptual preparation for college-level work. All portfolios must include a minimum of 10 pieces; at least five of those pieces must be drawings from direct observation. The remaining five or more pieces can represent your selected major or areas of strength.

Expenses

Tuition is $624 per credit hour.

Contact

College for Creative Studies, 201 East Kirby, Detroit, MI 48202. Telephone: 313-664-7425 or 800-952-ARTS. Email: kfuller@ccscad.edu. URL: http://www.ccscad.edu/

Eastern Michigan University

F/X Degrees Offered

Computer Science undergraduate major and minor (teaching, non-teaching). Graduate courses for M.S. in Math with concentration in Computer Science. Computer Graphics course offered.

Curricular

Computer Graphics.

Facilities

PCs and Macintoshes.

Student Body

There are 250 undergraduates and 30 graduate students in the department.

Faculty Profile

One teacher teaches in the area of Computer Graphics.

Deadlines and Financial Aid

Admission application deadlines: mid-April for the spring; mid-June for the summer; Aug. 1 for the fall; December 1 for the winter.

Admission Requirements

Undergraduates: application and fee, transcripts, and SAT or ACT. Graduates: contact the graduate studies office.

Expenses

Undergraduate tuition is $153.15 per credit hour for residents and $467.10 for non-residents.

Contact

511 Pray Harrold, Ypsilanti, MI 48197. Telephone: 734-487-1063. Contact person: H. Sachdev, Associate Professor. E-mail: harash.sachdev@emich.edu. URL: http://www.emich.edu/.

Grand Valley State University

F/X Degrees Offered

B.A. and B.S. in Film and Video Production. Majors emphasize one of four specialty areas: animation, audio, film and video, or writing for media. M.A. in Communication.

Curricular

Film and Video Production students gain practical hands-on experience through class projects, internships and independent studies. Courses in the history, theory and critical interpretation of media are offered. Media Production I, II; Animation I, II; Computer Image Making; Cinematic Multimedia; Television Studio Production; Documentary and

Field Production; Film and Video Art; 16 mm Film Production II; Scriptwriting II; Audio Production; Storyboarding; Web Design.

Facilities
Cameras, editing equipment, animation stands, and an optical printer for work in 16 mm film; VHS and S-VHS color portable video and editing equipment; Macintosh computers. Various Graphic Design and Web Design software packages.

Student Body
Total enrollment is 13,553; approximately 160 undergraduate film and video majors; 22 students in the animation emphasis.

Faculty Profile
There are 403 regular faculty members; 12 full-time faculty teach in the School of Communications; two teach courses in animation.

Deadlines and Financial Aid
More than 70 percent of the full-time students receive some kind of financial aid. The average award is approximately $4,100. To be considered for aid, a student must be admitted as a degree-seeking student and be enrolled for 12 credit hours or more per semester. Students planning to enroll for the fall semester, the following dates are important: February 1: freshman and transfer applicants must apply for admission to be considered for the major scholarship programs offered. February 15: renewal aid applicants and returning upper-class students must submit a completed FAFSA to the appropriate agency listed on the form. If planning to enroll beginning with the winter semester, the following dates are important: Oct. 1: entering freshman, graduate, transfer, renewal aid applicants, and upper-class students must submit a completed FAFSA to the appropriate agency listed on the form for winter semester aid. If the student plans to begin in the summer session, the following dates are important: February 15: entering freshman,

graduate, transfer, renewal aid applicants, and upper-class students must submit a completed FAFSA to the appropriate agency listed on the form for summer session aid.

Admission Requirements
Undergraduates: completed undergraduate application, fee, official high school transcript, and official results of the ACT or SAT. Graduate students: a baccalaureate degree from an accredited institution of higher education, completed graduate application for admission, $30 non-refundable application fee (unless you have previously applied to GVSU), official copies of transcripts from all institutions of higher education previously attended; unless otherwise indicated, applications should be submitted two months prior to the semester enrollment date.

Expenses
Undergraduate tuition is $5,353 per semester for residents and $12,216 for non-residents.

Contact
Computer Science Department, 1 Campus Dr., Allendale, MI 49401. Telephone: 616-895-6611 or 1-800-748-0246. Department: 616-895-3668. Fax: 616-331-2106. Contact person: Dr. Paul Leidig, Chair. E-mail: leidig@gvsu.edu. URL: http://www.gvsu.edu/.

Additional Information
A four-year undergraduate liberal arts school, GVSU combines career education within a solid liberal arts framework.
Lansing
Community College

F/X Degrees Offered
Associates in Applied Arts degree in Computer Graphics Animation, Computer Graphics Multimedia and Graphic Design.

Curricular

3D Modeling and Rendering; 3D Computer Animation; 2D Computer Animation; Multimedia/Interactive; Digital Painting/Drawing; Image Processing. Special Topic/Film Description: Non-linear Editing.

Facilities

Hardware: Pentium PCs; Macintosh workstations; Mitsubishi dye-sub printer; Tektronix Phaser III; assorted laser printers. JVC CD-ROM burners; Agfa PCR film recorder; assorted flatbed and slide scanners; two 3/4-inch video editing suites; 50 total stations. Software: Lightwave; 3D Studio; MacroMedia Extreme 3D; Crystal Topas; Fractal Design Painter; Adobe PageMaker; QuarkXPress; MacroMedia Freehand; Adobe Illustrator; MacroMedia Fontographer; MacroMedia Director; Adobe Photoshop; Adobe Premiere.

Student Body

There are 400 undergraduate students in the department.

Faculty Profile

Forty faculty members teach in the department.

Deadlines and Financial Aid

Various fellowships, and traditional state, federal and city aid are available to students. Contact the Financial Aid Office for details on obtaining financial assistance at the university.

Admission Requirements

SAT or ACT, transcripts, application and fee.

Expenses

Tuition is $54 per credit hour.

Contact

Art and Design Department, 419 N. Capitol Ave., Lansing, MI 48901-7210. Telephone: 517-483-1483. Fax: 517-483-9781. Contact person: Sharon Wood.

E-mail: SWood2@lcc.edu.
URL: http://www.lcc.edu/.

Additional Information

The Art Program at Lansing Community College provides training for professional artists; that is, for those who earn all or part of their livelihood from the creation of visual art objects or commercial art. Each art curriculum may be completed at the student's own pace on a full-time or part-time basis.

Michigan Technological University

F/X Degrees Offered

Computer Science Department. B.S. and M.S. in Computer Science, Ph.D. in Computational Science and Engineering.

Curricular

3D Modeling and Rendering; 3D Computer Animation; 2D Computer Animation; High-Level Programming; Geometric Modeling.

Facilities

The CS Department operates four labs with 80 workstations (the PizzaLab in Fisher 229, the ICU, in Fisher 232, the SciFiLab, in Fisher 233, and the LanguageLab, in Fisher 234). The Language, SciFi and Pizza Labs contain postscript compatible laser printers. The Department also operates four servers that are primarily for access over the MTU network (from other labs on campus, from dorm rooms, from dial-up lines, etc.), and a file-only server for student files. All machines have Internet access. The labs are generally open all day and evenings.

Student Body

There are 240 undergraduates and 30 graduate students in the department.

Faculty Profile
Nineteen full-time faculty members are in the department.

Deadlines and Financial Aid
Various forms of fellowships and teaching assistantships are available. Teaching assistants receive a stipend of $2,600 and a tuition waiver. Assistantship application deadline: February 15 for fall entrance. All students seeking optimum financial aid opportunities should apply for admission as soon as possible after Sept. 1, preceding the academic year in which they plan to enroll.

Admission Requirements
Undergraduates: application and fee, transcripts, and ACT or SAT scores. For details, contact the Admission Office. Graduate students: to be considered for admission to the Graduate School as a regular student, the applicant must be: a bachelor's degree recipient from an accredited institution, adequately prepared for advanced study in a chosen field of specialization as demonstrated by the previous program of study and the scholastic record, and recommended for admission by the head of a major or program.

Expenses
Tuition is $227 per credit hour for residents and $590.00 per credit hour for non-residents. Graduates pay $398 per credit hour.

Contact
1400 Townsend Dr., Houghton, MI 49931-1295.
Telephone: 906-487-2183. Fax: 906-487-2283.
Contact person: Dr. John Lowther, Director. E-mail: john@cs.mtu.edu.
URL: http://www.cs.mtu.edu/.

University of Michigan

F/X Degrees Offered
B.F.A. in Electronic Media, Graphic Design and Mixed Media. All programs are offered through the School of Art and Design. M.A. and M.F.A. in Medical and Biological Illustration are also available. M.S. and Ph.D. in Computer Science.

Curricular
Computing Introduction; Computer Modeling; Video; Animation.

Facilities
More than 40 computers are linked for easy access to extensive software and databases. Students use the Imaging Center for Advanced Computer Graphics. The Media Union building houses a virtual reality laboratory. Computer Science Department facilities--Hardware: 500 workstations--HP; DEC; IBM; Sun; 200 PCs. Macintosh and Windows NT Software systems and languages: C; C++; Lisp; SQL (Oracle); Smalltalk; Tcl; tk; Pascal; Fortran; GPSS.

Student Body
Total of 36,000 students are enrolled at the university.

Faculty Profile
Eleven faculty teach in the Computer Graphics and Animation areas.

Deadlines and Financial Aid
Scholarships and awards are available to qualified students in the School of Art and Design. They are administered on a merit basis. Undergraduate admission deadlines are April 1 for the fall, and November 1 for the winter term. Computer Science Admissions application deadline: June 1. Assistantship application deadline: Jan. 15. Fellowships--Rackham's Office of Student Recruitment and Support administers all fellowship and student financial support programs of the

Graduate School. The Fellowships Office, part of the Office Student Recruitment and Support, administers Rackham Fellowships and provides administrative services for other federal, state, university and private fellowships.

Admission Requirements
Maintain a B average shown in transcripts, SAT or ACT, complete application and fee, submit portfolio when requested, letters of recommendation, and essay.

Expenses
Tuition ranges from $6,100 to $7,800 per year for full-time residents, and approximately $14,000 per year for non-residents.

Contact
The University of Michigan, 527 East Liberty Street, Suite 204, Ann Arbor, MI 48104-2242. Telephone: 734-995-0221. Fax: 734-995-0548. Contact person: Sally Harris Lindsley, Assistant Director. E-mail: sallyhl@umich.edu.
URL: http://www.umich.edu/.

Wayne State University

F/X Degrees Offered
Department of Computer Science offers M.S. and Ph.D. degrees in Computer Science.

Curricular
Courses are offered in Biocomputing; Graphics and Simulation; Multimedia Information Systems; Introduction to Modeling and Simulation; Computer Graphics and Animation.

Facilities
Department facilities--Hardware: 45 SPARC workstations; MasPar 1024; 40 PCs. Software systems and languages: SunOS; UNIX; C; C++; CommonLisp; Prolog; Fortran; STP; Khoros;

Sybase and Oracle databases. University facilities--Hardware: Amdahl 5890/300E; two PC and Macintosh laboratories; Multimedia classroom; research support laboratories. Software systems and languages: MVS/ESA; VM/CMS; MTS; Fortran; Pascal; Cobol; APL; PLI; SNOBOL; PROFS.

Student Body
Total enrollment is 32,906; 340 graduate students in the Computer Science Department.

Faculty Profile
Fourteen full-time faculty members teach graduate-level courses.

Deadlines and Financial Aid
Admissions application deadline: November 1, March 1, July 1 of each year. Assistantship application deadline: February 15 for fall, Oct. 15 for winter.

Admission Requirements
Application and fee, transcript and GRE.

Expenses
Tuition is $155 to $296 per credit hour for undergraduate residents; non-residents pay $356 to $755 per credit.

Contact
5143 Cass Ave., Room 431, State Hall, Detroit, MI 48202. Telephone: 313-577-2477. Fax: 313-577-6868. URL: http://www.cs.wayne.edu/.

Western Michigan University

F/X Degrees Offered
Department of Computer Science offers a M.S. and Ph.D. in Computer Science.

Curricular

Several courses in Computer Graphics and Scientific Visualization.

Facilities

Department facilities--Hardware: 128-node nCube; Sparc server 20; three Sparc 20s; 30 Sparc 5s; approximately 25 other Sun workstations; assorted PCs. Software systems and languages: Solaris 2.4; DOS; Linux. Various packages for instructional, learning, and research. University facilities--Hardware: Sparc server 6/670, DEC Alpha 7000-620, DEC VAX 6000-620. Several Sun workstations; PCs and Macintoshes. Software systems and languages: SunOS 4.1.4; VMS 6.1; many high-level languages; specialized applications programs.

Student Body

Twelve Ph.D. students in the department; 26,537 total enrollment.

Faculty Profile

Sixteen full-time faculty members in the department; 1,263 faculty members teach at the university.

Deadlines and Financial Aid

Numerous forms of financial aid are available including grants, students loans, and even scholarships given directly from the school. Graduate assistantships are available to students ranging from teaching assistantships of $7,600 per year to research assistantships of $9,365 per year.

Admission Requirements

Admissions application deadline: July 1 for fall admission. Assistantship application deadline: March 15.

Expenses

Tuition is $144.08 per credit hour for residents and $366.90 per hour for non-residents.

Contact

Department of Computer Science, 3308 Friedmann, Kalamazoo, MI 49008. Telephone: 616-387-5645. Fax: 616-387-5997. Contact person: Dr. Agay Gupta, chair. E-mail: gupta@wmich.edu. URL: http://www.cs.wmich.edu/.

Minnesota

Minneapolis
College of Art and Design

F/X Degrees Offered
B.F.A. and M.F.A. Graduate students may elect to pursue creative work in the areas of Filmmaking, Video, Photography, Graphic Design, Advertising Design, Illustration, Computer Animation, Electronic Publication, Interactive Media, and other related or hybrid courses of study.

Curricular
Undergraduates: the curriculum emphasizes individual and group exercises; discussion and analysis of photographs, films and videotapes, and writings on theory and criticism. All Media Arts majors must participate in a professional, career-related internship through positions such as curatorial assistant, film editor, video production intern, or photographer's apprentice. In the past, students have worked with nationally recognized artists including Annie Liebovitz and Mark Seiger, and have had internships at Paisley Park, HBO Feature Films, Disney Productions, Harper's Bazaar Magazine, and public television's *Alive TV.* Graduate: the schools's M.F.A. degree in Visual Studies provides individuals seeking advanced study in the arts an opportunity to secure the recognized terminal degree in the studio arts. MCAD's program encourages graduate students to develop an interdisciplinary program of study, which meets their specific needs and interests. Grounded in a mentorship-style environment, the program utilizes individualized learning contracts; however, all students must take the required liberal arts seminars, studio critique sessions, and a thesis exhibition. Candidates also have the opportunity to participate in an internship program, which places them into working situations related to their study experiences or career goals. Computer Graphics I; Computer Graphics II; Film I-III; Video I; Film Photography III; Video II, III.

Facilities
Media Arts students use computers for video editing, electronic photography and sound composition. 3D Modeling programs are applied to sculpture projects; painting and drawing students explore the large array of color painting and illustration software. More than 120 workstations in seven laboratories; Silicon Graphics workstations form the basis of the 3D Animation laboratory. The Graphic Design laboratory, the CAD/3D laboratory, the Multimedia/Fine Arts laboratory, the Digital Media laboratory and the Foundation Studies laboratory have more than 50 Apple Macintoshes. These computers all feature full-color palettes and video output capability, and utilize network-computing software to render 3D scenes. Additionally, many of these computers are equipped with peripheral drives for removable optical and hard-disk cartridges, video input capabilities and pressure-sensitive tablets. Other facilities include PC Targa workstations, and 20 Macintoshes in the library dedicated to word processing. The Computer Center supports several CD-ROM workstations; five high-resolution color scanners; a video-frame-capture station, two slide scanners and a choice of color printers, including dye-sub technology for digital photography and prepress work. Animation can be output directly to videotape and laser disk. Support for the laboratories includes three multi-gigabyte file servers, five print servers and several high-resolution, grayscale laser printers. Everything is connected together using coaxial and fiber-optics networks and eight Internet routers. Complete facilities are available for producing Super-8 mm

and 16 mm films, both on location and in the production studios. There is equipment for silent synchronous sound films, animation facilities, and a professional color and b/w off-campus laboratory for processing motion picture film at cost. Post-production facilities include individual editing stations, including seven 16 mm flatbed editing tables, and 16 mm mag track mixing system, as well as projection facilities and auditoriums for presentations. Video production facilities allow students to shoot Hi8 or 3/4-inch formats on location with Sony camcorders and portapaks, or in the studios via the professionally equipped control room. The control room and editing suites are composed of four individual electronic track-editing stations, a dubbing room, and a computer-generated graphics station, which allows students to create still-video images, 3D model rendering and animation.

Student Body
There are 460 full-time students in the school.

Faculty Profile
Seventeen faculty in the Media Arts and Dimension Department teach undergraduate courses. 27 faculty teach graduate courses at MCAD.

Deadlines and Financial Aid
Candidates for the M.F.A. program are encouraged to apply in a timely manner. All application materials must be received by the Admissions Office by February 15. Admissions applications that are incomplete at the deadline will not be considered. Candidates who complete the applications will receive notice regarding their status by April 1. All candidates for the M.F.A. program are encouraged to apply for financial aid. MCAD uses the FAFSA to determine financial need. Scholarships will be awarded to full-time students (12 credits or more) showing financial need. Various loan programs are also available to graduate students. Teaching assistantships will be offered. For more information, contact the Financial Aid Office. Undergraduates: prospective students are encouraged to apply in a timely manner. If applying for the fall semester, it is beneficial to complete the application process by March 15 for priority scholarship and financial aid consideration. Applicants for the spring semester should complete the application process by November 1. Several forms of scholarships are available for undergraduates. Financial aid is awarded as financial aid files are completed; therefore, it is very important that the application is completed before April 1. Eligible students whose files are complete by April 1 will be considered priority applicants and will receive award notices indicating estimated grants, scholarships, loans and work-study by the last week of the spring semester. Late applicants will receive award letters approximately two weeks after the financial aid files are complete. Spring semester applicants also need to complete the applications for financial aid by April 1 to be assured of priority funding.

Admission Requirements
Application form and fee; statement of purpose; resume; letters of recommendation; portfolio; official college transcripts and interview. Undergraduates: admissions application form and fee; personal statement of interest; transcripts; test scores; letters of recommendation; admission portfolio and interview.

Expenses
Tuition is $11,200 per year.

Contact
Minneapolis College of Art and Design, 2501 Stevens Ave. S., Minneapolis, MN 55404. Telephone: 612-874-3760 or 800-874-MCAD. E-mail: admissions@mn.mcad.edu. URL: http://www.mcad.edu/.

University of Minnesota at Duluth

F/X Degrees Offered
Department of Art offers a B.F.A. and M.F.A. in Graphic Design.

Curricular
All graphic design classes involve the use of computers. Courses include: Computer Art and Animation; Design Using Computers; 3D Design; Computers, Graphic Techniques and Processes; Computer Studio; Digital Imaging; Motion Graphics.

Facilities
Three Macintosh laboratories (24 stations each) with b/w laser printers; color laser printers; color flatbed scanners; slide scanner; CD burner. The most used graphic design software: Adobe Illustrator; Adobe Photoshop; QuarkXPress; Fractal Design Painter; Macromedia Director.

Student Body
There are 250 art students, 135 of which are Graphic Design majors.

Faculty Profile
Four faculty in the Graphic Design area, one additional teaching Computer Studio. Two other faculty actively involved in Computer Mediated Art.

Deadlines and Financial Aid
Call 800-232-1339 for details. Fellowships and teacher assistantships are available for graduate students. Apply early for financial aid and submit all required documentation upon request. There are application deadlines and limited funding for some financial aid programs. For example, you will not be considered for a Minnesota State Grant if your FAFSA is received by the Federal Processing Center after the second week of the semester. If you apply late, you may also lose eligibility for other awards.

Admission Requirements
Admission is done in fall semester only. Students who wish to pursue the art education K-12 or graphic design B.F.A. degree program initially are admitted into the pre-art education or pre-graphic design program. Students are admitted directly into the art history and studio art-general majors. The pregraduate art major, with emphasis in either studio art or art and technology, has a separate application process, with the prerequisite of completion of 18 credits in art department studio courses; for transfer students to apply for this major, completion of 9 art department studio credits is required. During the second (spring) semester of art study at UMD, the pre-majors may seek admission to the majors in art education K-12 and graphic design through an application and review process. They enroll in the no credit, no cost portfolio review course appropriate to the major they seek. Students transferring into the department with at least 9 credits of art courses may apply during their first semester of study through the same process. This procedure is effective for students beginning their coursework as UMD art majors in the fall semester 2001 or later. Students who do not qualify for admission may reapply once in a subsequent spring semester.

Expenses
Tuition is $201.51 per credit hour for residents and $571.67 per credit hour for non-residents.

Contact
Department of Art & Design, 317 Humanities, Duluth, MN 55812. Telephone: 218-726-8225. Fax: 218-726-6532. Contact: Jim Klueg, Professor. E-mail: jklueg@d.umn.edu.
URL: http://www.d.umn.edu/art/.

Mississippi

Mississippi State University

F/X Degrees Offered
School of Architecture. M.S. degree in Architecture with a specialization in Digital Design/Computer Visualization. B.F.A. through the Department of Art in Computer Animation, Multimedia or Graphic Design. M.F.A. in Electronic Visualization through the Department of Art.

Curricular
2D and 3D Animation; Electronic Painting; 2D and 3D Graphics; Multimedia Authoring and Scripting; Digital Photography; CD Recording; Digital Video; World Wide Web Publishing and Design; Theory of Visual Communication and History of New Media.

Facilities
The Center for Visual Creation is currently housed in National Science Foundation Engineering Research Center. The Research Center's new 44,000-square-foot building is designed for interdisciplinary efforts that promote the synergistic research collaboration essential to the Center's success. It is networked with fiber optics and thin-net, connected by fiber with the rest of the campus, and by T1 lines on NSFnet via SURAnet. It has a video classroom, affording the use of video equipment in classes and allowing for the production of videotaped classes for live satellite transmission to remote sites. The Center also contains a workstation classroom designed for use as a Silicon Graphics Silicon Studio National Training Center, an Onyx RealityEngine 2, high-performance virtual environment viewing devices, high-resolution scanners, color printer, CD authoring tools, audio composition, and video-recording capabilities.

Department of Art facilities--contains graduate and faculty studios; a multimedia classroom and production laboratory; digital compositing laboratory; digital sound recording studio; media library and presentation center; a computer graphics laboratory; graphic design classroom and research center. The CoA Digital Research and Imaging Lab is a multi-platfrom visualization laboratory for inter-disciplinary research work conducted by the School of Architecture. The lab contains UNIX (SGI and Sun), Windows 2000/XP, and MAC OS workstations running a variety of modeling, rendering, animation, simulation, CAD and multi-media software. Packages include Alias|Wavefront Maya, 3D Studio Max, AutoCAD, ArchiCAD, Revit, Rhino, Form-Z, Studio Pro, Infini-D, Premiere, After Effects, Flash, Dreamweaver, Director, PhotoShop, MicroStation and others. Peripheral equipment and capabilities include RAID arrays, printers, plotters and video output, 3D probe digitizing, scanning and, through associated programs, digital photography, laser scanning, rapid prototyping and related technologies. DRIL also contains Internet servers delivering nationally recognized Web sites, including Digital Darwins developed in conjunction with the Smithsonian Institution.

Student Body
Twelve graduate students in the Architecture area. The Department of Art has 230 majors, and more than 1,000 students are enrolled each semester.

Faculty Profile
The College of Arts and Sciences employs more than 300 faculty and 60 staff members; 17 full-time faculty members teach in the Department of Art.

Deadlines and Financial Aid
Through the Mississippi Resident Tuition Assistance Grant program, or MTAG, the state of Mississippi awards as much as $500 per year for freshman and sophomore students, and up to $1,000 per

year for junior and senior students enrolled in state universities who meet certain eligibility requirements, including being a Mississippi resident for four consecutive years, being a full-time college student, and having a 2.5 high school GPA and 15 ACT score. Contact the Office of Student Financial Aid and Scholarships at 601-325-3990 for more information. The deadline for filing an application with the Financial Aid Office is February 15.

Admission Requirements

Fill out an application for admission and if considered, an out-of-state student, application fee, ACT or SAT scores, high school transcript, proof of immunization for measles and rubella, all no later than 20 days before registering for classes.

Expenses

Tuition is $1,937 per year for residents and $4,390 for non-residents.

Contact

College of Architecture, P.O. Drawer AQ, Mississippi State, MS 39762. Telephone: 601-325-2202. Fax: 601-325-8872. Contact person: Michael Fazio, Interim Associate Dean. Email: mfazio@sarc.msstate.edu. URL: http://www.msstate.edu/.

Additional Information

The M.S. degree in Architecture with a specialization in Digital Design offers an interdisciplinary, research-oriented academic experience for students from various fields who wish to use designed visualization as a method of inquiry. It draws upon a long history of representation in the discipline of architecture to develop principles of 3D visual investigation, and to apply them to a variety of problems and knowledge domains. The degree program is appropriate for students who have demonstrated a high level of success and potential for further development in their undergraduate studies, and can submit a significant portfolio of design work. The M.S. degree in Architecture is not a professional degree; that is, it does not lead to architectural licensing as does the school's five-year Bachelor of Architecture Degree. Rather, it trains specialists to enter a broad range of fields, including architecture, scientific research, education, and entertainment, or to pursue related studies at the doctoral level. Students will be given the opportunity and means to both develop individual research agendas and to collaborate with faculty and student colleagues on projects undertaken by the school. In the first year, students will be expected to present developing work in school colloquia and at appropriate conferences and, by the time of graduation, to prepare the findings for publication. Students will also be expected to master an appropriate level of computer programming and to achieve a basic understanding of the ways in which computers aid in accomplishing tasks.

University of Southern Mississippi

F/X Degrees Offered

M.S. and Ph.D. in Computer Science.

Curricular

Various courses in Computer Graphics, Advanced Scientific Visualization, Software Design, and Artificial Intelligence.

Facilities

Hardware: 90 PC clones; one TI 1500 UNIX computer; one Sun Sparc station; 14 Motorola 68,000 single-board computers attached to PCs. Software systems and languages: MS DOS; Windows; UNIX; Linux; X-Windows; C; C++; Turbo Pascal; Ada; Lisp; Fortran. University facilities--Hardware: 50 IBM PC clones; IBM RS6000; Bull mainframe; two Linux servers; VAX 3100. Software systems and languages: as above plus VMS and Cobol.

Student Body

There are 330 graduate students in the department. A total of 11,600 students attend the university.

Faculty Profile

Seventeen full-time faculty members in the department; total of 577 full-time faculty members at the university.

Deadlines and Financial Aid

Three types of assistance are available through the university: grants or scholarships, loans and student employment. Approximately 70 percent of students receive financial aid. Deadlines vary. Contact the addmissions office.

Admission Requirements

Application and fee, transcripts and GRE scores.

Expenses

Tuition is $1,944 per semester.

Contact

Department of Computer Science, Hattiesburg, MS 39406-5106. Telephone: 601-266-4949. Fax: 601-266-5148. Contact person: Dr. Frank Nagurney, Chair. E-mail: frank.nagurney@usm.edu. URL: http://www.usm.edu/css.

Missouri

University of Missouri at Columbia

F/X Degrees Offered
Environmental Design Department. Undergraduate academic program prepares students for careers in Interior Design. A pre-architecture option is also available. There is a graduate academic program that prepares students for positions in teaching and research. Design Communications (Computer Graphics) is also an option. M.S. and Ph.D. in Computer Engineering and Computer Science.

Curricular
3D Modeling and Rendering; 3D Computer Animation; Digital Painting/Drawing.

Facilities
At the Univ. of Missouri Dr. Zhuang and Dr. Palaniappan have recently established a $1.7 million Multimedia Communications and Visualization Laboratory (MCVL) in the Department of Computer Engineering and Computer Science (CECS) jointly funded by grants from the National Aeronautics and Space Administration, National Science Foundation, Raytheon, and Silicon Graphics Inc. (SGI). The MCVL currently consists of sixteen Silicon Graphics workstations including one Origin 2000 supercomputer, one four processor Onyx2, eight R10000 O2s, four dual processor Octanes, and two Indigo2s. The Origin 2000 includes InfiniteReality2 graphics with two raster managers (64MB and 16 MB of texture memory each), the Onyx2 includes InfinteReality2 graphics with 8 display channels, and the Octanes have MXI or SSI graphics. The rack-based Origin 2000 has a 360 GB Fibre-channel disk array storage system and the Onyx2 has a 54 GB 6-way striped disk array. The Octane and Onyx2 virtual reality workstations have stereo capability and are used to develop 3-D displays using the StereoGraphic CrystalEyes stereo hardware. The distributed MCVL cluster of workstations contains a total of over 4 gigabytes of memory (RAM), over 520 gigabytes of disk storage, over 30 CPUs, a variety of graphics capabilities, with 100BaseT (Fast Ethernet) network connectivity. A variety of high end networked Pentium III SGI, Dell and Compaq PCs are also available. High speed Gigabit Ethernet and ATM switches support distributed computing research over local area wired and wireless networks. Internet access optimized over the NSF vBNS or Internet 2 Abilene research networks is available at OC-3 (155 megabits/sec) or DS-3 speeds. Specialized nonlinear video processing and editing equipment are also available. The CECS MCVL was established to support research and training in (1) digital video over information networks applied to very low bit rate video coding using the wavelet transform, visual content analysis, coding and retrieval, and intelligent network access to compressed multimedia datasets in digital libraries; (2) scientific visualization applied to the analysis and interactive manipulation of geophysical datasets, video visualization and databases, distributed visualization, biomedical virtual reality, data mining, network topology visualization, and parallel algorithm development using the massively parallel Maspar cluster at NASA Goddard; (3) design of robust algorithms for image understanding including stereo analysis, nonrigid motion estimation, and scene classification.

Student Body
A total of 15,658 undergraduate and 5,800 graduate students attend the university; 150 undergraduates and 20 continuing-education students in the Design Department; 73 graduate students major in Computer Science.

Faculty Profile

Eighteen faculty teach in the Computer Engineering and Computer Science Department. Environmental Design: six faculty members, two teach classes in computer graphics.

Deadlines and Financial Aid

Financial aid is available to qualified degree candidates who are enrolled at MU. Financial aid includes: student loans, grants, curatorial and University Scholarships (as well as other scholarships), vocational rehabilitation, and some third-party billings. Graduate students may apply for a graduate assistantship and may receive a teaching assistantship stipend of $8,520, or a research assistantship of $12,000 per year. Admissions application deadline: May 1 for fall; Oct. 1 for winter. Assistantship application deadline: March 1 for fall; Oct. 1 for winter.

Admission Requirements

Graduate students must submit an application and fee, transcripts and GRE scores. Undergraduate students should contact the office of admission for detailed instruction on the application process.

Expenses

Tuition is $6,149 per semester for residents and $8,818 for non-residents.

Contact

313 Engr. Bldg. West, Columbia, MO 65211.
Telephone: 573-882-2382. Fax: 573-992-7887.
Contact person: Xinhua Zhuang, Professor. E-mail: zhuang@cs.missouri.edu.
URL: http://www.cs.missouri.edu/.

Montana

Montana State University at Bozeman

F/X Degrees Offered
B.A. in Studio Art. Other degree options available through the Department of Computer Science.

Curricular
Graphic Design I and II; Introduction to Graphic Design I and II; Advanced Graphic Design I; Computer Graphics; and Artificial Intelligence.

Facilities
Computer laboratory equipped with 22 Macintosh workstations. Software includes QuarkXPress, Photoshop, Flash, Dreamweaver and Adobe Illustrator. Color and b/w printers, and scanners.

Student Body
285 students in the Art Department; 150 of these students major in Graphic Design.

Faculty Profile
Three full-time faculty teach Graphic Design.

Deadlines and Financial Aid
Application deadlines for the fall semester is July 1; spring semester's deadline is December 1. Financial aid applications may be requested from the Office of Financial Aid.

Admission Requirements
Application and fee, SAT or ACT, and transcripts.

Expenses
Tuition for undergraduate residents is $4,145 per year and $12,707 for out-of-state residents.

Contact
School of Art, Department of Computer Science, PO Box 173880, Bozeman, MT 59717-3880. Telephone: 406-994-4780. Fax: 406-994-3680. Contact person: Michael Oudshoorn, Department Head. Email: michael@cs.montana.edu.
URL: http://www.cs.montana.edu/.

Additional Information
Located just north of Yellowstone National Park in a valley surrounded by mountains, MSU offers a course of study with options in Art Education, Art History, Fine Arts and Graphic Design.

Nebraska

College of Saint Mary

F/X Degrees Offered
B.A. through the Computer Graphics Department.

Curricular
Introduction to Computer Graphics; Graphic Design; Introduction to Software Systems; Advanced Computer Graphics; Business Graphics Applications; Practicum in Computer Graphics; Senior Thesis.

Facilities
Various hardware and software programs for creating Computer Graphics and Animation.

Student Body
A total enrollment of 1,000 students.

Faculty Profile
More than 130 faculty teach at the college.

Deadlines and Financial Aid
Various forms of financial aid are available including scholarships, CSM Grant Program, Tuition Assistance Program, Family Grant Program, and many others. The priority deadline for financial aid is March 1. Rolling admission for academic programs.

Admission Requirements
Application and fee, high school transcripts, ACT or SAT scores, and college transcripts if transfer student.

Expenses
Tuition is $7,885 per semester.

Contact
College of Saint Mary, 1901 S. 72nd St., Omaha, Nebraska 68124. Telephone: 800-926-5534. Fax: 402-399-2412. E-mail: enroll@csm.edu. URL: http://www.csm.edu/.

Nevada

University of Nevada at Las Vegas

F/X Degrees Offered
B.S., M.S. and Ph.D. in Computer Science.

Curricular
Courses include Advanced Computer Graphics; Computer Graphics; Introduction to Computer Grabhics; and Software Design.

Facilities
Most of the computing facilities on campus are available to Dartmouth computer-science students. The campus is extensively networked; all the computers mentioned below are tied together through Ethernet or fiber optic links. Every office and dorm room has network ports. The campus has a 60 Mbps connection to vBNS (Internet2), and Sudikoff lab has a gigabit fiber optic connection to the vBNS router on the edge of campus. The entire campus, indoor and outdoor, is covered by an 802.11b Wi-Fi wireless network. The Department of Computer Science is housed in the Sudikoff Laboratory, a modern building containing classrooms, seminar rooms, research laboratories, instructional laboratories, and offices for faculty and graduate students. Three instructional laboratories are accessible 24 hours a day to all graduate and undergraduate students of computer science. These labs provide access to 50 Linux workstations (regularly updated with new hardware - currently all running with 18inch LCD screens and 2.5ghz Pentium 4 processors) and 22 Macintoshes (Flatscreen iMacs running OS X). Each lab has a high-speed duplexing laser printer, and the Macintosh lab has a scanner. Graduate-student and faculty offices contain state-of-the-art computer workstations. Indeed, all graduate-student workstations were replaced in Winter 2003 to their choice of Linux, Windows XP, or MacOS X. Each office corridor has a high-speed duplexing PostScript printer, and there are several color printers for public use, one of which is a high quality solid ink printer. There are also six research laboratories and a machine room, which include equipment dedicated to specific research projects.

Student Body
More than 22,000 students attend the university.

Deadlines and Financial Aid
Federal and state aid, loans and scholarships are available to students. Graduate students may receive assistantships from the department.

Admission Requirements
Undergraduate students must submit an application and fee, high school transcripts, and SAT or ACT scores. Graduate students must submit an application and fee, transcripts, letters of recommendation and GRE scores.

Expenses
Tuition is $85 per credit hour for residents and $178.50 for non-residents.

Contact
Computer Science Department, 4505 S. Maryland Parkway, Las Vegas, NV 89154-5015. Telephone: 702-895-2206. Fax: 702-895-1672. Contact person: Hal Berghel, Director. Email: hlc@acm.org. URL: http://www.cs.unlv.edu/.

New Hampshire

Dartmouth College

F/X Degrees Offered
B.S., M.S. and Ph.D. in Computer Science.

Curricular
Courses are taught in Graphics and Multimedia.

Facilities
Department facilities--Hardware: instructional laboratories with 19 DEC Alphas, 17 SGIs, 20 Macintoshes, and other equipment. Research laboratory for robotics, multimedia, compression, parallel file systems, transportable agents, and signal processing. Software systems and languages: UNIX; VMS; C; C++; Pascal; Fortran; PL/I; Lisp; Macsyma; SPSS; SAS.

Student Body
There are 150 undergraduate, and 27 graduate students in the department. A total of 4,200 students attend the college.

Faculty Profile
Fourteen faculty members in the department.

Deadlines and Financial Aid
Graduate students may apply for the Dartmouth Fellowship that offers a stipend of $13,750. Assistantship application deadline: February 1.

Admission Requirements
Graduate students must submit an application and fee, transcripts and GRE score. Undergraduate students must submit an application and fee, transcript, and ACT or SAT score.

Expenses
Tuition is $27,600 per year.

Contact
Graduate Admissions Commissions Chair, Ph.D. Program in Computer Science, Department of Computer Science, Hanover, NH 03755-3510. Telephone: 603-646-2875. Fax: 603-646- 1216. E-mail: csphd@dartmouth.edu.
URL: http://www.cs.dartmouth.edu/.

New Jersey

Fairleigh Dickinson University

F/X Degrees Offered

Fine Arts Major (B.A.). The Department of Visual and Performing Arts offers four areas of concentration: Computer Graphics/Graphic Design; Electronic Filmmaking; Digital Video Design; and Theater Arts/Visual Arts.

Curricular

Computer Graphics; Video and Film Concepts; Computer Graphic Design; Computer Graphics in Communications. Electronic Filmmaking and Digital Video Design Concentration: This concentration offers three distinct tracks of study: A) Documentary and News; B) Corporate and Entrepreneurial; and C) Computer Science in Art. Tracks A and B stress the integration of video and graphic arts, such as 3D animation, video production and practices, non-linear post-production, paintbox technique, and scriptwriting. The program culminates in a senior project in Video Program Design. All courses offered build on foundations in the arts and humanities and on the general core curriculum. Track C requires the student to take a comprehensive Computer Science component: Introduction to Electronic Filmmaking; Video-Production Practices I; Video-Production Practices II; Post-Production Techniques I; 2D Design with the Computer; Scriptwriting for Video; Multimedia: Theory and Practice; 3D Animation; Video and Film Concepts.

Facilities

Lab facilities include 20 IBM NetVista PCs, printing via either laser printer or line printer, internet access, and use of university software (MS Office, Visual C++, Visual Basic, JAVA, etc.). Other facilities include: Avid Non-Linear Editing Systems; Electronic Paint Effects Systems; BetacamSP— Editing Suite; Sony U-Matic SP Editing Suite; S-VHS; VHS; Video Toaster. Camera: BetacamSP; Ikegami Studio Cameras; Sony 3/4-inch; S-VHS; VHS.

Student Body

A total of 10,000 students are enrolled in the university.

Deadlines and Financial Aid

The preferred filing date for fall applications is February 15; for the spring applicants, November 15. Applications continue to be processed on a rolling basis until the class is filled. Financial aid is available to qualified full-time and part-time students. New applicants for aid should file a Financial Aid Form (FAF) and a FAFSA with the College Scholarship Services (CSS). These forms should be filed preferably before March 15 for the fall semester. Financial aid awards are made annually and are based upon continued financial need, enrollment status, matriculation, availability of funds, satisfactory academic performance, and not being in default and/or not owing a refund on any Title IV and/or HEA loans and grants. Also, the university funds several types of specialized financial aid programs in addition to its large commitment to general need-based programs. Sixteen major forms of funding are available through the university.

Admission Requirements

First-time students must submit a completed application for undergraduate admission, application fee, either SAT or ACT scores, and an official copy of their high school transcript. Part-time students are encouraged, but not required, to submit SAT or ACT scores. The Department of Fine Arts requires a portfolio review for entrance into the B.A. program in Art that is separate from the general admissions procedure. All prospective students must arrange for a portfolio review with the department prior to being accepted into the program.

Expenses
Tuition is $382 per credit for undergraduate courses and $420 per credit for graduate courses.

Contact
Computers Science and Information Systems, Mail Stop T-BE2-01, 1000 River Road, Teaneck, NJ 07666. Telephone: 201-692-2261. Fax: 201-692-2560. E-mail: info@admit.fdu.edu.
URL: http://www.fdu.edu/.

Mercer County Community College

F/X Degrees Offered
Degree programs in Computer Graphics, Computer Science, and Visual Arts.

Curricular
3-D graphics and animation, multimedia and website design; also courses in film, video, or illustration.

Facilities
Most course work takes place in a studio using regularly updated professional-quality hardware and software on both Macintosh and PC computer platforms.

Student Body
There are 5,500 students enrolled. Many classes are seminars and small discussion groups.

Faculty Profile
Six faculty members teach at the Center for Advanced Digital Applications.

Deadlines and Financial Aid
The federal government, the State of New Jersey, and Mercer County Community College offer eligible students a range of financial aid opportunities. A student or applicant who needs financial aid should apply as early as possible even before completing an application for admission. Most student financial aid is provided in the form of grants through federal and state funded programs. This money is specifically awarded for education related expenses, including tuition, fees, books, and indirect costs such as living expenses and transportation. Eligibility depends upon financial need. Other grants are available through private scholarships and college sponsored grants-in-aid. The college administers only those scholarships and awards that comply with the Equality in Education mandates.

Admission Requirements
The college accepts applications throughout the year. Early application gives students the best chance for admission to a program of study and the best selection of courses. Each prospective student must complete an admissions application either online or mail in a printed form. Each student must arrange for high school transcripts (or GED scores), immunization records (for full-time students) and college transcripts to be sent to the Student Records office. The results of standardized tests the Scholastic Aptitude Test (SAT) or ACT Assessment are not required for admission, but SAT scores may be used for placement and should be sent.

Expenses
Tuition is $996 per semester for residents and $1,338 for non-residents.

Contact
West Windsor Campus, 1200 Old Trenton Road, West Windsor, NJ 08550. Telephone: 609- 586-4800.
URL: http://www.mccc.edu/.

New Jersey City University

F/X Degrees Offered
B.F.A. and M.F.A. in Art with a focus in Computer Graphics. B.A. in Art with a specialization in Communication Design, concentration in Design and Illustration.

Curricular
Visual Arts: Digital Imaging in Photography; Computer Graphics; Preparation of Art for Printing; Advertising Design; Typography/Desktop Publishing; Corporate Publication Design I and II; Electronic Illustration I and II; Presentation Graphics. Media Arts: Computer Graphics for Film and Video; Film Animation. Graduate: Computer Principles and Applications in the Visual Arts; 2D Computer Graphics; Electronic Drawing; Electronic Printing. The department offers courses in programming, programming language concepts, software engineering, computer architecture, artificial intelligence, operating systems, data base design, and microcomputer applications, as well as theoretical computer science. In addition, the department offers in-service undergraduate and graduate courses for elementary and secondary teachers.

Facilities
Macintoshes. All CPUs are equipped with access the campus Internet and Zip removable storage, CD-ROMs and 17-inch monitors; eight Wacom graphics tablets; four flatbed scanners including Agfa Arcus II w/transparency adapter; four laser printers all networked. Main Computer Laboratory Software: Photoshop; QuarkXPress; Illustrator; PageMaker; Painter; PageMill. Art Department Service Bureau: Cannon CLC500 Color Copier w/Fiery Interface for direct printing to 11x17, LaserMaster DisplayMaker Inkjet printer for direct digital printing to 36x72; Agfa SelectSet for direct digital film and paper output to 17x72. Related hardware and software for media production resides in the Media Department. Software includes: Inspiration 6; HyperStudio 4; Macromedia DreamWeaver 4; Adobe Acrobat Reader 5.0; Adobe Illustrator; Pcalc2; Graphing Calculator; PC (Dell) Software; Windows 2000; Office XP; Hyperstudio 4; and DreamWeaver 4.

Student Body
There are 350-375 students in the department, and 80-100 in Computer Graphics.

Faculty Profile
Four faculty members teach in the area of Computer Art and Animation.

Deadlines and Financial Aid
Academic scholarships, grants, loans and jobs. Students who wish to apply for financial aid are required to: enroll as a matriculated student in a degree-granting program, and take at least six credits each semester.

Admission Requirements
To be considered for any federal or state student financial aid programs, including student loans, students must first fill out the Free Application for Federal Student Aid (FAFSA). This form is used to determine your eligibility for all financial aid programs. There is no processing fee involved with this FAFSA application. Complete and submit the FAFSA as soon as possible after January 1 of the year you will be attending. In four to six weeks, you will receive a Student Aid Report (SAR) from the federal processing center. New Jersey City University will review your application for financial aid and offer you a financial aid package listing the different types of aid for which you may be eligible, including any University grants and scholarships. This financial aid package will be presented in the form of an Award Letter from our Office of Financial Aid. You will be sent this award letter when the application process is complete and you have been

admitted to the University. You will be required to return the award letter to the Office of Financial Aid to indicate whether you accept or decline the aid that is being offered. Each spring, as a community service, the University also offers a series of financial aid workshops to provide you with additional information and assistance with applying for financial aid. The priority filing deadline for the Free Application for Federal Student Aid (FAFSA), the prerequisite for any financial aid, is April 15.

Expenses
Tuition is $2,280 per semester for residents and $4,434 for non-residents.

Contact
Jersey City State College, 2039 Kennedy Blvd., Jersey City, NJ 07305-1597. Telephone: 201-200-2141 or 888-441-NJCD. Fax: 201-200-2294. Contact person: Dr. Charles Pratt,
Interim Director. Email: cpratt@njcu.edu.
URL: http://www.njcu.edu/.

Additional Information
Jersey City State College is located in the New York City metropolitan area, providing access to galleries, museums and cultural activities. Cooperative Education placements are a priority in all Art Department programs and provide internships in professional settings to prepare students for the world of work.

New Jersey Institute of Technology

F/X Degrees Offered
Undergraduate and graduate studio-based, NAAB-accredited professional degrees. M.S. in Architectural Studies. The department also offers a full range of degree programs in computer science (BA/BS, MS and PhD), in addition to emerging interdisciplinary graduate programs (Telecommunication and Biomedical Informatics).

Curricular
Animation; 2D Computer Animation; High- and Low-Level Programming; Digital Painting/Drawing; Image Processing; Digital Video; Computer-aided Architectural Design.

Facilities
CAD/graphics; 85 DOS/Windows Pentium computers; scanners; Inkjet plotter; thermal plotters; pen plotters; dye-sub printers; color Wax thermal printers; AutoCAD; Animator Pro; 3D Studio; MicroStation; MegaMODEL; I-Draw; upFront; Advanced Architect; PhotoFinish; Photoshop; PhotoStyler; Picture Publisher; Tempra Pro; Auto Architect; AccuRender; SGI workstations. Computer Science Department facilities--Hardware: three Sparc Center 2000 file servers; more than 100 workstations; PCs. Software systems and languages: Solaris 2.4 OS; C; C++; Pascal; Fortran; Lisp; Sybase; Ontos; Objectmaker; Oracle; Ingres; FrameMaker; Motif.

Student Body
There are 300 undergraduates and 50 graduate students in Architectural Studies; 496 undergraduate and 626 graduate students in the Computer Science Department.

Faculty Profile
There are 35 faculty members in the Computer Science Department.

Deadlines and Financial Aid
Graduate assistantships offer students a stipend of $12,000 per year. Admissions application deadline: November 1 for spring; June 5 for fall. Assistantship application deadline: Sept. 1 for spring; February 1 for fall.

Admission Requirements

Students are advised to contact the department of interest for details on the application process. Graduate students are required to submit an application and fee, transcripts and GRE scores.

Expenses

Tuition is $7,332 per year for residents and $12,700 per year for non-residents.

Contact

NJIT, Department of Computer and Information Science, University Heights, Newark, NJ 07102. Telephone: 973-596-3366. Fax: 973-596-5777. Contact person: Joseph Leung, Chairman. E-mail: leung@cis.njit.edu.
URL: http://www.cis.njit.edu/.

Princeton University

F/X Degrees Offered

B.S., M.S. and Ph.D. in the Computer Science Department. Students may also apply to the Program in Applications of Computing.

Curricular

Courses in Computer Graphics, Simulation, and Advanced Scientific Visualization.

Facilities

Department facilities--Hardware: 25 SGI workstations; 30 DEC Alphas; 90 terminals; Intel Hypercube; 10 Sun Sparcs; two Sun 3s; Auspex; 12 HP workstations; PCs; Macintoshes; four NeXT workstations; laser printers; Ethernet language. Software systems and languages: several UNIX formatters and editors; C; C++; Mathematica; Pascal; Prolog; ML; PostScript; Eiffel; Modula2; Scheme; GNU; OSF; IRIX; Ultrix; HPUX; SunOS; Solaris. University facilities--Hardware: SGI workstations; large IBM facility; Sun workstations; Macintoshes; Supercomputer access. Software systems and languages: UNIX; CMS.

Student Body

There are 80 undergraduate and 40 graduate students in the department.

Faculty Profile

Eighteen faculty members teach in the department.

Deadlines and Financial Aid

A financial resources statement is included in each application packet. All Ph.D. candidates are considered for university financial awards consisting of tuition plus a monthly stipend for the 10-month academic year. Summer support is determined separately. Financial support for students is reviewed each year. Graduate students may apply for a research or teaching assistantships. Assistantship stipends range from $12,000-$15,000 per year. Admissions application deadline: circa Jan. 3 for the fall semester. Assistantship application deadline: circa Jan. 3 for the fall semester.

Admission Requirements

Graduate applicants to the Science Department must submit an application and fee, transcripts, GRE scores and letters of recommendation. Students should contact the Graduate School for details on the admission requirements. Undergraduate students should contact the Undergraduate Admissions Office for information on the undergraduate program.

Expenses

Tuition and fees are $28,549 per year.

Contact

Director of Graduate Studies, Department of Computer Science, 35 Olden St., Princeton, NJ 08544. Telephone: 609-258-5030. Fax: 609-258-1771. E-mail: info@cs.princeton.edu.
URL: http://www.cs.princeton.edu/.

Additional Information

The Computer Science major at Ramapo is based on the philosophy that true learning occurs through active participation. This notion is incorporated throughout the curriculum. For example, almost all the courses require programming projects that illustrate and expand the course content. Before completing the major, each student must design and implement a significant piece of software as their senior project. Additionally, Computer Science students are encouraged to participate in one of the many experiential learning opportunities available through off-campus internships.

Ramapo College of New Jersey

F/X Degrees Offered

The school of Media Arts through Contemporary Arts offers a program of theory and practice courses in video, audio, writing, computer art, photography, film, sculpture, painting, graphics, music and theater.

Curricular

Computer Graphics courses and video production.

Facilities

SGI computer system; BetacamSP video decks and editing system, and film.

Student Body

Total enrollment of 4,700 students.

Faculty Profile

Ramapo College has 286 full- and part-time faculty members. The faculty is composed of working artists, writers, producers, composers and performers.

Admission Requirements

Students applying from high school must take the SAT of the College Board or the ACT examination of American College Testing and have test scores sent to Ramapo. Applying for admission as a matriculating student involves completing an application, having the high school and college (if a transfer student) forward transcripts, and sending a non-refundable fee to the admissions office. Students may obtain the forms and instructions by visiting or contacting the admissions office.

Deadlines and Financial Aid

Students may enter in September or January. Freshmen are encouraged to apply during the fall of their senior year. Applications for the freshman year are accepted until May 1. There are three forms of student financial aid for which application can be made: grants, loans and work/study payments. The package offered to a student is determined by financial need and college year. Students must first fill out the FAFSA, available from guidance counselors, before being considered for financial aid.

Expenses

Tuition is $3,705.60 per semester for residents and $4,762.40 per semester for non-residents.

Contact

Director of Admissions, Ramapo College of New Jersey, 505 Ramapo Valley Rd., Mahwah, NJ 07430. Telephone: 201-684-7500 or 201-684-7712. Fax: 201-684-7919. Contact person: Amruth N. Kumar. Email: amruth@ramapo.edu.
URL: http://www.ramapo.edu/.

Raritan Valley Community College

F/X Degrees Offered
A.A., with Studio Arts option; Commercial Art with a Computer Art option.

Curricular
Courses in Computer Graphics I and II; 2D Design; Computer Animation; Computer as an Art Tool; Web Design for the Graphic Artist; Digital Photography

Facilities
Eighteen PC workstations; laser printer; Kodak color printer; color copier and color scanners. Facilities also include: Networked PENTIUM Labs; Direct Internet/WWW Connection Through T1 Line; DVR & CDR (ability to create DVD & CD-ROM presentations); Audio/Video Capture; Web Page Development Software; and Network Labs (Windows 2000, UNIX, LINUX, Cisco Academy Router & Switch Lab). Arrangements can be made if specialized software is needed.

Student Body
There are 500 students in the Department of Art; 150 students in the Computer Graphics area.

Faculty Profile
Two full-time and six part-time faculty.

Deadlines and Financial Aid
Rolling admissions.

Admission Requirements
Open admission.

Expenses
Tuition is $1,034 per semester.

Contact
P.O. Box 3300, Somerville, NJ 08876-1265. Telephone: 908-218-8878. Fax: 908-595-0213. Contact person: Thomas Edmunds, Chair. E-mail: tedmunds@rarita nval.edu.
URL: http://www.raritanval.edu/.

Rutgers University, Camden

F/X Degrees Offered
B.A. in Art. B.A. and B.S. in Computer Science.

Curricular
Courses in Computer Animation; Computer Art; Computer Graphics Internship; Graphic Design; Desktop Publishing.

Facilities
Amigas; SGIs; Maya; Macintoshes; Wacom tablets; Sun workstations; slide scanner; polaroid slide maker.

Student Body
There are 2,600 undergraduate students attending the university.

Deadlines and Financial Aid
All students interested in applying for financial aid must submit a FAFSA. This form should be mailed no later than March 1 prior to the academic year for which aid is sought. Funds are available from a variety of sources for scholarship awards and grants, including university-endowed scholarships, federal and state grants.

Admission Requirements
Candidates are expected to have completed a minimum of 16 units of secondary school work that should include 4 units of English, 3 units of college preparatory mathematics, 2 units of a foreign language, and 7 additional units in some combination of foreign languages, history, social sciences or sciences. Candidates who have not completed the distribution units may also be

admitted by demonstrating proficiency in the subject matter. Students applying for the Visual Arts program must attend a portfolio review day. At this time, students submit a portfolio containing a minimum of 20 recent examples of work in whatever range of media is appropriate to personal interests and abilities. Out of state applicants may mail in a portfolio and $50 application fee.

Expenses
Tuition is $6,290 per year for residents and $12,804 for non-residents.

Contact
University College Office of Student Services, 311 N. Fifth Ave., Camden, NJ 08102. Telephone: 856-225-6077. Fax: 856-225-6498. Contact person: Jean-Camille Birget, Chair. Email: birget@camden.rutgers.edu.
URL: http://cs.camden.rutgers.edu/.

Rutgers University, New Brunswick

F/X Degrees Offered
B.A. and B.F.A. in Computer Art, Film and Video.

Curricular
Film as a Visual Art; Video, Art and Politics; Introduction to Computer Animation; Introduction to Computer Art; Film I, II; Video I, II, III; Computer Animation; Graphic Design I-III.

Facilities
The Rutgers high performance computing facility consists of two (2) interconnected 64 processor Sun Microsystems HPC-10000 systems in the facility, located side by side in CoRE 635. Also dubbed as Starfire, E10k, and E10000, they represent Sun's high-end multi-processor servers. The Rutgers configuration is the HPC-10000, which consists of

an Enterprise 10000 platform with the Sun HPC software installed. Total list price for the two systems is approximately $7 million dollars, although Sun made considerable contributions to the project including the donation of one system at no cost.

Student Body
There are 659 students attend the School of Arts.

Faculty Profile
Twenty-three faculty members in the Department of Visual Arts. Two full-time faculty teach CG courses.

Deadlines and Financial Aid
All students interested in applying for financial aid must submit a FAFSA. This form should be mailed no later than March 1 prior to the academic year for which aid is sought. Funds are available from a variety of sources for scholarship awards and grants, including university-endowed scholarships, federal and state grants.

Admission Requirements
Candidates are expected to have completed a minimum of 16 units of secondary school work that should include 4 units of English, 3 units of college preparatory mathematics, 2 units of a foreign language, and 7 additional units in some combination of foreign languages, history, social sciences or sciences. Candidates who have not completed the distribution units may also be admitted, by demonstrating proficiency in the subject matter. Students applying for the Visual Arts program must attend a portfolio review day. At this time, students submit a portfolio containing a minimum of 20 recent examples of work in whatever range of media is appropriate to personal interests and abilities. Out-of-state applicants may mail in a portfolio.

Expenses
Tuition is $6,290 per year for residents and $12,804 for non-residents.

Contact

Department of Computer Science, Rutgers University, 110 Frelinghuysen Road, Piscataway, NJ 08854-8019. Telephone: 732-932-INFO or 732-445-4176. Fax: 732-445-0237. Contact person: Dr. Haym Hirsh, Chair.
URL: http://www.rutgers.edu/.

William Paterson University of New Jersey

F/X Degrees Offered

B.A., B.F.A. and M.F.A. in Visual Arts with a concentration in Computer Art and Animation; B.A. and B.F.A in Graphic Design. B.A. and M.A. in Communication Arts.

Curricular

Visual Arts: Beginning to Advanced 2D Computer Art; Computer Art and Design; Introduction to 3D Computer Modeling; Advanced Computer Art and Animation; Advanced 3D Computer Modeling; Traditional Animation Techniques; Web Design and various Graphic Design courses. Communication Arts: Production Experiences; Film Production.

Facilitles

SGI, Macintosh and PC computer systems. Accom WSD workstation disk: Desktop real-time digital disk; recorder; 32 seconds of uncompressed storage; full-motion preview on workstation monitor; one BetacamSP video deck; three 3/4-inch video decks; two one-half video decks; one laser disk player; one audio tape deck player/recorder. A fully equipped Macintosh laboratory with 15 workstations, 17-inch monitors; Zip drives; Wacom drawing tablets. The laboratory has high-end color scanners, T1 network access to the Web, large format b/w printers, color laser and dye-sub printers. Software includes current versions of Macromedia Director; Sound Edit Pro;

Photoshop; Xres; Illustrator; Freehand; Dimensions; Extreme 3D; QuarkXPress; PageMaker; PageMill; Poser; Bryce, Maya, 3D Studio Max and others.

Student Body

More than 200 undergraduates in the Department of Art; 50 students in Computer Art and Animation program.

Faculty Profile

Four faculty members teach in the area of Computer Art and Animation.

Deadlines and Financial Aid

Students who wish to apply for financial aid are required to file the FAFSA with a need analysis servicer. This application should be filed by the April 1 priority deadline date for aid consideration for the subsequent year. Prospective graduate students may also apply for a graduate assistantship.

Admission Requirements

Undergraduates: must submit an application and fee, transcripts, SAT or ACT, and portfolio review. Graduate students: completed application form, prior to the closing date, to the Graduate Office. Applications are available from the Graduate Office; include with the application a fee payable to William Paterson University. Arrange to have official transcripts of all previous college work forwarded to the Graduate Office. Official transcripts should include evidence of a bachelor's and/or master's degree. Candidates must meet the following requirements: A bachelor's and/or master's degree awarded by an accredited college or university; an acceptable undergraduate cumulative GPA (see appropriate program for specific requirements), an acceptable score on the GRE, MAT or GMAT, and recommendations from two people chosen by the applicant.

Expenses
Tuition is $7,120 per year for residents and $11,352 for non-residents.

Contact
Department of Art, College of Art and Communications, William Paterson University, Wayne, NJ 07470. Telephone: 973-720-2404. Fax: 973-720-3273. Contact person: Russell Pensyl. pensylw@wpunj.edu.
URL: http://www.wpunj.edu/.

Additional Information
The school's proximity to New York City allows students easy access to its fine art galleries.

New Mexico

Highlands University

F/X Degrees Offered
The design studies program at New Mexico Highlands University is a four-year professional B.F.A. and B.A. degree program with an emphasis on the use of the computer as the primary design tool. Master of Science and Master of Arts Program in Media Arts and Computer Science (MACS); Master of Science or Master of Arts. This concentration area focuses on the skills required to do graphics programming. Students will be exposed to the programming language C++, software design and engineering principles, and the use of advanced graphics development tools. Design Studies (Master of Arts).

Curricular
At the undergraduate level, students in the program are taught traditional as well as computer-based design techniques, production methods and tools. The design courses are not restricted to conventional print media and may include experiences in areas such as display and exhibition systems, packaging design, signing or interactive multimedia communications systems. In addition to this program, many students take courses and earn a minor in fine arts, mass communication or other areas of interest to them. Basic Drawing; Fund. of Design; Intro. Electic Image; Electronic Paint; Design 380; Design History; Photography; Multimedia Design; Electronic Photo; Independent Study; Desktop Pub.; Video Graphics; Video Effects; Video Animation; Adv. Video Anim.; Scriptwriting; UNIX and Systems Adm.; Most of these courses are also offered at the graduate level. The following are offered exclusively at the graduate level: Principles of Media Arts and Computer Science; Seminar in Media Arts and Computer Science; Lighting Stage and Screen; Multimedia Presentations; Screen Writing; Video Animation; Special Topics; Introduction to Computer Graphics; Principles of Media Arts and Computer Science; Computer Science/MasCom/Design Computer Graphics Digital Audio and Video Production (Master of Arts). Students will become familiar with the computer-based production tools for audio and video, which may be used by themselves or integrated into a multimedia environment. They must choose four courses from the following list: Cinematography and Lighting; Non-Linear Audio/Video Editing; Screen Writing; 3D Video Animation. Design Studies (Master of Arts): Students in this concentration are provided opportunities for developing new and advancing existing design and artistic skills to meet the increasingly technical requirements of the visual communications industry professions. They will take four of the following courses: Advanced Visual Communications; Multimedia Design; Advanced Electronic Paint; Graphics for the Internet; Advanced Electronic Photography; Exhibition.

Facilities

The Computer Science Department currently has three main computer labs where a variety of systems and software are available. The main lab is located in the lecture hall and consists of twenty-five machines (mostly Gateway Pentiums), a multimedia projection system, and a suite of software from word processing to programming for class instruction. The Unix lab in Science 103 contains an HP-UX server, a handfull of HP workstations, two Sun Sparc Stations, and a Pentium running Linux. The Advanced CS Lab, known as the Dino Lab due to the names of the machines, is designed for upper division study. The machines there have development and experimental software installed for student use. Various operating systems are available at different times for study, including Windows 95, NT, OS/2, Linux, NextSTEP, and Sco Unix, and the Dino Lab houses the CS Department's Web server, Tricera.

Deadlines and Financial Aid

Financial aid for Media Arts and Computer Science Graduate Students: Computer Science Department-based Financial Assistance: assistantships--graduate research assistantships are available for students with concentrations in Networking Technology, Computer Graphics and Cognitive Science. Most assistantships are offered at the 75 percent level (a $4,500 stipend plus a full tuition waiver for 15 hours of work per week). Digital Audio and Video Production and Design Studies-based Financial Assistance. It is anticipated that assistantships will also be available for the Digital Audio and Video Production and Design Studies concentrations.

Admission Requirements

The University Graduate Catalog describes the general graduate admission requirements. To be accepted into the graduate program in Media Arts and Computer Science a student must: 1. have a bachelor's degree in an area related to one of the three disciplines involved in this program, or a bachelor's degree in some unrelated area AND extensive work experience in an area related to one of the three discipline areas. 2. have a Bachelor of Science degree or have a strong mathematics background including Calculus and either Discrete Mathematics or Linear Algebra to be accepted into the Master of Science track. 3. have a 3.2 GPA in their major. 4. have the Graduate Record Exam (GRE) General Test. (This is being re-evaluated in light of nation-wide problems with the GRE. Please check with a program advisor.) 5. submit a portfolio demonstrating their knowledge and accomplishments to be used as part of an evaluation of the depth and breadth of their undergraduate education and work experience. Students should contact an advisor in the area of concentration they wish to pursue to discuss the type of portfolio expected for that concentration area.

Faculty Profile

Six full-time faculty teach in the Master of Science and Master of Arts Program in Media Arts and Computer Science (MACS).

Expenses

Tuition is $1,092 per year for residents and $4,548 for non-residents.

Contact Information

Design Studies Program, New Mexico Highlands University, Las Vegas, NM 87701. Telephone: 505-454-3439 or 800-338-NMHU. Fax: 505-454-3511. URL: http://cs.nmhu.edu/labs/.

Additional Information

The disciplines of Computer Science and Communications Arts are seeing a significant convergence of interests. Computer Science, with its interest in exploring and developing new programming paradigms, user interfaces, computer networking models, and multimedia-based technologies, is constantly offering new forms of human communication. The communication arts professions, including graphics design, broadcasting, as well as video and audio production, have always sought new and more effective ways to express ideas, concepts and visions. Thus, they have a natural interest in the possibilities offered by the technologies coming out of Computer Science. It seems natural, then, for the Departments of Communication and Fine Arts and Computer Science to provide a program in Media Arts and Computer Science that, depending on one's area of concentration and background, leads to either a Master of Science degree or a Master of Arts degree.

University of New Mexico at Albuquerque

F/X Degrees Offered
The Computer Science Department offers B.S. (CSAB accredited), M.S. and Ph.D. programs. Departmental strengths include Computer Graphics and Visualization, Human Computer Interfaces, Complex Systems, and High-Performance Computing.

Curricular
3D Modeling and Rendering; High-Level Programming; Low-Level Programming; Image Processing; Virtual Reality; Volume Visualization; Human Computer Interfaces.

Facilities
UNIX workstations (SGI, Sun, IBM, DEC) and X-terminals. Most students program in C; C++; Scheme or Lisp. Graphics software includes: OpenGL; Open Inventor; Explorer; Khoros; Wavefront; PHIGS and Renderman.

Student Body
There are 200 undergraduates and 125 graduate students in the department.

Faculty Profile
Fifteen faculty are in the department.

Deadlines and Financial Aid
The department currently supports approximately 50 research and teaching assistants. Additional opportunities exist for cooperative work with the local National Laboratories (Sandia and Los Alamos) and the Maui High-Performance Computing Center, of which UNM is the prime contractor.

Admission Requirements
Undergraduate students must submit a completed application with the non-refundable application fee, official high school transcript with rank-in-class (and courses in progress if not yet graduated), or official GED scores, and official ACT or SAT scores. Graduate students must submit an application and fee, GRE scores and transcripts.

Expenses
Tuition is $1,513 per semester for residents and $5,712 for out-of-state residents.

Contact
Office of Admissions, Student Services Center 150, Albuquerque, NM 87131. Telephone: 505-277-2446 or 800-CALL UNM. Fax: 505-277-6686. Contact person: Ed Angel. E-mail: angel@cs.unm.edu. URL:http://www.unm.edu/.

New York

Alfred State College

F/X Degrees Offered
Two years A.A. in Engineering Technology. A.A. in Computer Art and Design.

Curricular
3D Modeling and Rendering; High-Level Programming; Solids and Parameters.

Facilities
Six Computervision CADDs 4x and 8 Sun Computervision CADDs 5.

Student Body
There are 50 undergraduate students.

Deadlines and Financial Aid
Students who wish to apply for financial aid must file FAFSA. Among the other forms of financial aid available are SEOG grants, Federal Perkins Loans, Federal Stafford (GSL) Loans, and Federal College Work-Study Program awards.

Admission Requirements
Application and fee, transcript, and SAT or ACT score.

Expenses
Tuition is $138.95 per credit hour.

Contact
Alfred State College, 10 Upper College Dr., Alfred, NY 14802. Telephone: 607-587-4630. Fax: 607-587-4620. Contact person: Jim Woughter. E-mail: WOUGHTJR @SNYAlFVA.cc.alfredtech.edu. URL: http://www.alfredstate.edu/.

City College of New York

F/X Degrees Offered
B.A. and B.F.A. Electronic Design and Multimedia.

Curricular
Computer Imaging and Illustration; Multimedia Design; Electronic Design; Design and Multimedia Portfolio; Design for the World Wide Web; 3D Imaging; Digital Video.

Facilities
Macintosh workstations in a graphics laboratory environment. The Atrium and Wolfe Computer Labs and classrooms at Brooklyn College are the largest and most accessible in CUNY and are open 7 days a week, up to 15 hours each weekday. The labs have several software operating environments and applications, and provide adaptive technology devices for students with disabilities.

Student Body
Two full-time faculty and eight part-time faculty.

Student Body
Student-teacher ratio is 15:1.

Deadlines and Financial Aid
Financial assistance is available for eligible City College students through state and federal programs. Students wishing to apply for financial aid must file the FAFSA. Other forms of financial aid available are Federal Supplemental Educational Opportunity Grants (SEOG), Federal Perkins Loans, Federal Stafford Loans (GSL), and Federal College Work-Study Program awards. The City College Fellowship, sponsored by the Ford Foundation, offers $2,000 per year for undergraduate study plus additional academic and financial support through graduate study.

Admission Requirements
Application and fee, transcripts, and SAT or GED.

Expenses

Tuition is $125 per credit hour for residents and $275 per hour for non-residents.

Contact

Department of Art, Compton-Goelhals Hall, 253, The City College of New York, 138th St. and Convent Ave., New York, NY 10031. Telephone: 212-650-7410. Contact person: Prof. Annette Weintraub. URL:http://www.cuny.edu/.

City University of New York-College of Staten Island

F/X Degrees Offered

B.S. in Computer Science with a focus in Advanced Visualization.

Curricular

Fundamentals of Computer Graphics; special topics in Computer Graphics and Visualization.

Facilities

SGI and Sun UNIX workstations; scanners; video capture; digital cameras; video recording equipment. Macintosh workstations in a graphics laboratory environment. The Atrium and Wolfe Computer Labs and classrooms at Brooklyn College are the largest and most accessible in CUNY and are open 7 days a week, up to 15 hours each weekday. The labs have several software operating environments and applications, and provide adaptive technology devices for students with disabilities.

Student Body

There are 450 students in the department.

Faculty Profile

Four faculty members teach Computer Graphics courses.

Deadlines and Financial Aid

The Office of Student Financial Aid administers federal, state and college-funded aid programs. Students should get in touch with the Office of Student Financial Assistance early in the admissions process to discuss eligibility requirements and responsibilities, and to obtain forms and up-to-date information on the various aid programs. Deadline is June 1 for the fall semester.

Admission Requirements

Application and fee, transcript and three letters of reference.

Expenses

Tuition is $125 per credit hour for residents and $275 per hour for non-residents.

Contact

College of Staten Island, 2800 Victory Blvd., Computer Science 1 N-215, Staten Island, NY 10314. Telephone: 718-982-2850. Contact person: Prof. Emile Chie.
URL: http://www.cuny.edu/.

Columbia University

F/X Degrees Offered

B.A., B.S., M.S. and Ph.D. in Computer Science.

Curricular

3D Modeling and Rendering; 3D Computer Animation; Multimedia/Interactive; High-Level Programming; Image Processing; Virtual Reality; Stereo Imaging; 3D User Interfaces; Knowledge-Based Graphics. Computer Graphics; Computational Techniques in Pixel Processing; Synthetic 3D Imaging; Computer Vision; Projects in Computer Science.

Facilities

Hundreds of HP, Sun and SGI workstations, X-terminals and Macintoshes are available as part of the academic computing facilities of Columbia University, the Engineering School and the Department of Computer Science. Graphics software ranges from professional systems, such as Maya, to teaching packages, such as SRGP and SPHIGS. Computer Graphics and User Interfaces Laboratory: 3D graphics workstations (SGI Maximum Impact; Sun Ultra Sparc Creator 3D; HP 735 CRX48Z); PCs (Pentium machines and Macintoshes; assorted 3D boards); 3D interaction devices (Digital Image Design Cricket; VPL DataGlove; Logitech 3D mice); 3D tracking systems (Ascension extended range Flock of Birds; Logitech ultrasonic trackers; Origin Instruments Dynasight optical radar trackers; Trimble DSM differential GPS receiver); 3D displays (StereoGraphics Crys-talEyes stereo eye wear; Electrohomem Marquee 100-inch diagonal rear-projection stereo display; locally-built and Virtual I/O see-through head-mounted displays); and 3D audio (Crystal River Beachtron sound processor). Students also have shared access to a four-processor SGI Onyx with Reality Engine 2; an 8-processor HP 9000/735 cluster with FDDI interconnect; and an Avid Media Composer. Software in use includes OpenGL; OpenInventor; Renderware; Photoshop and many locally developed systems.

Student Body

Thirty undergraduates and 60 graduate students in the department.

Faculty Profile

Twenty full-time faculty members in the department.

Deadlines and Financial Aid

Students and applicants for any of the Federal Student Aid Programs offered by the university must submit the FAFSA to the Federal Student Aid Programs' Processing Center no later than February 15th. Contact the office at 800-433-3243 for more information. Various forms of grants, loans, scholarships and research assistantships are available.

Admission Requirements

Application and fee, SAT or ACT, and transcripts for undergraduate admission. Graduate applicants must submit additional GRE scores.

Expenses

Tuition is $904 per credit hour.

Contact

500 W. 120th St., 450 CS Building, New York, NY 10027. Telephone: 212-939-7000. Fax: 212-666-0140. Contact person: Prof. Steven Feiner. E-mail: feiner@cs.columbia.edu. URL: http://www.columbia.edu/.

Additional Information

The Computer Graphics and User Interfaces Laboratory within the department has as it's goal the exploratory design and development of high-quality user interfaces. Research emphasizes virtual environments, created through the use of 3D interaction and display devices (including augmented reality, in which see-through displays overlay graphics on the real world), and the application of artificial intelligence techniques to design effective graphics and multimedia presentations. The university has active collaborations with the Natural Language Processing Laboratory, the Mobile Computing Laboratory, the Building Technologies Laboratory (in the Graduate School of Architecture), and the Center for Medical Informatics (in the School of Medicine).

Cornell University

F/X Degrees Offered
B.S., M.Eng. and Ph.D. in Computer Science; College of Engineering Arts and Sciences.

Curricular
Various software allows for research in the areas of Advanced Computer Graphics and Animation; Advanced Scientific Visualization; Networking; Distributed Systems; Artificial Intelligence; Software Engineering; Human Language Systems; and Human-Computer Interaction.

Facilities
The SimLab brings together technologies such as geometric modeling, symbolic mathematics, numerical analysis, compilation/code generation, and formal methods to create tools that raise the semantic level at which it is possible to create scientific software. The CS undergraduate laboratory currently features 50 Intel PCs equipped with Pentium processors operating under an NT-network and OS. In addition the laboratory contains approximately 40 HP and Sun workstations. All CS majors are given a special CS laboratory account upon acceptance to the major. Cornell Theory Center: the CTC supports a range of graphics facilities and software for both local and remote users. Interactive devices include SGI workstations and Macintoshes. Hard-copy devices include videotape production, 35 mm slides and color printers. Workstation graphics software includes: DataExplorer, Maya and RenderMan, plus other utilities.

Student Body
Approximately 4,000 undergraduates and 1,500 graduate students are majors in the College of Arts and Sciences at Cornell University.

Faculty Profile
Thirty-two faculty members in the Computer Science Department.

Deadlines and Financial Aid
The application deadline is November 1, for spring admission, and May 1 for fall admission. Most M.Eng. students are self-funded or have obtained their own corporate support. Every year the Engineering College gives three full-tuition fellowships (open to all M.Eng. students) plus one fellowship that covers approximately one quarter of the tuition for a Cornell graduate going into the C.S. M.Eng. program. Prospective students interested in financial aid must apply to the program by March 1. Top applicants should consider submitting extra letters of recommendation to improve fellowship chances. The department also awards a few (paid) teaching assistantships in which students perform various duties that aid faculty in the teaching of Cornell CS courses. If considering a teaching assistantship, indicate when applying as well as any pertinent experience.

Admission Requirements
Graduate students must submit: a completed application form and the application fee, two letters of recommendation, an official transcript of undergraduate degree, a statement of purpose and GRE official test results.

Expenses
Tuition is $27,270 per year.

Contact
Undergraduates: Office: 4148 Upson Hall, Cornell University, Ithaca, NY 14853-7501. Telephone: 607-255-5418. Fax: 607-255-4428. Contact person: Charles Van Loan, Director. E-mail: cv@cs.cornell.edu.
URL: http://www.cornell.edu/.

Fashion Institute of Technology

F/X Degrees Offered

B.F.A. in Illustration, Toy Design, Graphic Design and Interior Design. A.A.S. in Photography, Illustration and Graphic Design. B.F.A. in Computer Animation and Interactive Media.

Curricular

Computer-Assisted Design; Introduction to 3D Modeling; 3D Computer Image Generation; Independent Study in Computer Graphics; Advanced 2D Computer Animation; Advanced 3D Computer Animation; 3D Computer Animation Production; Introduction to Film Animation; Film Animation II, and various other computer graphics-based courses are offered.

Facilities

FIT has 23 computer labs housing over 500 PC workstations and over 200 Mac workstations along with printers, color printers, and scanners. Many departments have their own computer labs where students learn technology specific to their major. In the Peter G. Scotese Computer-Aided Design and Communications Center, for instance, you'll see the kind of state-of-the-art computer facilities FIT students use as they explore technology's applications to the design of textiles, toys, interiors, fashion, advertising, photography, packaging, jewelry, and much more. There are computers, printers, and copiers on all three floors of the library, as well. Primarily used for locating and using information from the Internet, CD-ROMs, and other specialized resources to which the Library subscribes, they are also available to aid students in their classwork.

Student Body

There are 350 students attending computer graphics studio classes.

Faculty Profile

Twelve faculty members teach in the Computer Graphics Program.

Deadlines and Financial Aid

Students should complete applications by Oct. 15 for the spring semester, or by Jan. 15 for the fall semester. F.I.T. directly administers its own institutional grants and scholarships, which are provided by the Educational Foundation for the Fashion Industries. Federal funding administered by the college may include Federal Supplemental Education Grants and Federal Perkins Loans (formerly National Direct Student Loans), as well as the Federal College Work-Study program. New York State residents who meet state guidelines for eligibility may also receive Educational Opportunity Program funds through F.I.T. Students seeking financial assistance should file the appropriate forms, available in the Financial Aid Office, designating F.I.T. as a college choice. The forms must be filed by March 15 for the fall semester and November 15 for the spring semester. Tuition Assistance Program for New York State Residents: New York State residents should apply for TAP, and may receive a grant of as much as the full tuition. A student must be registered for at least 12 credits at the time of TAP certification. Three factors are involved: 1) academic progress in the previous semester; 2) program pursuit in the previous semester; 3) a minimum of 12 credits in the current semester.

Admission Requirements

Application, transcripts, SAT/ACT, standardized test scores. Artwork evaluation: the annual Portfolio Day, for applicants whose applications have been received by F.I.T. before Jan. 1, is the second Saturday in February.

Expenses
Tuition is $1,450-$5,150 per year.

Contact
Director of Admissions, Fashion Institute of Technology, Seventh Ave. at W. 27th St., New York City, NY 10001-5992. Telephone: 212-217-7938 or 800-468-6348. Fax: 212-217-7160. Contact person: Prof. Leslie Blum.
URL: http://www.fitnyc.edu/.

Long Island University-C.W. Post Campus

F/X Degrees Offered
B.F.A. in Art with a focus in Computer Graphics; M.A. in Interactive Multimedia through the Art Department. B.F.A. in Film through the Film Department.

Curricular
Digital Layout; Digital Illustration; Motion Graphics I; Digital Imaging; 3D Modeling; Desktop Video; Advanced Digital Illustration; Motion Graphics II; Digital Imaging Synthesis; Multimedia on the Internet.

Facilities
The campus supports 25 campus-wide labs for student use with more than 525 computers. These labs offer free LaserJet printing services and a wide range of software. All dormitory rooms are connected to the network with more than 1,000 computers currently in use. There are approximately 5,000 ports available with more than 1,700 computers for staff and faculty. Every member of the campus community has an account on the university-wide integrated E-mail system with a web interface. Students have the ability to access their grades, registration, financial aid, account status, class schedules, and job bank listings through the Student Information System (SIS). Most classrooms are wired with at least two network connections for faculty, staff and student access. Twenty-seven smart classrooms connected to the Internet include a high-resolution projection overhead digital projector and screen. Four classrooms are equipped with projection units and a network connection at every seat. Other equipment includes: Macintosh workstations; one Video Toaster; 14 Amiga computers; three laser printers; one Dye-sub printer; two Epson color printers. Software programs include the latest versions of Adobe Illustrator; Premiere; Photoshop; QuarkXPress; Strata Studio Pro; and Macromedia Director programs. Systems provide students with access to the Internet and e-mail.

Student Body
There are 200 students in the Art Department, and 30 undergraduates in the Computer Art area.

Faculty Profile
Seven faculty teach Computer Graphics courses in the department.

Deadlines and Financial Aid
Rolling admissions. Scholarship deadlines: summer and fall semesters is March 1; spring semester deadline is October for freshmen students. Deadline for transfer students is July 1 for the summer and spring semesters, and Oct. 1 for the spring semester. Students seeking financial aid must file a FAFSA and CSS/ Financial Aid Profile annually by the dates mentioned.

Admission Requirements
Application and fee, high school transcript, and SAT or ACT scores. Transfer students must submit transcripts from all former colleges.

Expenses

Tuition is $19,510 per year.

Contact

Art Department, Long Island University-CW Post, 720 Northern Blvd., Brookville, NY 11548. Telephone: 516-299-2000. Fax: 516-299-3829. Contact person: Prof. John Fekner. Email: jfekner@liu.edu. URL: http://www.cwpost.liu.edu/cwis/cwp/.

New York Institute of Technology

F/X Degrees Offered

M.A. in Communication Arts with a concentration in Film and Video; Animation; Multimedia Technology. B.F.A. in Fine Arts and Communication Arts.

Curricular

Courses are taught in UNIX Animation 1-3; Multimedia Production; Web Page Design; Internet Uses; Art and Design 1-3; Cartooning; Modeling and Rendering 2D and 3D; Computer Graphics and Animation; C Programming.

Facilities

Two SGI laboratories; two Macintosh laboratories; Accoms; scanners; printers; Softimage; Maya. Software: QuarkXPress; Illustrator; Photoshop; Director. The school has many of the newest software titles including Adobe AfterEffects, Alias, Dreamweaver, and more.

Student Body

There are 200 graduate students in the area of Computer Graphics; 200 Fine Arts students in Computer Graphics.

Faculty Profile

Eight faculty members teach in the area of Computer Graphics.

Deadlines and Financial Aid

Fellowships are available on the basis of need and academic achievement. Applications are accepted through Aug. 31 of each year. Financial aid programs of scholarships, grants-in-aid, loans and employment are drawn from college, state and federal funds. Awards are designed to recognize scholastic achievement, financial need, character and promise of the applicant, competence in a particular field, or distinctive contributions to the college or the community.

Admission Requirements

An undergraduate applicant must submit an application and fee, SAT or ACT, and transcript. Graduate students must submit a portfolio, application and fee, transcript, 3.0 GPA, and GRE score.

Expenses

Tuition is $8,463 per semester.

Contact

Communication Arts, NYIT, 1855 Broadway, New York, NY 10023. Telephone: 212-261-1576. Fax: 212-977-3460. URL: http://www.nyit.edu/.

New York University The Center for Advanced Digital Applications

F/X Degrees Offered

M.S. in Digital Imaging and Design; Certificate programs.

Curricular

3-D Computer Animation for Doctors and Medical Professionals; 3-D Modeling Workshop; Advanced 3-D Computer Animation and Visual Effects Using

Maya; Advanced Compositing and Visual Effects with Shake; Character Animation; Computer Animation Using 3D Studio Max; Computer Animation Using SoftImage XSI. Other courses include: Intermediate 3D Computer Animation; Film Post-Production Workshop; Animation Action Analysis; Advanced Animation Production; Stop-Motion Animation. Various workshops are taught on weekends.

Facilities

Six state-of-the-art, advanced digital studios support students in the process of making a film or a work of art, with a complete range of 2-D, 3-D, audio and editing visual effects software.

Student Body

There are 5,500 students enrolled. Many classes are seminars and small discussion groups.

Faculty Profile

Six faculty members teach at the Center for Advancede Digital Applications.

Deadlines and Financial Aid

Undergraduates: early-decision candidates for fall entry should complete the application procedure by December 1. The regular freshman application deadline for fall entry is February 1, while transfers should apply by April 1. The spring semester deadline is December 1. Applications for the summer semester should be received by April 1. Applications are due by December 15. For those interested in the animation track, the deadline is Jan. 7. Financial aid in the form of fellowship points and assistantships are available to students who are not U.S. citizens. Various forms of grants, loans, and scholarships are available.

Admission Requirements

Undergraduates: applicants to the Undergraduate Division are required to present 16 acceptable units of secondary school work, to be distributed as follows: English (four years), 4 units; Mathematics (elementary algebra and plane geometry), 2 units; two years of a foreign language, 2 units; electives, 8 units. The 8 elective units are to be so distributed that at least 3 units are offered from the following: (1) additional classical and modern languages other than English; (2) additional mathematics; (3) social studies: history, civics, economics, etc.; and (4) sciences. Admission to the department is based on 1) an academic review; 2) portfolio review of such creative materials as film, video, photography, painting, dramatic or creative writing; 3) co-curricular activities, teacher recommendations, evidence of leadership qualities.

Expenses

Tuition is $6,300 per semester.

Contact

School of Continuing and Professional Studies, Office of Admissions, 145 4th Avenue, Room 201, New York, NY 10003. Telephone: 212-998-7200. Fax: 212-995-4124. Contact person: David Finney, Dean. URL: http://www.scps.nyu.edu/departments/department.jsp?deptId=9.

New York University Tisch School of the Arts

F/X Degrees Offered

B.F.A., M.F.A. and Certificate in Film Production and Animation; B.F.A. in Television and Photography; M.P.S. in Interactive Telecommunication. As part of the College of Arts and Sciences (CAS) at NYU, the department offers a Bachelor of Arts (BA) degree, a minor in computer science and a minor in computer applications.

Curricular

Undergraduates: Production Courses--Program Development; Frame and Sequence; Introduction to Animation Techniques; Fundamentals of Sight and Sound: Video; Introduction to Computer Graphics and Multimedia; Community Video and Public Access; Editing Workshop; Producing the Short Screenplay; Camera Technology; Editing I: Techniques of the Film Cutting Room; Video Tech; Animation Story Visualization; Animation Camera Technology; Experimental Workshop; Advanced Production Workshop; Camera I: Fundamentals of Lighting for Film and Television; Directing I and II; Production for Film; Advanced Seminar in Computer-Assisted Electronic Editing; Introduction to 3D Computer Animation; Intermediate Video Editing; Introduction to Computer Animation on the Macintosh; Intermediate 3D Computer Animation; Film Post-Production Workshop; Animation Action Analysis; Advanced Animation Production; Stop-Motion Animation. Graduate students: the curriculum has these objectives: 1) to provide students the opportunity to develop their creative talent through actual production experience. The primary format is 16 mm with access to 35 mm and video; 2) to provide not only artistic and technical knowledge, but also familiarity with business procedures used in the profession, 3) the emphasis of the curriculum is on gaining experience in the actual process of making films. Graduate courses are available in Film Editing; Motion Picture Production Technique; Motion Picture Camera Technique; Directing Workshop; Producing Technique; Directing Actors in Scene Studies; Sound Editing, Mixing and Recording; Feature Film Script Workshop; Short Film Script Workshop; Advanced Applications Workshop; Advanced Directing Workshop with Writing; Advanced Digital Sound Design and Mixing. Courses are available in beginning, intermediate and advanced levels.

Facilities

Undergraduates: video, film and sound production equipment is issued to students. Space is provided for equipment testing and training. A screening amphitheater and two screening theaters are devoted to class screenings and lectures for the fundamental-level film courses. The animation studio incorporates an Oxberry animation stand, optical printer, roto-scope and video animation system. The department's computer animation production studio is equipped with high-end Macintosh computers, an IBM computer and Sun workstations, plus a variety of peripherals including a color scanner and video input. There is a film post-production center, featuring four-, six- and eight-plate flatbed editors, screening rooms and complete post-production support facilities used by students involved in fundamental, intermediate and advanced film production projects. A floor is devoted to video post-production activity. Students have access to complete half-inch Beta and 3/4-inch U-matic editing systems. Film/video transfer facilities, and computer and time-coded editing systems are available for all levels of video post-production. Two teaching television studios are outfitted with three-camera, time-base-corrected video inputs, character generators and a full complement of studio lighting with computerized lighting board. Advanced-level video and film student production is conducted in the Todman Center. The center is capable of single-camera video or film, as well as multiple-camera bidie chain. A complete support floor is housed under the sound stage, including makeup and rehearsal rooms as well as a scene shop and greenrooms.

Student Body

There are 5,500 students enrolled in the College of Arts and Science. The faculty/student ratio is 1:13, and many classes are seminars and small discussion groups.

Faculty Profile

More than 66 undergraduate faculty in the area of Film and Television Arts; 22 faculty members teach graduate courses.

Deadlines and Financial Aid

Undergraduates: early-decision candidates for fall entry should complete the application procedure by December 1. The regular freshman application deadline for fall entry is February 1, while transfers should apply by April 1. The spring semester deadline is December 1. Applications for the summer semester should be received by April 1. Applications are due by December 15. For those interested in the animation track, the deadline is Jan. 7. Financial aid in the form of fellowship points and assistantships are available to students who are not U.S. citizens. A complete application for financial aid consists of two separate forms: 1) The Tisch School of the Arts: Graduate Financial Aid Form should be submitted with the application for admission to the Office of Graduate Admission at 721 Broadway, 7th Floor, New York, NY 10003, no later than February 1 of the year for which financial aid is desired for the fall term.

Admission Requirements

Undergraduates: applicants to the Undergraduate Division are required to present 16 acceptable units of secondary school work, to be distributed as follows: English (four years), 4 units; Mathematics (elementary algebra and plane geometry), 2 units; two years of a foreign language, 2 units; electives, 8 units. The 8 elective units are to be so distributed that at least 3 units are offered from the following: (1) additional classical and modern languages other than English; (2) additional mathematics; (3) social studies: history, civics, economics, etc.; and (4) sciences. Admission to the department is based on 1) an academic review; 2) portfolio review of such creative materials as film, video, photography, painting, dramatic or creative writing; 3) co-

curricular activities, teacher recommendations, evidence of leadership qualities. To be enrolled, an admitted undergraduate candidate must do the following: 1) accept the University's offer of admission and pay the required non-refundable $200 tuition deposit; 2) have the high school or college forward the final transcript to the New York University Office of Undergraduate Admissions. Graduate students: a student matriculating in the Tisch School of the Arts must be admitted at two levels: 1) as a student within the department of specialization or major; 2) as a student of New York University. Applicants are asked to submit a creative portfolio, which may include videotapes, creative writing, graphic art, still photography or demonstrated experience in the theater. Important note: All Super 8, 16 mm, and 35 mm films must be transferred to half-inch VHS only. Current Graduate Application for Admission and non-refundable application fee. Applicants to the Department of Film and Television Graduate Division should obtain supporting materials such as letters of recommendation and transcripts, and enclose these with the application in a single package.

Expenses

Tuition is $31,270 per year.

Contact

NYU, College of Arts and Science, Computer Science Department, Warren Weaver Hall, Room 405, 251 Mercer Street, New York, NY 10012. Telephone: 212-998-3011. Fax: 212-995-4124. Contact person: Margaret Wright, Chair.
URL: http://cs.nyu.edu/csweb/index.html.

Additional Information

The Institute of Film and Performing Arts: The Department of Film and Television offers undergraduate training in film, television, video, animation and radio. The department also offers a graduate program that concentrates on film production. The Department of Photography offers professional training on the undergraduate level. The Department of Cinema Studies is devoted to the scholarly study of film and media at both the undergraduate and graduate levels. The Dramatic Writing Program offers intensive study in writing for film, theatre, television and radio for both undergraduate and graduate students. The interactive Telecommunications Program focuses on the development of new uses of interactive telecommunications systems. The Alternate Media Center focuses on applied research, primarily in cable television and interactive telecommunications. At NYU, several other schools offer course work in the study or use of computers including: Department of Information, Operations and Management Sciences at Stern School of Business, (212) 998-0800; Information Technologies Institute at the School of Continuing and Professional Studies (212) 998-7190; Communications Technologies at the School of Continuing and Professional Studies (212) 998-7100; Interactive Telecommunications Program (ITP) at Tisch School of the Arts (212) 998-1880; Graphic Communications at the Steinhardt School of Education (212) 998-5125; and Educational Communication and Technology at the Steinhardt School of Education, (212) 998-5220. These departments offer a variety of course and degree alternatives for students who seek an understanding of computers directed towards a particular application area.

Parsons School of Design

F/X Degrees Offered
B.F.A. in Communication Design and Digital Design with a focus in Computer Graphics. M.F.A. in Design and Technology with a concentration in Multimedia; Animation and Visualization; Fashion and Textile Computing.

Curricular
B.F.A. courses in Advanced Computing Techniques: Computing Procedures; Multimedia Workshop; Multimedia Design; Advanced Digital Seminar in Language of Sound and Picture; Network Design, Integrated; Game Design with mTropolis; Virtual Reality; Scripting and Java. M.F.A. courses include Computer Technology; Creativity and Technology; History of Computer Graphics; Collaboration Studio I and II.

Facilities
Computer platform networked via high-speed fiber optics, includes Macintoshes; SGI; Sun; Windows NT; Plan 9 and Linux. Laboratories include: Foundation Computing Laboratory; Parsons Computing Center (200 Macintoshes with QuarkXPress, Adobe's Photoshop, Illustrator and more.). University Computing Center contains Macintosh and Windows applications. 3D Modeling and Animation Center (Maya, Softimage, Electric Image Studio) AutoCAD Laboratory; 3D Studio Max. The Experimental Multimedia Center houses eight non-linear audio and video stations; Avid; Media100.

Student Body
There are 350 art students.

Faculty Profile
Varies, as most of the faculty are part-time.

Deadlines and Financial Aid
Priority Financial Aid deadline is April 1 for the fall, and December 1 for the spring. Rolling admissions deadline, B.F.A. only, July 1. Contact the Financial Aid Office for possible outside scholarships and grants.

Admission Requirements
M.F.A. candidates must submit an application and fee, portfolio, statement of intent, two letters of recommendation, resume and transcripts.

Prospective B.F.A. students must submit high school transcripts, application and fee, and portfolio and SAT scores.

Expenses
B.F.A. tuition is $21,200 per year.

Contact
Office of Admissions, Parsons School of Design, 66 Fifth Ave., New York, NY 10011. Telephone: 212-229-8960. Fax: 212-229-5995. Contact person: William Bevington. E-mail: bevingtw@newschool.edu. URL: http://www.parsons.edu/.

Pratt Institute

F/X Degrees Offered
M.F.A. in Computer Graphics. Other M.F.A. programs include Industrial Design; C Programming; Packaging Design. B.A. in Fine Arts.

Curricular
Fundamental Concepts of Computer Graphics; 2D Computer Graphics Workshop; 3D Modeling Workshop; Computer Graphics in Context; Computer Graphics; Programming Workshop; Interactive Media I; 3D Computer Animation Workshop; Video Editing and Special Effects; Interactive Media II; Advanced 3D Computer Animation Workshop.

Facilities
Macintosh computers with graphics boards. A large selection of graphics software including interactive multimedia, drawing, animation and electronic prepress programs. Eight Silicon Graphics workstations running the Maya and Softimage 3D Modeling and Animation software; 15 PC-compatible computers with Targa graphics boards, graphics tablets, and assorted input and output peripherals. All of these graphics workstations run the TIPs paint and image processing program.

One Sony 3/4-inch Video Editing System with A/B-roll and special effects capabilities. Many other computer resources include a DEC VAX 6210 minicomputer; three Skok CAD systems; 10 Sun Sparc stations, and dozens of additional PC and Macintosh systems.

Student Body
Eighty undergraduates and 70 graduate students in the department.

Faculty Profile
Seventeen faculty members teach graduate courses in the Department of Computer Graphics.

Deadlines and Financial Aid
Financial Aid Office, 200 Willoughby Ave., Brooklyn, NY 11205. Deadline: May 15.

Admission Requirements
Request that all educational institutions that you have attended since graduating from secondary school send official transcripts to the Office of Graduate Admissions; submit three letters of recommendation; submit a brief, signed statement of your long-range goals and your reasons for applying to Pratt Institute for advanced study.

Expenses
Undergraduate tuition is $22,196 per year. Tuition is $802 per credit hour for graduate students.

Contact
Pratt Institute, Office of Admission, 200 Willoughby Ave., Brooklyn, NY 11205. Telephone: 718-636-3669 or 800-331-0834. Fax: 718-636-3670. E-mail: info@pratt.edu.
URL: http://www.pratt.edu/.

Additional Information
Among the Computer Graphics program's objectives are the following: A) link the traditional art and design concepts with the new technology of computer graphics; B) offer four areas of

concentration including: Interactive Systems (multimedia and interface design), Experimental Media (fine arts), Computer Animation (mostly 3D techniques), and Print-oriented Media (2D techniques); C) provide students with state-of-the-art hardware, software and instruction to experiment and become proficient in computer graphics technology.

Rensselaer Polytechnic Institute

F/X Degrees Offered
B.A. and M.F.A. in Integrated Electronic Arts. M.S. in Computer Science.

Curricular
Video Art Studio; Image Processing/Animation Studio; Integrated Studio; Electronic Arts Theory; Advanced Independent Study Projects in Electronic Arts; Topics in Electronic Arts.

Facilities
The Undergraduate Studios are designed to accommodate the needs of introductory non-professional students. The Image Processing/Animation Studio and the Undergraduate Media Studio can also be used by graduate students, faculty and visiting artists as a sketchpad environment for preliminary work on some aspects of a project. The Graduate Studios provide facilities for production of CD-quality sound, and broadcast-quality video and graphics. Multimedia project development through the Computer Music Studio, the Off-line Edit Suite, the Image Processing/Animation Studio, and Integrated Studio. The Integrated Studio is equipped for video production and audio recording, with a large production space acoustically isolated from the control room. Computer Science Department facilities--Hardware: 35 Sun workstations; Sequent Symmetry 81; Ardent Titan; Vision processing workstations; Maspar MP-1; various micros and peripherals. Software systems and languages: UNIX; C; C++; TeX; Mathematica; Maple; Lisp; Prolog; DOS applications; Macintoshes, etc. University facilities--Hardware: IBM 3090VF; 500 UNIX workstations; various micros; Sun; DEC; IBM; HP; SGIs. Software systems and languages: UNIX; DOS; MTS; MacOS. As often as possible, all of the Department's Sun workstations run the Solaris 8 operating system. All of the Department's Sun workstations are configured for MPI, making the 36 machines in public labs as well as the other computers in student offices a large distributed parallel computer. The Department's network provides 100Mbit full-duplex Ethernet to the desktop from a gigabit Ethernet backbone. All of this equipment is on a Class B Internet network which is connected to the Rensselaer Class B network. This in turn connects to the worldwide Internet, giving all students access to an astonishing variety of information resources. There is a wide variety of computing equipment available in other laboratories as well, and students who need specialized hardware or software for their research can get accounts on whatever systems are appropriate. There is also a 32-node IBM SP2 on campus to satisfy larger parallel computing needs.

Student Body
There are 1,800 full-time and 600 part-time graduate students, and 4,200 undergraduates. There are 60 undergraduates and 24 graduate students in the department.

Faculty Profile
There are 27 faculty members in the Computer Science department.

Deadlines and Financial Aid
Applicants requesting financial aid for the fall term should submit the application and all supporting materials by Jan. 15. Later applicants with strong

credentials will be considered pending aid availability. Although the M.F.A. does not require GRE scores, applicants who wish to be considered for financial aid should plan to take the GRE General test.

Admission Requirements

Applicants are expected to have completed a bachelor's degree and to display exceptional ability in either musical composition or the visual arts. The application procedure requires: transcripts of courses previously taken; two letters of recommendation from people who can comment on the applicant's artistic or musical training, accomplishments, and potential, a background and goals statement describing the applicant's artistic and/or musical experience, reasons for wanting to pursue an M.F.A. degree in Electronic Arts, long-term artistic and professional goals, and submission of a portfolio of creative work. Previous experience with electronic media is not a requirement for acceptance into the program.

Expenses

Tuition is $24,820 per year.

Contact

Department of Computer Science, Rensselaer Polytechnic Institute, 110 8th Street, Troy, NY 12180-3590. Telephone: 518-276-8326. Fax: 518-276-4780. Contact person: Laura Garrison. E-mail: garril@rpi.edu. E-mail: info@cs.rpi.edu. URL: http://www.cs.rpi.edu/.

Additional Information

The M.F.A. program at Rensselaer is conceived as an electronic arts program in an integrated artistic and technological environment. The program offers the opportunity to combine computer music, video art, computer imaging techniques, animation, installation and performance. The curriculum stresses creative studio-based work and emphasizes the unique problems presented by performance and public presentation of these media.

Rochester Institute of Technology

F/X Degrees Offered

B.F.A. in Film and Video with an emphasis in Production or Animation. M.F.A. in Imaging Arts with concentration in Computer Animation or Photography; M.S. in Information Technology. Advanced Certificate in Interactive Multimedia Development.

Curricular

Undergraduates: Film/Video freshman Seminar; Film/Video Production I, II, and III; Materials and Processes of the Moving Image; Film Language; Writing for Film/Video I, II; Introduction to Animation; Film/Video Electives; Advanced Animation; Film/Video History and Aesthetics; Video Tools and Technology; Introduction to 16 mm Sync. Sound; Film/Video Production Workshop; Introduction to Computer Animation; Introduction to Color Animation; Experimental Animation Workshop; Advanced Animation Workshop II. Graduate students: Interactive Media Design; Fundamentals of Interactive Multimedia; Interactive Multimedia Development; Programming for Interactive Multimedia. M.F.A. in Imaging Arts: Film/Video Photography Core; Animation and Graphic Film Production I, II and III; Video Tools and Technology; 2D Computer Animation I, II; 3D Computer Animation; Film/Video Special Topics Workshop; Film/Video Photographic Workshop; Film/Video Graduate Seminar; Film/Video Alternative Processes; Film/Video Contemporary Issues; Film/Video Independent Study; Film/Video Research Seminar.

Facilities

Computer Science: six Motorola 68000-based microcomputers (the Operating Systems Laboratory); 32 Sun Sparc 2 color workstations; 20 Sun Sparc 2 monochrome workstations; SGI workstations; three Sparc file servers; a 64-processor Transputer-based parallel processing platform; 30 Apple Macintosh systems; 35 PC compatibles. These computers operate under the UNIX operating system and the Macintosh operating systems on Windows. A laboratory devoted exclusively to graduate Computer Science students have 18 Sun SLC workstations; two Sparc stations. Software includes: Acrobat Professional by Adobe 6.0; After Effects by Adobe 5.5; Better Telnet by NCSA; EMacs; Easy CD Creator by Roxio 5; Illustrator by Adobe 10.0.3; ImageReady by Adobe 7.0.1; Internet Explorer by Microsoft 6.0; Java Developers Toolkit 1.4.0; Keyserver Client; Maya Unlimited by Alias Wavefront 5; Netscape Navigator by Netscape Communications Corp. 7; Photoshop by Adobe 7.0.1; Premiere by Adobe 6.5; Quicktime Pro by Apple; Smedge by Uberware; StudioTools by Alias Wavefront 10.1; VirusScan by Network Associates 4.5.1SP1; and XnView 1.61.

Student Body

There are 11,000 undergraduates and 1,500 graduate students enrolled in the university.

Faculty Profile

The M.F.A. in Imaging Arts program is supported by a staff of 45 faculty members within the School of Photographic Arts and Sciences, and adjunct faculty members at the International Museum of Photography, George Eastman House, and the Visual Studies Workshop, as well as RIT's Image Permanence Institute.

Deadlines and Financial Aid

Financial aid resources include: Scholarships; New York State-Tuition Assistance Program (TAP); Bureau of Indian Affairs Higher Education Program Fellowships; Loans--Federal Direct Loan, Federal Direct Unsubsidized Loans, Federal Perkins Loans; Private Lender Loans; Work--Federal College Work-Study Program, Institutional Employment. Portfolios must be postmarked by March 15 and mailed to the Chairperson.

Admission Requirements

Graduate students: Students with a baccalaureate degree or equivalent from an accredited college or university, or equivalent, are eligible for admission, provided they present a portfolio of work that demonstrates their skills, visual sophistication and aesthetic awareness. Acceptance depends on the strength of portfolios as judged by the graduate faculty, past academic performance, letters of recommendation, and personal statements of purpose.

Expenses

Tuition is $20,445 per year for undergraduates.

Contact

School of the Art and Design, Rochester Institute of Technology, Bldg. #7, P.O. Box 9887, Rochester, NY 14623-5604. Telephone: 585-475-6631. Fax: 585-475-7424. URL: http://www.rit.edu/.

Additional Information

Undergraduate B.F.A. Program: the degree program in film, video and animation will acquaint students with film, video and animation as creative media, and develop their production skills. The curriculum emphasizes production. Freshmen begin working in 16 mm film their very first quarter, continue with actual production every quarter until they graduate, and may specialize in motion pictures, video, traditional or computer animation. Through lectures and laboratories, students develop individual skills in moving-image communications, and learn the aesthetic principles governing the art. Technology and technique are taught as tools necessary to achieve a creative goal in relation to the audience. The curriculum also recognizes the increasing interrelationship between the technologies of film, video, animation and computers. Students typically produce several short films or videos, working through all phases of production: scripting, production planning, budgeting, shooting, sound editing and working with a laboratory. Students combine their learning of visual and sound artistry through hands-on experience with camera and sound equipment. Graduate: the M.F.A. program in Imaging Arts emphasizes a broad interpretation of photography as an art form. The program provides each student an opportunity to pursue graduate study in photography and other imaging arts as a means to personal, aesthetic, intellectual and career development. The M.F.A. curriculum is based on a flexible pattern of study continually sensitive to the needs of each student, and which builds upon the strengths that he or she brings to the program. The degree in Imaging Arts is offered with two areas of academic concentration: Photography and Computer Animation. Graduates obtain careers in education, museum or gallery work, business, broadcasting, A/V production, advertising or as self-employed professionals.

St. Bonaventure University

F/X Degrees Offered
Computer Science Department offers a B.S. degree in Computer Science.

Curricular
3D Modeling and Rendering; 3D Computer Animation; High-Level Programming.

Facilities
Sun workstations and PCs. Many pieces of digital equipment are available to students including scanners, cameras, video editing machines, and many software choices.

Student Body
Ten undergraduate students in the computer graphics area.

Deadlines and Financial Aid
Students at St. Bonaventure University receive financial aid from a variety of sources. More than 90 percent of our students receive some type of financial assistance. Some students receive aid that is generated by St. Bonaventure. The most highly qualified applicants will be offered academic scholarships, which are granted for academic achievement. Priority is given to students who apply for admission to the University before February 1. Notification of academic scholarship eligibility begins during the first week of February for prospective freshmen. St. Bonaventure Grants-in-Aid and other University sponsored grants and scholarships are available to students demonstrating financial need, as determined by the FAFSA (Free Application for Federal Student Aid). St. Bonaventure University also sponsors a work study program, which is dependent upon availability of funding and willingness to work. The Federal and New York State governments award grants, scholarships and loans. St. Bonaventure University participates in the Supplemental Education Opportunity Grants (SEOG) and Pell Grant programs and the Perkins Loan program, which are sponsored by the Federal government and New York State's TAP. TAP is limited to New York State residents. In addition, the Federal government sponsors the need-based Federal Work Study Program. Lending institutions, such as banks, provide financial assistance in the form of the Federal Stafford Loan program (subsidized and unsubsidized), and the Parent Loan for Undergraduate Student (PLUS) program. Applicants who wish to begin college in the fall semester should apply during the fall term of the senior year in high

school. Students graduating at mid-year who wish to begin college in the spring semester should apply no later than December 1.

Admission Requirements
An applicant must arrange for an official high school academic transcript to be submitted to the Admissions Office. The results of the SAT or the ACT battery must be sent.

Expenses
Tuition is $17,190 per year.

Contact
St. Bonaventure University, St. Bonaventure, NY 14778. Telephone: 716-375-2000. Fax: 716-375-4005. URL:http://www.sbu.edu.

School of Visual Arts

F/X Degrees Offered
The M.F.A. Computer Art Program is broken up into three focus sections: Animation, Interactivity, and Telecommunication and Installations. B.F.A. in Film/Video/Animation; B.F.A. and M.F.A. in Computer Art. Other degrees offered include Photography, Illustration and Cartooning, Advertising and Graphic Design.

Curricular
Graduate students: Animation--Animation Mechanics; 3D Modeling; Surfaces and Lighting; Computer Art in Context; UNIX or C Programming I; Computer Systems, Production Issues in Animation Techniques. Interactivity--Interactive Techniques, Interactive Design, Computer Art in Context; UNIX or C Programming I. Telecommunication and Installations--Production Issues: Interactivity. Telecommunication--PC Hacking and Engineering; Computer Art in Context; UNIX I or C Programming; Computer Systems. Undergraduate Courses: Computer Art: Introductory Computer Workshop; Introduction to Desktop Publishing; Media Communications; Introduction to Paint Systems on the IBM; Desktop Animation I; Computer-Assisted Illustration; Computers and Animation; Introduction to Video; Introduction to Computer Systems; Introduction to C Programming; Interactive Programming; Issues in Electronic Publishing/Business Graphics; Issues in Multimedia; Introduction to 3D Modeling and Animation; Advanced Computer-Based Typography. Undergraduate Courses in Film, Video and Screen Writing--Introduction to Film History; Introduction to Film; Storytelling; Introduction to Video; Film Editing; Film Production Workshop; Acting and Directing; Scriptwriting for Film; Advanced Editing; The Director's Workshop; Video Post-Production; Film and Entertainment Law; Advanced Video Computer Editing; Lighting for Video; Writers Workshop for the Short Film.

Facilities
Maya and TDI on the SGI; Macintosh; IBM. There are many labs to choose from that offer up-to-date equipment as well as many software choices.

Student Body
There are 5,000 undergraduates and 100 graduate students.

Faculty Profile
There are 700 faculty members; 29 members teach graduate students in the area of Computer Art. More than 60 faculty members teach undergraduate Computer Art courses. More than 80 faculty teach Film/Video/Animation undergraduate courses.
Deadline and Financial Aid
New York State residents may be eligible for the TAP (Tuition Assistance Plan). Scholarships and assistantships are awarded through the admissions process for new students, and by the department chair and faculty for continuing students based

upon individual merit and performance. There are no additional application forms for these awards. New students are notified in their letter of acceptance if they have been selected to receive such an award. Undergraduates: The application period begins in September for students applying for the fall. Applications for the spring semester may be submitted beginning in January. The completed application deadline for the fall semester for Film, Video, Animation and Computer Art is March 15. Three major scholarships are available to undergraduates: Silas H. Rhodes Scholarships for Freshmen and Transfer Students; Chairman's Merit Award; Scholastic Art Awards for freshmen.

Admission Requirements
Applicants to the M.F.A. program in Computer Art are not required to have any previous formal training in computer graphics or computer sciences. Official transcripts from all colleges and universities attended are required. Letters of recommendation from three instructors or practicing professionals are required. A written statement of the applicant's intent and reason for graduate study is required. Completed applications for admission, accompanied by application fee, must be received no later than February 1. Computer Art Program requirements: examples of recent work are required of all applicants; at least 10 and no more than 20 slides. In addition, applicants may submit a VHS tape, Zip, optical or floppy disk. Please do not submit oversized binders, portfolio, prints or original work. Undergraduates: the application for Admission and Statement of Intent, accompanied by the application fee, an official transcript, letter of recommendation (optional), results from the ACT or SAT, a personal interview (required of all applicants living within 250 miles of New York City). A portfolio of 12 to 15 pieces of artwork is required of all Animation and Computer Art; applicants; portfolios are not required of applicants to the Video and Film Department,

however, these students are required to submit a one- to two-page description of a significant dream. Based upon that dream, the student must write a two- to three-page essay on how they would translate that dream into a film or video.

Expenses
Tuition is $9,100 per semester.

Contact
School of Visual Arts, 209 E. 23rd St., New York, NY 10010-3994. Telephone: 212-592-2532. Fax: 212-592-2509.
URL: http://www.schoolofvisualarts.edu/main2.html.

State University of New York at Buffalo

F/X Degrees Offered
M.S. and Ph.D. in Computer Science.

Curricular
Courses are offered in Computer Graphics and Computer Vision.

Facilities
In addition to the specialized facilities in the research centers and labs, the general research facilities include more than 100 Sun workstations, PCs, thin-client workstations and SPARC-server systems including two V880s, four Ultra60/2360s, three Ultra Enterprise 450s, and several Ultra 10s, totaling 1.2 terabytes of disk space. Computer-intensive processing is handled by two Sun Ultra 80s with four CPUs and 4 gigabytes of memory each. Power Macs, Windows NT machines, and laser printers are all readily available. The Center for Computational Research is equipped with an SGI Origin2000 and an IBM SP2. Our other centers and labs have extensive dedicated infrastructure,

including notably the 20 terabyte online high-performance data storage system being developed for the MultiStore project. Department systems are connected to the university backbone by a gigabit Ethernet port directly on a gigabit router. The internal networking is a mix of 100BaseT and gigabit Ethernet. The university has an OC3 link to the Internet and an additional OC3 link to Internet2. Other Department facilities include: 65 Sun workstations; three SS2-/712S; one SS10/512; one SS10/51; one SS10/514; two 4/670S; X-window terminals; 60 Macintoshes; 25 LCIIs. Software systems and languages: C; Lisp; Add; Prolog; UNIX; VMS. University facilities--Hardware: VMS cluster with DEC Alpha running Open VMS; IBM 3090J-300; X-terminals; workstations; several Sun time-sharing systems.

Student Body
There are 406 graduate students enrolled in the department.

Faculty Profile
Nineteen faculty members teach in the department.

Deadlines and Financial Aid
Graduate students may apply for an assistantship that offers a stipend of $9,970 per year. Graduate students may also receive $10,000-$13,000 in the form of fellowships. Admissions application deadline: December 31. Assistantship application deadline: December 31.

Admission Requirements
Application and fee, transcripts and GRE scores.

Expenses
Tuition is $4,350 per year.

Contact
Department of Computer Science, 201 Bell Hall, Buffalo, NY 14260-2000. Telephone: 716-645-3180. Fax: 716-645-3464. Email: cse-dept@cse.buffalo.edu. URL: http://www.cs.buffalo.edu/.

State University of New York at Potsdam

F/X Degrees Offered
B.A. in Computer and Information Sciences.

Curricular
3D Modeling and Rendering; Multimedia/Interactive; 2D Computer Animation; Digital Painting/Drawing; High- and Low-Level Programming; Image Processing; Virtual Reality.

Facilities
The College has over 400 computers for student use in computer labs and classrooms located throughout the campus. The main facility is always staffed, has color printing available and is open approximately 100 hours a week. In addition, each dorm room has a direct network connection for students who bring their own computer. This allows for access to campus resources as well as the Internet. Faculty use technology extensively, with access to 36 smart classrooms that include networked computers, multimedia resources and projectors which allow for advanced instructional presentations. All faculty and staff offices have Internet access.

Student Body
Twenty undergraduate students in the department.

Faculty Profile
One full-time faculty and one adjunct in the department.

Deadlines and Financial Aid
The Office of Student Financial Aid administers federal-, state- and college-funded aid programs. Students should get in touch with the Office of Student Financial Assistance early in the admissions process to discuss eligibility requirements and responsibilities, and to obtain forms and up-to-date information on the various aid programs.

Admission Requirements
Application and fee, transcripts, and SAT or ACT scores.

Expenses
Tuition is $4,350 per year.

Contact
Computer and Information Sciences Department, State University of New York at Potsdam, Potsdam, NY 13676. Telephone: 315-267-2900. Fax: 315-267-3140. Contact person: Dr. John Dalphin, Chair. Email: dalphijf@potsdam.edu.
URL: http://www.potsdam.edu/.

Syracuse University

F/X Degrees Offered
B.F.A. and M.F.A. College of Visual and Performing Arts, Department of Media Studies, Computer Graphics Program.

Curricular
The computer art program stresses artistic expression using digital technology. The program takes a fine arts and experimental approach to the creation of art using the computer. The courses merge the technical and aesthetic aspects of computer art. Students learn digital image making, graphics programming, 3-D modeling, 2-D and 3-D computer animation, World Wide Web technologies, and other contemporary computer art techniques. In the programming courses, students write their own animated and interactive work.

Facilities
Hardware: 14 Silicon Graphics; one Silicon Graphics Personal Iris; 40 Macintosh computers; three Zenith 386 Computers; DEC Computers; six 3/4-inch video editing decks; five half-inch video editing decks; two full-color scanners; three digital film video in/outboards; Radius Video Vision video in/outboard; Dyquest frame-by-frame recording; Audio Media card with CD quality output to video or cassette or disk; digital camera; Yarc card; CD players; all computers networked. Software: includes Maya; Macromedia Director; Adobe Photoshop; Adobe Premiere; CoSA After Effects; Macromedia MacroModel; Specular Infini-D; Specular TextureScape; Fractal Painter; Gryphon Morph; Presenter Professional; Electric Image; Turbo Pascal; Asymetrix Toolbook; Pandemonium; Macintosh Renderman; Sound Edit Pro; Sound Designer; BackBurner; Gallery FX; JagII; Sketcher; StudioVision; Swivel 3D; Debabilizer; Dynamic Effects; Paint Alchemy.

Student Body
Approximately 110 Computer Graphics undergraduate majors, and eight Computer Graphics graduate students in the department.

Faculty Profile
Three faculty members teach in the Computer Graphics area.

Deadlines and Financial Aid
Undergraduates: contact VPA Admissions at 315-443-2769. Fax: 315-443-1935. E-mail: admissu@vpa.syr.edu. College of Visual and Performing Arts, Office of Recruiting, 202 Crouse College, Syracuse University, Syracuse, NY 13244. Deadline for undergraduate application: February 1; late admission is on a space-available basis. To be considered for admission, you must submit an art portfolio consisting of slides, videotape or labeled disks (interactive or programmed work). Graduate students: deadline for graduate fellowship applicants is Jan. 1; non-fellowship graduate applicants' deadline is March 1. For more information: College of Visual and Performing Arts, Office of Graduate Student Services, 200 Crouse College, Syracuse University, Syracuse, NY 13244-1010. Telephone:

315-443-3089. Graduates must hold a B.F.A. or equivalent (75-90 credits of studio work).

Admission Requirements
To be considered for admission to the undergraduate or graduate program, all candidates must submit an art portfolio consisting of slides, videotape or labeled disks (interactive or programmed work) with application.

Expenses
Tuition is $25,142 per year.

Contact
102 Shaffer Art Building, Syracuse University, Syracuse, NY 13244. Telephone: 315-443-1033. Fax: 315-443-1303. Contact person: Edward Zajec. E-mail: ezajec@mailbox.syr.edu. URL: http://vpa.syr.edu/schools/soad/artcgr.html.

Tompkins Cortland Community College

F/X Degrees Offered
Associate in Applied Science in Graphics Design and Computer Graphics through the Department of Art.

Curricular
Graphic Design I and II; Computer Graphics I and II.

Facilities
Workstations include a mixture of Macintoshes and PCs, printers and scanners. Recently, new Pentium IV (1.7GHz) computers were installed.

Student Body
There are 65 students in the Computer Graphics area.

Faculty Profile
Three faculty teach in the area.

Deadlines and Financial Aid
No deadline for filing. Several financial aid programs are available including New York State TAP and Federal programs (FAFSA).

Admission Requirements
Application and fee, high school official transcript and prior college transcript, if applicable.

Expenses
Tuition is $2,800 per semester for residents and $5,900 per semester for non-residents.

Contact
Tompkins Cortland Community College, P.O. Box 139, Dryden, NY 13053. Telephone: 607-844-8211. 888-567-8211. Contact person: Janik Carol, Professor. URL: http://sunytccc.edu/.

University at Albany

F/X Degrees Offered
B.S., M.S. and Ph.D. in Computer Science.

Curricular
Courses in Computer Graphics and Advanced Visualization.

Facilities
Department facilities--Hardware: 50 Sun workstations; three SGI workstations; one DEC station; various terminals and PCs. Software systems and languages: UNIX; C; C++; Scheme; Common Lisp; Prolog; Modula-3; VLSI Tools; DOS; Lotus 123; Maple V; GAP; Interviews; GCC; G++; KCL; Perl; tcl/tk; Spice; SPIM; Logo; HPF; Fortran77; 90. University facilities--Hardware: VMS cluster; IBM mainframe; UNIX cluster; 19 Sun Sparc classics; 78 DEC PCs; 25 macintoshes; 97 terminals. Other classrooms contain 12 Macintosh G3s, 12 Orange PC boards, 2 superdisk drives, a large format laser printer, a color printer, 12 6x8 pen tablets, 3 MIDI keyboards, a flatbed scanner

and a LCD video projector. Specialized software such as Light Shop, Sound Hack, AutoCad, Finale, etc., is also available. Other classrooms contains 26 Dell Pentium III 733Mhz classroom computers with DVD drives, 3 Dell XPS 800Mhz authoring workstations, a media control center, a LCD video projector, a document camera, VCR, sound system, a high speed laser printer, 3 high speed scanners and a digital video camera. Additionally, specialized software such as Dreamweaver, Flash, Micromedia Director, Shockwave media, etc., are available.

Student Body
There are 78 graduate students in the department; 17,000 students attend the university.

Faculty Profile
Fourteen faculty members in the department.

Deadlines and Financial Aid
Graduate assistants can receive a stipend of $8,000-$14,000 per year. Assistantship application deadline: March 15.

Admission Requirements
Requirements for admission to M.S. program: open to students holding a bac- calaureate degree with at least a minor or its equivalent in Computer Science or Mathematics, or a combination thereof. Students whose preparation in undergraduate Mathematics or Computer Science is deficient are required to take undergraduate courses during the first year of graduate study as specified by the department. Scores from the aptitude portion of the GRE are required from all applicants. Requirements for admission to Ph.D. program: an applicant must have a bachelor's degree from an accredited college or university. A bachelor's degree in Computer Science or Mathematics is desirable, but not necessary. Deficiencies in Computer Science or Mathematics, as determined by the departmental faculty, must be made up during the first year of graduate study. Admission is normally in the fall semester, but

those applicants with exceptional qualifications may be admitted at any time. Applicants are required to submit scores for the Verbal, Quantitative and Analytic portions of the GRE.

Expenses
Tuition is $213 per credit hour for residents and $351 per hour for non-residents.

Contact
Computer Science Department, 1400 Washington Ave., Albany, NY 12222. Telephone: 518-442-4270 or 800-440-GRAD. Contact person: George Berg, Associate Professor. Email: berg@cs.albany.edu. URL: http://www.cs.albany.edu/.

Additional Information
Courses offered by the Department of Computer Science provide an introduction to the theory and practice of computing. Familiarity with computer languages and data structures is developed in appropriate courses by the completion of programming assignments related to course material. Students may elect a short sequence of courses in a particular aspect of computer science, complete a minor for broader competence, or obtain a foundation in both theory and practice by completing either a major in computer science or in computer science and applied mathematics. Among the majors that combine well with either elective course work or a minor in computer science are mathematics, any science major, economics, geography, linguistics, rhetoric and communication, psychology, and sociology. A major in business administration (such as the management science concentrations) would also be appropriate, but students should be aware that they will also have to satisfy the School of Business admission requirements.

University of Rochester

F/X Degrees Offered
B.A., B.S., and Ph.D. in Computer Science.

Curricular
Particular emphasis on theory of computation, AI, programming systems, and a wide range of topics related to parallel and distributed computing.

Facilities
The Department maintains a high-speed local network of computers for the research use of its faculty, staff, and students. In 2002 the computers on the network included approximately sixty high-end PCs running Linux, twenty Sun workstations, and another twenty miscellaneous workstations (SGI machines, Apple Macintoshes, and PCs running Windows NT), together with an extensive collection of file and compute servers. Most of the servers are connected by switched Gigabit Ethernet; almost all of the remaining machines are on 100Mb switched Ethernet. All department space is also covered by an 802.11 wireless network. The showcase resource for the Computer Systems Group is a 32-processor IBM pSeries 690 Regatta multiprocessor, with 1.3GHz Power-4 processors (currently the fastest microprocessors available from any manufacturer), 32GB of physical memory, and 128MB of cache. Other parallel computing facilities include a 32-processor IBM-branded Linux cluster, a 32-processor Compaq Alpha-Server cluster, an 8-processor SunFire v880, an 8-processor Sun Ultra 4500, and miscellaneous other 2- and 4-processor machines. Other facilities include several high-end Pentium servers, a flock of Compaq iPAQ hand-held computers, and high-end lab equipment for power measurement in mobile systems. The Vision and Robotics Laboratory is equipped with 2 Unimation Puma 700 series robot arms, a Utah four-fingered anthropomorphic hand, 4 SensAble Phantom virtual force feedback devices, a TRC robot head, a dataglove, a Digicolor color digitizer, and 2 DataCube (MV-200) real-time image processing boards. The Virtual Reality Lab contains a binocular display helmet equipped with an eye-tracker and head-position transducers, Infinite Reality Silicon Graphics machines for real-time graphics generation, an instrumented go-cart on a hydraulic motion-tilt platform for performing human studies in driving, and an additional head-eye tracking station for studying human visual strategies. The Speech Lab contains equipment for digitizing, storing, and analyzing audio signals. The flagship Theory Group resource is state-of-the-art black (currently the darkest color available) ballpoint pens each containing a 13.6cm, 0.08oz ink cartridge that have been clocked at up to 1.2 words per second; dozens of these pens are clustered in an array-of-boxes architecture within the Supply Closet Facility. Undergraduate majors and those taking upper level computer science courses are given accounts in two computing labs reserved solely for undergraduate use. All workstations in these labs were replaced in the summer of 2001 with high-end Pentium III PCs and cycle servers running Red Hat Linux. File service is provided by RAID-equipped Sun servers. One of the labs, reserved for majors only, doubles as undergraduate lounge and library space.

Student Body
Forty-three graduate students in the Computer Science Department; 5,420 undergraduates and 2,940 graduate students are enrolled in the university.

Faculty Profile
Twelve faculty members teach in the department.

Deadlines and Financial Aid
Graduate students may qualify for graduate assistantships, research assistantships and fellowships. The assistantships offer stipends

ranging from $10,000-$16,400 per year. Admissions application deadline: February 1. Assistantship application deadline:
February 1.

Admission Requirements
Application and fee, GRE scores and transcripts.

Expenses
Tuition is $2,175 per semester for residents and $3,800 for non-residents.

Contact
Department of Computer Science, University of Rochester, 365 5th Avenue, New York City 10016, Room 4319. Phone: 212-817-8190. Fax: 212-817-1510. Contact person: Thomas J. LeBlanc, professor and chair. E-mail: compsci@gc.cuny.edu. URL: http://www.cs.rochester.edu/.

Additional Information
The Department of Computer Science at the University of Rochester is well known for its research production and collegial atmosphere. Degrees offered include an elite undergraduate major and an intense program leading to the doctor of philosophy. Particular emphasis is placed on computer vision and robotics, natural language understanding and knowledge representation, systems and architecture, and theory of computation.

North Carolina

Appalachian State University

F/X Degrees Offered
B.S. and M.S. in Computer Science.

Curricular
2D Computer Animation; Multimedia/Interactive; High-Level Programming; Digital Painting/Drawing; Computer Graphics.

Facilities
The Department's computing laboratories currently house: a Compaq Alpha ES40 server with two 667MHz processors and 2GB of error correcting RAM running Compaq Tru64 UNIX, Most classwork is run on this system; a DEC Alpha 2100A server with two 250 MHz processors running Compaq Tru64 UNIX; a lab with 24 PCs configured to run Matlab or an X-Server; a teaching (closed) lab with 29 PCs; specialized labs for real-time systems and for operating systems. The central computing system is a cluster of AXP-based servers. Every enrolled student receives an account on this system. In addition, the university provides a number of public computer laboratories (PC and Macintosh) with connections to campus networks and the Internet. Every student has University-supplied email access through a web-interface called AppalNET. The AppalNET interface provides access to a lot of other information, including some official notices that are not sent by either hard-copy or email students are encouraged to check this portal regularly and warned that they might miss important information if they fail to do so. The user identification for AppalNET is the same as for the AXP-based servers. Several buildings on campus have open (public) labs. Most of these labs have PCs, although a few have Macs. Computers in these labs connect to Novell servers. The open (public) lab in CAP (where the CS Department has its offices) currently has 23 PCs, 4 X-terminals, and 2 Macs.

Student Body
There are 250 undergraduate students in the department.

Faculty Profile
Ten faculty members teach in the department.

Deadlines and Financial Aid
Scholarships: the Department of Mathematical Sciences awards several scholarships each year to current students, and one scholarship to an incoming freshman (the Patterson Scholarship). Applications from current majors must be received by February 17, and awards are made by the department's Scholarship Committee by March 15. Applications for the Patterson Scholarship must be received by March 25, and awards are made by April 30. Types of Scholarships: Computer Science Scholarship; G.T. Buckland Scholarship; Inez Harris Mathematics Education Scholarship; Paul B. Patterson Scholarship; Taylor Memorial Scholarship. Approximately 50 percent of all students receive financial aid in the form of grants, loans, scholarships, jobs and/or minority grants.

Admission Requirements
The completed application form with a check or money order made payable to Appalachian State University, and an official copy of your high school transcript, which includes grades 9 through 12. The Transcript Supplement is required for high school seniors if the information requested by the supplement is not on your transcript. Freshman applicants must submit SAT results directly from the Educational Testing Service to Appalachian.

Expenses

Tuition is $585 per semester for residents and $5,045 tuition per semester for non-residents.

Contact

Appalachian State University, College of Arts & Sciencesm, I.G. Greer Room 100, Boone, NC 28608. Telephone: 828-262-8629. Fax: 828-265-8617. Contact person: Kenneth H. Jacker. E-mail: khj@cs.appstate.edu.
URL: http://www.cs.appstate.edu/.

North Carolina A&T State University

F/X Degrees Offered

M.S. and Ph.D. in Computer Science.

Curricular

Courses in Scientific Visualization, Computer Programming, and other basic computer science courses.

Facilities

Department facilities--Hardware: Pentium; Sun; VAX; X-windows; networks. Software systems and languages: C++; Ada9x; Smalltalk.

Student Body

There are 300 students in the department.

Faculty Profile

Twelve full-time faculty members in the department.

Deadlines and Financial Aid

Graduate assistantships range from teaching assistantships of $1,200 to various forms of research assistantships. Admissions application deadline is June. Assistantship application deadline is March.

Admission Requirements

Application and fee, transcripts and GRE.

Expenses

Tuition is $1,340 per semester for in-state students and $5,801 per semester for non-residents.

Contact

Computer Science Department - Graham Hall, North Carolina A&T State University, 1601 East Market Street, Greensboro, NC 27411-0002. Telephone: 336-334-7245 or 800-443-8960. Fax: 336-334-7244. Contact person: Kenneth A. Williams, Chair. E-mail: williams@ncat.edu.
URL: http://www.comp.ncat.edu/.

North Carolina State University

F/X Degrees Offered

B.S., M.S. and Ph.D. in Computer Science.

Curricular

3D Modeling and Rendering; 3D Animation; 2D Animation; Multimedia/Interactive; High- and Low-Level Programming; Virtual Reality; Volume Visualization; Digital Video; Stereo Imaging.

Facilities

Department facilities--Hardware: Laboratories for algorithms, database, multimedia, operating systems, software systems and voice i/o. University facilities--Hardware: College of Engineering maintains EOS (integrated network of 700 UNIX/X-windows workstations); access to North Carolina Supercomputing Center. The Computer Science Department at NCSU has extensive computing facilities that span three buildings and are mostly connected to the campus ethernet to provide faculty, staff, and students with the best interconnectivity possible. Students, faculty, or staff members can be in any of the buildings (or even off campus) and log onto machines in the other buildings.

Macintosh and PC users can print to Unix printers, and Unix users can print to AppleTalk printers if they are conveniently located. File sharing is possible between platforms. The multimedia lab currently has 20 PC workstations with a variety of software available on them, dependant on the classes using the lab. There are two video capture stations that allow capture from both digital and analog sources. Adobe Premiere is available for editing video. Other resources of the lab include a flat-bed scanner and access to several CD burners. There are also two I-Macs available. Current Multimedia Software in the lab includes: Adobe Photoshop 7.0 (all machines, except HP XAs); Adobe Premiere 6.5 (all machines, except HP XAs); Cakewalk Pro Audio 9 (one machine); 3D Studio Max 5 (5 machines); and Sound Forge 6.0 (all machines, except HP XAs).

Student Body
There are 450 undergraduates and 125 graduate students.

Faculty Profile
Twenty-seven faculty members in the department.

Deadlines and Financial Aid
Graduate assistantships range from teaching assistantships with stipends of $10,000 to research assistantships with stipends of $10,000-$15,000 dollars. Admissions application deadline: fall, April 1; spring, November 1. Assistantship application deadline: fall, February 1; spring, Sept. 1.

Admission Requirements
Undergraduate students must submit an application and fee, transcripts, and ACT or SAT score. Graduate students must submit an application and fee, letters of reference, transcript and GRE.

Expenses
Tuition is $1,581.50 per semester for residents and $7,580.50 per semester for non-residents.

Contact
North Carolina State University, Department of Computer Science, 226 Withers Hall, Box 8206, Raleigh, NC 27695-8206. Telephone: 919-515-2858. Fax: 919-515-7896.
URL: http://www.csc.ncsu.edu/.

School of Communication Arts in Raleigh

F/X Degrees Offered
Certificate and Associates Degrees in Computer Art and Animation, Multimedia and Advanced 3D Computer Animation.

Curricular
Computer Graphics courses are offered through Graphic Design, Multimedia, Animation and Advanced Animation. DIGITAL FILMMAKING for the study in classic film moved into total digital production, but containing far reaching exploration of new digital trends including 24p and more. DIGITAL MEDIA ARTS & INTERNET ARTS taking students into extended application in advertising, audio, video, and internet creative and technical production.
DIGITAL AUDIO PRODUCTION & DESIGN acts as a technical program with creative components giving the recording engineer the added edge in the job market... with varied skills for film, TV, and the Internet. ART & ANIMATION for 3D modeling plus special FX motion graphics and advanced animation study along with broader skills in 2D internet animation and art.

Facilities
PC laboratories; Macintosh workstations; SGIs. Design and multimedia software programs such as Flash, Director, Quark, Illustrator and Photoshop.

Student Body

There are 320 students in the Computer Graphics area.

Faculty Profile

Twelve faculty members teach in the Computer Graphics area.

Deadlines and Financial Aid

Attending the School may be facilitated through working with a Financial Planner within the Student Services office at the School. Financial planning includes reviewing grant and loan eligiblity for candidates for enrollment. A menu of options is usually reviewed, giving students a comprehensive view of the qualifications required for both tuition assistance and living cost allowances. The School is authorized to participate in Federal grant and loan programs. Such programs are usually based on need. In addition to Federal programs, the School participates in various private lending programs. The process of reviewing financial support usually begins with the Admissions Office who will provide contact with Student Services and a Financial Planner. A limited number of Scholarship opportunities may be available at select times during the School year. Most Scholarships are based on merit and/or need.

Admission Requirements

Interview, portfolio review, creative writing sample, general aptitude test, high school transcript, application and fee.

Expenses

Tuition is $12,400 per year.

Contact

School of Communication Arts, 3220 Spring Forest Rd., Raleigh, NC 27616. Telephone: 919-981-0972 or 800-288-7442. Fax: 919-981-0946. URL: http://www.ncsca.com/.

Additional Information

Since its founding more than 10 years ago, the School of Communication Arts has grown to graduate students who have gained impressive credentials in the worlds of film, advertising, computer gaming and beyond. They have gone to work on leading features, history making computer generated movies, leading computer games, moved into important positions in network and information technology roles at leading companies and much more.

University of North Carolina at Chapel Hill

F/X Degrees Offered

Department of Computer Science.

Curricular

Courses are taught in algorithms and their analysis; theory of languages and computation; files and databases; operating systems; translators; digital logic techniques; numerical computing methods; programming languages; software engineering; 3D Modeling and Rendering; High-Level Programming; Image Processing; Virtual Reality; Volume Visualization; Stereo Imaging.

Facilities

The computing environment includes more than 450 computers. These systems are integrated by means of high-speed networks, and by software that is consistent at a user-level over the many architectural platforms. In addition, the department's research laboratories include specialized equipment and facilities. General computing systems include more than 38 Sun workstations, 140 DEC workstations, 70 HP workstations, 7 IBM workstations, seven SGI workstations, 180 Apple Macintosh systems, and 30 IBM personal computers. Output facilities include laser printers, color printers and plotters, slide makers, and transparency-making equipment. The parallel computing facilities comprise the Department's own designs, such as the two Pixel-Planes 5 multicomputers, and a commercial MasPar MP-1 computing system, a massively parallel computer. The latter provides 8,192 processors and 512 megabytes of main memory in a SIMD architecture. The primary software environment consists of the UNIX operating system, Andrew File System (AFS), and X-windows. Languages most commonly used include C++, C and Prolog. Document preparation is usually accomplished via Macintosh systems. The Department's computer systems are connected by high-speed networks, including an integrated voice/data switch, and video switches, which serve as the hubs of an extensive cabling network that reaches into each office to provide voice, data and video networking capabilities. The campus broadband provides extended service to other facilities on campus and connects the department to the North Carolina Research and Education Network (NC-REN), allowing users to reach any network in the world. NC-REN is the statewide network that links research and educational institutions. A two-way video classroom and teleconference room allows connection to any institution served by the network. Courses are shared among the institutions via two-way, interactive video teleclassing, and NC-REN substantially widens the course, concentration and advising opportunities available to students at participating universities. The Graphics and Image Laboratory supports research and teaching in computer graphics, image processing, virtual environments, computer vision and pattern recognition. Specialized image-generation systems include two of UNC-Chapel Hill's unique Pixel-Planes 5 machines; scalable 3D graphics multicomputers that each contain more then 250,000 processors; Silicon Graphics Onyx computers with Reality Engine 2 graphics; Other SGI computers; and a Division ProVision 100 system. Other graphics computers in the laboratory include 11 Hewlett Packards, and DEC workstations . Some systems are equipped with high-precision color monitors. Viewing devices include several Virtual Research head-mounted displays (HMDs); a Kaiser full-immersion HMD; D'glasses, an ultra-compact video display designed and built in the department; alternative polarized stereo glasses; a large rear-projection screen. Tracking of head and hand movements is accomplished with Polhemus and Ascension magnetic tracking systems and the large-area optoelectronic ceiling tracker that was designed and built in the department. Interaction devices include three PHANTOM force display devices, an Argonne Remote Manipulator, a voice recognition system, joysticks, mouse devices, data tablets and other commercial and in-house-designed manual input devices. The laboratory has extensive facilities for recording, editing and producing high-quality video.

Student Body

There are 150 graduate students and more than 400 undergraduates in the department.

Faculty Profile

Forty-five faculty members teach in the department.

Deadlines and Financial Aid

Admission Deadlines: The fall semester runs from late August to late December; the spring semester from early January to early May. Graduate courses in computer science are not offered during the summer. Application for admission is due at Graduate School no later than Jan. 31. To ensure meeting that deadline, the GRE should be taken no later than December. A few assistantships are sometimes available to begin in the spring semester. To be considered for these assistantships, completed applications should be received no later than Oct. 15

and the GRE taken no later than June. Admissions application deadline: fall--Jan. 31; spring--Oct. 15. Assistantship application deadline: fall--Jan. 10; spring--Oct. 15.

Admission Requirements

Applications for fall admission, complete with a personal statement, and all transcripts and recommendations. Entering students must have a substantial background in both Mathematics and Computer Science. This normally includes at least six semester courses in mathematics, and six in Computer Science. Standard preparation for the graduate program includes: differential and integral calculus; discrete mathematics: sets, relations, functions, algebra; linear algebra or matrix theory; mathematical probability, preferably calculus-based; structured programming techniques; data structures and abstract data types; computer organization.

Expenses

Tuition is $4,072 per year for students and $15,920 per year for non-residents.

Contact

University of North Carolina, CB# 3175, Sitterson Hall, Chapel Hill, NC 27599-3175. Telephone: 919-962-1700. Fax: 919-962-1799. Contact person: Janet Jones. E-mail: admit@cs.unc.edu. URL: http://www.cs.unc.edu/.

Additional Information

The Department of Computer Science at UNC-CH was established as an independent department in 1964. The primary objectives are graduate teaching and research, and it offers graduate degree programs only. Most of the 150 students are full-time. Undergraduate instruction is limited to service courses and to participating in the Computer Sciences options of the Applied Sciences and Mathematical Sciences curricula. Two closely related graduate degrees are offered. The Ph.D. program prepares teachers and researchers for positions with universities, government and industry. The curricula are oriented toward the design and application of real computer systems and toward that portion of theory that guides and supports practice.

University of North Carolina at Greensboro

F/X Degrees Offered

B.A. and B.S. through the Department of Mathematical Sciences.

Curricular

3D Modeling and Rendering; 3D Computer Animation; 2D Computer Animation; High-Level Programming; Image Processing.

Facilities

Fully networked PC-compatible, Macintosh and Sun workstations.

Student Body

There are 100 undergraduate students in the department. Approximately 12,000 students attend the university.

Faculty Profile

There are 22 faculty members in the department.

Deadlines and Financial Aid

Approximately half of all UNCG students receive some form of financial aid to assist them in meeting the cost of college. Financial aid resources include scholarships, loans, work (part-time campus jobs in academic and administrative departments), and private sources with a private lender. For eligible students, the financial aid package may include a combination of aid, such as a loan and a part-time campus job, depending upon the availability of funds. Applications are reviewed and admissions decisions are made on a rolling basis. For priority consideration for fall admission, freshmen and transfers should apply by March 1; the final deadline is Aug. 1. For priority consideration for the spring admission, candidates should apply by November 1; the final deadline is December 1.

Admission Requirements
Official high school transcript, official results of the SAT I, official transcripts of all college course work, list of courses in progress, application and fee.

Expenses
Tuition is $4,072 per year for students and $15,920 per year for non-residents.

Contact
University of North Carolina, Greensboro, NC 27412. Telephone: 336-334-5836. Fax: 336-334-5949. Contact person: S. M. Lea. E-mail: leasue@iris.uncg.edu.
URL: http://www.cs.uncg/edu.

Wake Forest University

F/X Degrees Offered
B.S. and M.S. in Computer Science. B.A. in Fine Art.

Curricular
Computer Graphics; Digital Systems Architecture. Art Department offers courses in Digital Media.

Facilities
Macintosh and PC workstations including Sun UltraSparc 170E/2D systems, scanners, and laser printers.

Student Body
There are 3,898 undergraduates, and 2,103 graduate students.

Faculty Profile
There are 308 full-time faculty members teaching in the university; 12:1 student-to-faculty ratio.

Deadlines and Financial Aid
Undergraduates: college scholarships are as much as the cost of tuition, and are available to applicants on the basis of need. Numerous federal, state and institutional scholarships, loans and work programs exist to support Wake Forest's need-blind admissions policy. Generally, need-based awards consist of the following: scholarship or grant; loan: federal, state, private or institutional funds with low-interest rates and deferred payment; federal work-study. The admissions application deadline for fall enrollment is Jan. 15. The application date for the spring semester is November 1. Graduate: approximately 90 percent of full-time enrolled graduate students receive financial support to assist in the cost of graduate education; scholarships ($16,300), fellowships ($20,300) and assistantships ($23,300-$29,800) are awarded annually to qualified students in graduate programs on the Reynolda Campus. The completed applications for graduate admission should be received by February 15.

Admission Requirements
Undergraduates: candidates for admission must furnish evidence of maturity and educational achievement including academic records, test scores, plus evidence of character and motivation for study in the college. High school academic performance and SAT scores. Graduate: students must complete an application and fee, GRE, and submit all college transcripts.

Expenses
Estimated tuition is $26,490 per year.

Contact
Computer Science Department, 1832 Reynolda Rd., Winston-Salem, NC 27109. Telephone: 336-758-4892. Fax: 336-758-4324. Contact person: Jennifer Burg, Chair. Email: burg@cs.wfu.edu.
URL: http://www.cs.wfu.edu/.

Wake Technical Community College

F/X Degrees Offered
A.A.S. in Desktop Publishing; Internet Programming; Visual Basic Programming.

Curricular
3D Modeling and Animation; Maya: Level 1.

Facilities
SGI workstations with Maya; PC laboratories.

Student Body
There are 7,000 students are enrolled in the college.

Faculty Profile
Twelve faculty members in the Computer Information Systems Division.

Deadlines and Financial Aid
Various forms of financial aid are available. These include grants and scholarships such as: NC Student Incentive Grant; Supplemental Educational Opportunity Grant; grants for non-traditional courses of study; Federal College Work-Study Program; Veterans Educational Benefits; Vocational Rehabilitation; Job Training Partnership Act; Child Care.

Admission Requirements
File a completed application with the college, have an official high school transcript or copy of GED scores sent directly to the Admissions Office. Submit an official transcript of all previous college work to be evaluated for transfer credit. (Transfer credit will be given when applicable), schedule a conference with a counselor to review test scores and placement. A conference with an academic department representative may also be required.

Expenses
Tuition is $568 per semester for residents and $3,152 for non-residents.

Contact
Admissions Office, Wake Technical Community College, 9101 Fayetteville Road, Raleigh, NC 27603-5696. Telephone: 919-662-3500. URL: http://www.wake.tec.wc.us/.

Winston-Salem State University

F/X Degrees Offered
BA degree in Art with Computer Graphics concentration. Computer Science degrees.

Curricular
Introduction to Computer Art and Design; Electronic Imaging; Desktop Publishing I (PageMaker); Desktop Publishing II (QuarkXpress); Designing for the Web; 3D Modeling; Multimedia I; Multimedia Authoring; Computer Animation I; Computer Animation II; Desktop Virtual Reality; Immersive Virtual Reality; Internship; Art Co-Op; Studio Problems I-IV; Portfolio/Résumé Seminar; Senior Exhibit Project.

Facilities
The Computer Science Department is located in Carolina Hall. The department computing facilities include two PC Labs (002 and 104); Visualization Lab (142), Distributed Computing Lab, Networking Lab, and Microprocessor Lab. The GAMMA Lab uses Macintosh workstations dedicated to graphic design, desktop publishing and multimedia authoring. Silicon Graphics Indigo workstations support 3D Modeling and Animation and Virtual Reality applications. The Amiga Video Toaster workstation is utilized with a Sony Betacam animation deck,

a green screen, video capture equipment and editing systems. Applications include: Photoshop, Illustrator, Freehand, Streamline, Dimensions, PageMaker, QuarkXPress, PageMill, DreamWeaver, Bryce, Swivelman 3D, Director, Morph and Virtus Walkthrough Pro, Softimage Creative Environment, Softimage Eddie for multimedia, Softimage Creative TOONZ for 2D cell animation and LightWave 3D. The acquisition of Softimage animation. Software infrustructure for Computer Science courses is provided via a variety of operating systems, language interpreters, compilers, and numerous applications packages. Languages include: Assembler, C, C++, COBOL, FORTRAN, Pascal, Prolog, XLISP and Microsoft Visual Studio Professional which includes Visual C++, J++, BASIC. Application Packages include: Microsoft Office Professional 97 and 2000, which includes Word, Excel, Access, and PowerPoint. Other software includes Graphics, MODSIM, Maple, SQL Server, AVS, Adobe Graphics Suite, and Netscape. Computer Science students also use the Mathematics Symbolic Algebra Lab (CH 112) for access to Maple Software.

Student Body

Undergraduate program only: 30 art majors with concentration in computer graphics.

Faculty Profile

Four full-time faculty members and five adjunct faculty.

Deadlines and Financial Aid

College scholarships range up to tuition and are available to applicants on the basis of need. Numerous federal, state and institutional scholarships, loans and work programs exist to support Winston-Salem Stat University. Generally, need-based awards consist of the following: scholarship or grant; loan: federal, state, private or institutional funds with low-interest rates and deferred payment; federal work-study.

Admission Requirements

In addition to the general requirements for admission to the university, entering freshmen and transfer art students must submit a special supplementary application to the Art Program; submit slides and/or a portfolio to the Art Program; arrange for a personal interview with art faculty, prior to arrival on campus, if possible.

Expenses

Tuition is $613 per semester for residents and $4,745.50 per semester for non-residents.

Contact

Winston Salem State University, 130 Carolina Hall, CB 19438, Winston-Salem, NC 27110-0001. Phone: 336-750-2485. Fax: 336-750-2499. Contact person: Dr. Elva Jones, Chair. E-mail: jonese@wssu.edu.
URL: http://www.wssu.edu/.

North Dakota

North Dakota State University

F/X Degrees Offered
B.A., B.S., and M.S. in Computer Science.

Curricular
Computer graphics, computer science, artificial intelligence, software engineering, and other related courses.

Facilities
Various hardware and software platforms that include many computer graphics tools. The NDSU Computer Science Department is a member of the Microsoft Developer Network Academic Alliance. The MSDN Academic Alliance program is designed specifically for academic labs, faculty, and students in the curriculum areas of Computer Science, Engineering, and Information Systems to make it easier and less expensive to get Microsoft developer tools, platforms, and servers for instructional and research purposes.

Student Body
Total undergraduate enrollment is 10,000.

Deadlines and Financial Aid
Office of Financial Aid assists in finding loans, grants and work-study programs. Non-residents often find that NDSU's costs are similar to their own state schools. In addition to loans and grants, NDSU students may be eligible for a number of scholarships. To recognize outstanding academic achievement, NDSU makes scholarship awards ranging from $1,000 for two years to $8,000 for four years. These Development Scholarships, Presidential Scholarships and National Merit Scholarships are based on high school grades, test scores and out-of-class accomplishments. In addition, a number of academic departments award scholarships. New Student Scholarship Applications may be obtained from the Office of Admission. The application deadline is February 1.

Admission Requirements
Application and fee, SAT or ACT score, and transfer.

Expenses
Tuition is $3,374 per year for residents and approximately $8,000 per year for non-residents.

Contact
North Dakota State University, Computer Science Department, 258 IACC, Fargo, ND 58105. Telephone: 800-488-NDSU or 701-237-8011. Fax: 701-231-8802. URL: http://www.cs.ndsu.nodak.edu/.

Ohio

Art Institute of Cincinnati

F/X Degrees Offered
Associate Degree offered in Applied Science/ Computer Graphics.

Curricular
Perspective; Drawing; Illustration; Color I, II, III and IV; Typography; Media; Type Design; Illustration Workshop; Production; Corporate Design; Poster Design; Computer Basics; QuarkXPress; Adobe Illustrator and Photoshop; Environment Design; Ad Campaign; Brochure Design; CD Design; Web Page Design; Interactive Resume Design.

Facilities
Twenty Macintosh workstations; Sony multiscan monitors on all computers; scanner; b/w printers; color printer. All students in the second year have a computer on their desk. Students have separate cubicles.

Student Body
Total enrollment: 65 students.

Faculty Profile
Four full-time faculty, four specialist, two part-time and four general education faculty.

Deadlines and Financial Aid
Approximately $8,400 in scholarship funding each year. Open to High School seniors, High school Graduates or those who have earned a GED and toured the Institute, been interviewed and excepted for admission. The enrollment fee is not required to be paid in advance of entering the competition. The scholarship is not transferable is good only for September or February starts of the year it is awarded. The scholarship may be used only at The Art Institute of Cincinnati. Any person who wins a scholarship and then decides not to attend AIC will forfeit their scholarship. All scholarships are credited to the students accounts in eight (8) equal quarterly disbursements. In the case of the Ron Long Scholarship there are four (4) quarterly disbursements. Second year February students are eligible for half of the award or $1,000. The remainder may be awarded to a second student. In case of a tie students will spilt the scholarship. A student who drops out or is dismissed by AIC forfeits all rights to the remaining scholarship credits. Contact the Financial Aid Office to discuss eligibility for federal and state aid programs. Deadline is six weeks prior to the start of the program. Last week in August for the September admission, and last week in February for the March admission.

Admission Requirements
The student must be a high school graduate (or GED), and must present a portfolio of art. Entrance is based on talent and availability of space. Students who wish to transfer from another college may submit their credits for approval to ACA; approval is based on matching curriculum and quality of art.

Expenses
Tuition is approximately $12,996 per year.

Contact
ACA College of Design, 1171 Kemper Lane. Cincinnati, OH 45206. Telephone: 513-751-1206. Fax: 513-751-1209. Contact person: Stephen J. Enzweiler, Computer Graphics Director. Email: aic@theartinstit uteofcincinnati.com.
URL: http://www.theartinstituteofcincinnati.com.

Additional Information
ACA College of Design is a two-year career college that is devoted to the individual. The small size allows individual attention to students' needs. Students learn in a studio/agency atmosphere. Students must complete first-year foundation before

entering the second year, at which time the computer applications are taught.

Bowling Green State University

F/X Degrees Offered
The School of Art offers a B.F.A. degree in Computer Art with three tracks: 1) Computer Animation: both 2D and 3D with a strong emphasis on 3D animation including non-linear digital video editing and compositing; 2) Imaging: computer-generated still images with 2D digital imaging and 3D modeled and still images; 3) Interactive Multimedia: with an emphasis on Internet and Web Development, including HTML, VRML and JAVA programming, as well as traditional multimedia development. Future M.F.A. in Computer Art, through the Center for Advanced Visualization and Education.

Curricular
Introduction to Computer Art; Computer Art; Applications of Computer Art; Problems in Computer Art; Advanced Computer Art. Courses are also offered through the Design Technology and the Visual Communication Technology Departments.

Facilities
The computer art laboratory is part of the Center for Advanced Visualization and Education (CAVE) in the School of Art and includes: 20-seat SGI lab; another lab with 22-seat SGI Studio lab; 20 Macintoshes; seven Media100xs non-linear digital video editing stations with 80 GB storage; one BetacamSP Video Recorder; one S-VHS and SIX VHS Video Decks; six Hi-8 Sony Camcorders; one Sony Digital DVCam; two Sony 8 mm Camcorders; one Shinko dye-sublimation printer; one large-format Epson color inkjet printer; three laser printers; one Tektronix Thermal wax printer; five full-color scanners; one Agfa film recorder; one CD-ROM Burner. All computers are networked via 10/100 baseT Ethernet to the university's fiber backbone. Software includes: Maya, Artisan, MayaLive, Studio, Maya, Composer, StudioPaint 3D, 3Design, Softimage, Eddie, Media100xs, Photoshop and Illustrator for SGI & Mac, Fractal Design Painter, Macromedia Director, SoundEdit, PageMaker and Quark. BGSU's design and art resources include a modern $11 million School of Art facility which serves 13 applied arts and fine arts disciplines

Student Body
Eighty students in the B.F.A. program.

Faculty Profile
Four full-time faulty members teach courses at the center.

Deadlines and Financial Aid
All types of financial aid including scholarships, grants, loans and work opportunities are coordinated through the Office of Financial Aid and Student Employment. Freshmen who are admitted by March 1 and submit the FAFSA by the February 15 priority date are given first consideration for instructional, need-based financial aid for the following summer, fall and spring semesters.

Admission Requirements
Application and fee, transcripts, ACT or SAT, and portfolio. Admission to Bowling Green State University as an art major, involves both admission to the University (University Application) and approval to the School of Art through a portfolio review. While it is not necessary to be fully accepted by the University at the time you schedule your portfolio review, it is recommended that your undergraduate application be on file when you come for your review. Further information on the portfolio review process is available at: http://www.bgsu.edu/departments/art/admissions/portfolio/portfolio.html. All pre-digital arts candidates

---

complete two-dimensional foundations, drawing foundations and three-dimensional foundations during their first year. In their second semester, pre-digital arts candidates will take the Introduction to Digital Arts course which will give a sampling of the digital arts focus area at BGSU. In this course students will develop a portfolio that will be used to determine entry into the digital arts major. The review board will select the top 40 to 50 students based on the relative merits of their portfolios. These students will be admitted into the digital arts program and be allowed to pursue further studies in this area.

Expenses
Tuition is $3,780 per semester for residents and $7,260 for non-residents.

Contact
Bowling Green State University, 1000 Fine Arts Center, Bowling Green, OH 43403. Telephone: 419-372-2293 or 866-CHOOSW BGSU. Fax: 419-372-6955. Contact person: Dr. Dena Eber, chair and assistant professor. E-mail: deber@bgnet.bgsu.edu. URL: http://www.bgsu.edu/.

College of Mount Saint Joseph

F/X Degrees Offered
B.F.A., B.A. and A.A. in Graphic Design as well as Computer Science.

Curricular
Traditional Graphic Design courses that implement the computer technology include Computer Graphics and PageMaker/QuarkXPress.

Facilities
Macintosh laboratory.

Student Body
There are 180 in the department; 70 major in Graphic Design.

Faculty Profile
Fifteen faculty in the department.

Deadlines and Financial Aid
May 1 deadline for the fall admission.

Admission Requirements
High school transcript, portfolio, application and fee. Presentation of a portfolio to the art faculty by prospective students is encouraged but not required. Formal admission to the Art Department is contingent upon submission of a portfolio of college-level work to the art faculty for its review and determination. The portfolio is to be submitted after completion of 18 hours of art courses at the Mount. This procedure usually occurs in the second semester of the sophomore year. Transfer students may apply after the completion of 18 hours of art courses at the college level, with the last 6 hours completed at the Mount.

Expenses
Tuition is $16,000 per year.

Contact
Department of Art, College of Mount St. Joseph, 701 Delhi Rd., Cincinnati, OH 45233. Telephone: 513-244-4200 or 800-654-9314. Fax: 513-244-4601. Contact person: Dan Mader, Chair. E-mail: dan_mader@mail.msj.edu. URL: http://www.msj.edu/academics/art/.

Additional Information
The Computer Science program is a synthesis of a traditional computer science major at a four-year college and a new field of study, computer network systems. It attracts students interested in computer science, networking and systems analysis, and has been designed with a delicate balance between the theoretical and applied areas of computer science.

Graduates will have gained practical marketable skills allowing for success upon entering the work force. They will have also gained a solid foundation of theoretical expertise enabling continued education at the graduate level. To strengthen the quantitative and analytical skills of the major, the program includes sufficient coursework for a minor in mathematics. This addition to the computer science curriculum provides a maturity in problem-solving and critical thinking that gives graduates a competitive edge in the workplace. The skills and knowledge gained through completion of this program have immediate application in areas of great demand in the computer science and networking industry. In addition, the technical features of the curriculum have a synergy with liberal arts concepts such as critical thinking, decision-making, analytical skills, organizational and management techniques, and interpersonal communication. Graphic design majors at the Mount have the opportunity to explore new techniques and develop their ability to communicate ideas into images in a highly artistic environment. This career-oriented program familiarizes students with the field of graphic design and its application to visual communication. The program also offers opportunities to study new technologies in the field. Students are encouraged to explore cooperative education work assignments in their concentrations. All art majors are eligible to study and work abroad through an agreement with London's Huron University and the school's affiliation with British institutions and businesses.

Columbus College of Art and Design

F/X Degrees Offered
B.F.A. Division of Photography with a concentration in Video and Film, Storyboard and Computer Animation. Other areas include: Computer Graphics (CADD); Photography; Media Illustration; Cartoon Comic Book Illustration and Advertising Design.

Curricular
Introduction to Computer Graphics; Computer Graphics-CAD; Computer Graphics-CAM; Design for Computer Animation; Storyboard Design for Film and Animation; Introduction to Animation; Introduction to Computer Animation; Video; Video Studio; Motion Picture; Advanced Video; Freehand; PageMaker; QuarkXPress; Illustrator; Multimedia; Photoshop; Advanced Computer Graphics.

Facilities
Macintosh laboratory; Commodore Amiga laboratory; SAI Work Station; Film and Video Facilities. Advanced PageMaker; Advanced QuarkXPress; Advanced Illustrator; Advanced Multimedia; Advanced Photoshop; Advanced Studies.

Student Body
The student body is comprised of high school graduates representing most states in the nation and a great number of foreign countries.

Faculty Profile
The faculty of the college is composed of a large body of artist-designers with extensive professional experience and appropriate degrees in the divisions of art offered. Faculty members are professionally oriented, practicing artist-designers with broad teaching experience in the diversities of the world of art.

Deadlines and Financial Aid

There are 133 Art scholarships: four tuition scholarships, value (divided equally over four years) of 30,000; six tuition scholarships value (divided equally over four years) of $24,000; 17 tuition scholarships value (divided equally over three years) of $18,000; 49 tuition scholarships, value (divided equally over two years) of $12,000; 30 tuition scholarships, value (divided equally over two years) of $10,000; 27 tuition scholarships value (divided one year) of $8,000. Scholarship material for 133 Art scholarships are due before March 1. CCAD National Scholarship Competition: this annual competition of The Columbus College of Art and Design offers a substantial number of tuition scholarships applicable to one, two, three and four years. This competition is open to high school seniors; basic art ability is the criterion. Art work to be submitted for this competition is submitted in the spring of each year. Several other forms of scholarships are available.

Admission Requirements

Complete the application for admission, send high school transcript. Applications for admission may be made in advance for the fall semester or for the spring semester. Request the scores for the SAT or the ACT be sent directly to the Director of Admissions. An appointment to show a portfolio personally can be arranged through the Admissions Office, and is suggested for applicants living within a reasonable distance. Students are encouraged to submit letters of recommendation.

Expenses

Tuition is $8,940 per semester.

Contact

Director of Admissions, The Columbus College of Art and Design, 107 N. Ninth St., Columbus, OH 43215-1758. Telephone: 614-224-9101. Fax: 614-232-8344. URL: http://www.ccad.edu/.

Kent State University

F/X Degrees Offered

B.S., M.S. and Ph.D. in Mathematics and Computer Science.

Curricular

Computer Graphics and Advanced Scientific Visualization.

Facilities

Departmental Computing facilities--the department has three general-purpose laboratories, an undergraduate laboratory with 19 Hewlett Packard X-terminals and 15 Suns, a graduate laboratory with 10 X-terminals and 11 Suns, and a teaching laboratory with 20 486DX-33 PCs and projection facilities. The teaching laboratory with AMD K590s processors, and a new teaching laboratory with 24 Pentium 200s, with 32 MB memory each and 17-inch monitors, is planned. In addition, there are four special purpose laboratories: a Graphics Laboratory with seven Hewlett Packard multimedia X-terminals; a Scientific Visualization Laboratory with a Hewlett Packard J-210 workstation with Visualize-24 graphics enhancement and two multimedia X-terminals; an Operating Systems and Systems Programming Laboratory with Hewlett Packard; Sun and IBM RT workstations; and a Distributed Operating Systems Laboratory with a 4-processor Sequent Symmetry, two Silicon Graphics workstations, and PCs. The departmental general purpose computing facilities currently include a four-processor Sun; a two-processor HP/Apollo J200, two HP/Apollo 730s; a Hewlett Packard 735/125; a Wavetracer DTC SIMD machine, with 8,192 processors and 256 MB of memory; and three HP/Apollo 715s and 705s. In addition, there are 18 HP and NCD X-terminals, 35 Sun 3s, and three Macintosh SE30s in faculty and graduate student offices. Peripherals include six laser printers, a

Hewlett Packard Color 5m laser printer, a plotter, a scanner and four annex terminal servers, which are used for modems and terminals. The Wavetracer DTC is extensively used for undergraduate and graduate education in parallel programming. The Sun 4/670 and the HP/Apollo 730s and 735 act as file servers for all faculty, undergraduate and graduate computer accounts. The Sun 3/50s are used as X-terminals to access the departmental file servers, and are in the process of being replaced by X-terminals. The departmental research equipment includes a Wavetracer DTC SIMD computer, with 16 384 processors and 512 MB of memory, a General Electric Warp systolic array processor, and a shared memory MIMD machine, the 26-processor Sequent Balance. Several other workstations are available in the department.

Student Body
There are 212 undergraduate Computer Science majors, and 88 graduate students are in the department.

Faculty Profile
Sixteen faculty members teach in the department.

Deadlines and Financial Aid
Graduate assistantship stipends range from $8,100 to $9,400 per year. Fellows receive a stipend of $9,400 per year. Admissions application deadline: rolling admission. Assistantship application deadline: March 1.

Admission Requirements
Undergraduate students should contact the office of admissions. Graduate students: application and fee, transcripts and GRE scores. Freshman applicants must submit the following items: a completed and signed application for admission, non-refundable application fee, an official high school transcript; ACT or SAT scores; final high school transcript.

Expenses
Tuition is $3,441 per semester for residents and $6,657 per year for non-residents.

Contact
Kent State University, Department of Mathematics and Computer Science, Kent, OH 44242. Telephone: 330-672-2430 ext. 343. Fax: 330-672-7824. Contact person: Prof. Johnnie Baker, Chair. E-mail: jbaker@mcs.kent.edu.
URL: http://www.cs.kent.edu/.

The Ohio State University

F/X Degrees Offered
Advanced Computing Center for the Arts and Design. Graduate educational opportunities are offered through the departments of Art (M.F.A.), Design (M.A. or M.F.A.), and Art Education (M.A./ Ph.D.), with specialization in Art and Technology, Computer Animation, Computer Visualization, Multimedia, and the Use of Technology in Arts Education. B.F.A. and M.F.A. degrees in Expanded Arts (including Computer Art). In addition, the Computer and Information Science Department offers B.S., M.S. and Ph.D. degrees in Computer Science. Students enrolled in these programs share the up-to-date environment of ACCAD to perform their advanced research and coursework. While at ACCAD, students collaborate with other students and faculty from such diverse areas as Computer Science, Medicine, and Education.

Curricular
3D Modeling and Rendering; 3D Computer Animation; Multimedia/Interactive; High-Level Programming; Low-Level programming; Digital Painting/Drawing; Image processing; Digital Video; Stereo Imaging.

Facilities

Silicon Graphics, Sun, Macintosh and IBM. Motion capture system. A variety of proprietary and commercial programs; coursework is taught using proprietary software. Equipment includes graphics workstations from Macintosh Computer, IBM, Sun Microsystems and Silicon Graphics. Peripherals include specialized processors from AT&T and Sun, and frame buffers from Raster Technologies. An Abekas digital storage system and a Panasonic WORM Optical Disc are used for video output, and a Solitaire film recorder is used for film output. Several brands of scanners and digitizing equipment are used, including a Polhemus 3D digitizer. The physical facility is shared with the Ohio Supercomputer Center (OSC). ACCAD personnel participated in the development of the apE visualization software that is used as the visual front end to the Cray Y/MP Supercomputer, and continue to provide consulting support for OSC and its industry and institutional clients. This relationship with OSC provides access to the Cray and to the Ohio Visualization Laboratory (OVL), with its collection of workstations and the video and film recording and editing facilities mentioned above.

Student Body

Forty graduates are at the Advanced Computing Center for the Arts and Design.

Faculty Profile

Currently, the Department of Art consists of approximately 22 full-time studio faculty, as well as an additional four to six lecturers and/or visiting artists per year. At present there are 20 full-time graduate faculty. Seven full-time faculty members teach at the Advanced Computing Center for the Arts and Design.

Deadlines and Financial Aid

Graduate: deadline for material is Jan. 20. All application materials must be submitted before application can be reviewed. Graduate Associateships: associateships are renewed on the basis of satisfactory performance in assignments, no academic probation, and continued University monetary support to the Department. The standard graduate associateship contract appointment covers fall, winter and spring quarters on a 50 percent contract (up to 20 hours per week). GTA contracts shall be awarded only for full academic year periods (three quarters--fall, winter, spring). University fellowships: Awarded on a competitive basis throughout the University. They are subject to variations in number and stipend each school year. Special information for fellowships can be obtained from the Fellowship Office of the Graduate School at The Ohio State University. Graduate students will receive no more than six quarters of support (during fall, winter, spring), whether fellowship or graduate associateship or any combination. Additional summer quarters of support are possible, but not to be expected. Undergraduates: various forms of financial aid are available including grants, loans and scholarships. Contact the Office of Financial Aid for information.

Admission Requirements

Undergraduate students are required to submit an application, transcripts, and SAT or ACT scores. Graduate students: mail to Graduate Admissions Office: Complete Graduate School Admission Application (including GRE scores if accumulative point hour is below 2.7 or if you attended a pass/non-pass institution), one transcript from each college and/or university attended, a carbon or photocopy of Statement of Purpose (substituted for the autobiography). Graduate applicants to the M.F.A. must mail to Department of Art: Department of Art Graduate application; slide portfolio (20 slides and slide identification sheet), Statement of Purpose, three letters of recommendation, and self-addressed stamped envelope.

Expenses

Tuition is $6,624 per year for residents and $16,488 per year for non-residents.

Contact

ACCAD, 224 Kinnear Rd., Columbus, OH 43212-1154. Telephone: 614-292-3416. Fax: 614-292-7776. Contact person: Dr. Wayne Carlson. E-mail: accad@cgrg.ohio-state.edu. URL: http://www.osu.edu/.

Additional Information

The Advanced Computing Center for the Arts and Design (ACCAD) at The Ohio State University was formally established in 1987 for the specific purpose of: applying advances in computing technology to the processes, values and ideals of the arts; promoting interdisciplinary projects and programs with visual and performing artists, designers, arts historians, and critics, and with computer scientists, engineers, mathematicians and others with related interests; employing sophisticated computing and visualization technologies for the investigation of artistic production and evaluation, and for modes of dissemination. ACCAD was originally called the Computer Graphics Research Group, which began in the early '70s, with research and instruction in computer graphics and animation. The Center has a true interdisciplinary character and attempts to merge scientific investigation with aesthetic ideals. While it is administratively located in the College of the Arts, it provides leadership in computer graphics and animation development to support instruction and research in both the arts and the sciences. The Center offers a context in which students and faculty representing both disciplines can learn the power of the digital syntax. It promotes the study of an aesthetic message design in such diverse areas as computer software development, advertising and television promotion, the visual and performing arts, human factors and interface design, multimedia and emerging media technologies, and scientific computing and visualization.

University of Cincinnati

F/X Degrees Offered

School of Art. The University of Cincinnati offers a B.F.A. and an M.F.A. in Electronic Arts. The program encourages a cross-disciplinary approach to art. The Electronic Arts major offers classes in computer animation and interactive art.

Curricular

3D Modeling and Rendering; 3D Computer Animation; 2D Computer Animation; Multimedia/Interactive; Digital Painting/Drawing; Image Processing; Virtual Reality (immersive); Virtual Reality (non-immersive).

Facilities

The DAAP Computer Graphics Center is a state-of-the-art university facility with hardware that includes Sun Sparc-stations and SGI graphics workstations, PCs, Macintoshes, and various peripherals such as 2D and 3D digitizers, scanners, and plotters. The center is a place where university researchers have access to sophisticated graphics equipment and high levels of technical support for computer visualization, advanced computer graphics, and virtual reality. Five computer graphics instructional studios provide hands-on instruction labs for individual classes. Scanning, digitizing, and other research and instructional support activities take place in the multi-platform open lab area. Various additional resources are provided through satellite components such as animation studios and an industrial shop for milling 3D models. All computing equipment is linked by switched ethernet to facilitate access across the university campus.

Student Body

Twenty undergraduates, six graduate students, approximately 200 students in the School of Art and 40 in the M.F.A. Program. A total of 1,800 graduate and undergraduate students attend the university.

Faculty Profile

Seventeen full-time faculty members teach in the Department of Art; two full-time Electronic Arts faculty.

Deadlines and Financial Aid

Application deadline: March 1. Contact: Office of Admissions, University of Cincinnati, Cincinnati, OH 45221. Graduate M.F.A. students: admission will be in the fall quarter only. Applicants must have completed their bachelor's degree by March 1 of the preceding school year. The majority of first- and second-year graduate students are awarded with either a graduate scholarship, which covers the annual tuition, or a teaching assistantship, which covers tuition and general fees, plus a cash stipend. In addition to theses awards, first-year M.F.A. graduate students are eligible to compete for the Isabel Meta Wolfstein Scholarships of $2,500 and $1,000 to support international and national travel in the study/practice of fine art.

Admission Requirements

Undergraduate Admission applicants must provide ACT (preferred) or SAT scores, application fee, transcripts, and any other information necessary to process your application. The following items are required for evaluation by the School of Art Graduate Admissions Committee prior to March 1 of each academic year: completed university application form with application fee and portfolio.

Expenses

Tuition is $7,623 per year for residents and $19,230 for non-residents.

Contact

University of Cincinnati, College of Engineering, 665B BALDWIN, PO Box 210018 Cincinnati, OH 45221-0018. Telephone: 513-556-0286. Fax: 513-556-2887. Contact person: Diane Buhr. Email: Diane.Buhr@uc.edu.
URL: http://www.ececs.uc.edu/~apattana/WEB/ENG/eng.htm.

Additional Information

Merging art and technology, undergraduate students in Electronic Arts explore creative applications of computer animation and interactive art. The program also provides an understanding of the role media plays in our culture. Students in the area can produce both animation and interactive projects. This program uses the DAAP Computer Graphics Center, a continually developing multi-platform facility designed for the creation of computer generated work. In the Electronic Arts area, classroom demonstrations are combined with individualized instruction from faculty members. Introductory students take classes which are designed for the initial development of technical skills along with the development of the individual's thinking about Electronic Art. Advanced students create portfolio projects, developing concepts and techniques of their own choosing. Advanced projects can extend over several quarters. Students in Electronic Arts are encouraged to explore and expand their understanding of the changing role of technology and art. This program supports students who have experience with computing as well as those who have a considerable background in the traditional arts with an interest and desire to develop electronic work.

University of Toledo

F/X Degrees Offered
Art Department. B.F.A. in 2D and 3D studies. The Cyber Art program is a multimedia program, which encourages the mixing of technology and traditional media.

Curricular
3D Modeling and Rendering; 3D Computer Animation; 2D Computer Animation; Multimedia/Interactive; Digital Painting/Drawing; Image Processing; Digital Video; Mixed Media.

Facilities
The Digital Studio is a Macintosh-based facility dedicated for use by fine arts students in the Cyber Arts program with 15 networked Macintosh computers, film recorder, color scanner, and laser and color printers. Adjacent to the Digital Studio is a 3D fabrication room and a complete workshop. All computers have Internet access and all Cyber Arts students have e-mail accounts. The Digital Studio's unique arrangement allows for highly flexible usage and is available for student use anytime the Center for the Visual Arts is open.

Student Body
There are 225 undergraduate students in the Department of Art.

Faculty Profile
Fifteen full-time faculty members teach in the department.

Deadlines and Financial Aid
Financial aid awards are valid only for one academic year, beginning with summer quarter and ending with spring quarter. Financial aid funds are to be used by the student to pay tuition, fees, room, board, books, and other educational costs including personal expenses. The Ohio Instructional Grant is used to pay tuition and fees before any other financial aid.

Admission Requirements
Application, college preparatory curriculum completion form, official high school transcript (from guidance office), ACT/SAT test scores, non-refundable application fee.

Expenses
Tuition is $3,207.36 per semester for residents and $7,526.76 per semester for non-residents.

Contact Information
Electrical Engineering and Computer Science Department, 620 Grove Pl., Toledo, OH 43620. Telephone: 419-530-8300. Contact person: Dr. Demetrios Kazakos, Chair. URL: http://www.eecs.utoledo.edu/.

Additional Information
The focus of the Cyber Arts program at the University of Toledo is a B.F.A. curriculum, which prepares fine arts students for graduate studies and/or a career in the fine arts. Addressing both 2D and 3D studies, the Cyber Art program is a multimedia program, which encourages the mixing of technology and traditional media. In addition, students in this program become part of a larger community of artists working with technology through an active Internet connection, maintained by the university, with which students are required to be highly involved. Using this connection, students participate with other universities around the country in course work and independent study projects. Students are actively encouraged to participate in exhibitions and performances outside the university both as individual artists and as groups.

Wright State University

F/X Degrees Offered

Computer Science and Engineering. B.S., M.S. and Ph.D. The Department of Computer Science and Engineering offers a CSAB-accredited B.S. in Computer Science, and an ABET-accredited B.S. in Computer Engineering degree. The department also offers a M.S. in Computer Science (M.S.C.S.), a M.S. in Computer Engineering (M.S.C.E.), and Ph.D. in Computer Science and Engineering. The M.S.C.S. and M.S.C.E. programs are available with or without a thesis.

Curricular

3D Modeling and Rendering; 3D Computer Animation; 2D Computer Animation; High-Level Programming; Low-Level Programming; Virtual Reality; Volume Visualization; Stereo Imaging.

Facilities

A Silicon Graphics (SGI) Reality Engine 2; many DEC, Sun and SGI workstations; and numerous PCs and X-terminals. The facility is separated into several specialized laboratories, including: Optical Computing Laboratory; Computer Architecture Laboratory; Mobile Robotics/Cybernetics Laboratory; Hardware Projects Laboratory; Microprocessor-based Systems Design Laboratory; PC Network Laboratory; Computer Software Laboratory I; Project 2000 Laboratory; Digital Design Laboratory; Computer Networking Laboratory; Adaptive Vision Laboratory; Fuzzy Systems Laboratory; Parallel Computing Laboratory; Software Engineering Laboratory; Neural Networks Laboratory, Room 448.

Student Body

There are 445 undergraduates, and 129 graduate students. Total enrollment at the university is 16,000 students.

Faculty Profile

Seventeen full-time faculty members in the department.

Deadlines and Financial Aid

Financial aid available to graduate students includes graduate assistantships, graduate fellowships, Federal Perkins Loans, Federal Subsidized and Unsubsidized Stafford Loans, and work-study employment. Undergraduates may qualify for various state, federal and university aid.

Admission Requirements

Undergraduate application: application fee; high school transcript, School Equivalence Diploma scores, College Preparatory Curriculum Completion Form, ACT or SAT scores. Graduate admission—complete an application form, pay a non-refundable application fee, have an earned bachelor's degree from an accredited college or university, request all colleges/universities previously attended to send one official transcript directly to the School of Graduate Studies. Official transcripts are required for all previous undergraduate and graduate (if applicable) college work. Graduate Record Examinations (GRE).

Expenses

Tuition is $5,892 per year for residents and $11,364 per year for non-residents.

Contact

Computer Science Department, 405 Russ Engineering Center, Dayton, OH 45435. Telephone: 937-775-5001. Fax: 937-775-5009. Contact person: Dr. Oscar N. Garcia, chair. E-mail: ogarcia@cs.wright.edu. URL: http://www.cs.wright.edu/.

Youngstown State University

F/X Degrees Offered
B.S. in Computer Science and B.F.A. in Art with a focus in Graphic Design, and Art and Technology. B.S. in Web Communications.

Curricular
Courses offered through the Department of Art include Digital Imaging 1, 2, 3 and 4; Time-based Digital Imaging; and Multimedia Design. 3D Computer Animation, 2D Computer Animation, Web Design as well as other related courses.

Facilities
PC, Macintosh and SGI workstations. Multimedia laboratory with 30 workstations, combination of Macintoshes and IBMs; one SGI laboratory. Software include Maya, Photoshop, Web-based design software, print-based design software.

Student Body
There are 75 students in the Art & Technology area of the department.

Faculty Profile
Four full-time faculty teach in the Art & Technology area.

Deadlines and Financial Aid
Rolling admission. The admission application process must be complete in order to be considered for YSU scholarships and receive a financial aid package. There are several forms of financial aid available in the form of grants, loans, scholarships, and federal aid.

Admission Requirements
High school transcript, application and fee, SAT.

Expenses
Tuition is $5,448 per year for residents and $10,656 for non-residents.

Contact
Youngstown State University, One University Plaza, Youngstown, OH 44555. Telephone: 330-742-3627. Fax: 330-742-7183. Contact person: Thomas A. Bodnovich, Professor. E-mail: tom@cis.ysu.edu. URL: http://www.cs.wright.edu/.

Oklahoma

Northeastern Oklahoma A&M College

F/X Degrees Offered
A.S. in Drafting and Design; A.A. in Business Administration with the Interior Design transfer program. An Associate in Applied Sciences degree in Computer Science is available with an option in Computer Support Specialist.

Curricular
Computer Aided Drafting, and Design I and II.

Facilities
Four Computer-Aided Design and Computer workstations in a design laboratory.

Student Body
Fifteen students in the Computer Graphics-related majors, and 300 students in the department.

Faculty Profile
Two faculty members teach in this area of studies.

Deadlines and Financial Aid
April 15 application deadline for the fall semester.

Admission Requirements
Open enrollment. Prospective students must submit a copy of the ACT or SAT scores, application and fee, high school and/or college transcript.

Expenses
Tuition is $59.25 per credit hour for residents and $147.25 per credit for non-residents.

Contact
Northeastern Oklahoma A&M College, 200 I Street Northeast, Miami, OK 74354. Telephone: 918-540-6259 or 888-GO-GO-NEO. Fax: 918-540-6946.

Contact person: Ron Combs, Program Director. Email: rcombs@neoam.edu. URL: http://www.neoam.cc.ok.us/.

Oklahoma Christian University

F/X Degrees Offered
B.F.A. in Advertising Design with an emphasis in Multimedia. B.S. in Mass Communication with an emphasis in Electronic Media/Multimedia.

Curricular
Computer Graphics I; Computer Graphics II; Graphic Design; Typography; Computer-Aided Interior Design; Computer Graphics for Multimedia; Theories of Hypermedia/Multimedia Environments; Multimedia Production Concepts and Practices; Advanced Multimedia; Multimedia Workshop

Facilities
Four computer-aided design workstations running AutoCAD. Fifteen multimedia design and production workstations running PhotoShop, Freehand, Painter, Flash, Authorware, Infini-D, AfterEffects, DreamWeaver, MusicLab, Premiere, PageMaker, Vision, and Finale. Peripherals include Flatbed Scanners and MIDI Keyboards.

Student Body
There are 100 students in computer graphics/multimedia related majors.

Faculty Profile
Five faculty members teach in this area.

Deadlines and Financial Aid
Records for a recent year show that more than 80 percent of OC students received financial assistance. More than 50 percent were eligible for federal aid and received an average of $7,300 per year through

grants, loans, and work-study jobs. Programs include Federal Pell Grants, Federal Supplemental Educational Opportunity Grants, Oklahoma Tuition Aid Grants, Academic Scholarships, Merit Scholarships, and a variety of others. Contact the OC Financial Aid Office, 405-425-5190 for complete details. Application deadline for the fall semester is April 30.

Admission Requirements

Open enrollment. Students must submit a completed application, high school transcripts, and ACT or SAT scores.

Expenses

Tuition is $4,320 per semester.

Contact

Oklahoma Christian University, Admissions Office Box 11000, Oklahoma City, OK 73136-1100. Telephone: 405-425-5548 or 800-877-5010. Fax: 405-425-5069. Michael O'Keefe, Art & Design Chair. E-mail: michael.okeefe@oc.edu. URL: http://www.oc.edu/.

Oregon

Mount Hood Community College

F/X Degrees Offered
A.A. in Art, Graphic Design, and Television Production.

Curricular
Courses are a mixture of technology and art with a strong emphasis on design. 3D Modeling and Rendering; 3D Computer Animation; 2D Computer Animation; Multimedia/Interactive; Image Processing; Digital Painting/Drawing; Desktop Publishing. Television Production courses offer many related skills.

Facilities
Macintosh computers; Quark XPress; Adobe Illustrator; Aldus Freehand; Adobe Photoshop; Macromind Director; Diva Videoshop; Swivel 3D.

Student Body
There are 130 undergraduate students in the department, and 200 students in Continuing Education. A total of 10,500 students are enrolled in the college.

Deadlines and Financial Aid
Federal and state aid and various scholarship options.

Admission Requirements
Application, placement test. Open admission college.

Expenses
Tuition is $37 per credit for residents and $147.50 per credit for non-residents.

Contact
26000 SE Stark, Gresham, OR 97030. Telephone: 503-669-6968. Fax: 503-669-6949. URL: http://www.mhcc.edu.

Oregon Graduate Institute of Science and Technology

F/X Degrees Offered
M.S. and Ph.D. in Computer Science and Engineering.

Curricular
Advanced 3D Modeling and Animation, Human-Computer Interfaces, and Software Systems.

Facilities
Department facilities--117 systems including Sun, DEC, NeXT and Macintosh; 99 X-terminals. The school provides several specialized labs: Center for Human Computer Communication (CHCC) Human-computer interaction through sound and gesture; Database and Object Technology Lab (DOT) Databases and object-oriented systems; Pacific Software Research Center (PacSoft) Programming language technology and formal methods; Systems Software Lab (SySL) Distributed and mobile computing, operating systems, and networking; Center for Spoken Language Understanding (CSLU)Spoken language systems; Visualization and Geometric Computing, Computer graphics, computational geometry and scientific visualization.

Student Body
There are 57 graduate students.

Faculty Profile
Twenty-one full-time faculty members in the department.

Deadlines and Financial Aid

Full-time students typically finance their education with a combination of personal finances and loans. The Office of Student Services maintains information on student loan programs and can assist you in applying for them. Graduate assistantships are offered in the form of research assistantships and teaching assistantships of $14,000 per year. Admissions application deadline: Ph.D.—March 1. Master's accepted on quarterly basis. Assistantship application deadline: Ph.D.—March 1. M.S.—quarterly.

Admission Requirements

Application and fee, transcripts, letters of recommendation, statement of purpose and GRE score.

Expenses

Tuition is $3,223 per semester for residents and $5,192 per semester for non-residents.

Contact

Department of Computer Science and Engineering, OHSU, 20000 NW Walker Rd., Beaverton, OR 97006-8921. Telephone: 503-748-1151. Fax: 503-748-1553. E-mail: csedept@cse.ogi.edu. URL: http://www.cse.ogi.edu.

Additional Information

The Department of Computer Science and Engineering offers an outstanding educational opportunity for those planning or engaged in careers in computing technology or research. Study in the department integrates the discipline of computer science, which focuses on algorithms, architectures, programming and theory of computation, with engineering, which is about using this science to create useful artifacts. Students learn skills that can be transferred immediately to the workplace, conceptual knowledge that will be valuable throughout their careers, and an understanding of the fundamental principles underlying all computer systems, past, present, and future...

Pacific Northwest College of Art

F/X Degrees Offered

Department of Design. B.F.A. program in the visual arts (Sculpture, Ceramics, Glass, Painting, Printmaking, Photography, Design, and Digital). Currently in the process of organizing an M.F.A. curriculum.

Curricular

Computer Animation; Multimedia/Interactive; Digital Imaging; Desktop Publishing.

Facilities

Twenty-four Macintosh workstations. All of the machines are equipped with CD-ROM and Zip drives. Three Tektronix printers; two Apple Color Laser and two Laser printers. Adobe Photoshop; Illustrator; Painter; QuarkXPress; Freehand; Fontographer; Macromedia xRes; and PageMaker. 12 Macintoshes in the Design Building; which are used mainly for typography. Our extensive Computer Arts Center provides students access to the latest digital technology and industry standard software. Students also have access to animation, video and audio editing labs.

Student Body

There are 50 undergraduate students in the Computer Graphics area.

Faculty Profile

Seven faculty members teach in the Computer Graphics area.

Deadlines and Financial Aid

Various fellowships and traditional state, federal and city aid are available to students. Students who have completed their application for admission to the BFA program and who have submitted their FAFSA form before March 1 will receive "Priority Attention" in the Financial Aid process. These students will be the first to receive their financial aid award notices, and are more likely to receive funding from our exhaustible financial aid funds, such as Federal Work Study, STEP, PNCA Tuition Remission Grants, and Federal SEOG. Students who apply by March 1 will also be eligible for PNCA's new student scholarship programs the Leta Kennedy New Student Scholarship, and the Hearst Foundation Transfer Student Scholarship. Students who meet the Priority Application Deadlines will receive their financial aid award notices by June. Students who do not meet the March 1 deadline may not receive funds for which they are otherwise qualified, as Priority Attention Applicants may exhaust these funds. Current BFA students qualify for Priority Attention by submitting their FAFSA forms by March 1.

Admission Requirements

Application and fee, portfolio, two recommendations, essayn and transcripts.

Expenses

Tuition is $14,270 per year.

Contact

1219 S.W. Park Ave., Portland, OR 97204. Telephone: 503-226-4391 Fax: 800-818-7622. E-mail: pncainfo@pnca.edu.
URL: http://www.pnca.edu.

University of Oregon

F/X Degrees Offered

Fine Art and Applied Arts Department. Three bachelor's degrees are offered by the department: a four-year program leads to the B.A. or B.S. degree, and a five-year program leads to the B.F.A. degree. The department offers the M.F.A. degree in several areas of instruction. Computer studies are offered through the Visual Design area.

Curricular

3D Modeling and Rendering; 3D Computer Animation; 2D Computer Animation; Multimedia/ Interactive; High-Level Programming; Digital Painting/Drawing; Image Processing; Digital Video.

Facilities

The departmental computing environment is a mix of Unix, Apple Macintosh, and Intel-based computers. First year undergraduates use Intel-based computer labs in the Computing Center, while upper-division undergraduates and graduate students use a Sun Ultra SPARC workstation lab. Research labs operate a variety of Unix workstations and Intel-based computers. The Human-Computer Interaction Lab is equipped with Sun workstations, Macintoshes, and several Pentium processors. Specialized equipment for interactive systems research includes a PHANToM force feedback control device and the DecTalk speech synthesizer. Usability studies are supported by a laboratory with multiple video cameras, video cassette recorders, and audio recording. The Computer Graphics Laboratory includes color scanners, color film recorders, color calibrated monitors and video-editing equipment, and high-performance Unix and PC graphics workstations. Research in high-performance computing is supported by the facilities in the Computational Science Institute. The institute has a Power Onyx with 8 R10000 CPUs, Reality Engine graphics, and Sirius Video; and, two Silicon Graphics Power Challenge systems with ten and twelve CPUs. These machines are connected with 100mb Fast Ethernet to a dedicated Ethernet switch. Research in the institute is also supported by a four-proccssor Origin 2000, four Indigo2 High Impact workstations, and eight 02 desktop workstations. The Network Research Lab contains a model of a wide-area network that is used to develop and prototype new Internet applications. Any of the computers may be used for simulations and as general-purpose workstations. The network is composed of custom-built PCs running the FreeBSD operating system. The department network is primarily a switched 100-Base-T network, connected to the UO's one-gigabit network. The university is a member of Internet2, a high-speed network, connecting major research institutions.

Student Body
There are 65 undergraduates (Visual Design only), and 12 graduate students (Visual Design only).

Deadlines and Financial Aid
Jan. 1 is the earliest time to apply for financial aid. February 1 is the deadline for General University Scholarship Applications and required materials.

Admission Requirements
Students must apply directly to the Department of Fine and Applied Arts for admission as majors. Write or call the department for the application form and deadlines. Admission screening takes place each term for admission the next term.

Expenses
Tuition is $1,561 per semester for residents and $5,173 per semester for non-residents.

Contact
CIS Department, University of Oregon, Eugene, OR 97403. Telephone: 541-346-4408. Fax: 541-346-5373. Contact person: Zena M. Ariola, Associate Professor. E-mail: ariola@cs.uoregon.edu. General Information: 541-346-3111.
URL: http://www.cs.uoregon.edu/.

Pennsylvania

Art Institute of Pittsburgh

F/X Degrees Offered
A.A. and B.S. in Computer Animation, Multimedia, Video Production, and Game Design.

Curricular
Computer Animation/Multimedia: Computers in 2D Animation I; Character Drawing; Computers in 2D Animation II; Audio Recording and Production I; Background Rendering; Image Manipulation; Introduction to Video. Animation: History and Principles; Cel Animation I; Computer 3D Modeling; Interactive Authoring; Video Production I; Cel Animation II; Computer Modeling and Animation; Animation Production II; Computer Animation Workshop. Interactive Media and Games Video Production: Introduction to Video Production; Video Production I; Video Production II; Advanced Lighting Techniques; Scriptwriting; Advanced Videography; Video Engineering; Advanced Video Editing; Video Graphics; Filmmaking I, II and III; Non-Linear Editing; Directing; Multi-camera Field Production; MIDI and Sequencing; Digital Audio Technology.

Facilities
Equipment provided at The Art Institute of Pittsburgh is specific to the program of study. This includes, but is not limited to: four-by-five cameras; projectors; color and b/w enlargers; editing decks; camcorders; 24-track recorder; blueprint machine. Gateway and Macintosh computers; typewriters; light tables; and various sanding, milling, cutting; and modeling tools.

Student Body
There are 25 students in the average class size; 2,325 total enrollment.

Faculty Profile
More than 100 faculty members teach at the institute.

Deadlines and Financial Aid
Awards under these programs are based on individual need and the availability of funds. A number of states, including Pennsylvania and Ohio, also offer educational grants. Some states permit their residents to use the grants at schools outside of the state. Contact The Art Institute of Pittsburgh's Student Financial Services Office for complete details about financial aid resources.

Expenses
Tuition is approximately $345 per credit hour.

Admission Requirements
A student must be a high school graduate or possess the recognized equivalency (i.e., GED). Proof of graduation or passing equivalency exam scores are required by the end of the student's first quarter. All Art Institute of Pittsburgh applicants are evaluated on the basis of their previous education, background, and stated or demonstrated interest in art, animation, interior design, fashion illustration, photography, fashion marketing, industrial design, music and video business, video production, or multimedia. Portfolios are welcomed, but not required. Applicants who have taken the SAT or ACT are encouraged to submit scores to the Admissions Office for evaluation.

Contact
Director of Admissions, The Art Institute of Pittsburgh, 420 Boulevard of The Allies, Pittsburgh, PA 15219. Telephone: 800-275-2470 or 412-263-6600. Fax: 412-263-6667.
URL: http://www.aip.aii.edu/index2.asp.

Additional Information

The Art Institute developed Computer Animation/ Multimedia, a 24-month program, to prepare students with interests in computer and media technologies for creative careers that require specialized skills. Students will receive training in 3D animation, cel and stop-motion animation, computer imagery, and interactive programming, as well as film and video production for the motion picture, advertising, and educational/entertainment game industries. Computer Animation/Multimedia graduates are prepared for entry-level positions such as effects artists, title artist, animation artist, prepress artist, post-production artist, multimedia specialist, and presentation specialist in the graphic arts or media departments of businesses related to recording, film, television, advertising, simulation, animation, design, engineering and architectural fields.

Bucknell University

F/X Degrees Offered

B.S., B.S.E.G. and B.A. in Computer Science and Engineering.

Curricular

3D Modeling and Rendering; 3D Computer Animation; 2D Computer Animation; High-Level Programming; Low-Level Programming.

Facilities

Dana 319 has 3 SGI graphics UNIX workstations and other graphics and video production equipment. The SGI workstations are interconnected by a local network and connected to the campus internet. The equipment in this room is used in the Computer Graphics course and for graphics research. Dana 318 contains instructional and research systems that are accessed remotely from other locations in Dana and across campus through the campus internet. There is a parallel computing system of Transputer processors connected to a local network and accessible through the campus network. The Transputer processors can be reconnected into a variety of configurations for studying parallel processing architectures, and are used in the Parallel Computation course and for research. There are also two Linux workstations connected to a local network and the campus internet that are used for parallel processing. Other equipment includes: Fifty Sun Sparc Stations/10/20/LX; several Silicon Graphics workstations, Indigo/Indy; many Macintosh; Windows PC; PHIGS; OpenGL; Maya.

Student Body

There are 120 undergraduate students major in Computer Science and Engineering; 3,400 undergraduates and 200 graduate students attend the university.

Faculty Profile

10 faculty members in the department.

Deadlines and Financial Aid

December 1: Early decision applications must be submitted. December 20: Announcement of all early decisions. Jan. 1: Regular applications should be filed; applications received after Jan. 1 will be reviewed and considered on an availability basis. April 1: Admissions decisions are announced. May 1: Response date for students offered admission. A $200 deposit is required to confirm enrollment intentions. Institutional scholarship assistance is awarded to 35 percent of the student body; 60 percent receive general financial aid. Nearly $17.6 million in institutional scholarship assistance is available. The average student award is approximately $18,000 (including scholarships, loans, and employment).

Admission Requirements

Bucknell focuses on the content of a high school experience, particularly the student's grades and recommendations. Applicants are required to take the SAT-I of the College Board or the ACT prior to January of their senior year.

Expenses

Tuition is $28,764 per year.

Contact

Computer Science Department, Lewisburg, PA 17837. Telephone: 570-577-1394 Fax: 570-577-3533. URL: http://www.bucknell.edu. Contact person: Patricia Wenner. E-mail: wenner@bucknell.edu.

Additional Information

One of the first universities to introduce computer science into its curriculum - in 1957 - Bucknell continues its commitment to providing students with a state-of-the-art computer science curriculum. For students majoring in computer science there are three degree options: a bachelor of science in computer science and engineering in the College of Engineering, and both a bachelor of science in computer science and a bachelor of arts in computer science in the College of Arts and Sciences. A minor in computer science also is available. These degree options allow students to choose a program compatible with their curricular interests. All the computer Science degree programs share a common core of six courses. In the first two courses, students are introduced to problem-solving and program design using C++. The second year includes courses in computer organization and assembly language as well as the structure of computer programming languages. The final two courses in the core provide introductions to advanced data structures and algorithm analysis as well as operating systems. Following the common first semester in engineering, students begin the B.S. in computer science and engineering curriculum with the common core

of computer science courses. A required course in computer architecture is taken in the fall of the senior year. An important part of the program for engineering majors is a required senior design project that deals with the design of a solution for an open-ended problem on a topic of current interest in computer science. The curriculum in the junior year for both bachelor of science programs includes a course on the societal impact of computer science. Elective courses available in all programs allow students to choose from such topics as graphics, software engineering, parallel computation algorithms, computer networks, database management systems, artificial intelligence, functional programming, object-oriented languages, and new topics of current interest.

Carnegie Mellon University

F/X Degrees Offered

B.F.A. and M.F.A. in Art. Electronic and Time-Based Work Master of Design in Interaction Design (with specialization in Human-Computer Interaction Design and Human-Machine Interaction Design); and M.A. in Communication Planning and Design (a joint degree with the Department of English).

Curricular

Using five categories of courses, the curriculum presents art-making in a unique manner that respects tradition and encourages innovation. The course categories are: 1. Concept Studies; 2. Media Studios; 3. Advanced Studios; 4. Art Academic Courses; and 5. University Academic Courses. Studio courses comprise over sixty percent of the course of study and academic courses comprise the remainder. The studio curriculum is divided into conceptually-driven and media-driven courses.

Facilities

Media Studios: The Media Studios can be viewed as the foundation courses for the program. Students take two Media Studios each semester during the freshman and sophomore years for a total of eight courses. These studios ensure that all students have an exploratory experience with all of the media resources of the department. They also serve as preparation for advanced studio work. 2D Media Studios introduce drawing during the freshman year, and painting and printmaking during the sophomore year. Electronic Media Studios introduce computer-related work during the freshman year, and video in the sophomore year. 3D Media Studios introduce ceramics, welding, and wood during the freshman year, and foundry, metals, and construction during the sophomore year.

Student Body

There are 4,440 undergraduates and 2,710 graduate students; of these 7,150 students, 2,190 are women and 4,960 are men; 200 undergraduate majors and 18 graduates make up the student body of the Art Department. The College of Fine Arts has a 9:1 student-faculty ratio.

Faculty Profile

There are 865 full-time faculty and 200 part-time faculty, 30 active professionals teach in the Art Department.

Deadlines and Financial Aid

The deadline to be considered for admission for fall is February 1. There are no spring admissions. Materials to be considered for admission for fall will be accepted starting Sept. 1.

Admission Requirements

High school classes (four years English, two years Foreign Language is preferred), Pre-college Tests, SAT I or ACT, portfolio, application and fee.

Expenses

Tuition is $14,595 per semester.

Contact

Department of Computer Science, 5000 Forbes Avenue, Carnegie Mellon University, Pittsburgh, PA 15213-3890. Telephone: 412-268-6795. Fax: 412-268-6436. Contact person: Jessica K. Hodgins Associate Professor. Email: jkh@cs.cmu.edu. URL: http://www.cs.cmu.edu/.

Drexel University

F/X Degrees Offered

B.S. and M.S. in Computer Science; B.S., M.S. and Ph.D. in Mathematics; Dual M.S. in Mathematics and Computer Science; B.S. in Computer Science accredited by CSAB.

Curricular

3D Modeling and Rendering; high level programming; Computer Graphics I; Computer Graphics II.

Facilities

Sun workstations and servers; Tektronix X-terminals; Macintoshes.

Student Body

There are 15,000 students are enrolled in the department.

Faculty Profile

The full Drexel teaching staff includes more than 1,200 educators. Of that total, more than 560 are full-time teaching faculty and more than 450 are adjunct faculty (many of whom are working professionals who teach in their area of expertise). The ratio of students to full-time faculty is about 9:1. Thirty-seven faculty members teach in the department.

Deadlines and Financial Aid

Graduate students for fall admission seeking assistantship: February 1. Total amount provided to Drexel undergraduates is $56 million. Amount awarded by Drexel to new students is $6 million. Percentage of the freshman class receiving financial assistance: 87 percent. Average financial assistance package offered: $11,173. Percentage of entering class awarded academic (merit) scholarships: 38 percent. Types of aid available at Drexel includes: Federal grants (including Pell and SEOG Grants), state grants, Drexel University grants/scholarships, federal loans, work-wtudy funds and outside scholarships.

Admission Requirements

Undergraduates: application and fee, transcripts, ACT or SAT. Graduate students are advised to contact the graduate office for details on Admission Requirements.

Expenses

Undergraduate tuition is $16,726 per year. Graduate tuition is $894 per credit.

Contact

Computer Science Department, 3241 Chestnut Street, Drexel University, Philadelphia, PA 19104. Telephone: 215-895-2668 or 800-2DREXEL. Fax: 215-895-1582. Contact person: Jeffrey L. Popyack. E-mail: jeffrey.lee.popyack@drexel.edu. URL: http://www.cs.drexel.edu.

Edinboro University of Pennsylvania

F/X Degrees Offered

B.F.A. and A.M.A. in Animation/Cinema; Graphic Design; Photography.

Curricular

Introduction to Computer Graphics Software; Graphic Design Studio Skills; Principles of Typography; Publish Design; Corporate Identity; Graphic Design Practicum; Introduction to Illustration; Beginning Animation; Intermediate Animation; Advanced Animation; Computer Animation I and II.

Facilities

The Art Department Computer Laboratory houses 14 Macintoshes, 17-inch monitors, and Zip drives. The system software is system software includes QuarkXPress, Illustrator, Freehand, Photoshop, and Suitcase. Extensions include Zip DL Viewer, Imagery and Stuffit Expander. In addition, the laboratory includes two scanners; a Cannon color copier; Fiery Interface and laser printer. Deluxe Paint, Lightwave; 30 Animation Master Animator; 3D Animation; Brilliance; Art Department Pro; Disney Animation Studio; Take Two; 11 Amiga computers; three DEC Alpha Computer with Windows NT 4.0. operating software; two Video Toaster Flyer Non-Linear Video Editors; one cel scanner; four Line Testers.

Student Body

There are 300 students in Graphic Design/ Animation and Photography; 700 students in the Art Department; 7,100 total enrollment.

Faculty Profile

Eight faculty members teach in the area of Graphic Design/Animation; 408 total faculty at the university.

Deadlines and Financial Aid

Open admissions. Apply through the Financial Aid Office. Telephone: 814-732-2821.

Admission Requirements

Admission and fee, transcript, SAT or ACT test scores, to the Admission Department. Graduate: Have a B.F.A. degree in one of the studio areas available for graduate work at Edinboro or be judged to have an equivalent background; three letters of recommendation from faculty members whom the applicant has had for studio courses; submit the application for admission to the Graduate Office; forms of recommendation can be obtained from the Graduate Office; if applying for Studio Art concentration, submit at least 10 slides of studio pieces recently completed by the applicant; submit to the Art Department Chairperson in transparent 8.5x11 slide sheet(s) by March 15; complete a personal interview, if required; must enroll as a full-time graduate student for at least two semesters, summers not included; If necessary, submit a request for transfer credit, up to 15 credits may be accepted.

Expenses

Tuition is $4,598 per year for residents and $6,898 for non-residents.

Contact

Art Department, Doucette Hall, Edinboro University of PA, Edinboro, PA 16444. Telephone: 814-732-2406 or 888-8GO-BORO. Fax: 814-732-2629. Contact person: Mr. William Mathie, Department Chair. E-mail: cmullineaux@edinboro.edu. URL: http://www.edinboro.edu/cwis/Art/GenInfo.html.

Additional Information

The Art Department operates three galleries; the Bruce Gallery, the Bates Gallery, and a small space in the lounge area of Hamilton Hall. The Bruce Gallery in Doucette Hall is the major campus gallery. Each year competitive and invitational exhibitions of contemporary art work are brought to the campus from around the nation and the world. Individual and group exhibitions are held at the gallery, as well as faculty shows and regional student competitions. Bates Gallery, in Loveland Hall, is operated by the Student Art League and features weekly exhibitions by individual students or groups of students. Both galleries are funded and sponsored by the Student Government Association. STUDENT ORGANIZATIONS. Within the Art Department many student organizations exist, expanding the activities of the department and allowing for greater involvement of the student. The STUDENT ART LEAGUE is the primary student organization in the department. The Art League sponsors guest speaker programs, the Bates Gallery, and the annual field trip to New York City. The National Art Education Association student chapter is a professional organization which participates in state and national conferences, and provides guest lecturers on current topics, and trips to art museums. OTHER ORGANIZATIONS, representing specific interests within the department, include the Pulpbusters (Printmaking), the Clay Club, the Photo Club, Studio 118 (Graphic Design), the Drawing & Painting Club, and the Imagination Station (Animation). Participation in these activities not only provides needed services to each area, but also creates a valuable networking opportunity for the students involved. THE ALTERNATIVE FILM SERIES is another important facet of the department, bringing in foreign films, works by independent and documentary filmmakers, and festivals such as the annual animation film festival. All of these activities and organizations receive some funding from the Edinboro University Student Government Association. The Art Department is a member of the College Art Association and the National Art Education Association (NAEA). Students often attend national and regional conferences and meetings of these organizations as well as conferences of the NCECA (National Council for Education in the Ceramic Arts), and the SPE (Society for Photographic Education). Membership is also available in the Northwest Pennsylvania Artists Association (NPAA). ACADEMIC ADVISEMENT.Students in the art programs are assigned academic advisors from the faculty of the

Art Department. The faculty advisor is generally from the student's emphasis or degree concentration area, and provides scheduling and career guidance for the art student. Other advisement is available from the chairperson or the assistant chairperson of the department, from the Academic Advisement Center, or from the Career Counseling Center. Students are encouraged to seek the advice of their faculty advisor as often as necessary to help ensure that the required and most beneficial courses are completed.

La Salle University

F/X Degrees Offered
Mathematics and Computer Science Department. LaSalle University has an undergraduate component for the B.A. and B.S. degrees in Computer Science. The department also offers an M.A. in Computer Information Science, Digital Arts, and Multimedia.

Curricular
3D Modeling and Rendering; Multimedia/ Interactive; High-Level Programming; Low-Level Programming; Digital Painting/Drawing; Image Processing; Digital Video.

Facilities
New networked computer laboratory with 20 Pentium 60 PCs, two 486 PCs, and laser printer. Networked computer classroom with 25 486 PCs and printer. Networked computer laboratory with 20 486 PCs. Networked computer laboratory with 40 386 and 30 486 PCs. Software supported among these laboratories includes: MS Windows and Office; C++; Toolbook; science application packages. DEC Alpha with terminals. All PCs are connected on the campus network and to the DEC Alpha. Languages supported on the PCs and Alpha are: C; C++; Visual Basic; Pascal; LISP; Cobol; SmallTalk; MS Office Suite. The campus LANs are connected via a fiber backbone.

Student Body
Sixty undergraduates and 65 graduate students in the department.

Faculty Profile
Eleven full-time faculty members in the department.

Deadlines and Financial Aid
Various fellowships and traditional state, federal and city aid are available to students. Contact the Financial Aid Office for details on obtaining financial assistance at the university.

Admission Requirements
All applicants must have: A completed application and essay; high school transcript (or your most recent college transcript if you're transferring); SAT 1 or ACT scores; A letter of recommendation from a teacher or counselor; An application fee (checks can be made out to La Salle University). The fee is waived if you apply online. For students applying for Early Action, our application deadline is November 15th.

Expenses
Tuition is $11,380 per year.

Contact
La Salle University, 20th and Olney Avenue, Box #258, Philadelphia, PA, 19141.
Telephone: 215-951-1130 or 215-951-1222. Fax: 215-951-1805. Contact person: Linda Elliott. Email: elliott@lasalle.edu.
URL: http://www.lasalle.edu/.

Additional Information
The department supports three major Computer Science programs. Two of these major programs provide a traditional, strong foundation in the discipline of Computer Science; one leads to a B.A. degree and the other to a B.S. degree. The

third major program leads to a B.S. in Information Technology. A major goal of these programs is the preparation of graduates for direct entry into the computing profession with sufficient background to make continuing contributions. The B.S. program in Computer Science provides the foundation for remaining current in Computer Science. It requires courses in related fields and provides breadth and depth in the discipline. The B.A. program is applications-oriented and has fewer required courses to provide greater flexibility. It is strongly recommended that students in the B.A. program in Computer Science choose an appropriate minor in consultation with a departmental advisor. The Information Technology major is designed for those students interested in the study of networks and client support systems. It is recommended that students in the B.S. program in Information Technology choose a concentration in one of several areas including Mathematics, Technical Writing, Communication, Management, or Digital Arts and Multimedia Design. Students selecting Computer Science or Information Technology as a major will normally choose the focus of their program during their sophomore year.

Pennsylvania State University

F/X Degrees Offered
M.S. and Ph.D. in Computer Science and Engineering.

Curricular
Advanced Computer Graphics and Scientific Visualization courses.

Facilities
Department facilities--Hardware: Two DEC Alphas; 10 Sun 4 file servers; six DEC file servers; 100+ Sun workstations; 85 DEC stations; 16-node nCube; Internet and bitnet access. Software systems and languages: UNIX and associated programs; C++; Magic; Common Lisp; Prolog; SML; Smalltalk; Modula; Cantata. University facilities--Hardware: IBM ES9000/740 running VM/ESA; 32-node IBM Scalable Parallel 1. Software systems and languages: Pascal; Fortran; Lisp; Ada; C. 101 Pond houses 46 Sun Ultra 5's running Solaris 7, and a high-speed laser printer. The facility is available 7x24 to CSE students with an active PSU ID card and CSE computer account. 304 Hammond houses 58 Sun Ultra 5's running Solaris 8, and a high-speed laser printer. The facility is available 7x24 to CSE students with an active PSU ID card and CSE computer account.

Student Body
128 graduate students major in Computer Science.

Faculty Profile
31 faculty members teach in the department.

Deadlines and Financial Aid
Graduate students may apply for fellowships, teaching assistantships, and research assistantships. These graduate assistantships offer stipends ranging from $10,260 to $11,000 per year. Various supplemental fellowships are available, ranging from $2500 to $5000 per year. Admissions application deadline: July 1. Assistantship application deadline: Jan. 1 for fellowships; February 1 for assistantships.

Admission Requirements
Students must submit an application and fee, transcript, and GRE score.

Expenses
Tuition is $9,296 per year for residents and $18,918 for non-residents.

Contact
220 Pond, University Park, PA 16802. Telephone:
814-865-9505. Fax: 814-863-7590
URL: http://www.cse.psu.edu/.

Temple University

F/X Degrees Offered
Film and Media Arts undergraduates. B.A. and
M.F.A. and an interdepartmental Ph.D.

Curricular
Media Arts I and II; The Production of Media
Culture; Videography; Filmmaking; Lighting for
Film and Video; Audio Production; Experimental
Video and Multimedia; TV Studio Production;
Editing Film and Video; Computerized Editing;
Independent Film and Video; Animation Workshop;
Writing for Media II; Screen Directing; Screen
Performance.

Facilities
Three broadcast-quality television studios;
camcorders for field production; video and
computer-based editing suites with graphics and
special effects; AVID non-linear computerized
film/video editing; and hypermedia laboratories
for computer-controlled and computer-generated
media. Film facilities include 16 mm film processing
laboratory; 16/35 mm synchronous multi-track
mixing studio; digital sound; animation facilities;
optical printers; Arriflex, Bolex, Canon, Eclair,
and CP-16 cameras. Steenbeck editing stations;
professional lighting and support equipment; and
cultural studies libraries of films, videos, and laser
discs. Students in Film and Media Arts begin hands-
on experience in the freshman year.

Student Body
There are 24,900 undergraduates and 10,000
graduate students enrolled in the university.

Faculty Profile
Ten faculty members teach courses in the areas of
Film and Media Arts.

Deadlines and Financial Aid

**Various forms of financial aid are
available, including time payments,
student loans, work-study and
scholarships. Contact Temple's Office of
Financial Aid: 215-204-1492. Fax: 215-
204-5897.**

Admission Requirements
Application and fee, SAT or ACT, recommendation,
transcript and portfolio. Graduate students are
advised to consult the Graduate Office.

Expenses
Tuition is $8,134 per year for residents and $14,894
for non-residents.

Contact
Film and Media Arts Department, Annenberg Hall
011-00, Temple University, Philadelphia, PA 19122.
Telephone: 215-204-3859 or 888-340-2222. Fax:
215-204-5694. Contact person: Jeff Rush, FMA Chair.
Email: jrush@thunder.temple.edu.
URL: http://www.temple.edu/fma/xba.html.

Additional Information
Film and Media Arts offers a rounded core
education: balanced training in both cultural studies
and production, a wide range of courses, personal
attention; professional film/video/computer
facilities, hands-on experience every semester, the
opportunity to build a professional portfolio, new
approaches and new technologies, an advanced
senior project or thesis and internship opportunities.
After filling basic departmental requirements in the
freshman and sophomore years, students choose
one of three sequences for their final two years.
The Production Sequence: training to take creative
control of media as writers, directors, filmmakers,

video-makers and media artists. This sequence builds toward a Senior Project in the form of a completed 16 mm film, video project, screenplay, or computer-based work for which the student has primary creative control. The Media Culture Sequence: critically studies media, examining how both media producers and consumers create cultural meaning. In this sequence each student completes a written, research-based Senior Thesis, or a produced script based on research. The Non-Thesis Sequence is a balanced, liberal arts approach to both media studies and production where, in lieu of a thesis or senior project, the final two years are designed as an individual program of study under the close guidance of a faculty advisor.

University of Pennsylvania

F/X Degrees Offered
B.S.E. in Engineering; M.S. Ph.D. in Computer Science through the Department of Computer and International Science.

Curricular
Current research in the center can be viewed in several broad categories: Simulated Humans in 3D Virtual Environments; Locomotion and Navigation; Automatic Animation; Physics-Based Modeling and Analysis; Biomedical Modeling and Applications; Rendering Techniques for Complex Environments. Simulated Humans in 3D Virtual Environments projects here include: A Quick Introduction to Jack: Integrating Virtual Humans in VR Applications; Controlling a Virtual Human Using Minimal Sensors; Jack LISP-API and Pat-Nets; Human Figure Modeling; Free Form Deformation. Undergraduates: courses include Introduction to Programming; Programming Languages and Techniques; Programming Languages and Techniques laboratory; Introduction to Cognitive Science;

X-window Programming laboratory; Introduction to Algorithms and Data Structures; Introduction to Computer Architecture; Mathematical Foundations of Computer Sciences; Automata, Computability and Complexity. Expert Systems: Applications of Artificial Intelligence; Scientific Visualization; Digital System Organization and Design; Digital laboratory; Computer Operating Systems; Robotics; Introduction to Artificial Intelligence; Distributed and Real-Time Systems. Graduate students: Programming Languages and Techniques; Computer Architecture; Analysis of Algorithms; Theory of Computation; Introduction to Artificial Intelligence; Database and Information Systems.

Facilities
The primary educational equipment is a collection of Sun workstations and servers, running Sun's version of UNIX. In addition to the vast array of utilities provided with manufacturer's UNIX, the department provides various software packages and languages including C++, C, Lisp, Scheme, Prolog, Standard ML, Fortran 77, most GNU utilities, the MIT/X Consortium release of the X window system, LaTeX, and elm. Each CIS computer is connected to an Ethernet network and supports the TCP/IP protocol. The Ethernet is gatewayed to the Penn Campus Network and to the Internet. Every faculty member and all graduate students have workstations or terminals in their offices capable of accessing any system in the department. The CIS Computing Facility has several groups of computers configured for specific applications. The General Robotics and Active Sensory Perception (GRASP) Laboratory includes a Sun Sparcserver 10/512, several Sun Sparcstations, and numerous smaller Sun and SGI machines, all running the manufacturer's version of UNIX. They are used mainly for research in robotics and manipulator control and vision. Users are CIS researchers in robotics and vision. The Language Information

and Computation (LINC) Laboratory includes an six-processor Sun Sparcserver 1000, a Sun 4/690MP, and many Sun Sparcstations running the manufacturer's version of UNIX, plus numerous X terminals. The primary applications are for research in artificial intelligence. Users are researchers in artificial intelligence. The Logic and Computation Group includes a Sun Sparcserver 1000 with two M61 SuperSPARC processors, running Solaris plus numerous X terminals. The primary applications are for research in programming languages and information structures. The Graphics Laboratory includes about twenty Silicon Graphics workstations and an SGI Onyx with Reality Engine. The primary applications are for research in computer graphics and animation. The user community consists of CIS researchers in graphics, and non-CIS researchers sponsored by CIS faculty. The · Distributed Systems Laboratory (DSL) includes numerous IBM RS/6000's, HP 9000/700's, and Sun workstations, all running the manufacturer's version of UNIX. Some of the computer systems include special-purpose sub-systems for distributed or parallel operations. The primary applications are for research in digital design and distributed systems. The user community for this lab includes graduate and undergraduate students in Electrical Engineering and Computer Science taking classes assigned to the lab, and CIS researchers in distributed systems. The General Research Computing Facilities of CIS include a Sparcserver 10/61, and several desktop Sun workstations, all running the manufacturer's version of UNIX. In addition, numerous X terminals are used to connect to server machines. The primary applications used are general programming and research, and administration support (text formatting, electronic mail, etc.). The user community includes CIS faculty, staff, graduate students, and non-CIS researchers as sponsored by CIS faculty. Laser printers are distributed throughout the department for high-quality hard copy. All systems are interconnected to the SEAS/Penn Ethernet network. A number of systems are connected to a high-speed (155Mb/s) ATM network.

Student Body
More than 30 students are Ph.D. candidates in CIS: the Center educates a large fraction of the Ph.D.s in the CIS Department. Undergraduate students also do independent study or senior project work in the Center. All students taking the Computer Graphics courses learn to use Jack as the fundamental interaction and rendering system, and can utilize the film and video facilities of the center.

Faculty Profile
Five full-time support staff and 22 faculty members are associated with the Center for Human Modeling and Simulation.

Deadlines and Financial Aid
Ph.D. program admissions deadline (for Financial Aid consideration): Jan. 15. M.S.E. program admissions deadline for fall term: July 1.

Admission Requirements
Graduate students: GRE scores, application and fee, transcripts, and letters of recommendation. Undergraduates: application and fee, high school transcripts, SAT or ACT scores.

Expenses
Tuition is $14,608 per semester.

Contact
University of Pennsylvania, Department of Computer & Information Science, Levine Hall, 3330 Walnut Street, Philadelphia, PA 19104-6389. Telephone: 215-898-8560. Fax: 215-573-0587. Contact person: Dr. Norman Badler. E-mail: badler@central.cis.upenn.edu. URL: http://www.cis.upenn.edu/.

Additional Information

The overall goals of the Center for Human Modeling and Simulation are the investigation of Computer Graphics Modeling, animation, and rendering techniques. Major focus is in behavior-based animation of human movement, modeling through physics-based techniques, applications of control theory techniques to dynamic models, illumination models for image synthesis, and understanding the relationship between human movement, natural language, and communication. Jack may be described as a non-immersive virtual reality system upgradeable to fully immersive interaction. The structure of the software makes it ideal for use with VR input and output devices which enable the user to become the Jack figure and inhabit the virtual environment. For the past 17 years, research has been carried out at the Center for Human Modeling and Simulation, University of Pennsylvania with the aim of creating an interactive and intelligent virtual human model. This goal is realized in the Jack system and has involved expertise from the fields of computer science, computer graphics, biomechanics, robotics, psychology, physiology, and cognitive science. Development in Jack is driven by the demands of the end user, with the majority of funding from military and NASA sources. Other reference users of Jack include General Motors, Ford, General Dynamics, John Deere, Caterpillar, Volvo, British Aerospace, MOD Defense Research Agency, GEC Macroni and Vickers.

University of the Arts

F/X Degrees Offered

B.F.A. in Media Arts; Multimedia; Communication; Writing for Media and Performance; Photography; Film/Video; Animation. Master's of Industrial Design.

Facilities

SGI laboratory; Amigas; Macintosh laboratories; and Multimedia laboratory with both 8500 and 9500 Macintoshes and PCs. The department of Academic Computing is dedicated to the support and integration of digital technology within the University's academic programs. Academic Computing maintains a variety of labs (33) including those dedicated to high-end graphics work and animation, and to music, and four dual-platform digital laboratories in the New Media Center. The University provides ample open access to computer labs, and students are not required to bring personal computers, though some may find it beneficial depending on their major and individual schedule and needs. Students interested in purchasing their own computers are welcome to contact the Academic Computing office for advice on hardware and software selection and information on educational discounts available. Two of the University's labs in Anderson Hall (333 South Broad Street) and in the Terra Building (211 South Broad Street) are dedicated solely to open access for students.

Student Body

Undergraduate faculty/student ration of 1:9. Graduate faculty-student ration: 1:4.

Faculty Profile

Six full-time faculty teach in the area of Animation, and seven full-time faculty teach in the area of Film/Video.

Deadlines and Financial Aid

Undergraduates: priority consideration is given to students who file their aid applications by March 15. Applicants who wish to be considered for the Talent Scholarships should submit their applications for admission by March 15 and complete all admission requirements by April 1. Selection is made on the basis of academic achievement, artistic presentation and potential.

Admission Requirements

Freshmen must be graduates of an accredited secondary school or the equivalent. A curriculum of college preparatory subjects is recommended and students are strongly advised to include courses in languages, mathematics, science, humanities, art history, psychology and sociology in their studies. All applicants must submit the scores of the SAT, SAT 1 or ACT, and an official high school transcript or a general education diploma (GED). There are no minimum score requirements, and scores are waived if the applicant has been out of school for five years or more, or if the applicant has completed a college-level course in English composition with a grade of C or better, submit a one-page statement describing your goals, motivation, and commitment to studying the visual arts, a teacher recommendation, a personal interview with an admissions officer (recommended but not required), and a portfolio review of your art work. Call or write for an appointment. If a visit is impossible, you may submit a slide portfolio.

Expenses

Tuition is $20,860 per year.

Contact

University of the Arts, 320 S. Broad St., Philadelphia, PA 19102. Telephone: 800-616-ARTS. Fax: 215-717-6045. URL: http://www.uarts.edu.

Additional Information

Undergraduate Film/Video: the goal is to prepare students to be an independent film and video artist, to master basic techniques as well as experiment with images and time/motion; and view films of historical and critical importance, and learn the essentials of film and video production: scripting, budgeting, shooting, sound recording, editing, and releasing the final print. By the senior year, students produce independent films or videos to exhibit their creative vision. The program prepares its graduates to enter the profession as a freelance editor, sound recordist, cinematographer, animator, screen writer, or director. Undergraduate Animation: using the technologies of filmmaking, animators draw upon a diverse palette of materials created by drawing, painting, sculpture, illustration, graphic arts and still photography to produce animated films. The students' enhanced drawing skills and knowledge of computer animation enable them to create an animated film in their junior year, first in a pencil test, then in a full-color version with synch-sound. Students produce a short thesis film in a proposed style and topic. This video portfolio of animated sequences is used to illustrate the students' skills, sense of style, and creative ability when applying for work in the field. Master of Industrial Design: two years, 60 credits. This is a research-oriented degree. However, students also receive intensive studio and classroom instruction, as well as coaching in conceptualization, organizational and management skills, computer-aided design, multimedia presentation, human factors systems integration, advanced technologies and production. The focus is on developing the knowledge and computational expertise important to the future of design management, design education, and design research. The program is organized around product development teams, with members selected on the basis of the individual's interests and skills. Each class is selected so that among the participants there is a balance of the following design elements: management, information, methods, presentations, simulation, assessment, systems development and interface.

Villanova University

F/X Degrees Offered
M.S. and Ph.D. in Computer Science.

Curricular
Courses in Computer Graphics and Advanced Scientific Visualization.

Facilities
Department facilities--Hardware: Microvax II Cluster; ATT 3B2 cluster; 17 Sparcs; 65 PC compatibles; seven UNIX PCs; three HP workstations; X-terminals; HP plotter; seven laser printers; 12 color printers; scanner. Software systems and languages: UNIX; X-windows; MSWindows; Oracle7; PC DOS; C; Pascal; Perl; Lisp; Modula-2; Prolog; Logo; Ada; TeX; Minitab; PHIGS; AutoCAD; FrameMaker; RN; Macsyma; Mathematica; Miranda; SML; C++; Renderman; SunVision; Maple; Scheme; Netscape.

Student Body
There are 200 graduate students major in Computer Science.

Faculty Profile
Twelve faculty members teach in the department.

Deadlines and Financial Aid
This year, Villanova will provide over $21.6 million in direct grants to students, including nearly $6.8 million to the freshman class. These grants are based only on financial need and do not include the substantial scholarship funds that are also available. Contact the admssions office for more details. Graduate students may receive a graduate assistantship through the department. Graduate Assistants receive a yearly stipend of an estimated $8,400.

Admission Requirements
GRE scores, application, fee, and transcripts.

Expenses
Tuition is $26,300 per year.

Contact
Villanova University, Department of Computing Sciences, 161 Mendel Science Center, 800 Lancaster Avenue, Villanova, PA 19085-1699. Telephone: 610-519-7310 or 800-338-7927 Fax: 610-514-6450. E-mail: csdept@villanova.edu. URL: http://www.csc.villanova.edu/csc/index.jsp.

Rhode Island

Brown University

F/X Degrees Offered
M.S. and Ph.D. in Computer Science Research.

Curricular
Courses in Scientific Visualization, Animation, and Computer Graphics.

Facilities
The department maintains a computing infrastructure that is separate from the rest of the University. Facilities include: Sun Microsystems machines; four dual-processor Sparc station 10s with Leo Boards; three quad processor Sparc station 10s with Leo Boards; one single processor Sparc station 10; one dual-processor; UltraSparc with Creator3D board. Other machines: dual-processor SGI Onyx with Reality Engine; SGIs; five Hewlett Packard workstations with CRX 24 graphics; three Pentium machines running Windows 95; two dual-processor Pentium Pros running WindowsNT; Abekas A60 Digital Frame Store; 750 frame (25 sec) 720x486 pix; Abekas A20 Analog-to-Digital Converter (YUV Abek); Lyon Lamb RTC Real Time Scan Converter (monitor RGB NTSC); Sony BVW-40 Betacam tape player/recorder; Sony Umatic 3/4-inch NTSC videotape player/recorder; Panasonic AG-2510 half-inch NTSC VHS videotape player/recorder; S-VHS JVC BR8-S22U; JVC transcoder YC, YRB, Composite; Lyon Lamb ENC-VI Encoder; Faruda Transcoder R,B,G to Y, Y-R, Y-B, NLE; Data Translations Media100 non-linear editing system; routers sierra: audio; component video; composite video; (4X) Sony TR101 Hi8 Video camcorders; Canon L1 Hi8 video camcorder; Mackie 1202 Audio Mixer. Input/Output Devices Ascension Bird 6D tracker; Vertex Cyber glove; (4X) Logitech 3D Mouse; flymouse; Logitech/StereoGraphics Crystal-Eyes VR; Fakespace Boom 2-CM virtual reality display device; Polhemus Isotrack 3D tracker; SensAble two-handed Phantom.

Student Body
There are 100 students in the Computer Science Department.

Faculty Profile
Seventeen faculty members teach in the department.

Deadlines and Financial Aid
Office of Financial Aid offers aid (loan, work and scholarship) on the basis of the candidate's need/eligibility as determined from the College Scholarship Service Profile Form (registration forms are available from most secondary school guidance offices or directly from Brown), the FAFSA (also available from secondary schools guidance offices), information provided on parent and student tax returns, and the Brown Application for Financial Aid--Form 5. Applicants who wish to be considered for any type of financial support, including assistantships, should submit an application and necessary credentials to the Graduate School Admission Office no later than Jan. 1 of the year they wish to enter Brown. Applications for admission without financial support, as well as for assistantships, will be considered after that date, but only so long as departments remain willing to evaluate them. Applications for admission in the second semester should be filed by November 1, but it should be noted that financial aid is normally not available to students who enter at that time.

Admission Requirements
Applicants who want to be evaluated by more than one department must submit a separate application fee for each. Applicants should submit with the application original transcripts from all colleges and universities previously attended or presently being

attended. Required also are a personal statement and three letters of recommendation written on the forms provided by persons well-qualified to speak from first-hand knowledge about the applicant's potential for graduate study. At least two of these letters must be from professors at the institution of current study or, if the applicant is not in school at the time of application, at the institution most recently attended. Applications must also include, when required, the official reports of the General and Subject Tests of the GRE.

Expenses
Estimated tuition is $30,078 per year.

Contact
Postal Address: Box 1910, Computer Science Department, Brown University, Providence, RI 02912. Street Address: 115 Waterman St., Fourth Floor Providence, RI 02906. Telephone: 401-863-7600. Fax: 401-863-7657. Contact person: Eli Upfal, Departement Chair. Email: eli@cs.brown.edu. URL: http://www.cs.brown.edu/.

Additional Information
Brown University is part of the Graphics and Visualization Center, one of 24 National Science Foundation Science and Technology Centers founded to promote fundamental interdisciplinary research. The Center comprises five universities: Brown University, the University of Utah, the University of North Carolina at Chapel Hill, Cornell University, and the California Institute of Technology. The Brown Computer Graphics Group is directed by Professors Andries Van Dam and John F. Hughes. The Group is composed of Ph.D., master's, and undergraduate students, as well as full-time research staff. Professor Van Dam is also the director of the NSF Graphics and Visualization Center, one of 24 NSF Science and Technology Centers founded to promote fundamental interdisciplinary research.

Rhode Island Schoolof Design

F/X Degrees Offered
B.F.A. in Film/Animation/Video.

Curricular
Film/Animation Video: Introductory Film; Puppet Animation; Computcr-Gcncratcd Imagcry; Documentary Film/Video; Film II; Video I; Film Animation I-A; Animation II; Film Special Effects; Writing the Short Script; Animation Degree Project; Beginning Computer Animation; Film/Video Degree Project; Introduction to Sound; Time, Light and Sound; Animation 1-A; Creature-Creation/Performance; Advanced Film Production; Advanced Animation Production; Autobiographical Video. The Film/Animation/Video curriculum emphasizes the form, context, and structure of images moving in time, and teaches students the technical skills and concepts necessary to produce artistic and professional photographic, electronic, and animated motion pictures. Students learn to work in art film/tape, experimental narrative, and animation, and may also choose to produce work that encompasses film and video installations as well as performance pieces. Students work with both film and video in their sophomore and junior years. In both senior year students concentrate in one of these areas to design and complete a degree project in live-action film, animation, video, or combined media.

Facilities
RISD's comprehensive studio facilities and extensive equipment have an excellent international reputation. Facilities in over 40 buildings include computer labs, darkrooms, kilns, printmaking studios, jacquard and computer design looms, woodworking shops devoted to industrial design, furniture design and sculpture. Other facilities

include: Two Filmmaker and one Master Series animation stand; 12 SGI computer workstation running Maya, Photoshop and various other software program; a variety of graphics hardware and software including Macintosh II; Amigas; video digitizers; printers; plotters; complete range of film and video production and post-production equipment; MIDI system with 8-tracks.

Student Body
Approximately 2,000 undergraduates and 100 graduate students are enrolled in the school.

Faculty Profile
More than 140 full-time faculty, and over 140 part-time faculty teach at RISD.

Deadlines and Financial Aid
Questions concerning financial aid should be addressed to: Financial Aid Office, Rhode Island School of Design, 2 College St., Providence, RI 02903-2784. Telephone: 401-454-6635.

Admission Requirements
Application and fee, transcript, a visual presentation representing the applicant's art and design experience and accomplishments, a statement of purpose concerning the applicants educational goals and interests, scores from the SAT I or the ACT may be submitted in place of the SAT, letter(s) of recommendation.

Expenses
Tuition is $25,734 per year.

Contact
Admissions Office, Rhode Island School of Design, 2 College St., Providence, RI 02903-2791. Telephone: 401-454-6300 or 800-364-7473. Fax: 401-454-6309. E-mail: admissions@risd.edu. URL: http://www.risd.edu.

South Carolina

Bob Jones University

F/X Degrees Offered
B.S. and M.A. in Cinema and Video Production, Art, and Graphic Design. B.S. and M.S. in Radio and Television Broadcasting. B.A. in Computer Science.

Curricular
Undergraduate: Introduction to Computer Graphics; Computer Graphics; Fundamentals of Motion Picture and Video Production; Beginning Sound Recording; Editing for Film and Video I; Film and Video Camera; Editing for Film and Video II; Video Production Seminar; Cinema Directing; Cinema Seminar; Cinematography; Animation Camera; Art of Animation; Advanced Editing I; Advanced Editing II; Motion Picture Production Techniques; Cinema Workshop; Cinema Directing; 3D Computer Animation; Makeup for Motion Picture and Video Production. Graduate students: Editing and Post-Production I and II; Seminar in Creative Cinema; Advanced Art of Animation; Special Effects; Advanced 3D Animation; Advanced 3D Animation Workshop. Computer Science courses.

Facilities
Video and video editing equipment with computer graphics stations. In addition to the general-access labs available to all BJU students, a computer lab is available exclusively to computer science/engineering majors and minors. Several networked workstations host the Microsoft Windows XP Professional and Linux operating systems (the current workstation configuration features 1 GHz Intel Pentium CPUs with 256 MB RAM, 20 GB hard drives, multimedia hardware, and dual monitor displays). The department administers its own network with Windows 2000 and Linux servers.

Student Body
Approximately 5,000 students attend the university.

Deadlines and Financial Aid
The Student Work Program is available to undergraduate dormitory students in the amounts of $125 to $325 per month in even $25 increments. Academy students who are sixteen years of age and older are limited to a maximum of $250 per month. Earnings will be credited to the tuition accounts biweekly. The University cannot guarantee work for all students and cannot guarantee that each student will earn the stated amount each month. Each job is to be considered a ministry as well as a privilege.

Admission Requirements
Undergraduates: secure an application for by writing the director of admissions, Bob Jones University, Greenville, SC 29614-000. Fill in the application form completely. Send this form with a non-refundable application fee to the director of admissions. Arrange to take the ACT if applying to an undergraduate program. Graduate students must request each college or university they attended to send a complete, official transcript of their work to Bob Jones University.

Expenses
Tuition is $7,380 per year.

Contact
Bob Jones University, Greenville, SC 29614-0001. Telephone 864-242-5100 or 800-BJ-AND-ME. Fax: 864-235-6661. Contact person: Dan Wooster, Chairman. Email: : dwooster@bju.edu. URL: http://www.bju.edu.

Clemson University

F/X Degrees Offered
Department of Graphic Communications offers a B.S. in Graphic Communication, Printing Process. B.A. and B.S. in Computer Science.

Curricular
All computer graphics include computer operations to generate prepress images. Introduction to Graphics; Approaches to Imaging; Photograph and Digital Images; Specialty Printing; Advanced Lithography; Advanced Color. Various Computer Science courses.

Facilities
The college Information Technology Services (ITS) maintains college laboratories and a help desk. The department also maintains over 150 Unix and Windows based systems in various department labs and classrooms. All systems are connected to the department network, which in turn is connected to the campus-wide university network and the internet. Department servers provide shared file space and numerous other shared resources. Laser printers, color printers, scanners and other facilities are provided for classwork, projects and research. Other equipment includes: Fifty-seven Macintosh computers; 10 Digital scanners; Color printer; six Macintosh LaserWriters; seven digital cameras; one disc writer.

Student Body
The department enrolls 315 undergraduate students, 31 masters, and two doctoral candidates. Total enrollment is 16,400

Faculty Profile
Twelve faculty members teach in the department.

Deadlines and Financial Aid
Federal and state financial aid is available. Graduate students may attain a graduate assistantship.

Approximately 15 students are employed by the Department. An additional 10 Graphics students are employed by the university.

Admission Requirements
Application and fee, $100 deposit, SAT or ACT scores. Contact the department for more information.

Expenses
Tuition is approximately $780 per credit hour for residents and $1389 per credit hour for non-residents.

Contact
G-01 Tillman Hall, Clemson University, Clemson, SC 29634. Telephone: 864-656-2287. Fax: 864-656-2464. Contact person: Pradip Srimani, Chair. Email: srimani@cs.clemson.edu. URL: http://www.cs.clemson.edu.

University of South Carolina

F/X Degrees Offered
Department of Art offers a M.M.A. (Master of Media Arts) and a B.M.A. (Bachelor of Media Arts). Computer Graphics courses can be taken through the M.F.A., B.F.A., B.A. and M.A. programs. The Department also offers MS, ME, and PhD degrees in Computer Science and Engineering.

Curricular
Computer Visualization; Computer Imaging; Graphic Design; Interactive Learning Workshop; Animation; Non-Linear Editing.

Facilities
The department maintains several computer laboratories for instruction and research. Laboratories used to support undergraduate work include two Windows 2000 labs, a Solaris Ultra 10 lab, and a Solaris Sunblade 100 lab; the latter two labs use Unix. CSCE 145 and 146 (the first

two courses for majors) use Java in a Windows environment; CSCE 245 then introduces C++ in a Unix environment. Appropriate programming languages and software are used in other courses.

Student Body

There are 200 Studio Arts majors and 260 students in the Media Arts major.

Faculty Profile

Ten faculty members teach courses in Computer Graphics.

Deadlines and Financial Aid

Graduate degree applications are due by November 2 for the spring, and March 1 for the fall. Undergraduate admission is rolling.

Admission Requirements

Undergraduate students must contact the admissions office. Graduates must submit an application and fee, transcripts, and two letters of recommendation. Art Studio majors are required to submit 20 slides.

Expenses

Tuition is $5,778 per semester for residents and $7,558 per semester for non-residents.

Contact

Department of Art, University of South Carolina, Columbia, SC 29208. Telephone: 803-777-4236. Fax: 803-777-0535.
URL: http://www.sc.edu.

South Dakota

South Dakota State University

F/X Degrees Offered
Department of Visual Arts offers a B.A. and B.S. in Graphic Design; B.S. and B.A. in General Art with a minor in Computer Science.

Curricular
Digital Painting/Drawing; Image Processing; Page Layout Design; Computer Graphics I and II; Design Media I and II.

Facilities
One Computer studio containing Macintosh computers; Apple Laser printer; HP Workgroup Laser printer; Sharp Scanner. Adobe Photoshop; Adobe Illustrator; QuarkXPress; Fractals (A Tree Shareware); 18 workstation Macintosh computer studio for Graphic Design courses only; other IBM and Macintosh resources on campus are available. VHS video editing equipment and multimedia stations.

Student Body
Approximately 130 students in the department.

Faculty Profile
Two faculty members teach in the area of Computer Graphics.

Deadlines and Financial Aid
All visual arts scholarships and awards are based on an annual adjudicated competition for full-time majors only. Ten scholarships are awarded every year. Contact the Financial Aid Office for additional information on scholarships and aid.

Admission Requirements
Baccalaureate candidates must be at the top 60 percent of high school class; or score 18 or above on the ACT; or have a GPA of at least 2.6 on a 4.0 scale in required high school courses. Contact the admissions office. Telephone: 605-688-4121.

Expenses
Tuition is $1,730 per semester for residents and $3,666 for non-residents.

Contact
Department of Visual Art, Box 2223 Solberg Hall, Brookings, SD 57007. Telephone: 605-688-4103. Fax: 605-688-6769.
URL: http://www3.sdstate.edu/.

Additional Information
South Dakota State University, the land-grant school for the state, is the largest university in the state. The Visual Arts Department has been committed to Computer Graphics since the mid- to late-'80s.

Tennessee

East Tennessee State University

F/X Degrees Offered
M.S. and Ph.D. in Computer Science, Information Sciences, and Software Engineering.

Curricular
Courses in Human-Computer Interface, Computer Graphics, and Advanced Scientific Visualization.

Facilities
PC laboratory as well as a UNIX lab with many software titles.

Student Body
One hundred graduate students in the department.

Faculty Profile
Fourteen full-time faculty members teach in the department.

Deadlines and Financial Aid
Apply for financial aid early! This is the best way to enhance your chances to receive financial assistance. The university recommends the following dates as guidelines: January 1: Complete online or mail the Free Application for Federal Student Aid (FAFSA). Average processing time is four weeks if mailed; about two weeks if completed online. List Title IV Code: 003487 for ETSU. February 15: Tennessee residents applying for the Tennessee Student Assistance Awards (TSAA) are encouraged to complete the FAFSA by this date. The Office of Financial Aid mails inquiry forms to students asking their summer school plans and their interest in financial aid assistance. March 1: The priority deadline to apply for scholarships, unless otherwise stated in the ETSU Financial Aid and Scholarship Brochure. Applications received after April 15 may not be processed. April 15: The priority deadline preceding each school year for student financial aid files to be complete. Aid funds may not be available for students who apply after July 1. Please contact of Office of Financial Aid for other means to assist you with your cost of education. November 15: The priority deadline to receive financial aid for the Spring Semester. All student financial aid files in the Office of Financial Aid must be complete by this date. 30-Day Hold: Delayed disbursement of Federal Stafford Loans for first-time freshmen. These funds are released to student accounts thirty days after classes start. Please contact of Office of Financial Aid for other means to assist you with your cost of education. Graduate students in the department may qualify for various forms of graduate assistantships and may receive a stipend of $2,500 to $5,000.

Admission Requirements
GRE scores, application and fee, transcripts, and letters of recommendation.

Expenses
Tuition is $1,919.50 per semester for residents and $5,885.50 per semester for non-residents.

Contact
Department of Computer and Information Sciences, Box 70711, Johnson City, TN 37614-0711. Telephone: 423-439-5328. Fax: 423-439-7119. Contact person: Dr. Donald Sanderson, Assistant Professor. E-mail: sanderso@etsu.edu.
URL: http://www-cs.etsu.edu/.

Additional Information
The Department of Computer and Information Sciences has the goal of producing outstanding computing professionals, contributing significant advancements in the computing sciences, and providing notable professional service to the academic and general communities. Our

undergraduate Computer Science program is accredited by the Computing Sciences Accreditation Board. Our graduate program is offered as an on-campus evening program for both full-time and part-time students. The BS program has Computer Science, Information Systems, Information Technology options while the MS has Applied Computer Science and Information Technology options. Coursework spans a broad spectrum including software engineering, database systems, object-oriented and client/server technologies, data communications, security, computing ethics, human-computer interfaces, real-time systems, computer graphics, artificial intelligence, and computer science education.

Middle Tennessee State University

F/X Degrees Offered
Radio, Television and Photography Department. Undergraduate program in Television Production with a specialty in Digital Animation. Degrees in Computer Science.

Curricular
3D Modeling and Rendering; 3D computer animation; 2D computer animation; multimedia/interactive; digital painting/drawing; image processing; digital video.

Facilities
SGI with Maya and other software; Abekas 82 and video equipment; PC and Macintosh laboratories.

Student Body
Fifty undergraduates, and a total of 290 students are enrolled in the department.

Faculty Profile
Twenty-seven faculty members teach in the department.

Deadlines and Financial Aid
Rolling admission.

Admission Requirements
Application and fee, SAT or ACT, transcript and portfolio.

Expenses
Tuition is $1,955 per year for residents and $5,921 for non-residents. Tuition for graduate is $2,492 per year for residents and $6,458 for non-residents.

Contact
P.O. Box 25, Murfreesboro, TN 37132. Telephone: 615-898-5628 or 800-433-6878. Fax: 615-898-5682. Contact person: Marc J. Barr. E-mail: mjbarr@mtsu.edu.
URL: http://www.mtsu.edu.

Memphis College of Art

F/X Degrees Offered
M.F.A. in Computer Arts with concentration in Imagery Publication Arts, Visual Presentations, and Multimedia. B.F.A. in Design Arts with concentration in Graphic Design and Illustration.

Curricular
Introduction to Computer Systems; Intermediate Computer Graphic Design; Electronic Photo Imaging; Beginning Animation; Intermediate/Advanced Animation. Graduate students: Computer Arts I-IV. Fundamentals of computer operations, graphical user interface, image scanners, and image recorders. Concentration on painting and collage applications, typographic and vector-based illustration applications. Current software tools

include: Microsoft Word, Adobe Photoshop, Adobe Illustrator.

Facilities

Three computer laboratories have Macintosh and Amiga color workstations, Laser Writer printers; grayscale and color scanners; high-resolution film recorders, and high-end multimedia facilities.

Student Body

There are 220 undergraduate students, 30 graduate students. Students come from 25 states and 10 foreign countries; 60 percent of the students come from the South.

Faculty Profile

Thirty-nine faculty members in the department. The Fine Arts and Design Arts faculty are professional artists who exhibit frequently and stay abreast of industry standards through their professional projects; 86 percent of full-time faculty have earned terminal degrees.

Deadlines and Financial Aid

A student need only submit all required application materials to be considered for institutional scholarships, grants, and work study based on merit. Students will be notified of merit awards along with acceptance replies. With the exception of merit scholarships, the financial assistance you receive is based on your financial need. This need is determined by an evaluation of your Free Application for Federal Student Aid (FAFSA). The FAFSA form is available from high school counselors or directly from MCA's Financial Aid Office. Analysis of the confidential information submitted on this form is standard throughout the nation. Scholarships: awarded by MCA based on the merit of an art portfolio during the admission process. Grants: determined by federal or state formulas based on the EFC. Federal Pell, Federal SEOG, TSAC Tennessee residents. Loans: Federal Stafford, Federal PLUS, Federal Perkins, Nellie Mae EXCEL, P.L.A.T.O.

Work-Study: based on your EFC as determined by federal formulas. Federal work-study: determined by MCA based on the merit of your art portfolio during the admission process.

Admission Requirements

Undergraduates: application, application fee, high school transcript, ACT or SAT scores, and portfolio.

Expenses

Tuition is $14,500 per year for undergraduate and $14,900 per year for graduate students.

Contact

Memphis College of Art, Overton Park, 1930 Poplar, Memphis, TN 38104. Telephone: 800-727-1088. URL: http://www.mca.edu.

The University of Memphis

F/X Degrees Offered

M.S. and Ph.D. in Applied Mathematics through the Mathematical Sciences Department.

Curricular

Advanced Visualization.

Facilities

Department facilities--Hardware: more than 90 PC workstations; seven Macintoshes; Intel 16-node Hypercube; five Sun workstations; SGI workstation; four VAX stations; seven laserjet printers. Software systems and languages: VMS; Solaris; Ultrix; IRIX; UNIX; Xenix; MS DOS; MSWindows; Macintosh System 7; Pascal; C; C++; Fortran; Ada; Modula-2; Prolog; Lisp.

Student Body

There are 125 students in the department.

Faculty Profile

There are 38 faculty members in the department.

Deadlines and Financial Aid
Graduate assistantships range from teaching assistantship with stipends of $8,500 to $12,000 and research assistantships of $9,500 to $12,000 per year; fellowships of $12,000 per year. Admissions application deadline: Aug. 1; assistantship application deadline: March 15.

Admission Requirements
Application and fee, transcripts, GRE scores.

Expenses
Tuition is $1,058.50 per semester for residents and $3,097 per semester for non-residents.

Contact
University of Memphis, Mathematical Sciences Department, Winfield Dunn Building, Memphis, TN 38152. Telephone: 901-678-2482 or 800-669-2678. Contact person: Lisa Eldin, assistant to the chair. E-mail: lisa@hermes.msci.memphis.edu. URL: http://www.msci.memphis.edu.

University of Tennessee at Knoxville

F/X Degrees Offered
B.F.A. in Art through the Art Department. M.S. and Ph.D. in Computer Science.

Curricular
3D Modeling and Rendering; 3D Computer Animation; 2D Computer Animation; Multimedia/ Interactive; Low-Level Programming; Digital Painting/Drawing; Image Processing; Digital Video; Desktop Publishing.

Facilities
The Department of Computer Science (CS) operates the Cetus, Crux, and Hydra computer laboratories (labs) for instructional and research purposes by CS students, faculty, and staff. Other equipment includes: a Computer Graphic laboratory equipped with high-end Macintosh work stations; flatbed scanners; color printer and b/w laser printer. Film and video facilities are also available to students. Computer Science Department facilities--Hardware: about 150 networked workstations including Sun, HP and SGI. Software systems and languages: UNIX systems with C and Fortran compilers.

Student Body
There are 150 undergraduates in the Graphic Design Department, 45 in Computer-Enhanced Design, and 10 graduate students. A total of 18,850 students are enrolled in the university.

Faculty Profile
Sixteen full-time faculty members in the Computer Science faculty.

Deadlines and Financial Aid
Rolling admission, several forms of federal and state aid, scholarships, and loans available. Dille Scholarship is available for undergraduate students. Graduate assistantships through the Computer Science Department range from teaching assistantship with a stipend of $8,500 to $9,500 per year to research assistantships of $10,000 to $16,000 per year.

Admission Requirements
Undergraduates: application and fee, ACT or SAT, transcripts, and portfolio. Admissions application deadline: March 1.

Expenses
Tuition is $4,450 per year for residents and $13,532 per year for non-residents.

Contact
Computer Science Department, 1715 Volunteer Blvd., Knoxville, TN 37996-2410. Telephone: 865-974-3407. Fax: 865-974-3198. Contact person: Jack Dongarra,

Professor. E-mail: dongarra@cs.utk.edu.
URL: http://www.cs.utk.edu.

Texas

Art Institute of Dallas

F/X Degrees Offered
A.A. applied degree in Animation, Multimedia and Graphic Design.

Curricular
Drawing design; 2D and 3D Animation; Character Animation; Special Effects; Compositing and Non-Linear Editing.

Facilities
Silicon Graphics workstations; PCs and Macintosh workstations.

Student Body
There are 200 undergraduate students in the department; 1,200 total enrollment in the institute.

Faculty Profile
Eighty faculty members teach at the institute.

Deadlines and Financial Aid
Various fellowships and traditional federal aid available to students. Contact the Financial Aid Office for details on obtaining financial assistance at the university.

Admission Requirements
Application and fee, interview, high school diploma, and recommendation from admissions.

Expenses
Tuition is $342 per credit hour.

Contact
8080 Park Lane, Dallas, TX 75231. Telephone: 214-692-8080 or 800-275-4243. Fax: 214-692-6541. URL: http://www.aii.edu.

Southwest Texas State University

F/X Degrees Offered
The Department of Art and Design offers eight programs leading to the following degrees: Bachelor of Fine Arts (BFA) with a major in Communication Design that includes areas of study in advertising art direction, graphic design, multimedia, and illustration; Bachelor of Fine Arts with a major in Studio Art that offers specialization in ceramics, drawing, fibers, metals, painting, photography,printmaking, sculpture, and watercolor; Bachelor of Fine Arts leading to All-Level or Secondary Certification or the Bachelor of Arts (BA) leading to Secondary Certification (two options) that prepare students for teaching art in elementary and secondary schools; Bachelor of Art with a major in Art with an emphasis in Art History that provides an intellectual foundation and a broad background in the history of art, aesthetics and art criticism; and a Bachelor of Arts with a major in Art that provides broad exposure to art.

Curricular
Communication Design Foundation III; Multimedia I-III; Digital Illustration; and other various courses.

Facilities
Communication Design students have access to the COMDES Digital Imaging laboratory: 19 Macintosh workstations; one Apple 16/600PS Laser Writer; one Apple Color One Scanner. A second laboratory contains 19 Macintoshes; LCD projection system; Pinnacle Writeable CD-ROM; Apple Quicktake digital camera. Kodak DC50 digital camera and Iomega removable storage. All workstations are connected via and linked to the Internet through university fiber optic backbone. Both laboratories utilize Apple Network Administrator Toolkit to enhance instruction through monitor sharing. Tektronix

Phaser color output services. QMS color printer, a film recorder and a b/w VariType Laser Writer. Software includes Adobe's Illustrator; Photoshop; Dimensions; Acrobat; FilmMaker; Fontographer; Director; Sound Edit 16; QuarkXPress; Swivel 3D Pro; Extreme 3D; Netscape and Premiere.

Student Body

There are 480 Art and Design majors; 280 Communication Design majors.

Faculty Profile

Three full-time and two part-time faculty.

Deadlines and Financial Aid

Undergraduate application deadlines are: July 1 for the fall; December 1 for the spring; May 1 for summer I; and June 15 for summer II. Graduate application materials should be submitted to the Graduate School no later than: July 15 for the fall; November 15 for the spring; April 15 for summer I; and June 1 for summer II. Various federal and state programs are available through the Financial Aid Office. The priority date for filing a Financial Aid Application is April 1 prior to fall or spring semester.

Admission Requirements

Application and fee, high school transcript and college if transfer student, SAT or ACT score.

Expenses

Tuition is $1,104 per semester for residents and $3,936 per semester for non-residents.

Contact

Department of Art and Design, 601 University Dr., San Marcos, TX 78666-4616. Telephone: 512-245-2611. Fax: 512-245-7969. Contact person: Erik Nielsen, Acting Chair. Email: en04@txstate.edu. URL: http://www.swt.edu.

Stephen F. Austin State University

F/X Degrees Offered

M.S. and Ph.D. in Computer Science.

Curricular

Various subject areas in Computer Science including computer graphics and parallel, distributed processing, and scientific applications.

Facilities

Department facilities--Hardware: 40 terminals; 100 microcomputers; six Macintoshes; six Sun Sparc stations; one Sun Sparc server. Software systems and languages: DOS; Windows; UNIX; OpenVMS; Basic; Pascal; C; C++; Fortran; Cobol. University facilities--Hardware: DEC 4720 Alpha AXP; 10 terminals; 150 microcomputer systems; 100 Macintosh. Software systems and languages: Fortran; Cobol; Basic; Pascal; Lisp; Macro; C; C++; DOS; VMS.

Student Body

There are 270 Computer Science students in the department. A total of 10,200 students are enrolled in the university.

Faculty Profile

Twelve full-time faculty members in the department.

Deadlines and Financial Aid

Graduate teaching assistantships are available through the department. These positions offer a yearly stipend of $5,600 to $6,000. Assistantship application deadline: April 1. Admission deadline: Submit application to the Graduate Office at least 30 days prior to entering.

Admission Requirements

Application and fee, transcripts, and GRE scores.

Expenses

Tuition is $2,639 per year for residents and $8,307 per year for non-residents.

Contact

P.O. Box 13063, SFA Station, Computer Science Department, Nacogdoches, TX 75962-3063. Telephone: 936-468-2504 or 800-731-2902. Fax: 936-468-3849. Contact person: Craig A. Wood, Chair. E-mail: woodca@sfasu.edu. URL: http://www.cob.sfasu.edu/csc/.

Texas A&M University

F/X Degrees Offered

M.S. in Visualization Sciences.

Curricular

Concepts of Visual Communication I and II; Computing for Visualization I and II; 3D and Animation; Design Communication I; Video/Photography; The Digital Image; Visualization Systems; Foundations of Research; Computer Animation; Character Animation; Design Communication; Color Photography; Computer Animation; Experimental Visual Techniques.

Facilities

Data and images are input via component analog, digital, video and high-resolution scanning cameras, as well as 2D and 3D digitizing devices. Complex commercial software, such as Maya, Softimage, and Renderman, along with custom applications, are used to structure and process data for output. With digital video techniques, computed sequences can be compiled, composited, and edited with other sources to realize production objectives. Two video studios are linked by and video routing to advanced graphics computing resources. The studios total more than 2,000 sq. ft. with complete studio lighting and cyclorama systems. These studios constitute a unique node in a distributed network and serve the Visualization Laboratory as a production research facility. Hyper-media, photographic output, post-production, and an electronic presentation room are supported in a recent building addition. The electronic presentation room is equipped with multiple high-resolution, multiscan projectors. This space is also furnished with a multi-channel, high-fidelity audio system. The Visualization Laboratory has a combined area of specially designed facilities approaching 17,000 sq. ft.

Student Body

Thirty-five graduate students.

Faculty Profile

Six full-time faculty teach in the Visualization Sciences Program.

Deadlines and Financial Aid

The deadline for completed applications for fall admission is Jan. 15 of the year in which admission is desired. Applications for spring admission are not accepted.

Admission Requirements

In addition to the normal application materials required by the university, students must submit the following materials: Resume of academic and/or professional experience, 300- to 500-word statement of intent, a brief autobiographical statement (one page) detailing the development of the candidate's interest in electronic visualization, and either or both of the following: 1) a portfolio of visual design work in 2D or 3D media (work should be presented on 35 mm slides or VHS videotape); and 2) a portfolio of computer work. This should include a hard copy of code, with a 10-page limit. Running applications with a graphical orientation are most helpful; include source code and instructions with submission. The labs can accommodate most Macintosh, PC or UNIX applications.

Expenses

Tuition is $184 per credit hour for residents and $656 per credit hour for non-residents.

Contact

Texas A&M University, Visualization Laboratory, 216 Langford Center, College Station, TX 77843. Telephone: 979-845-3465. Fax: 979-845-4491. Contact person: Donald House, Academic Coordinator. E-mail: house@viz.tamu.edu. URL: http://www-viz.tamu.edu/.

University of Houston at Clear Lake

F/X Degrees Offered

Mechanical Engineering Technology Department. Major and minor in Computer Drafting and Design Engineering Technology. B.S. in Engineering Technology. Minor to accompany any B.A./B.S. major. M.S. and Ph.D. in Computer Science.

Curricular

3D Modeling and Rendering; 3D Computer Animation; High-Level Programming; 2D Drafting Design; Graphics and Visualization; Virtual Reality.

Facilities

Department facilities--Hardware: DEC, Sun, and NeXT workstations (100+). Software systems and languages: UNIX; all major languages for teaching and research. University facilities--Hardware: KSR-1; iPSC/860; Cray Y/MP; VAXs; Macintoshes; PCs; and other types of workstations. Software systems and languages: VMS; UNIX; all major languages and packages.

Student Body

There are 250 undergraduates and, 235 graduate students.

Faculty Profile

Fifteen faculty members in the department.

Deadlines and Financial Aid

The mission of the Office of Scholarships and Financial Aid is to provide financial assistance to students through grants, loans, scholarships, and employment. Graduate assistantships range from teaching assistantships with stipends of $7,650 to $10,800 to research assistantships of $6,300 to $9,000 per semester. Admissions application deadline: July 3 for fall; December 4 for spring. Assistantship application deadline: March 1 for fall; Oct. 1 for spring.

Admission Requirements

Application and fee, transcripts, ACT or SAT. Graduate students must submit an application and fee, transcripts and GRE scores.

Expenses

Tuition is $8,960 per year.

Contact

University of Houston, College of Technology, Houston, TX 77204-4083. Telephone: 713-743-4097. Fax: 713-743-4032. Contact person: Ronald C. Pare. E-mail: ronpare@uh.edu. URL: http://www.cs.uh.edu.

University of Houston at Houston

F/X Degrees Offered

M.S. and Ph.D. in Computer Science.

Curricular

Courses are offered in Computer Graphics, Advanced Visualization, Interactive Computer Graphics and Virtual Reality.

Facilities

Department facilities--Hardware: DEC, Sun, and NeXT workstations (over 100 workstations). Software systems and languages: UNIX; all major languages for teaching and research. University facilities--Hardware: KSR-1; iPSC/860; Cray Y/MP; VAXs; Macintoshes; PCs; all types of workstations. Software systems and languages: VMS; UNIX; all major languages and packages.

Student Body

There are 235 graduate students in the department, and a total of 5,436 graduate students in the university.

Faculty Profile

Fifteen faculty members teach in the department.

Deadlines and Financial Aid

The mission of the Office of Scholarships and Financial Aid is to provide financial assistance to students through grants, loans, scholarships, and employment. Graduate assistantships are available for teaching assistants and research assistants. Stipends range from $6,300 to $10,800 per year. Admissions application deadline: July 3 for fall; December 4 for spring. Assistantship application deadline: March 1 for fall; Oct. 1 for spring.

Admission Requirements

Application and fee, transcripts, letters of recommendation and GRE scores.

Expenses

Tuition is $8,960 per year.

Contact

Department of Computer Science, U. of Houston, Houston, TX 77204-3475. Telephone: 713-743-3350. Contact person: Dr. Stephen Huang, Director. E-mail: gradinfo@cs.uh.edu.
URL: http://www.cs.uh.edu.

University of North Texas

F/X Degrees Offered

The School of Visual Arts offers a B.F.A. and M.F.A. in Communication Design as well as other art-related majors.

Curricular

Undergraduate Computer in Art courses include: Computer Application in Visual Arts; 3D Modeling and Animation; Digital Photo Imaging; Interactive Multimedia Authoring and Design for www; Art and Design of the Computer Game; Studio Application in Graphic Design; Computer Illustration; Computer Art Studio. Graduate students' coursework is specifically directed by the graduate director and major professor.

Facilities

Computer laboratories and studios with an extensive array of software design programs; professional internships in Dallas/Ft. Worth Metroplex. The 90,000-square-foot Art Building on the UNT campus includes classrooms, three computer labs, faculty offices, studios, a workshop, the University Art Gallery and a visual resources library. A major addition to the Art Building is scheduled to be built within the next few years, doubling the amount of classroom and studio space. Three other campus buildings house additional classrooms and laboratories, as well as the Texas Fashion Collection and the Cora Stafford Gallery. The North Texas Institute for Educators on the Visual Arts, also located on the UNT campus, provides a unique outreach to metroplex area schools and museums. The Art Building is located at the corner of Avenue A & Mulberry on the Northeast corner of campus. It houses the Dean's Office, the Office of Student Services, the Division Offices, the University Art Gallery, the Visual Reseources Library, Computer Laboratories, the Fabrication Facility; and the instruction space for art education, art history, commmunication design, the core drawing and design programs, drawing and painting, interior design, metals and jewelry, printmaking, and sculpture.

Student Body
There are 1,500 undergraduates and,120 graduate students in the School of Visual Arts; Communication Design is the largest undergraduate major.

Faculty Profile
Five to seven faculty members teach in the Computer Graphics area.

Deadlines and Financial Aid
Undergraduate admission deadlines are: June 15 for the fall semester; December 2 for the spring semester; May 15 for summer I; and June 27 for summer II. Graduate admission deadlines are: February 15 for the fall semester; Oct. 15 for the spring semester; some graduate Art programs only accept students in the fall Semester. General UNT Financial Aid and Scholarships: consult the Financial Aid Office. The School of Visual Arts awards scholarships annually to currently enrolled Art students.

Admission Requirements
Graduate students: Application and fee, slide portfolio, letters of recommendation, artist statement, and declaration of major to the School of Visual Arts. Graduate students must apply to both UNT graduate school and the School of Visual Arts. The ideal candidate to the M.F.A. in Communication Design should have an undergraduate degree in Communication Design with two years of experience in the field beyond the B.F.A. Undergraduates: Application and fee, SAT or ACT, and transcripts.

Expenses
Tuition is $75 per credit hour for residents and $292 per credit hour for non-residents.

Contact
UNT School of Visual Arts, P.O. Box 305100, Denton, TX 76203. Telephone: 940-369-7234 or 800-UNT-8211. Fax: 940-565-4717. Contact person: Cynthia Mohr, Division of Design, Chair. E-mail: mohr@unt.edu.
URL: http://www.art.unt.edu/.

University of Texas at Austin

F/X Degrees Offered
B.S., M.A., M.F.A. and Ph.D. in Radio-Television-Film. M.S. and Ph.D. in Computer Science.

Curricular
The Department of Radio-Television-Film offers courses in: Internship in Film and Electronic Media; Multimedia; Film/Video Production; Studies in Film and Electronic Media Industries; Digital Animation and Graphics; Film Animation and Graphics; Research Design in Film and Electronic Media; Advanced Research in Film and Electronic Media; Electronic Editing.

Facilities
A nine-level, 110,000-square-foot production building to accommodate studios for training students in radio, television, and production facilities for the University Cable System. Computer Science Department facilities--Hardware: 65 Quadra 800s; 130 Sparc stations; 90 IBM X-terminals; 25 PCs; one Alpha; one IBM SP2-3A4; one Intel Paragon XP/E/4; 10 DEC station 5000s; 20 Dell 486/66s; 28 Pentiums; one Sparc server 1000. Software systems and languages: AIX; Solaris; Ultrix; OSF/1; Windows; C; C++; Lisp; Fortran; Pascal; Ada; Miranda.

Student Body

There are 220 graduate students enrolled in the Computer Science Department.

Faculty Profile

Twenty-four full-time faculty members in the department; 40 faculty members in the Science Department.

Deadlines and Financial Aid

The College of Communication has a large number of scholarships that are awarded annually. Students interested in receiving one of these scholarships should apply by February 15 for scholarships to be awarded in the fall semester. Each department also awards scholarships. Department of Science offers various forms of fellowships with stipends of $30,000 per year, and teaching assistantships with stipends of $9,000 to $10,098 per year, and research assistantships of $9,000 to $11,595. Undergraduate admission deadlines: February 1 for the fall semester; Oct. 1 for the spring semester; and February 1 for the summer session.

Admission Requirements

Undergraduates must submit an application and fee, SAT I or ACT scores, and transcripts. Graduate students must submit an application and fee, two transcripts, GRE scores.

Expenses

Undergraduates tuition is $5,340 per year for residents and $11,446 per year for non-residents.

Contact

Department of Computer Science, Taylor Hall, 2.124, Austin, TX 78712-1188. Telephone: 512-475-7440. Fax: 512-475-7475. Contact person: J. Strother Moore, Professor and Chair. Email: chair@cs.utexas.edu.
URL: http://www.cs.utexas.edu.

West Texas A&M University

F/X Degrees Offered

Art/Communication/Theatre Department. Fine Arts program, B.A., B.F.A., M.A. and M.F.A. in Studio Art with major emphasis in Computer Art; other areas include Drawing, Painting, Printmaking, Metalsmithing, Sculpture and Ceramics.

Curricular

3D Modeling and Rendering; 3D Computer Animation; 2D Computer Animation; Multimedia/Interactive; Digital Painting/Drawing; Image Processing; Virtual Reality; Digital Video; Computer Automated Engraving (with concurrent enrollment in Printmaking).

Facilities

Macintoshes and Pentiums. Software: Photoshop; Painter; Bryce; Premiere; and Strata Studio Pro taught in classes. AutoCAD; 3D Studio; Corel Draw; Lightwave; and many others available to students.

Student Body

Seventeen undergraduates major in computer graphics; 40 in classes per semester. Five graduate students in the department.

Deadlines and Financial Aid

Various fellowships and traditional state, federal, and city aid are available to students. Contact the Financial Aid Office for details on obtaining financial assistance at the university.

Admission Requirements

Application and fee, transcripts, ACT or SAT, and the Texas Academic Skills Program (TASP) scores.

Expenses

Tuition is $1,386 per semester.

Contact

WTAMU Box 747, Canyon, TX 79016. Telephone: 806-651-2789 or 800-99-WTAMU. Fax: 806-651-

2779. Contact person: Sven Anderson. E-mail:
sven@wtamu.edu.
URL: http://www.wtamu.edu.

Utah

University of Utah

F/X Degrees Offered
Department of Computer Science. B.S., M.S., and Ph.D. in Computer Science.

Curricular
Courses are offered in the following research areas including Asynchronous Digital Systems; Computer Aided Geometric Design; Computer Graphics; Computer Vision; Constraint-based Modeling; Educational Computing; Formal VLSI Design Methods; High-Speed GaAs Circuits; Information-based Distributed Complexity; Information Retrieval; Natural-language Processing; Numerical Analysis; Operating Systems, Robotics; Scientific Visualization; Scientific Computing; VLSI Design; and Virtual Reality and Tele-operation. Courses offered in the Department include: Computer Architecture; Computer Vision; Robotics; Programming Languages and Data Structures; Compiler Construction; Natural Language Processing; Machine Learning; Logic Design; Program Verification; Switching Circuit Theory; Digital Systems; Theoretical Computer Science; Operating Systems; LSI Circuits Design; Computational Complexity; Software Engineering; Multisensor Integration; VLSI tools; Scientific Computing; and Scientific Visualization.

Facilities
The computing facilty at the School of Computing consists of over 500 desktop machines and servers, running a variety of operating systems (Solaris, IRIX, Linux, Windows NT and 2000). Six laboratories: Computer-Aided Design and Graphics; Computer Systems Laboratory;

Asynchronous Digital Systems and VLSI; Robotics and Vision; Scientific Computing and Imaging; and Information Retrieval and Natural Language Processing. The department is divided into two computing environments: one is dedicated to research computing, and the other is for general/instructional computing. The Research Computing Facility: A heterogeneous network comprised of 20 file and application servers, with more than 600 GB of disk storage. These servers utilize AFS and NFS and are connected by 18, five fast, and four FDDI rings to more than 200 workstations from DEC, Hewlett Packard, Sun, IBM, and Silicon. General research equipment includes a six-processor Power Challenge with an Extreme Graphics console, a processor SGI power Onyx with two RE2 Graphics consoles, and a two-processor SGI DM file server. Individual laboratories contain specialized equipment dedicated for research. The latter includes high-end graphics workstations; a 60-CPU Origin 2000 with eight infinite reality engines; three FDDI, IBMs, HPs, and SGIs; and a multi-source video-editing environment. Robot arms and a variety of specialized equipment for image analysis, plus specialized equipment for real-time signal processing, are also housed in departmental laboratories. The General Computing Facilities--include more than 100 UNIX workstations from HP, Sun, SGI, and DEC and 30 Hewlett Packard Pentium/NT machines for instructional use, connected to 10 file and application servers with a total of 75 GB of disk storage using ASF and NFS file systems. The Department of Computer Science also has access to the College of Engineering Workstation Laboratory, which consists of five servers, 100 Sun workstations, and 25 HP workstations. The machines are divided into two separate rooms and are used for undergraduate and graduate instruction.

Student Body

There are 103 graduate students, and 300 undergraduate students.

Faculty Profile

Six faculty members teach in the area of Computer Graphics or closely related areas.

Deadlines and Financial Aid

The deadline for undergraduate students to apply for major status is at the end of the spring quarter. They must have completed all the prerequisite courses for the major. Deadline for graduate students is February 1 of each year to be considered for fall admission. Teaching and research assistantships are available to full-time graduate students. Undergraduate students can apply for various scholarships offered through the department, and a teaching assistant position for a lower-level course.

Admission Requirements

Requirements for students to the Graduate program are: Application for admission, official transcripts, three letters of recommendation, GRE scores on the General Test and Advanced Subject Test in Computer Science, and a personal statement listing specific research goals and academic background. Undergraduates must submit an application and fee, high school transcript, and SAT or ACT scores.

Expenses

Tuition is $1,271.20 per semester for residents and $4,465.76 per semester for non-residents.

Contact

Department of Computer Science, University of Utah, Salt Lake City, UT 84112. Telephone: 801-581-8224. Fax: 801-585-6742. Contact person: Chuck Hansen, Professor. E-mail: hansen@cs.utah.edu. URL: http://www.cs.utah.edu.

Utah State University

F/X Degrees Offered

Instructional Technology; B.S. and M.S. in Computer Science.

Curricular

Computer Graphics and Advanced Computer Graphics.

Facilities

SGI workstation laboratory; Macintosh and UNIX workstations.

Student Body

There are 20,800 students enrolled in the university.

Faculty Profile

There are 776 faculty members teaching at the university.

Deadlines and Financial Aid

Various forms of federal aid are available in the form of federal aid, loans, grants and scholarships.

Admission Requirements

Undergraduates: high school transcripts, SAT or ACT score, application, and fee. Graduate students: submit an application and fee, transcripts, GRE scores and letters of recommendation.

Expenses

Tuition is $2,898 per year for residents and $14,376 per year for non-residents.

Contact

Utah State University, Computer Science Department, Logan, UT 84321. Telephone: 435-797-1000 or 435-797-3280. Fax: 435-797-4077. Contact person: Dr. Donald Cooley, Chair. Email: don.cooley@usu.edu. URL: http://www.usu.edu.

Weber State University

F/X Degrees Offered
Visual Arts. B.S., B.A., and B.F.A. degrees in traditional areas of studio concentration, including Visual Communication. Students can also pursue a bachelor's degree or an associate degree in Computer and Design Graphics Technology.

Curricular
3D Modeling and Rendering; 2D Computer Animation; Multimedia/Interactive; Digital Painting/Drawing; Image Processing.

Facilities
Three large labs are available for students in the major to explore applications in the 3D modeling, CAD/CAM, graphical presentations and animation. Facilities include: Macintosh computers capable of running high-end software; scanners; video system using a Targa 2000 card. Software: Adobe Photoshop; Adobe Illustrator; Adobe PageMaker; Adobe Streamline; QuarkXPress; Macromedia Director; Super 3D; Strata Studio Pro.

Student Body
Fifty undergraduate students in the department.

Faculty Profile
Eleven full-time and 15 half-time faculty members in the department.

Deadlines and Financial Aid
Various fellowships and traditional state, federal, and city aid are available to students. Contact the Financial Aid Office for details on obtaining financial assistance at the university. Weber State University awards scholarships for achievement of excellence in either academics or specific activities. Unless otherwise specified, all scholarships are for one year and are not renewable. Students must apply each consecutive year for consideration. Scholarship applications must be received at the Scholarship Office by February 1 for the following academic year. The admission process must be completed by February 1 for the fall semester.

Admission Requirements
Application and fee, transcripts, ACT scores.

Expenses
Tuition is $2,130 per year for residents and $7,456 for non-residents.

Contact
Weber State University, Department of Visual Arts, 2001 University Circle, Ogden, UT 84408-2001. Telephone: 801-626 6455. Fax: 801-626 6976. Contact person: Larry Leavitt. E-mail: lleavitt@weber.edu. URL: http://www.weber.edu.

Additional Information
The university began with electronic painting and image processing in 1983, and currently offer three courses which focus specifically on digital media. Computing tools have been integrated to support foundation courses, advance studio emphases, and as media concentrations (Animation and Multimedia/Interactive).

Vermont

University of Vermont

F/X Degrees Offered
B.F.A. through the Art Department.

Curricular
3D Modeling and Rendering; 2D Computer Animation; High-Level Programming; Digital Painting/Drawing; Image Processing.

Facilities
Access to laboratory with 50 Windows workstations. Silicon Graphics Teaching Laboratory with 12 SGI workstations and three 8-processor server engines; IBM Power laboratory. Adobe Photoshop; Fractal Design Painter; Morph by Gryphon; Infini-D; Director. A pool of postscript printers serves the facility. Several other computer laboratories are available across the campus.

Student Body
There are 9,000 undergraduates, and 1,000 graduate students attend the university.

Faculty Profile
Approximately 1,002 full and part-time faculty teach at the university.

Deadlines and Financial Aid
Early Decision: November 1 to mid-December. General Admission: February 1 to March 15. International: February 1, rolling. VT Scholars: November 1 to mid-December.

Admission Requirements
Application and fee, transcripts, counselor and teacher recommendations, and SAT I or ACT scores.

Expenses
Tuition is $4,348 per semester for residents and $10,874 per semester for non-residents.

Contact
University of Vermont, Williams Hall, 72 University Place, Burlington, VT 05405. Telephone: 802-656-2014. Fax: 802-656-8429. Contact person: Nadine E. Carpenter, Art Department Secretary. E-mail: ncarpent@moose.uvm.edu. URL: http://www.uvm.edu.

Additional Information
Studio Art majors take introductory courses in drawing, 2D design, 3D design, and/or film/video production. Other optional introductory courses are offered in ceramics and fine metals. Students then choose intermediate level classes from a broad variety of offerings which includes drawing, painting, printmaking, film and video, photography, computer art, sculpture, clay and fine metals. These classes are followed by advanced coursework in drawing, painting, photography, or sculpture, or by independent tutorials with faculty guidance in projects of special interest to the student.

Virginia

College of William and Mary

F/X Degrees Offered
B.S., M.S., and Ph.D. in Computer Science.

Curricular
Courses in Scientific Visualization, Advanced Computer Graphics, and Digital Image Processing.

Facilities
The department runs a heterogenous network of Unix computers, including Intel-based computers running Linux, Sun Sparc's running SunOS and Solaris, and SGI's running Irix.

Student Body
Forty undergraduate students, and 70 graduate students major in Computer Science.

Faculty Profile
Fifteen full-time faculty members in the department.

Deadlines and Financial Aid
Financial assistance is available to undergraduates who need additional resources to meet the costs of education at the College. Demonstrated need is established through the analysis of the Free Application for Federal Student Aid (FAFSA). In most cases, Virginia undergraduates may expect sufficient support to enable them to attend the College for four years, while out-of-state undergraduates may in many cases expect partial support, with the level depending upon financial need and the availability of funds. Assistance is offered for one year only, but may be renewed for each succeeding year if need continues and the student otherwise qualifies. Renewal requires the completion of the FAFSA for each succeeding year.

The College's standard of satisfactory academic progress, which is generally the same as that required for continuance in the College, is outlined in the Guide to Financial Aid, available from the Office of Student Financial Aid. Entering students include early decision, regular decision and transfers. Early decision students should file the College's Early Decision Financial Aid application by November 1 of the senior year in high school. Regular decision and transfer students should file the FAFSA by February 15. Returning students should file by March 15. Late applicants will be considered on a funds available basis. Graduate teaching assistantship offers a stipend of $12,000 in addition to a tuition waiver. Admissions application deadline: May 1, fall; November 15, spring. Assistantship application deadline: March 1, fall. In addition, other forms of financial aid are available to graduate and undergraduate students through the Financial Aid Office.

Admission Requirements
Undergraduates must submit an application and fee, high school transcript, and SAT or ACT score. Graduate students must submit an application and fee, GRE scores and transcripts with evidence of an undergraduate degree.

Expenses
Undergraduate tuition is $2,544 per semester for residents and $9,646 for non-residents.

Contact
Department of Computer Science, Williamsburg, VA 23185. Telephone: 757-221-3455 or 757-221-4223. Fax: 757-221-1242. Contact person: Xiaodong Zhang, Chair.
URL: http://www.cs.wm.edu.

James Madison University

F/X Degrees Offered
M.S. degree in Computer Science. The School of Media Arts and Design offers both B.A. and B.S. degrees with concentrations in Multimedia and Mediated Visual Expression.

Curricular
Computer Graphics courses through the art and science curricular.

Facilities
Computer Science Department facilities--Hardware: eight UNIX workstations; 30 Windows workstations. Software systems and languages: Sun OS; MS Windows; C/C++; numerous others.

Student Body
There are 11,643 undergraduate students and 759 graduate students enrolled in the university.

Faculty Profile
Nine faculty members teach in this area.

Deadlines and Financial Aid
Stipends are offered in the form of graduate assistantship and teaching assistantships. These stipends range from $5,300 to $6,300 per year. Admissions application deadline: July 1. Assistantship application deadline: April 1. Undergraduate students should contact the Financial Aid office for information on obtaining scholarships, loans, and grants.

Admission Requirements
Undergraduates must submit an application and fee, high school transcripts, and the SAT or ACT scores. Application and fee, transcripts, and GRE scores.

Expenses
Tuition is $2,529 per semester for residents and $6,640 for non-residents.

Contact
Department of Computer Science, Harrisonburg, VA 22807. Telephone: 540-568-2770 or 540-568-5681. Fax: 540-568-3332. Contact person: Chris Fox. E-mail: foxcj@jmu.edu.
URL: http://www.cs.jmu.edu.

Additional Information
The program puts students in the middle of the exploding information revolution where they study technological advances, such as object-oriented software, communication networks, multimedia systems, information and knowledge management and artificial intelligence. Students learn about computing technologies used by today's professionals and how to use these technologies to solve real-world problems. They learn to analyze problems, design solutions, implement solutions using multiple computing technologies, test and install those solutions and communicate those solutions to others in written and verbal presentations.

George Mason University

F/X Degrees Offered
New Century College awards the following degrees: B.A. or B.S. in Integrative Studies, B.A. in Interdisciplinary Studies, bachelor of Individualized Study. B.F.A. and M.F.A. through the Center for the Arts

Curricular
Beyond the general education requirement students generally work with an advisor to design their own curriculum. The interims and the intersession are built into the curriculum to allow for optional, intensive, one-credit courses such as Network Computer Graphics, TV Workshop, or Leadership Development, to name a few. The winter intersession

also allows for special intensive courses and provides a period for study abroad, individualized projects, research with faculty, or experiential learning outside the college.

Facilities

Two advanced Macintosh labs for teaching couses in multimedia, Web site production and animation. An advanced lab with more than 15 SGI workstations with advanced animation applications. Several multimedia PC labs with video editing equipment. Software programs include Maya, Director, Infini D, Sound Edit, Flash, Photoshop, Illustrator, Quark, Dreamweaver, Pagemill, Premiere.

Deadlines and Financial Aid

Students interested in applying for financial aid should complete the Free Application for Federal Student Aid (FAFSA) and submit it to the Federal Processor by March 1. Applications should be submitted as soon as possible after Jan. 1.

Admission Requirements

The Integrative Studies program has a self-selecting admissions policy. Any student who meets George Mason University's admissions requirements may select this program. Admission is based on the appropriateness of the student's academic objectives and the likelihood that the student will benefit from the curriculum of the college. The curriculum is designed not only with the full time student in mind, but is also committed to offering learning communities on weekends and evenings to fit the needs of students who can only attend classes part time. When applying to George Mason University, you should identify which of the New Century College programs you are interested in (Integrative Studies, Individualized Study, Interdisciplinary Studies) from the list of available programs. Freshman Review Process: the scores submitted for the Scholastic Aptitude Test (SAT) and/or the American College Test (ACT). These may

be supplemented by the SAT Subject Tests (SAT II) results in English (essay required), mathematics (level I or II), and a foreign language or science (foreign language is preferred for students seeking a bachelor of arts degree). Test of English as a Foreign Language (TOEFL) scores from non-native English-speaking applicants to supplement other standardized test results; a student essay; any additional elements you wish to submit; results of the personal interview.

Expenses

Tuition is $2,556 per semester for residents and $7,476 per year for non-residents.

Contact

New Century College, George Mason University, 4400 University Drive, Fairfax, VA 22030-4444. Telephone: 703-993-1436. Fax: 703-993-1439. URL: http://www.ncc.gmu.edu.

Additional Information

Located in Northern Virginia, George Mason is convenient to all the resources of the nation's capital and the Washington metropolitan area. Situated on 677 wooded acres near the City of Fairfax, the university's Fairfax Campus combines the quiet of a suburban setting with accessibility to Washington's libraries, galleries and museums; Virginia's historic sites; and Fairfax County's high-technology firms. Metrorail, the Washington area's subway system, enables GMU riders to reach the U.S. Capitol in 35 minutes. It also provides a quick ride to GMU's 5.2-acre Arlington Campus, which houses the law school, a professional center, and a conference center. Its campus in Prince William County offers academic, community, and business support programs. The Center for the Arts complex includes a 2,000-seat Concert Hall, two experimental theaters, three dance studios, and music and fine arts studios. Five hundred concert hall tickets are available free to students for each performance.

Old Dominion University

F/X Degrees Offered
B.S., M.S., and Ph.D. in Computer Science, Computer Information Sciences, and Computer Engineering.

Curricular
Courses include networks and communications; software engineering; high-performance scientific computing; foundations; distributed systems; databases; artificial intelligence; multimedia.

Facilities
Department facilities--Hardware: Sun; SGI workstations; access to NASA Langley's IBM SP-2; Paragon; ATM networks; electronic multimedia classrooms. Software systems and languages: UNIX; Solaris; C; C++.

Student Body
There are 12,000 undergraduates, and 5,000 graduate students; 250 undergraduates, and 100 graduate Computer Science students in the department.

Faculty Profile
Thirty-four faculty members teach graduate courses in the department, and 18 faculty members teach undergraduate courses in the department.

Deadlines and Financial Aid
The Office of Student Financial Aid administers need-based financial assistance programs for eligible students funded by federal, state, university, and private sources in the form of grants, Federal Direct Stafford/Ford Subsidized Loans, Federal Perkins Loans, employment through the Federal Work-Study Program, and need-based as well as merit-based scholarships. In addition, the office administers non-need-based options for education financing through the Federal Direct Unsubsidized Stafford/Ford Loans and Federal Direct PLUS Loans for parents of dependent students. Students must file a FAFSA by February 15 of the spring preceding the academic year of the award. Graduate students may receive graduate research assistantships and fellowships, and may receive stipends of $10,000 to $16,000 per year. Admissions application deadline: June 15 for the fall semester; November 1 for the spring semester. Graduate assistantship application deadline: April 1 for the fall semester.

Admission Requirements
Undergraduates must submit an application and fee, SAT or ACT scores, and transcript. Graduate students may be required to submit GRE scores, transcripts, and an application with fee.

Expenses
Tuition is $159 per credit hour for residents and $464 per credit hour for non-residents.

Contact
Department of Computer Science, Norfolk, VA 23529. Telephone: 757-683-3915. Fax: 757-683-4900. Contact person: Kurt Maly, Chair. E-mail: office@cs.odu.edu.
URL: http://www.cs.odu.edu/.

University of Virginia

F/X Degrees Offered
B.S., M.S. and Ph.D. in Computer Science.

Curricular
Various computer graphics courses and advanced visualization courses are taught in the department. Digital Picture Processing.

Facilities
Department facilities--Hardware: 22 Sun 3 X-terminals; 44 Sun 4 workstations; seven SGIs; six Macintoshes; 13 NCD X-terminals; 80 486s; 32-node Intel iPSC/2; two IBM RS6000; 12 Sparc 10 and 20 systems. Software systems and languages: UNIX;

X-windows; extensive software. University facilities-
-Hardware: Several RS/6000; one IBM 3090; IBM
SP/2; cooperative agreement with Supercomputer
Centers; large number of Sun workstations,
IBM-compatibles and Macintoshes. The VINTLab
consists of the following equipment: 5 Cisco 7000
IP routers; (7 more will be added); 2 Lightstream
2020 ATM switches; 2 Cisco 2500 routers; 4 T-1 DSU/
CSUs; 2 FDDI concentrators; 6 workstations.

Student Body
Total of 11,949 undergraduate, and 4,403 graduate
students attend the university; 150 undergraduate,
and 86 graduate students are Computer Science
majors.

Faculty Profile
Seventeen faculty members teach in the Computer
Science Department.

Deadlines and Financial Aid
Financial aid is based on the premise that the
primary responsibility for financing a college
education rests with the student and parents.
Therefore, a portion of the student's and parents'
resources is expected to be available for college
expenses each year. Need-based scholarships
and grants come from a variety of sources. When
students complete the FAFSA and UFAA forms,
they are applying for federal, institutional and, in
some cases, state financial aid programs. Eligibility
for financial aid is automatically considered for
every applicant. Awards made to students are
based on a number of factors including federal
regulations, demonstrated financial need, student
enrollment status, and availability of funds. Students
are automatically considered for all types of aid
programs (grants, loans, and work-study) when they
have valid FAFSA records and complete UFAA forms.
Graduate assistantships are available with a stipend
of $10,000 to $12,800 per year.

Admission Requirements
Undergraduates must submit an application and fee,
SAT or ACT scores, and transcript. Graduate students
must submit an application and fee, transcripts and
GRE scores.

Expenses
Tuition is $6,150 per year for residents and $22,170
per year for non-residents.

Contact
Department of Computer Science, School of
Engineering & Applied Science, University of
Virginia,
151 Engineer's Way, P.O. Box 400740, Charlottesville,
VA 22904-4740. Telephone: 804-982-2200. Fax: 434-
982-2214. Contact person: Ruth Anderson. E-mail:
ruth@cs.virginia.edu.
URL: http://www.cs.virginia.edu.

Virginia Commonwealth University

F/X Degrees Offered
B.F.A. in Communication Arts and Design with
a focus in Electronic Media. M.F.A. in Visual
Communications.

Curricular
Computer technology is integrated into the design
of most courses in the Department. The curriculum
includes courses such as: Computer Graphics
I-III; Computer Techniques for Graphic Design;
Introduction to Video; Electronic Animation
I-III; Video I and II; Art Direction I-IV; Video
Editing; Multimedia Communication Systems;
Virtual Reality; Integrated Electronic Information/
Communication Systems; Film Pre-production and
Post-production; Filmmaking I-III; The Film Image;
Film Animation; Motion Picture Special Effects.

Facilities

Eight departmental computer laboratories.

Student Body

There are 450 students in the department, and 130 in the Electronic Media area.

Faculty Profile

Four full-time faculty and six part-time faculty teach in the area of Electronic Media.

Deadlines and Financial Aid

Various fellowships and traditional state, federal and city aid are available to students. Applications received after the recommended deadline will be considered if space is available and there is sufficient time for processing, review and notification. Transfer applicants planning to apply for financial aid or to the School of the Arts should use freshman deadlines. Contact the Financial Aid Office for details on specific deadlines. VCU uses all available funds to help students gain access to a college education. Eligibility for financial aid varies depending on a student's academic and financial circumstances. In most cases, each student will qualify for some form of financial assistance.

Admission Requirements

Candidates for admission to VCU are reviewed based on their academic performance in an accredited high school and either SAT I or ACT scores. The college preparatory curriculum is highly preferred, and a minimum of 20 units is required for admission to all programs on the Academic Campus. Undergraduate applicants for the department must first complete freshman art foundations. Extracurricular activities and employment experience may strengthen an application. Essays are required for scholarship consideration.

Expenses

Tuition is $4,869 per year for residents and $17,213 per year for non-residents.

Contact

Department of Communication Arts and Design, Virginia Commonwealth University, 325 N. Harrison St., Box 842519, Richmond, VA 23284. Telephone: 804-828-1709. Fax: 804-828-6930. Contact person: Matt Woolman, Acting Chair. E-mail: mwoolman@vcu.edu. URL: http://www.vcu.edu/artweb/.

Additional Information

This concentration is designed for students who desire major study in video, computer graphics, and audio-visual communications. Emphasis is placed upon the artistic and communicative uses of media in contemporary society. VCU's School of the Arts is one of the largest and most comprehensive art schools in the United States. The only state-supported professional school of the arts in the South, the VCU School of the Arts is one of few in the country offering a professional curriculum within a combined academic and professional environment. U.S. News & World Report recently ranked the School of the Arts as one of the top six art schools in the nation.

Virginia Polytechnic Institute and State University

F/X Degrees Offered

Computer Science Department. B.S., M.S. and Ph.D. The Department of Computer Science offers a wide range of courses in various aspects of Human-Computer Interaction.

Curricular

Undergraduate senior-level electives in both Computer Graphics and HCI. At the graduate level, a series of courses in HCI are offered covering both theory and practice, as well as frequent special-topics classes. Both graduate and undergraduate courses in Multimedia and Image Processing. 3D Modeling and Rendering; 2D Computer Animation; Multimedia/Interactive; High-Level Programming; Image Processing.

Facilities

Near-infinite supply of smaller workstations, including Sun, DEC, IBM-compatible and Macintosh. An Intel Paragon Multi-processor. Specially equipped research laboratories in the department and around the Blacksburg campus support work across all areas of the discipline. These facilities include a usability engineering laboratory designed for meta-evaluation; head-mounted virtual reality displays; the VT-CAVE (a 3-D audio/visual environment driven by an eight-processor SGI Power Onyx); and connectivity through Virginia Tech's advanced networking infrastructure and Internet2 access. Department faculty play a lead role in the university's terascale computing facility (a world-class supercomputer consisting of 1,100 dual 2.0 GHz Apple G5s). A second large (400 processor) cluster is located in the department's Laboratory for Advanced Scientific Computing and Applications.

Student Body

There are 600 undergraduates, and 100 graduate students in the department.

Faculty Profile

Eighteen faculty members teach in the department.

Deadlines and Financial Aid

The Department of Computer Science at Virginia Tech is home to an extremely competitive program with one of the highest enrollments of any department in the university. Graduate assistantships are available to qualified graduate students. These assistantships range from teaching assistantships with a yearly stipend of $9,600 to $10,400, to research assistantships of $9,630, and others forms of funding such as fellowships in the Human-Computer Interaction are available. Admissions application deadline: February 1. Assistantship application deadline: February 1.

Admission Requirements

Undergraduates must submit an application and fee, SAT or ACT scores, and transcript. Graduate students are required to submit the following materials for admission: GRE scores, application, fee, transcripts, letters of recommendation.

Expenses

Tuition is $4,190 per year for residents and $14,074 per year for non-residents.

Contact

Virginia Polytechnic Institute and State University, Department of Computer Science, Blacksburg, VA 24061-0106. Telephone: 540-231-6932 or 540-231-6000. Contact person: Shawn A. Bohner, Associate Professor. E-mail: sbohner@vt.edu. URL: http://www.cs.vt.edu.

Additional Information

The Department of Computer Science is home to one of the largest groups of undergraduate majors in the university as well as to graduate students in Blacksburg and at the Northern Virginia Center. The B.S., M.S., and Ph.D. degrees provide in-depth exposure to the core body of knowledge in the computing discipline, preparing graduates for careers or further study. In July 2003, the department joined the College of Engineering after more than 30 years in the College of Arts and Sciences. The department's focus on the fundamental properties and processes associated with software is complemented by the discipline-centered application of software systems in other departments within the college. The computer science major is software oriented, in contrast to the hardware-oriented computer engineering major. Computer science majors design and develop software, from the software systems that control the functioning of the computer such as operating systems and compilers to applications software for areas such as numerical analysis, graphics, and data bases.

Virginia State University

F/X Degrees Offered
B.F.A. through the Art and Design Department. The Virginia State University Art and Design Department offers low-end electronic publishing.

Curricular
Courses in Computer Graphics.

Facilities
Computer Graphics laboratory with both Macintosh and IBM workstations.

Student Body
There are 76 undergraduate students in the department.

Deadlines and Financial Aid
Various fellowships and traditional state, federal and city aid are available to students. Contact the Financial Aid Office for details on obtaining financial assistance at the university.

Admission Requirements
Application and fee, transcripts, portfolio, ACT or SAT scores.

Expenses
Tuition is $890 per semester for residents and $4,237 per semester for non-residents.

Contact
Art and Design Department, 1506 Jacquelin St., Richmond, VA 23220-6010. Telephone: 804-524-5000. Fax: 804-524-5055. Contact person: Mark W. Phillips, Chair.
URL: http://www.vsu.edu.

Additional Information
The mission of the Art and Design unit is structured to prepare students to operate in the dynamics of a visual world in a most expeditious and creative manner. The Unit's mission extends to the larger community through exhibitions, seminars, lectures, artists-in-residence programs, and extra curricular activities. The unit periodically updates its programs as it relates to the needs of industry and education. Further, the mission is to develop the students as well-rounded human beings with knowledge, skills, and self assurance to function as responsible citizens in society. Moreover, the unit seeks to be responsive to the needs and aspirations of those who may otherwise not have the opportunity to develop to their fullest potential. Further, the mission involves the development and enrichment of students who do not seek careers in visual arts.

Virginia Western Community College

F/X Degrees Offered
A.A.S. in Commercial Art.

Curricular
Courses in: Advertising Design; Graphics I and II; Topics in Computers; Introduction to the Macintosh; Photoshop; Introduction to Computers-PC; QuarkXPress.

Facilities
Eighteen Macintosh workstations; three color scan stations; three b/w, 600 dpi printers, 8.5x11; one b/w 600 dpi printer, 11x17; two color printers, 8.5x11; one Cannon color copier; two digital cameras; one video camera.

Student Body

More than 45 students in the Commercial Art area.

Faculty Profile

Two faculty members teach courses in this area.

Deadlines and Financial Aid

Federal grant programs and Virginia and local scholarship programs available; work-study opportunities.

Admission Requirements

Open college system.

Expenses

Tuition is $57 per credit hour for residents and $120 per credit hour for non-residents.

Contact

Commercial Art Department, Virginia Western Community College, 3095 Colonial Ave. S.W., P.O. Box 14007, Roanoke, VA 24038-4007. Telephone: 540-857-6082. Fax: 540-857-6096. Contact person: Diane Wolff. Email: dwolff@vw.vccs.edu. URL: http://www.vw.cc.va.us/.

Washington

Eastern Washington University

F/X Degrees Offered
B.S. and M.S. in Computer Science.

Curricular
Classes offered in Computer Graphics in the Art Department. The Computer Science Department offers courses in Advanced Visualization and Computer Graphics.

Facilities
SGI workstations are available through the Science Department. Three main computer labs are available to all Computer Science Students. All of the labs are equipped with state of the art equipment.

Student Body
There are 8,000 undergraduate students, and 300 graduate students.

Faculty Profile
Nine faculty members teach in the department.

Deadlines and Financial Aid
Priority Application dates for freshmen are February 15 for fall quarter, Oct. 15 for the winter quarter, and February 1 for the spring quarter.

Admission Requirements
Freshman applicants: complete the Washington Uniform Application for Admissions (available from EWU and high schools throughout Washington state) and submit the application, official copies of high school and any college transcripts, a non-refundable fee, and an official score report of the SAT or ACT. Graduate admission: a completed Application for Admission with an application fee, two official copies of transcripts from all colleges and universities attended, score reports from the GRE General Test, and evidence of scholarly ability.

Expenses
Tuition is $3,582 per year for residents and $12,438 per year for non-residents.

Contact
Department of Computer Science, Eastern Washington University, MS-86, 526 5th Street, Cheney, WA 99004-2431. Telephone: 509-359-6260 or 888-740-1914. Fax: 509-359-6692. Contact person: Ray Hamel, Chair. Email: rhamel@ewu.edu. URL: http://acm.ewu.edu/csd/.

University of Washington

F/X Degrees Offered
Department of Computer Science. B.A., B.S., M.S., and Ph.D. in Computer Science, Computer Graphics, and Geometric Modeling.

Curricular
3D Modeling and Rendering; 3D Computer Animation, Multimedia/Interactive, Digital Painting/Drawing; Virtual Reality (immersive and non-immersive); Digital Video.

Facilities
The Department maintains a wide variety of state-of-the-art computing facilities for research and instructional use. These include several platforms: nearly 500 Intel Pentium systems, and several dozen SPARCs, Alphas and SGIs. Server infrastructure is comprised of general-purpose compute, file and print servers, running Linux, FreeBSD, and Windows 2000. Departmental networking utilizes a gigabit backbone with switched 100mb Ethernet connections to servers and desktop machines, targeted gigabit connections to specific labs, and a

gigabit connection to the campus backbone and the Internet. A wireless network provides connectivity in the general vicinity of our building. A 13'x7' video wall provides high-definition video display used in conjunction with networking and graphics research. Research in computer systems (including architecture, networking, and distributed systems) involves a wide and constantly updated variety of hardware, software, and networks. Current hardware includes high-performance Intel uniprocessor and SMP platforms, a 65-processor Intel cluster, a networking testbed cluster, and several Alpha, Sun, SGI and PC workstations. Our facilities include Linux, FreeBSD, Windows, and Alpha support, and our clusters enjoy gigabit switched Ethernet connectivity and an Abilene network feed. In addition, the Systems lab provides a common workspace for systems, networking, and architecture students, and features Windows workstations, a video projector, and floor-to-ceiling whiteboards. Research in VLSI, digital hardware, and embedded systems is supported by a set of PC and SPARC workstations and multiprocessor compute servers. A large collection of both commercial and university computer-aided design tools form the core of the design environment providing capabilities for the design of CMOS VLSI chips, various forms of programmable logic, microprocessor-based systems, and printed-circuit boards. A variety of specialized equipment for the prototyping, debugging, and testing of microelectronic systems is also available and is housed within the Laboratory for Integrated Systems (LIS). These resources are utilized by research projects involved in the design of programmable logic architectures, devices to support ubiquitous and invisible computing, embedded systems, neurally-inspired computing and learning devices, and by graduate and undergraduate courses including VLSI and embedded system design. Research in graphics, image processing, and user interfaces, centered in the Graphics and Imaging Laboratory (GRAIL), utilizes a set of high-end graphics workstations, a multiprocessor compute server, and a variety of special-purpose devices, including a real-time motion capture system, digital cameras (still and video), a computer-controlled lighting grid, a Cyberware 3D laser scanner, a video projector for shape capture, and rotational and translational motion control platforms. Most of the lighting and imaging hardware resides in GRAIL's blackout room, which is ideal for experiments that require controlled illumination. In addition, GRAIL's sound-dampened video editing room is host to an audio/video hardware suite with non-linear digital video editing. The workstations in the lab are also used as development stations for experimental teaching software in graphics and vision. Research in robotics is carried out in the Robotics Laboratory, which is equipped with several mobile robots, ranging from an RWI B21 robot to ActivMedia Pioneer robots to a team of four Sony AIBO dogs. All robots utilize wireless networking to communicate with each other and to the lab PCs running Linux. The department also operates four special-purpose laboratories containing approximately 60 Intel Pentium PCs running Windows 2000, each backed by dedicated file servers. To support digital system design courses, the Integrated Digital Design Laboratory contains 12 Pentium workstations for design entry and simulation along with Tektronix logic analyzers, digital oscilloscopes and other test equipment. Computer graphics courses utilize the Instructional Graphics Lab, containing approximately 20 high-end Intel Pentium workstations. The Laboratory for Animation Arts includes 18 Intel PCs and digital video production equipment, and is used for teaching interdisciplinary courses in computer animation. The Special Projects Lab contains 20 Intel PCs, and is used to teach capstone courses in VLSI design, software system design, computer telephony, and other courses requiring specialized equipment or dedicated access. The SPL runs different systems and software: including Linux: at different times, depending on course needs.

Student Body
In Architecture area: 40 undergraduates and 30 graduate students. In the Engineering area: 300 undergraduates and 150 graduate students.

Faculty Profile
Four faculty members teach in the area of Computer Graphics in the Computer Science Department.

Deadlines and Financial Aid
For students wishing to enter the program in the fall quarter, the deadline is the preceding July 1. For students wishing to enter the program starting in the spring quarter, the deadline is the preceding February 1.

Admission Requirements
Application and fee, transcripts, statement of purpose, GRE scores.

Expenses
Tuition is $4,167 per year for residents and $14,868 per year for non-residents.

Contact
Computer Science & Engineering, University of Washington, AC101 Paul G. Allen Center, Box 352350, Seattle WA 98195-2350. Telephone: 206-543-1695. Fax: 206-543-2969. Contact person: Brian N. Bershad. E-mail: bershad@cs.washington.edu. URL: http://www.cs.washington.edu/.

Washington State University

F/X Degrees Offered
Computer Science Department. Undergraduate (B.S.C.S., B.S.) and Graduate programs (M.S., D.Sc.) in Computer Science. Particular research strengths are in networking, distributed computing, visualization and biomedical engineering.

Curricular
3D Modeling and Rendering; 3D Computer Animation; 2D Computer Animation; Multimedia/Interactive; Digital Painting/Drawing; Image Processing; Digital Video; Stereo Imaging.

Facilities
Facilities exist for non-linear NTSC video editing for animation, walk through, etc. More than 150 workstations (Sun, Silicon Graphics, Pentium PCs) and associated file and computer servers linked by combination of switched and ATM (approximately 50 machines on ATM currently). ATM-based multimedia units supporting integrated studio-quality two-way real-time video and CD-quality audio, with multi-party conference control software. Software: Photoshop; 3D studio; Accurender; AutoCAD; Animator Pro, etc. Animation courses are taught on Indys, with its own dedicated server. Architecture, Architectural Studies, and Construction Management programs students can expect computer facilities to be available at all levels, for most courses.

Student Body
School of Architecture has 930 undergraduates and eight graduate students (Architecture and Construction Management). Computer Science has 200 undergraduates and 80 graduate students.

Deadlines and Financial Aid
Various fellowships and traditional state, federal, and city aid are available to students. Contact the Financial Aid Office for details on obtaining financial assistance at the university.

Admission Requirements

Undergraduate students must submit an application and fee, transcript, and SAT or ACT scores. Graduate students should contact the department of interest.

Expenses

Tuition is $4,836 per year for residents and $12,938 per year for non-residents.

Contact

School of Electrical Engineering & Computer Science, Washington State University, P.O. Box 642752, Pullman, Washington 99164-2752. Telephone: 314-335-6602. Fax: 314-335-3818. Contact person: Tom Fischer, Director. E-mail: fischer@eecs.wsu.edu. URL: http://www.eecs.wsu.edu/.

Western Washington University

F/X Degrees Offered

The Department of Art offers a number of degree programs with major and minor concentrations in graphic design. Computer Science Department offers a B.S. and M.S. in Computer Science.

Curricular

Internet Resource Creation And Management; Scientific Computing; Programming Project; Computer Architecture III; Computer Modeling And Simulation; Software Engineering I (C++/ Windows); Computer Networks; Computer Graphics; Complexity Theory; Advanced Compiler Design; Advanced Topics In Operating Systems; Advanced Computer Architecture; Communications Networks; Artificial Intelligence; Advanced Computer Graphics.

Facilities

Western's Computer Science department currently operates six student laboratories devoted exclusively to computer science course support. The laboratory consists of 10 Tangent 486DX2/66 workstations, each with 8 MB of memory, a 340 MB IDE drive, an NE2000+ ether card, and a 15-inch MicroScan monitor. These 10 computers are connected together. The workstations are served by a Tangent 486DX2/66 workstation with 16M of memory, 8G disk, a CD-ROM, and a tape drive for a backups. Haggard Hall has a twenty seat lab running Sun Workstations.

Student Body

More than 10,000 students are enrolled in the university.

Faculty Profile

Twelve full-time faculty members in the department.

Deadlines and Financial Aid

Initial application with all supporting materials (see below) must be received in the Graduate School Office by June 1 for the fall, Oct. 1 for the winter, February 1 for the spring, and May 1 for the summer. Fall quarter is March 1; winter quarter is Oct. 15; spring is Jan. 15; summer is March 1. Western makes every effort to provide assistance to students to meet the full cost of college. During previous years, more than sixty percent of Western students received over $40,000,000 in federal, state, institutional, and private funds, in the forms of need-based grants, tuition waivers, employment, and loans. To apply for need-based financial aid, complete the FAFSA. For priority consideration, the FAFSA must be mailed to the federal processor by February 15.

Admission Requirements

Undergraduates: Applicants are required to submit an official high school transcript or GED Certificate and SAT or ACT scores. Graduate: Application materials, including official transcripts, GRE scores and the application fee.

Expenses

Tuition is $4,181 per year for residents and $12,955 per year for non-residents.

Contact

Western Washington University, Computer Science Department, Bond Hall 302, Bellingham, WA 98225-9009. Telephone: 360-650-3805. Fax: 360-650-7788.
E-mail: csdept@cs.wwu.edu.
URL: http://www.cs.wwu.edu.

Washington, D.C.

George Washington University

F/X Degrees Offered

Electrical Engineering and Computer Science. B.S., M.S. and Ph.D. degrees in Computer Science.

Curricular

VR; animation; user interfaces; Rendering; Modeling natural phenomena; procedural methods and sound synthesis; procedural textures and models. Computer Graphics I, II, III; Computer Animation; Design of User-Computer Dialogues; Computer Graphics Programming Tools; Procedural Methods; Modeling Natural Phenomena.

Facilities

SEASCF is a modern engineering computing center consisting of up-to-the-minute Unix-based servers and workstations from Sun, Hewlett-Packard, and Silicon Graphics, interconnected using the Network File System architecture running on Ethernet. SEASCF also has well-equipped microcomputer facilities with Apple Macintosh, IBM PS-2, and HP Vectra PC equipment. Other equipment includes: Seven Silicon Graphics Workstations; Management Graphics Sapphire film recorder; single-frame animation recording equipment; video editing suite; scan converter; CrystalEyes stereo; Logitech ultrasonic head tracking and 6-DOF mouse. Software: Vertigo; Maya; BRTMan (RenderMan renderer with global illumination support) Custom versions of Optik and Rayshade ray tracers. In-house

motion control, rendering, and sound synthesis and synchronization system.

Student Body

Thirty graduate students in the department; 6,000 undergraduate and 12,000 graduate students attend the university.

Deadlines and Financial Aid

Various fellowships and traditional state, federal and city aid are available to students. Contact the Financial Aid Office for details on obtaining financial assistance at the university.

Admission Requirements

In considering freshman applicants, the review includes a review of academic background, the strength of the high school program, and the grades earned in those courses. In addition, the school also takes into consideration standardized test scores, essay(s), letters of recommendations, extracurricular activities, interviews (if applicable), and interest in the University. Important admission dates and procedures apply.

Expenses

Total expenses are approximately $27,790 per year.

Contact

Department of Computer Science, The George Washington University, Phillips Hall, 801 22nd Street, NW, Suite 703, Washington, DC 20052. Telephone: 202-994-5920. Fax: 202-994-8259. Contact person: James K. Hahn. URL: http://www.cs.seas.gwu.edu/.

Additional Information

The program is augmented by various local institutions: George Mason University, for relevant courses in an art department; the Naval Research Laboratory, for state-of-the-art computing and VR facilities; NASA Goddard, for co-op positions and computing facilities; The National Crash Analysis Center, for supercomputing facilities and experience with real-world applications; and the GWU Medical school for actual VR-applications research.

Howard University

F/X Degrees Offered
Department of Art, College of Fine Arts. B.F.A. and M.F.A. in Art with a focus in Computer Graphics.

Curricular
Computer in the Arts; Desktop Publishing; Presentation Graphics; Animation; Image Processing; Digital Photography; Multimedia I and II; Workshop; Independent Study I and II; Digital Media and Multimedia Application; Internship; Advanced Animation.

Facilities
Electronic Studio (15 PCs, 15 Macintoshes, three servers); CLDC (Computer Learning Design Center) with 25 PCs; IBM laboratory with 15 SGIs with Maya and other animation software.

Student Body
There are 220 students in the Department of Art; 35 undergraduate students in the Electronic Studio; three graduate students.

Faculty Profile
Five faculty members teach in Computer Art and Animation.

Deadlines and Financial Aid
All scholarships and financial aid deadline: fall and spring semesters is February 15. spring semester only is November 1.

Admission Requirements
Application forms are available from the Director of Admission's Office. Application and payable to Howard University. Application fees are non-refundable. All official transcript and SAT scores are forwarded to the Admission Office.

Expenses
Tuition is $5,160 per semester.

Contact
Director for Admission, Department of Art, College of Fine Arts, Howard University, 2400 Sixth St. N.W., Washington, D.C. 20059. Telephone: 202-806-7047. Fax: 202-806-9258. Contact person: Dr. C.C. Lee, Computer Graphics Coordinator. Email: clee@fac.howard.edu. URL: http://www.howard.edu.

Additional Information
The Department of Art offers undergraduate courses leading to the Bachelor of Arts degree in Art History, Art Management, Fashion Merchandising, and Interior Design; the Bachelor of Fine Arts degree in Painting, Design, Printmaking, Photography, Ceramics, Sculpture, Electronic Studio, and Experimental Studio; graduate courses in Art history that lead to the Master of Arts degree; and graduate art studio courses that lead to a Master of Fine Arts degree. The Howard University Art Department is an accredited institutional member of the National Association of Schools of Art and Design. Howard University is located in proximity to the downtown area of Washington, D.C., and many businesses, advertising agencies and museums provide intern opportunities for advanced students.

West Virginia

West Virginia State College

F/X Degrees Offered
B.A. in Art with a concentration in Graphic Design.

Curricular
Graphic Design; Computer Graphics; as well as Drawing and Design courses.

Facilities
Three PCs; 12 Macintosh workstations; two scanners; four Zip drives; color and b/w printers.

Student Body
There are 45 students in the Computer Graphics area.

Faculty Profile
One faculty member teaches in the Computer Graphics area.

Deadlines and Financial Aid
Admissions deadline is Aug. 15 for the fall semester, and Jan. 15 for the spring. Contact the Financial Aid Office for more information on financial aid and scholarships.

Admission Requirements
Application, transcripts, ACT or SAT. There are no special admission requirements, though a review of a prospective student's portfolio of art work is preferred prior to admission for all art programs.

Expenses
Tuition is $2,851 per year for residents and $6,808 per year for non-residents.

Contact
West Virginia State College, Department of Art, Campus Box 4121, P.O. Box 1000, Institute, WV 25112. Telephone: 304-766-3198 or 800-987-2112. Fax: 304-766-5100. Contact person: George Trapp, Chair. Email: trapp@cs.wvu.edu. URL: http://www.wvsc.edu.

Additional Information
West Virginia University offers two Bachelor of Science degree options in Computer Science. The B.S. degree may be earned in either the Eberly College of Arts and Sciences (ECAS) or the College of Engineering and Mineral Resources (CEMR). Both degree options are offered via the Department of Computer Science and Electrical Engineering in the College of Engineering and Mineral Resources. The curricula are designed to qualify students for professional positions in business, industry research, government service, or graduate study in computer science. The requirements of the two CS degree options reflect the basic intent of the individual degrees. The degree offered in ECAS emphasizes software development, while the degree offered in CEMR has a more hardware-oriented flavor. Both degrees require a total of 128 hours to graduate; students must earn at least a C in every required course.

West Virginia University

F/X Degrees Offered
B.S. and M.S. in Computer Science.

Curricular
Courses include Computer Graphics and Interactive Graphics.

Facilities
Macintosh laboratories and various advanced hardware and software programs for producing

computer graphics. 15 Pentium 200 MHZ Dell Optiplex Machines with 32 meg of RAM with: Windows 98; Microsoft Office '97 (Word, PowerPoint, Excel, Access); SPSS; Eudora Pro 4.2; Netscape/FTP/Telnet, etc.; Internet Explorer. A limited number of stations have Corel Office and ArcView GIS. Software and systems are updated regularly.

Student Body

There are 21,743 students are enrolled in the university.

Faculty Profile

Undergraduate student-to-faculty ratio is 17:1.

Deadlines and Financial Aid

Undergraduates: applications are accepted after Sept. 15 for admission the following fall; WVU has a rolling admission policy. Jan. 15 for freshman Scholarships; February 1 for financial aid (Priority Date); February 15 for summer financial aid; March 1 for financial aid. Graduate students: most graduate programs offer research or teaching assistantships. West Virginia University annually employs 1,400 graduate students. These positions obligate the student to work between 12 and 20 hours, depending on the assigned duties. All graduate assistants are also eligible to apply for a remission of tuition and most fees. The departments encourage the students to apply for these positions beginning in the fall. Graduate assistantships are generally granted for a period of nine to 12 months. W.E.B. DuBois Fellowships are also available for graduate and professional students who are black citizens of the United States. Arlen G. and Louise Stone Swiger Doctoral Fellowships are available for doctoral students. In addition, grants, loans, work-study and other types of scholarships are available. Awards are based on financial need and academic ability. About 70% of WVU undergraduates receive some financial aid; 47% of aid given to resident undergraduates is as grants and scholarships.

Admission Requirements

Undergraduates: admission to WVU is based on a combination of high school GPA and ACT or SAT scores. Graduate students: submit an Application for Graduate Admission. This form requires a $45 non-refundable Service Fee. Have official transcripts sent directly to the WVU Office of Admissions and Records from the institution where you received your baccalaureate degree, as well as all institutions that you attended in the course of undergraduate or graduate study. Contact the school or college that offers your program to determine additional requirements of that program.

Expenses

Tuition is $3,548 per year for residents and $10,768 per year for non-residents.

Contact

Department of Computer Science and Electrical Engineering, West Virginia University, P.O. Box 6109, Morgantown, WV 26506-6109. Telephone: 800-344-WVU1. Fax: 304-293-8832. URL: http://www.arc.wvu.edu.

Wisconsin

Milwaukee Area Technical College

F/X Degrees Offered
A.A. in Visual Communications.

Curricular
Computer Graphics for Multimedia; Digital Darkroom Techniques; Multimedia Presentations; Interactive Multimedia Systems; Digital 3D Modeling and Animation.

Facilities
Six Macintosh and PC-based laboratories, with flatbed scanners; color printers including Dyesub; audio and video capabilities; video capture; CD and film recording; laser disc; digital cameras; film scanners.

Student Body
Sixty students in the department.

Faculty Profile
Eight faculty members teach in the department.

Deadlines and Financial Aid
FAFSA, FAAS and SAR available. Applications are available from Oct. 1 for the following fall, and March 1 for the following spring.

Admission Requirements
High school diploma or GED, proficiency in mathematics, language, and reading, application and fee, high school and/or college transcripts.

Expenses
Tuition is $75.57 per credit hour for residents and $495.32 per credit hour for non-residents.

Contact
MATC, 700 W. State St., Milwaukee WI 53233. Telephone: 414-297-6267. Fax: 414-297-8143. Contact person: Alain DeMars. E-mail: demarsa@milwaukee.tec.wi.us. URL:http://www.milwaukee.tec.wi.us/.

Additional Information
Five other campuses in the Milwaukee area.

University of Wisconsin at Madison

F/X Degrees Offered
B.S., B.F.A. and M.F.A. in Art.

Curricular
3D Modeling and Rendering; 3D Computer Animation; 2D Computer Animation; Multimedia/Interactive. Madison provides beginning and advanced study in the theory, history, and practice of computer-mediated art, ranging from computer-assisted publishing to interactive multimedia applications.

Facilities
Computer graphics laboratory is equipped with various hardware and software programs including Amiga workstations, digitizers, video toaster and Macintosh computers.

Student Body
There are 400 undergraduate, and 120 graduate Art majors in the department.

Faculty Profile
Thirty-two faculty members in the department.

Deadlines and Financial Aid
Various fellowships and traditional state, federal, and city aid are available to students. Contact the

Financial Aid Office for details on obtaining financial assistance at the university.

Admission Requirements
Applicants must submit an application and fee, transcript, and ACT or SAT score. Portfolio may also be requested. Graduate applicants are advised to contact the Graduate Office.

Expenses
Undergraduate tuition is $2569.35 per semester for residents and $9569.55 per semester for non-residents.

Contact
6241 Humanities Bldg., 455 N. Park St., Madison, WI 53706. Telephone: 608-262-1660. Fax: 608-265-4593. URL: http://www.arts.wisc.edu/.

Additional Information
The Department of Art is dedicated to education, research and service in the visual arts. The faculty and staff of professional visual artists, designers and art educators provide a stimulating educational environment to prepare students for careers in a broad array of creative fields. These include Art Education, Graphics (Printmaking, Photography, Graphic Design, Book, Artist), 2 D (Painting, Drawing and Computer Mediated Art) and 3 D (Sculpture, Wood, Metals, Glass, Ceramics), Video, Performance and Electronic Sculpture. The Department of Art's Visiting Artists/Critics Program presents public lectures usually given in room 2650 Humanities. The department's two galleries, Gallery 734 and the Seventh Floor Gallery, located regularly feature exhibitions in all visual media. Tandem Press is a self supporting studio established in 1987 to encourage research, collaboration, experimentation and innovation in the field of printmaking.

University of Wisconsin at Milwaukee

F/X Degrees Offered
B.F.A. in Fine Art with a concentration in Graphic Design; and B.F.A. in Film through the Film Department. B.F.A. in Inter-Arts.

Curricular
Foundations of Computer Art; Graphic Design I, II and III; Computer Graphics; Animation I; Animation Workshop; Advanced Media Production Workshop; Video and Film Production.

Facilities
Animation stand; magnetic film to optical sound recording; film and video production and post-production; film and video studio; film archives. Computer animation laboratory with a variety of systems and software.

Student Body
There are 23,000 students are enrolled in the university.

Faculty Profile
Forty-six faculty members teach in the Art Department; nine faculty members teach in the Film Department.

Deadlines and Financial Aid
The Financial Aid Office administers or coordinates several federal and state financial student-assistance programs. FAFSA must be submitted to the federal processor by March 1 for priority application filing.

Admission Requirements
Application and fee, transcripts, letters of recommendation or other documentation. Additional testing and a personal interview may be required.

Expenses

Undergraduate tuition is $2,219.40 per semester for residents and $8,595.00 for non-residents.

Contact

Peck School of the Arts, University of Wisconsin, Milwaukee, P.O. Box 413, Milwaukee, WI 53211. Telephone: 414-229-4762. Fax: 414-229-6154. Contact person: Leslie Vansen, Chair. Email: lvansen@uwm.edu.
URL: http://www.uwm.edu/PSOA//.

University of Wisconsin at Oshkosh

F/X Degrees Offered

Computer Science Department. The Computer Science program offers course work leading to a B.S./B.A. degree. Computer Graphics is an elective course within the Computer Science major.

Curricular

3D Modeling and Rendering; High-Level Programming.

Facilities

A laboratory of Sun Sparc stations is the primary hardware resource for the Computer Graphics courses; several PC and Macintosh laboratories are also available. Software includes: C/C++ compilers (Sun, gnu); Renderman (Pixar, Sunvision); OpenGL (Mesa); Tcl/Tk; xv; pbm package; gnuplot; POVray. New hardware and sofware includes: a new version of Linux; 2.4GHz Pentium 4 with 512MB of RAM, 17" flat screen; RedHat Linux 9; and a new LaserJet printer.

Student Body

There are 160 undergraduates in the department.

Faculty Profile

Sixty faculty members teach in the department.

Deadlines and Financial Aid

Various fellowships and traditional state, federal and city aid are available to students. Contact the Financial Aid Office for details on obtaining financial assistance at the university.

Admission Requirements

Application and fee, transcripts and ACT score.

Expenses

Tuition is approximately $3,500 per year for residents and $12,915 per year for non-residents.

Contact

University of Wisconsin, Computer Science Department, 800 Algoma Blvd, Oshkosh, WI 54901. Telephone: 920-424-2068. Fax: 920-424-0045. Contact person: Peter Worland, Chair. Email: worland@uwosh.edu.
URL: http://www.uwosh.edu.

University of Wisconsin at Stout

F/X Degrees Offered

Art and Design Department. Graphic Design concentration in Art and Design leading to a B.F.A. degree. B.A. in Fine Arts.

Curricular

3D Modeling and Rendering; 3D Computer Animation; 2D Computer Animation; multimedia/Interactive; Digital Painting/drawing; Digital Video; 3D Modeling and Rendering; Design for the Internet. The curriculum is based on foundation courses in general education and the visual arts, including mathematics, social sciences, humanities (including art history), drawing and design. Students in the

Bachelor of Fine Arts program may opt to pursue advanced studies in the studio arts emphases of ceramics, drawing, metals, painting, printmaking, and sculpture; or a concentration in graphic design, industrial design, interior design, or multi-media design. Regardless of emphasis or concentration, students in the program engage in a curriculum which is grounded in the fine arts, which values the critical and perceptual dynamics of art-making, the relevance of art history to contemporary art and design, and the analytical principles of aesthetics.

Facilities
Computer Facilities dedicated to Art and Design: Macintosh computer laboratory with 25 Macintoshes. Video Spigot; digital cameras; color scanners; CD authoring facilities. Primary software programs covered include: Add-Depth; Adobe Illustrator; Adobe Pagemill; Adobe Photoshop; Adobe Premiere; Adobe Streamline; Aldus Persuasion; Ashlar Vellum; Macromedia Fontographer; Macromedia Freehand; Macromind Director; Morph; QuarkXPress; Sculpt 4-D; Virtus Walk-through.

Student Body
There are 250 undergraduate students in the department.

Faculty Profile
Four full-time and two adjunct faculty members in the department.

Deadlines and Financial Aid
Various fellowships and traditional state, federal, and city aid are available to students. Contact the Financial Aid Office for details on obtaining financial assistance at the university.

Admission Requirements
Application and fee, SAT or ACT score, and transcripts.

Expenses
Tuition is $5,679 per year for residents and approximately $16,015.50 per year for non-residents.

Contact
University of Wisconsin, 323I Applied Arts Building, Menomonie, WI 54751. Telephone: 715-232-1693 or 800-44-STOUT. Fax: 715-232-1669. Contact person: Ron Verdon, Program Director. E-mail: verdonr@uwstout.edu. URL: http://www.uwstout.edu/.

Wyoming

University of Wyoming

F/X Degrees Offered
B.S., M.S. and Ph.D. in Computer Science.

Curricular
Computer Vision; Digital Imaging Processing.

Facilities
The fiber optic-based campus data network permits all computing systems on campus, including those in the Department of Computer Science, to communicate with each other. More than 2,000 personal computers and high-level workstations at several campus locations use the network and central computing facilities. The network can be accessed from off campus by a dialup service. At both the Department and University level, these computers provide a wide selection of languages and tools, including FORTRAN, Pascal, Prolog, C, C++, Microsoft Office, and WWW browsers. Within the Department, a variety of equipment is available for faculty and graduate student use. An open graduate student lab contains Pentium II 500s, running Microsoft Windows 2000 and Red Hat Linux. In addition, there is a computer classroom with removable hard drives that enable either Linux or Windows operating systems to be run, giving students exposure to either platform. The department also maintains a cluster of four dual processor Linux servers, a Linux file server, and four Windows 2000 servers. Two laboratories focus on specific areas of research and contain state-of-the-art equipment. The Knowledge Representation lab contains one Silicon Graphics (SGI) multiprocessor Challenge, several X-Terms and several Linux workstations. The High Speed Heterogeneous computing lab contains Windows and Linux workstations, SUN Ultras, and SGI O2s. These machines are connected to each other and to the campus network by a high-speed local network maintained within the Department. There are resources beyond computing equipment, of course. The University's Science Library has an extensive collection of over 8,000 computer-related volumes. In addition, the library maintains subscriptions to numerous journals in computer science and related areas of mathematics. The computer science collection is supported by a strong reference library and includes major collections of technical reports.

Student Body
A total of 11,000 students attend the university; 185 undergraduates, and 30 graduate students in the department.

Faculty Profile
There are 680 faculty members at the school; 14 faculty members in the department.

Deadlines and Financial Aid
Students of an alumni parent receive a discount on their tuition. $27 million is available for merit scholarships. Graduate assistantships and fellowships are available through the department.

Admission Requirements
ACT or SAT, application and fee for undergraduates. GRE scores, transcripts, application and fee for graduate students.

Expenses
Undergraduate tuition is $84 per credit hour for residents and $279 per hour for non-residents.

Contact
Department of Computer Science, Dept. 3315, 1000 E. University Avenue, Laramie, WY 82071-3315. Telephone: 307-766-5190. Fax: 307-766-4036. URL: http://www.cs.uwyo.edu/.

Appendix A

NASAD Recommended Institutions

The National Association of Schools of Art and Design was established in 1944 to improve educational practices and maintain high professional standards in art and design education. In order to assist educational institutions in fulfilling their responsibilities to students and the field of art and design, NASAD is guided by very strict values. The following schools have been recommended by NASAD as being institutions that uphold the values of this organization as well as the profession as a whole.

Academy of Art College

http://www.academyart.edu/

The Academy of Art College offers 11 majors, including Architecture, Advertising, Computer Arts, Fashion, Fine Arts, Graphic Design, Illustration, Industrial Design, Interior Architecture & Design, Motion Pictures & Television, and Photography. The hands-on art and design courses are taught by Department Directors and a Faculty of practicing professional artists and designers. The Academy's open admission policy allows all persons who wish to obtain an education in the visual arts access to an institute of higher learning; a portfolio is not required. Admission to the Academy is permitted during three yearly enrollment periods, prior to the start of the Spring, Summer, and Fall semesters.

Appalachian State University

http://www.appstate.edu/

Founded in 1899 as Watauga Academy, Appalachian State University evolved into a state teachers' college, later broadened its mission to include the liberal arts, gained regional university status, and in 1971 became a part of The University of North Carolina. Appalachian State University is a comprehensive university, offering a broad range of undergraduate programs and select graduate programs. Undergraduates receive a well-rounded liberal education and the opportunity to pursue a special field of inquiry in preparation for advanced study or a specific career. Graduate students engage in advanced study and research while developing and extending their academic or professional specializations.

Arcadia University

http://www.arcadia.edu/

U.S. News and World Report has ranked Arcadia University among the top colleges and universities in the Northern region. Founded in 1853 and located 25 minutes from Center City Philadelphia, Arcadia University offers undergraduate and graduate degrees in more than 30 majors and pre-professional programs. Non-sectarian, with strong ties to the Presbyterian Church, Arcadia University is committed to serving students of all ages and cultural backgrounds.

Art Academy of Cincinnati

http://www.artacademy.edu/

The Art Academy of Cincinnati is a long-established independent college of art and design providing professional degrees and community education programs for fine artists and designers. The Art Academy is enriched by the sharing of resources with the Cincinnati Art Museum and Mary R. Schiff Library. While preserving its history as a studio school, the Art Academy supports the students' artistic development with a strong liberal arts curriculum. The Art Academy recognizes that the most effective visual statements come from artists whose minds are broad and rich and can integrate the mind, eye and hand in the creation of art.

Art Center College of Design
http://www.artcenter.edu/

Art Center is internationally recognized for its programs in art and design. The college is a leader in exploring the digital and new-media frontier, and is equally committed to the acquisition of solid traditional skills. It offers the Bachelor of fine arts or Bachelor of science degree in Advertising, Environmental Design, Film, Fine Art, Graphic Design, Illustration, Photography, Product Design, and Transportation Design. Graduate programs in fine art, design, new media, and critical theory lead to the master of fine arts, master of science, or master of arts degree.

Art Institute of Boston at Lesley University
http://www.aiboston.edu/

The Art Institute of Boston at Lesley University is a professional college of visual arts, located in the Kenmore/Fenway area of Boston. An AIB education prepares students for a variety of artistic professions including: graphic design, web and multimedia design, book, advertising and editorial illustration, animation, documentary photography, photojournalism, fine arts photography, fine arts and art education. The Institute offers the Bachelor of Fine Arts degree, three-year Diploma, two-year post baccalau-

reate Advanced Professional Certificate programs, a low residency Masters of Fine Arts degree, as well as continuing and professional education, intensive workshops and pre-college courses.

Atlanta College of Art
http://www.aca.edu/

Founded in 1928, the Atlanta College of Art is a school of art and design in the Southeast. The Atlanta College of Art is the only accredited four-year art college in the nation which shares a campus with a noted museum, theatre company, and symphony orchestra. ACA students are immersed in a community of professionals who are dedicated to the development of thought, imagination and skills. Working with faculty who not only teach but are practicing professionals, students are challenged to synthesize new information, ideas and technology toward the pursuit of creative excellence. The Arts Center campus and the thriving city of Atlanta provide valuable professional opportunities for interns and graduates.

Auburn University
http://www.auburn.edu/

Auburn University is one of the South's premier land grant institutions. In 1856 the university first opened its doors for 80 students and a faculty of six. Today Auburn is the largest university in Alabama, with an enrollment of approximately 22,000. Students hail from all 50 states and nearly 100 foreign countries. Auburn University's mission is defined by its land-grant traditions of service and access. The liberal arts and sciences — introduced in the University's nationally recognized Core Curriculum — are the heart of Auburn's undergraduate programs. Auburn offers baccalaureate degrees in more than 130 areas across the spectrum of disciplines and provides the state's only publicly supported programs in many fields, including several in agriculture, architecture, building science, forestry, pharmacy and veterinary medicine. Particularly strong baccalaureate programs can be found in the Colleges of Business, Education, Engineering, Liberal Arts, and Sciences and Mathematics.

Ball State University

http://www.bsu.edu/cfa

Approximately 18,000 graduate and undergraduate students are enrolled, 56 percent of whom are women, are enrolled at Ball State University. Out-of-state students make up 8 percent of the total enrollment and international students 2 percent. The 950-acre residential campus in Muncie, Ind., includes more than 50 major buildings and a physical plant valued at nearly $710 million. A master plan calls for the entire campus to be developed as an arboretum. Ranked a research intensive institution by the Carnegie Foundation; seven academic colleges and a graduate school offer more than 140 undergraduate programs, 72 master's programs, and 15 doctoral programs.

Belhaven College

http://www.belhaven.edu/

Belhaven College is a Christian liberal arts college dedicated to helping students prepare for positions of leadership in a rapidly changing society. A community of professors and students working together in a Christian environment, Belhaven emphasizes the importance of the individual. In addition to a traditional, strong liberal arts program, Belhaven provides academic preparation and Christian experience. Belhaven College has a long and productive history of relationship with the Presbyterian Church. The college has a covenant relationship with the Synod of Living Waters of the Presbyterian Church (USA) and seeks to deepen its relationship with

various other Presbyterian bodies. Faculty and staff members are drawn from various denominations, with the primary Presbyterian denominations represented being the Presbyterian Church (USA), the Presbyterian Church in America, and the Evangelical Presbyterian Church. The college receives both financial support and students from these three denominations.

Bowling Green State University

http://www.bgsu.edu/departments/art

The School of Art is comprised of six major divisions (Art Education, Art History, Graphic Design, Digital Arts, Two-dimensional Studies, and Three-dimensional Studies), offering three distinct undergraduate degrees (BA in Art, BA in Art History, BFA in Studio Art) through the College of Arts and Sciences and the College of Education and Human Development as well as two graduate degrees (MA in Art History, MFA in Studio Art) through the Graduate College. Because of this diversity within the degree programs, the nature of courses varies to include professional training, academic/lecture formats, and studio involvement.

Bradley University

http://www.gcc.bradley.edu/art

Undergraduate studio and teacher preparation degrees offered by the Department of Art are the B.A., B.S., and the B.F.A. In undergraduate art history studies, the B.A. is offered. The department also offers both the M.A. and M.F.A. degrees in studio art. Admission to a program of study in the Department of Art begins with meeting the application requirements as provided by Bradley University for general admission. Students are accepted into the Department of Art as art majors receiving a Bachelor of Arts, Bachelor of Science, or Bachelor of Fine Arts degree. A portfolio review is not required but is recommended for entry into the studio art program. Upon completion of their second year of study, studio art majors declare an area of concentration from the following: ceramics, drawing, graphic design, painting, photography, printmaking, and sculpture.

California College of Arts and Crafts
http://www.ccac-art.edu/

CCAC offers programs that lead to a four-year Bachelor of Fine Arts (BFA) or a five-year Bachelor of Architecture (BArch). Programs are offered in the following areas: Fine Arts Program, Ceramics, Film/Video/Performance, Glass, Individualized Major, Jewelry/Metal Arts, Painting/Drawing, Photography, Printmaking, Sculpture, Textiles, Wood/Furniture, Design Program, Fashion Design, Graphic Design (concentration in Design & Media), Illustration, Industrial Design, Architectural Studies Program, Architecture (BArch), Interior Architecture (BFA). CCAC offers a two-year, Master of Fine Arts (MFA) program in the following fields: Design, Writing, Fine Arts, Ceramics, Drawing/Painting, Film/Video/Performance, Glass, Jewelry/Metal Arts, Photography, Printmaking, Sculpture, Textiles, Wood/Furniture. CCAC offers a two-year, Master of Arts (MA) program in the following field: Visual Criticism.

California Institute of the Arts
http://www.calarts.edu/

California Institute of the Arts was incorporated in 1961 as the first degree-granting institution of higher learning in the United States created specifically for students of both the visual and the performing arts. The Institute was established through the vision and generosity of Walt and Roy Disney and the merger of two well-established professional schools, the Los Angeles Conservatory of Music, founded in 1883, and the Chouinard Art Institute, founded in 1921. By 1971, degree programs in dance, film/video, and theater had been added to those in art and music; in 1995, a writing program in critical studies was added. Since its founding, the Institute has established a national and international reputation as a leader in the disciplines it represents.

California Polytechnic State University
http://www.calpoly.edu/

Cal Poly, San Luis Obispo is a nationally ranked, four-year, comprehensive public university that emphasizes a "learn by doing" educational experience for its more than 17,500 students. As a predominantly undergraduate, comprehensive, polytechnic university serving California, the mission of Cal Poly is to discover, integrate, articulate, and apply knowledge. This it does by emphasizing teaching; engaging in research; participating in the various communities, local, state, national, and international, with which it pursues common interests; and where appropriate, providing students with the unique experience of direct involvement with the actual challenges of their disciplines in the United States and abroad.

California State University, Chico
http://www.csuchico.edu/art

The Department of Art and Art History at California State University Chico is pleased to announce the offering of a new graduate level degree major program: Master of Fine Arts in Art Studio. The Master of Fine Arts (MFA) is a three-year, 60 unit, professional degree program which incorporates a comprehensive background in the fine arts as well as advanced development in patterns of studio specialization. The degree offers students progressive course work in critical theory, practiced criticism and art history. The combined studio and academic experience provides students with the opportunity to synthesize information at a higher level, while engaging in original research and a significant body of creative studio work. Candidates are accepted into the program in the following areas of concentration: Ceramics, Glass, Painting/Drawing, Printmaking, and Sculpture.

California State University, Fullerton

http://www.art.fullerton.edu/

The California State University Department of Art offers programs which include the scholarly fields of art history, theory, analysis and criticism; the studio fields of drawing and painting, printmaking, sculpture, crafts (including jewelry, wood and metal), ceramics (including glass), graphic design, creative photography, illustration, exhibition design, and entertainment art/animation; and the single subject teaching field of art education. Curricular plans for the Bachelor of Arts and the Bachelor of Fine Arts have been developed to meet the individual needs and interests of students in art.

Carson-Newman College

http://www.cn.edu/

Carson-Newman College offers a Christian, liberal arts education in an environment that encourages open intellectual inquiry and deeper spiritual maturity. Students receive a personalized education in small classes. Caring faculty and staff mentors get to know and nurture each student. The cultural heritage and geographic beauty of the Appalachian region enriches the Carson-Newman experience, and the college contributes to the environmental preservation and economic development of this national treasure.

Casper College

http://www.caspercollege.edu/

Casper College overlooks the city from the foothills of Casper Mountain. Beautiful red-rock terraces surround the campus. The 465-seat Kramert Theatre is a popular attraction for community residents and the Goodstein Foundation Library is one of the finest in the Rocky Mountain region. There is a student center on campus, three residence halls and a new fitness center.

Central Missouri State University

http://www.cmsu.edu/

Central programs are nationally or internationally known. Central gives you many opportunities to broaden your horizons intellectually, culturally, and socially. Central Missouri State University is located in Warrensburg, a town of approximately 15,000 residents, located 50 miles southeast of Kansas City at the intersection of U.S. Highway 50 and Missouri Highway 13. The campus is just 17 miles from Interstate 70. Nearly 11,500 students attend Central, with 55 percent of them female, 45 percent male, 9 percent ethnic minority and 4 percent international. Nearly 80 percent of the undergraduate campus population is made up of full-time students. The student-to-faculty ratio is 17 to one, and the average size of undergraduate classes is 25 students.

Cleveland Institute of Art

http://www.cia.edu/

The Cleveland Institute of Art was established in 1882. Over the years it has earned a reputation for being among the top ten professional colleges of art and design in the country. The CIA's academic structure and integrity allow for unusual success in realizing its goals. Its two-year foundation program strengthens existing skills and challenges students to explore the creative edges. Its broad-based liberal arts offerings give context to sixteen studio majors. The second year studio electives give students a chance to experiment with a major prior to third-year major selection. And the Internship program gives students real world exposure and contacts that contribute to a smooth transition to work or graduate school. With an enrollment of about 600 students, the Institute is a small artistic community. Eighty percent of classes have less than twenty students. The student-to-faculty ratio is ten to one which facilitates a master/apprentice teaching philosophy.

College for Creative Studies

http://www.ccscad.edu/

At CCS, students start with basic skills and core curriculum, then build out from there to more complex approaches—to higher levels of concept development, idea development and problem solving. Detroit is a great place for an art school. This art school derives a lot of its energy and character from the city of Detroit.

College of Saint Rose

http://www.strose.edu/

The College of Saint Rose is accredited by the Board of Regents of the State of New York and the Middle States Association of Colleges and Schools. Many of the academic departments hold prestigious additional accreditations including art, business, communication disorders, music and social work. The College's 39 undergraduate programs combine intellectual growth and learning with career preparation and are built on a foundation of study in the arts and sciences that create a context for advanced study in the major. Liberal education courses are characterized by attention to such skills as writing, critical thinking and information literacy.

The College strives to offer courses, programs and other opportunities (such as study abroad) that nurture value formation, spiritual development and responsible citizenship and well as an awareness of and respect for diversity. The College's 22 Graduate programs and 6 certificate programs are designed to move students to advanced levels in their chosen fields.

Columbia College

http://www.ccad.edu/

Columbia College is recognized as a leader in visual arts education and as a resource for artists. More than 1,500 students from 40 states and 30 foreign countries are enrolled in the four-year program of study, pursuing the Bachelor of Fine Arts degree in one or more of seven majors: Illustration, Advertising and Graphic Design, Media Studies (photography, digital imaging, video and film, storyboard and computer animation, photo illustration), Industrial Design, Interior Design, Fashion Design, and Fine Arts, including painting, drawing, ceramics, sculpture, printmaking, and glassblowing. In addition to major areas of concentration, they offer specialized courses of study in animation, art therapy, computer graphics, fashion illustration, product design, package design, and photography. Liberal arts courses are a large and vital part of their curriculum.

Cooper Union for the Advancement of Science and Art

http://www.cooper.edu/

The Cooper Union for the Advancement of Science and Art, established in 1859, is among the nation's oldest and most distinguished institutions of higher learning. The college, the legacy of Peter Cooper, occupies a special place in the history of American education. It is the only private, full-scholarship college in the United States dedicated exclusively to preparing students for the professions of art, architecture, and engineering.

Corcoran College of Art and Design
http://www.corcoran.org/

The Corcoran College of Art and Design is only a block from the White House and from the nation's historic Mall. It is a place where the past, present, and future of the visual arts come to life; the past in the museum's extensive collection of American and European masterworks, the present in its ongoing exhibitions of contemporary art, and the future in the classrooms and studios of one of the most distinguished colleges of art and design in the country. The largest non-federal art museum in the nation's capital, the Corcoran was founded in 1869 as an institution to be "dedicated to art, and used solely for the purpose of encouraging the American genius." It was Washington's first art museum and ranks with Boston's Museum of Fine Arts and New York's Metropolitan Museum of Art as one of the three oldest museums in the United States.

Cornish College of the Arts
http://www.cornish.edu/

For almost 90 years Cornish College of the Arts has educated students and nurtured artists who, as professionals, have consistently contributed to the culture of society. In 1977, the college, then called The Cornish Institute, became a fully accredited college offering Bachelor of Fine Arts and Bachelor of Music degrees. In 1986, the college was named Cornish College of the Arts. Prominent members of the Northwest School of Artists, including Mark Tobey, Morris Graves, Guy Anderson and William Cumming, taught at Cornish College. Martha Graham, the inventor of modern dance, also taught here. Merce Cunningham, the legendary contemporary

dancer/choreographer, and broadcast pioneer Chet Huntley were Cornish students. In more recent years, the college has nurtured the talents of Heart's Nancy Wilson, Brendan Fraser and award-winning composer Wendell Yuponce.

Del Mar College
http://www.delmar.edu/

Del Mar College offers many academic, occupational, technical, and continuing education programs. Each year, more than 24,000 students enroll in one of their credit and noncredit programs. Since their conception, they've helped more than a half million individuals build careers over the past 67 years.

Drake University
http://www.drake.edu/

Drake is a private, fully accredited, coeducational university on a 120-acre campus in Des Moines, the capital and largest city in Iowa. Drake offers more than 75 undergraduate majors and many graduate programs in its six colleges and schools - Arts and Sciences, including Fine Arts; Business and Public Administration; Education; Journalism and Mass Communication; Law; and Pharmacy and Health Sciences. Drake also offers many fine arts activities, from theater performances to music to art exhibits; campus visits by internationally known experts on a variety of topics; cultural celebrations; and NCAA Division I athletic events, highlighted by men's and women's basketball.

East Carolina University
http://www.ecu.edu/

East Carolina University, a constituent institution of The University of North Carolina, is a public doctoral university committed to meeting the educational needs of North Carolina. They offer baccalaureate, master's, specialist, and doctoral degrees in the liberal arts, sciences and professional fields, including medicine. East Carolina University is located in Greenville, North Carolina. The university is a center for education and medicine for the campus and local communities and contributes to the culture of the region through its popular performing arts series, a successful intercollegiate athletics program, and numerous educational and recreational events.

East Tennessee State University
http://www.etsu.edu/design

East Tennessee State University offers both graduate and undergraduate studies in studio arts, art education, and art history. They are fully accredited by the National Association of Schools of Art and Design. The "Kaplan/ Newsweek 2002" rates them as, "the best value for your tuition dollar." From humble beginnings in 1911 as a normal school educating teachers, with 29 students enrolled on opening day, ETSU has evolved into a regional university preparing students for the 21st century. East Tennessee State University is classified by the Carnegie Foundation as "doctoral research intensive." Over 100 degree programs offer a variety of educational possibilities through nine colleges and schools.

Florida State University
http://www.fsu.edu/index.html

Florida State University is a public and coeducational institution. It is a senior member of the ten state universities that compose the State University System of Florida. The main campus of the University is located in Tallahassee, the state's capital. Florida State University also offers degree programs in Panama City, Sarasota, and the Republic of Panama. In addition to the branch campuses, FSU offers a variety of overseas study opportunities for students during the regular academic year, as well

as in special summer programs. These include, during the academic year, the Florence, Italy; Panama, Republic of Panama; Valencia, Spain; and London, England programs. The colleges and schools offer courses of study in 25 major disciplines. In addition to the associate in arts certificate they now offer 96 authorized baccalaureate degree programs covering 198 fields, 100 authorized master's degree programs covering 193 fields, 1 authorized advanced master's degree program covering 1 field, 29 specialist degree programs covering 34 fields, two authorized professional degree programs covering eight fields, and 72 authorized doctoral degree programs covering 135 fields.

Francis Marion University
http://www.fmarion.edu/famc

The Department of Fine Arts and Mass Communication offers major programs in art education, mass communication, theatre arts, and visual arts. Minors are offered in mass communication, music, theatre arts, and visual arts. Collaterals are offered in music, theatre arts, and visual arts. Introductory courses in art and theatre are offered for nonmajors. Students majoring in art education, theatre arts, and visual arts combine general education courses with lecture courses in art education, art or theatre history, and upper-level courses emphasizing studio/performance. Theatre arts majors may specialize in performance areas or design and technical production areas. Visual arts majors may specialize in ceramics, graphic design, painting, or photography.

Grand Valley State University
http://gvsu.edu/ah/

The Arts & Humanities Department at Grand Valley State University provides rigorous academic programs that integrate liberal and professional learning and that provide artistic knowledge, skills, and values. For the people of west Michigan it provides public cultural events, educational programs, and community service that enhance the quality of life in the region. The mission of the Division of Arts & Humanities is to study, teach, and extend the artistic and intellectual achievements of humanity.

Harrington Institute of Interior Design
http://www.interiordesign.edu/

The Harrington Institute of Interior Design is an independent institution of higher learning. They boast a number of high achievers in both local and national competitions. Harrington students: Have won four of the last six national awards presented by the American Society of Interior Designers Yale R. Burge Student Competition; annually participate in the Chicago Chapter of the International Interior Design Association Gilbert Grants Competition, winning many scholarships and honorable mentions; won first place in the Institute of Store Planners (ISP) International Competition; is ranked 8th by The Almanac of Interior Design & Architecture of all FIDER-accredited programs by over 300 employers nationwide.

Hartwick College
http://www.hartwick.edu/

Last year, students at Hartwick College directed fifteen plays and seventy-five students exhibited their work in the Foreman Gallery, which is part of the Yager Museum. Some of the organizations and institutions that make Hartwick a rich and multi-dimensional experience: A totally student-run dance club, Orchesis performs to sell-out crowds, twice a year. Dance styles range from tap to reggae to modern/interpretive dance. Hartwick is home to a large number of music clubs and organizations open to all students. During the year, you can also attend performances at the Hartwick College Choral

Festival, which involves high school singers, as well as dozens of performances by the music majors, especially during senior thesis season. A Native American poet and a novelist from Trinidad have come to read their work and share their experiences as published writers and artists.

Herron School of Art
http://www.herron.iupui.edu/

Herron is a community of more than 700 students, 70 faculty, and a dozen staff members who work together to create a very special environment. Herron is a School of Indiana University Purdue University Indianapolis, which is particularly responsive to the needs of its 27,000 students. Herron students benefit from the comfortable size and the nurturing atmosphere of an independent art school wedded to a full complement of an exciting university and capital city.

Hope College
http://www.hope.edu/

Hope College is a distinguished and distinctive four-year, liberal arts, undergraduate college, affiliated with the Reformed Church in America. The curriculum offers a variety of courses in 56 majors leading to a Bachelor of Arts, Bachelor of Music, Bachelor of Science, or Bachelor of Science in Nursing degree. Hope College is accredited by the Higher Learning Commission and a member of the North Central Association. Hope is also accredited by the American Chemical Society, the National Association of Schools of Art and Design, the National Association of Schools of Music, the National Association of Schools of Theatre, the National Association of Schools of Dance, the National League for Nursing, the National Council for Accreditation of Teacher Education, the Council on Social Work Education, the engineering commission of the Accreditation

Board for Engineering and Technology for the Bachelor of Science Degree with a major in engineering, the Commission on Accreditation of Allied Health Education Programs, and other agencies.

Illinois State University
http://www.ilstu.edu/

At the heart of a modern American university is its liberal arts college; and at Illinois State that heart lies in the College of Arts and Sciences, home to almost half the faculty and source of approximately half the university's course credit hours generated. The College has three related but diverse divisions that correspond to the three traditional approaches to knowledge: the Sciences, the Social Sciences, and the Humanities. ISU offers students many avenues to pursuing their arts degree.

Indiana State University
http://www.indstate.edu/

Indiana State University offers more than 125 majors, small classes (80 percent of which are taught by full-time faculty), and nearly 200 clubs and activities. Indiana State also offers a variety of first-year programs designed to help students make a successful transition to college life, including special advising and orientation programs, first-year seminars and learning communities.

*Indiana University
http://www.fa.indiana.edu/fina/home.html

The School of Fine Arts, founded in 1894, is today considered one of the premier art schools in the country. Over 450 undergraduate and graduate students pursue courses in art history and studio practice. An internationally distinguished faculty of 42 artists and art historians direct a wide range of programs. Studio areas include ceramics, drawing and painting, graphic design, metalsmithing and jewelry design, digital media, photography, textiles, printmaking, and sculpture. The Department of Art History offers programs in classical art; medieval art; Renaissance and Baroque art; Modern art; the art of Africa, Oceania, and Pre-Columbia America; Asian art; and art theory. Facilities include large studios and classrooms specifically designed to present visual material. Among the resources available to students are a collection of over 320,000 slides, over 90,000 volumes of books in the Fine Arts Library, and the collections of the Indiana University Art Museum.

Institute of American Indian Arts
http://www.iaiancad.org/

Having served more than 3.500 students from most of the 557 federally recognized tribes in the United States, cultural values are an important part of this institute's curriculum. In 1998, the U.S. Congress recognized the remarkable success of the IAIA and moved it from under the BIA to be an independent, public/private partnership which continues to receive some federal support. The IAIA is one of only three congressionally chartered higher education institutions and is a member of the American Indian Higher Education Consortium.

Jackson State University
http://www.artdept@ccaix.jsums.edu/

Jackson State University is a historically Black, coeducational, research-intensive public institution of higher learning that has been designated by the Board of Trustees of State Institutions of Higher Learning as the urban institution of Mississippi. In many ways, Jackson State University is a metropolitan composite of the other IHL universities. Like the larger school, it offers a breadth of academic programs at all levels. Like the smaller schools, it has a special focus on the area where it is situated, the Jackson metropolitan area.

Jacksonville State University

http://www.jsu.edu/

JSU classes are led by Ph. D. level faculty members, not teaching assistants. They have nationally recognized programs in business and teacher education. Graduates of many of the degree programs are 100 percent employed. Among the alumni are Randy Owen, lead singer of the award-winning group Alabama and Heather Whitestone McCallum, the 1995 Miss America. JSU has the laid-back charm, beauty and security of a small southern village, yet has the big-campus feel. Located at the foothills of the Appalachians about 1.5 hours Northeast of Birmingham and 2 hours west of Atlanta, Jacksonville offers a beautiful, scenic location.

James Madison University

http://www.jmu.edu/art

The School of Art and Art History discerns the following five distinct goals for the teaching of art at JMU: To prepare future professional artists and designers. To educate future art historians and museum specialists with a global perspective on the visual arts. To develop and license future elementary and secondary art teachers. To enrich the general education of non-art majors. To supply professional instruction in the visual arts for students who wish to enrich their education by studying art as a second major or minor. Affirming the belief that a knowledge and understanding of the visual arts is an indispensable part of any higher education, the School of Art and Art History offers students a wide range of learning experiences designed to encourage independent thought and creativity, and to develop a deeper appreciation of important artistic achievements throughout world history.

Kansas City Art Institute

http://www.kcai.edu/

A college of art and design, Kansas City Art Institute is a private, independent, four-year college of fine arts and design founded in 1885. Ranked among the nation's top 10 art schools by U.S. News and World Report, KCAI is an accredited institutional member of the National Association of Schools of Art and Design (NASAD), the Association of Independent Colleges of Art and Design (AICAD) and the North Central Association of Colleges and Secondary Schools. In addition, KCAI belongs to the National Portfolio Day Association, the members of which host portfolio days and career-in-the-arts events throughout the United States and Canada. KCAI combines intensive time in the classroom, extensive experience in the studio, a broad liberal arts emphasis, focused learning opportunities, and a dynamic campus community. Kansas City Art Institute is comprised of nearly 600 students (representing more than 45 states and several foreign countries) and approximately 75 talented artists and educated scholars who serve as KCAI's faculty. Students pursue the Bachelor of Fine Arts degree, in which a comprehensive liberal arts program is complemented by emphasis in one of the following studio majors: Ceramics, Design, Fiber, Illustration, Painting, Photo & New Media, Printmaking, and Sculpture. Majors in Art History as well as Studio Art with an Emphasis in Creative Writing are also available.

Kansas State University

http://www.ksu.edu/art

At Kansas State University, some career opportunities include graphic design and illustration, scientific and medical illustration, teaching and scholarship, museum and gallery work, arts administrator and mental health and community service work. K-State offers a variety of degree options. Programs lead to B.F.A. and B.A. degrees with concentration in drawing, graphic design, printmaking, painting, metals and jewelry, sculpture, ceramics, art history, art education, and pre-art therapy. Graduate study leading to the M.F.A. degree represents the terminal graduate degree in visual art. Drawing, graphic design, printmaking, painting, metal and jewelry, sculpture, and ceramics are degree concentration options.

Kent State University
http://www.kent.edu/art

The School of Art at Kent State University is one of the largest university art departments in the state of Ohio. The Cleveland Museum of Art, one of the finest in the United States, is less than one hour away, as is the Cleveland Orchestra, whose summer home at Blossom Music Center is a thirty minute ride. Cleveland has a small but growing gallery scene. The Akron Art Museum is twenty-five minutes away, and the Butler Institute of American Art in Youngstown is forty-five minutes from Kent. Students will find an excellent faculty committed to education. All are practicing professionals in art, craft and design, or are scholars in the fields of art education and art history. Kent has one of the few art schools in Ohio offering a comprehensive studio curriculum—twelve media areas in art, craft, and design. Summer workshops (Kent Blossom Art), are also available, with nationally known visiting artists, craftsmen, and designers.

Kutztown University of Pennsylvania
http://www.kutztown.edu/academics/visual_arts/index.shtml

Located on 325 acres in Kutztown (population: 4,500), the university is 20 miles from both Reading and Allentown, 90 miles from Philadelphia, and 100 miles from New York City. LVI International Airport is 25 minutes from campus. Currently, some 8,200 students are enrolled at the university from 20 states and 40 countries. They have 330 full-time faculty members and boast a favorable 17:1 student-faculty ratio. Sixty percent of the faculty have doctorates, 39% earned master's degrees, and 1% have Bachelor's degrees.

Laguna College of Art and Design
http://www.lagunacollege.edu/

The Laguna College of Art and Design prepares students to meet the challenges of further study in one of the four majors: Drawing & Painting, Graphic Design, Illustration, and Feature Animation. Throughout the Foundation Program, students investigate five general areas of study: 1. The Drawing Component is made up of structured drawing classes that expose students to both perceptual and conceptual modes of drawing. 2. The Design Component is organized as an integrated series of studio experiences that emphasize Two-Dimensional Design, Color Theory, and Three- Dimensional Design. 3. The Technical Studies Component introduces students to the latest technological advances and stylistic innovations seen in electronic media today, bridging the gap between traditional foundation courses and technology. 4. The Intro to the Majors Component consists of introductory courses in Painting, Graphic Design, Illustration, and Feature Animation. 5. The Liberal Arts Component introduces students to information and ideas outside the studio, to encourage intellectual depth and substance in the creation of their work.

Lawrence Technological University
http://www.ltu.edu/

With an enrollment of nearly 5,000 students, Lawrence Technological University is among Michigan's largest universities. The University offers nearly

50 academic programs at the associate, Bachelor's, master's, and doctoral levels through Colleges of Architecture and Design, Arts and Sciences, Engineering, and Management. The University's full service 115-acre campus in Southfield offers a complete range of modern academic, residential, and recreational facilities along with plenty of free parking. Lawrence Tech was founded in 1932.

Louisiana State University

http://www.lsu.edu/

Since 1860, LSU has served the people of Louisiana, the region, the nation, and the world. Research at LSU is conducted by faculty in academic departments and through institutes, offices, centers for advanced studies, and other special units. At any given time, more than 2,000 sponsored research projects are under way at the University. In addition, faculty members pursue numerous research projects that are not sponsored by outside agencies, as do many graduate students. LSU conducts two semesters, a summer term consisting of one or more sessions, and a three-week intersession each year, offering a great number and variety of courses of study. Curricula leading to Bachelor's degrees are offered in 71 major fields, master's degrees are offered in 75 major fields, and doctoral degrees are offered in 54 major fields.

Louisiana Tech University

http://www.art.latech.edu/

Louisiana Tech University offers Bachelor of Fine Arts degree in Graphic Design, Studio (Ceramics, Drawing, Painting, Printmaking, Sculpture), and Photography. They also have a graduate program in each of these areas, offering the Master of Fine Arts degree. The School of Art is fully accredited by the National Association of Schools of Art and Design. The faculty all are working artists. Located in an

excellent 40,000 sq. ft. facility, areas of study have up-to-date equipment for student use. Their photography lighting studio is equipped with strobes and tungsten lights. The main darkroom is equipped with sixteen quality enlargers. Two galleries exhibit work of artists from across the nation. The School also has a 10,000 sq. ft. auxiliary building which houses sculpture, woodworking, printmaking, and the ceramics labs. Each of these areas is also well equipped.

Loyola Marymount University

http://www.lmu.edu/colleges/cfa/art

The Art Department at Marymount University is a community of artists and art historians, teachers and students, professionals, and aspiring creators. The Department's curriculum is carefully crafted to allow ample opportunity for intellectual inquiry and for a continuous and direct experience of art. The Department of Art and Art History provides students with conceptual and technical skills. Studio artists attain competence in technical and conceptual skills. Courses in liberal arts help students gain a perspective of self and art in relation to past, present, and future. The liberal arts courses place strong emphasis on developing critical reading, research and writing skills which provide an optimum balance of both scholarly study and creative activity.

Lyme Academy College of Fine Arts

http://www.lymeacademy.edu/

The mission of the Lyme Academy College of Fine Arts is to provide the best education in Drawing, Painting, and Sculpture through study of the history, traditions, and principles of the fine arts and the Liberal Arts & Sciences. The Academy's curriculum is based on a respect for traditional forms of teaching which have produced master artists throughout the ages. The studio curriculum is centered around the study of nature and the human figure. The liberal arts curriculum provides a strong academic foundation necessary for advanced critical and creative thought.

Maine College of Art
http://www.meca.edu/

Maine College of Art is a college of art and design where nationally recognized faculty, interdisciplinary programs, and state-of-the-art facilities create an educational experience that gives fresh vision to Maine's legacy in the visual arts. Founded in 1882 and fully accredited, MECA educates artists at all stages of their creative careers, offering both the Bachelor and Master of Fine Arts degrees as well as a wide range of professional institutes and continuing studies classes for individuals of all ages. The College gallery, the Institute of Contemporary Art at MECA, has been hailed as one of the finest art spaces in the Northeast for the exhibition of leading edge contemporary art.

Maryland College of Art and Design
http://www.mcadmd.org/

The Maryland College of Art and Design is a place where the visual arts and the study of various academic disciplines are meshed to give students the knowledge and ability to transform your dreams of becoming an artist into reality. Studio classes are demanding and liberal studies (general education) courses, which help to inform your art, require extensive reading and writing. Activities outside the studio and the classroom increase your understanding of art, careers in art, the life of artists, as well as help you to gain insight into your own work. The Maryland College of Art and Design's degree program offers a foundation curriculum taught by practicing artists and parallel to the first two years of study in four-year independent colleges of art.

They teach you the traditional and technical skills you need to begin in an entry level position in the graphic design industry or to transfer to a four-year Bachelor's in fine arts program. Fine art, graphic design, web page design, curating, art education, advertising, fashion design, and interior design are some of the career paths Maryland College of Art and Design students have taken.

Maryland Institute College of Art
http://www.mica.edu/

MICA's undergraduate and graduate programs have consistently been ranked among the nation's top art programs by US News & World Report. Founded in 1826, Maryland Institute College of Art celebrated its 175th anniversary in 2001 and is the oldest fully accredited art college in the nation. BFA programs in ceramics, drawing, environmental design (interior design concentration available), experimental animation, fiber, general fine arts, general sculptural studies, graphic design, illustration, interactive media, painting, photography, printmaking, sculpture, video. Undergraduate concentrations in experimental animation, interactive media, and video; liberal arts programs in art history, cross-disciplinary studies, humanities and sciences, language and literature, and writing/poetry.

Maryville University of Saint Louis
http://www.maryville.edu/

Maryville University of Saint Louis is an independent, comprehensive, community-oriented University founded in 1872 by the Religious of the Sacred Heart. Primarily an undergraduate teaching university, Maryville offers select graduate programs in professional fields, including those leading to professional degrees. Art and design goals are to provide: 1. Professional programs in graphic design, interior design, studio art and art education (K-12) in collaboration with the School of Education; 2. A liberal arts program in studio art; 3. Liberal studies in art and design in support of the University core curriculum.

Massachusetts College of Art
http://www.massart.edu/

Massachusetts College of Art is a public, free-standing college of art and design. The college's professional baccalaureate and graduate degree programs enable students to contribute to the New England economy as fine artists, designers, and art educators, and to engage creatively in the well being of their society. Continuing education classes, exhibitions, and cultural programs fulfill the college's public purpose of providing access to the arts for the citizens of the Commonwealth.

Memphis College of Art
http://www.mca.edu/

Memphis College of Art is accredited by the Commission on Colleges of the Southern Association of Colleges and Schools to award the BFA degree in Fine Arts and Design Arts, and the MFA degree in Studio Art and Computer Arts. Additionally, Memphis College of Art is an accredited institutional member of the National Association of Schools of Art and Design. The college is located in a 342-acre wooded park in midtown Memphis adjacent to the Memphis Brooks Museum of Art and the Memphis Zoo. The Fine Arts and Design Arts faculty are professional artists who exhibit frequently and stay abreast of industry standards through their professional projects. Degree programs include: Computer Arts, Decorative Design, Painting, Photography, Print/Papermaking, Sculpture, Computer Arts, Graphic Design, Illustration, Photography, Fiber/Surface, Design, Painting, Print/Papermaking, Sculpture, and Interactive Media.

Milwaukee Institute of Art and Design
http://www.miad.edu/

The Milwaukee Institute of Art & Design (MIAD) is a private, non-profit corporation chartered by the State of Wisconsin for the purpose of providing a professional education to students of the visual arts and related fields. The college offers a Bachelor of Fine Arts degree in Communication Design, Drawing, Illustration, Industrial Design, Interior Architecture + Design, Painting, Photography, Printmaking, and Sculpture. The Milwaukee Institute of Art & Design is accredited by the Commission on Institutions of Higher Education of the North Central Association of Colleges and Schools. MIAD is Wisconsin's only 4-year independent, coed, professional art and design college. We offer a BFA in: Fine Art: Drawing, Painting, Sculpture, Photography, and Printmaking. Design: Communication Design, Illustration, Industrial Design, and Interior Architecture + Design. Minors include: All art & design disciplines, art history, writing, business, and advertising.

Minneapolis College of Art and Design
http://www.mcad.edu/

Founded in 1886, the Minneapolis College of Art and Design, MCAD, offers prospects for careers in the arts. Students can choose between four programs: \t "_top" Bachelor of Science: Visualization, \t "_top" Bachelor of Fine Arts in 14 majors, a \t "_top" Master of Fine Arts in Visual Studies, and a one-year \t "_top" Post Baccalaureate certificate program. MCAD's studies in Design, Fine Arts, and Media Arts, at both the undergraduate and graduate level, encourage students to progress to higher levels of artistic expression and intellectual investigation. MCAD also offers educational opportunities to the general public through its Continuing Studies, distance learning, and exhibition programs.

Minnesota State University

http://www.mnstate.edu/

Minnesota State University provides baccalaureate-level programs in the liberal arts, natural and social sciences, teacher education, business and technology, the fine arts, and professional areas. It provides selected graduate programs in response to regional needs. The University enhances the quality of life of the region with the professional, cultural, and recreational services offered by its students, faculty and staff.

Mississippi State University

http://www.msstate.edu/dept/art

The MSU Department of Art offers both an undergraduate degree in Art (Fine Art and Graphic Design) as well as a graduate program leading to a terminal degree in Electronic Visualization. Whether your plans include fine art, computer animation, multimedia, or graphic design, the aim of this school is to give you the necessary aesthetic foundation, skills, and knowledge needed to fulfill your vision by attending the Mississippi State University Department of Art. The Bachelor of Fine Arts degree in Art is a 143 hour, 4 1/2 to 5 1/2 year, professional studio degree with a series of in-depth studio experiences balanced by classes in the humanities and sciences. Emphasis areas in the Art Major include Graphic Design and Fine Art, with selected emphasis areas of Sculpture, Photography, Ceramics, Printmaking, or Painting.

Mississippi University for Women

http://www.muw.edu/

Mississippi University for Women is a public institution funded primarily by the State of Mississippi. MUW is dedicated to the liberal arts and to professional education for all students, with an emphasis on academic and leadership preparation for women. MUW offers degrees at the associate, baccalaureate, and graduate levels. Students select a major from liberal arts and prè-professional programs administered through the eight academic divisions: Business and Communication; Education and Human Sciences; Fine and Performing Arts; Health and Kinesiology; Humanities; Interdisciplinary Studies; Nursing; Science, and Mathematics.

Montana State University- Billings

http://www.msubillings.edu/art

The mission of the Department of Art at Montana State University-Billings is to educate students in the understanding, production, and analysis of visual art and culture. The curriculum is designed to prepare students to face the challenges and diverse career opportunities that exist within the discipline and to give students the knowledge, practical skills, and maturity of critical thinking that is necessary to embark on study at higher levels. This mission is accomplished through classes in various studio media; in art history, theory, and criticism; through individual advisement and assistance from a concerned faculty; through exhibitions in the Northcutt Steele Gallery, the Yellowstone Art Museum and other museums and galleries in the area, through the activities of the Art Students' League and the Potters' Guild; through the visiting artist programs; and through career advisement. The areas of specialization—art history, ceramics, drawing, painting, photography, printmaking, and sculpture—lead to a Bachelor of Arts degree in Art that may include teacher certification.

Montana State University-Bozeman

http://www.montana.edu/wwwart

The School of Art is a professional school within the University and is one of four subdivisions of the

College of Art and Architecture. The department's fourteen faculty members (all actively exhibiting artists or publishing scholars) offer strong courses leading to a Bachelor of Arts degree with programs in ceramics, jewelry/metalsmithing, painting, drawing, graphic design, sculpture, art history, and art education. The department also offers a Master of Fine Arts degree in ceramics, jewelry/metalsmithing, painting, drawing, and sculpture. All programs are accredited by the National Association of Schools of Art and Design (NASAD).

Montclair State University

http://www.montclair.edu/

The second largest university in New Jersey, Montclair State offers the advantages of a large university—a broad undergraduate curriculum with a global focus, a wide variety of superior graduate programs and a diverse faculty and student body—combined with a small college's attention to students. Presently the University is in the midst of an ambitious expansion program that will enable it to accommodate 18,000 students by 2008, the year of its centennial. The first element, Science Hall, opened in 1999. The Graphic Design MacLab in Finley Hall is the result of a partnership between the University's graphic design faculty and Information Technology personnel, opened in the spring of 2001. Called by Apple Computer the most technologically advanced graphic design facility in the state of New Jersey, it contains a teaching lab, a studio and a print and production studio.

Montserrat College of Art

http://www.montserrat.edu/

Montserrat College of Art is a college devoted to the Arts. Students are encouraged to get involved, explore new ideas, express themselves, and have fun. There are regular events throughout the year including the Halloween, Tropical and Global Holliday Parties and the Fashion Show. There are a number of groups and clubs such as Student Council, International Language Partners, and the Mural Committee. All of Montserrat's groups and clubs are open to all students.

Mount Ida College

http://www.mountida.edu/

Mount Ida College was founded in 1899 as a women's private high school on Mount Ida Hill in Newton Corner, Massachusetts. In 1939, Mount Ida moved to its present campus in Newton Centre on the site of the former Robert Gould Shaw II Estate. The first associate degrees were awarded in 1967. More than 25 majors combine the college's philosophy of combining a strong liberal arts foundation with professional preparation. The Newton campus has expanded significantly since 1939 with 80 percent of the buildings constructed in the past 15 years including a new academic technology building and an athletic center.

Munson-Williams-Proctor Arts Institute

http://www.mwpi.edu/

For more than 60 years, the School of Art has provided students of all ages with instruction by an excellent faculty of academically qualified, experienced professional artists, using exceptional equipment and facilities. The School of Art was started to provide a quality community program of studio art instruction and has expanded to offer dance and a college degree program. The school's mission is to enhance artistic appreciation, understanding and skill in people of all ages.

Murray State University

http://www.murraystate.edu/

For three-quarters of a century, Murray State University has educated students from around the world. They have grown from an enrollment of 202 students when the college was founded in 1922 to almost 10,000 today. US News consistently ranks Murray State among the leading universities in the South, and Barron's college guide lists MSU as "very competitive." Murray has also been singled-out as a "best value" by Kiplinger's Personal Finance magazine, ranking among the top nine public universities in the nation for quality education with affordable out-of-state rates. And MSU was one of only six public universities in America to make the prestigious "Hidden Treasure" list, just published by Kaplan Inc. Murray State is located in western Kentucky and features five academic colleges—Business and Public Affairs; Education; Health Sciences and Human Services; Humanities and Fine Arts; and Science, Engineering and Technology—as well as a School of Agriculture.

New England School of Art and Design at Suffolk University
http://www.suffolk.edu

Suffolk University is a comprehensive private university located on Boston's historic Beacon Hill. This global university offers a wide range of undergraduate and graduate degrees in over 70 areas of study. Distinguished by its teaching, the university utilizes the intellectual contributions of its faculty to provide a diverse, challenging and uniquely supportive environment in which motivated and capable students flourish. The school offers 56 undergraduate and graduate degree and certificate programs; it was one of 300 schools nationwide named in Barron's Best Buys in College Education; and named one of the Best 201 Colleges for the Real World. The New England School of Art & Design at Suffolk University, offers B.F.A. and diploma programs in Interior Design, Graphic Design and Fine Arts, as well as an M.A. program in Interior Design; B.F.A. and diploma programs in Interior Design accredited by the Foundation for Interior Design Education Research (FIDER); granted membership in the National Association of Schools of Art and Design (NESAD).

New Jersey City University
http://www.njcu.edu/

The mission of New Jersey City University is to provide a diverse population with access to an excellent university education, and the support services necessary for success. In conjunction with each of the liberal arts and professional studies programs is the opportunity for a practical application of the knowledge and skills gained in class. Paid internships allow students to develop their talents in professional settings. The New Jersey City University Cooperative Education Program is a national leader in this merging of academic development and applied learning. Its compact campus and low student/faculty ratio foster a congenial atmosphere. Through individualized support services in such areas as orientation to college, academic advisement, personal counseling and career counseling, the University helps students to define and expand their personal and academic goals.

New World School of the Arts
http://www.mdcc.edu/nwsa

New World School of the Arts was created by the Florida Legislature in 1984 as a Center of Excellence in the visual and performing arts. A unique collaborative venture of the University of Florida, Miami-Dade Community College, and Miami-Dade County Public Schools, the school provides a comprehensive program of artistic training, academic development and preparation for careers in dance, music, theater, and visual arts. New World School of the Arts is an accredited institutional member of the

National Association of Schools of Dance, National Association of Schools of Music, National Association of Schools of Theatre, National Association of Schools of Art and Design. Students have easy access to firsthand experiences in the arts, both as audience and participants. Miami-Dade Community College's Wolfson Campus, adjacent to the school, provides classroom space and a library for the general studies curriculum as well as other student services.

New York School of Interior Design
http://www.nysid.edu/

Founded in 1916, NYSID is one of the country's leading interior design schools. Because the college is totally devoted to interior design, NYSID students receive a rigorous and in-depth education that covers everything from the fundamentals of color and spatial relationships to the most sophisticated computer-aided design methods. NYSID graduates acquire the skills designers need to meet the demands of this global profession, along with a rich education in liberal arts and design history. With an average enrollment of 650 students, the college retains a close environment. Recent expansion of the school's facilities by the distinguished architectural firm of Hardy Holzman Pfeiffer Associates includes a new library equipped with Internet and other computer access, an improved atelier for independent student work, a new CAD center, the Whiton Student Center with a lounge, café and gallery devoted to the exhibition of student projects, as well as the complete renovation of the 70th Street building for academic purposes.

Northern Illinois University
http://www.vpa.niu.edu/art

The School of Art, with a faculty of more than 60 artists, designers, and scholars, and an enrollment of more than 800 undergraduate and 130 graduate

students, is one of the best and most comprehensive public university art schools in the United States, with a nationally established reputation in a number of fields. Graduates from the School of Art are sought by employers ranging from large and small businesses, to public school systems throughout Illinois, to colleges and universities, as well as museums and galleries.

Northwestern State University of Louisiana
http://www.nsula.edu/

Northwestern State University has a long history of academic excellence, dating back more than 110 years. Founded in 1884 as the Louisiana State Normal School, Northwestern's initial mission was to train teachers. Today NSU offers degrees in more than 50 areas, each offering a mix of the class room training and practical experience needed for students to get a job after graduation. The university is up to date on the latest trends in the job market and has recently developed degree programs in computer information systems, hospitality management and tourism, criminal justice and liberal arts to meet the needs of employers throughout the country. NSU has a diverse student body made up of residents from all 64 parishes in Louisiana and more than 70,000 alumni in all 50 states and 50 foreign countries.

Ohio State University
http://www.arts.ohio-state.edu/

The College of the Arts at Ohio State is recognized as one of the finest, most diverse, and most comprehensive higher education arts institutions in America. The student body includes 1,500 undergraduate and 500 graduate scholars from all over the world. The College of the Arts at Ohio State (OSUArts) embraces all aspects of both the performing and visual arts, offering students an educational experience and the opportunity to study with distinguished faculty in diverse fields.

Oregon College of Art and Craft

http://www.ocac.edu/

Drawing is a tool that defines an artist as a visual creator. OCAC guides students to work fluently between two- and three-dimensionality. This includes offering sculpture-based courses within the drawing curriculum. Students are encouraged to incorporate their evolving skills in craft media with drawing, painting or printmaking. Facilities include a large open studio; two-story window facing an outdoor courtyard; easels and drawing boards; tool bench; a variety of hand and power tools; human skeleton; and large supply of still-life props. A large, open studio is often available for temporary work space, when class is not in session.

Otis College of Art and Design

http://www.otisart.edu/

Otis reinforces creativity through integrated learning; students take advantage of a coordinated set of offerings and disciplines to gain deep training in each discipline. They graduate with cross-boundary thinking and the ability to formulate trans-disciplinary solutions to problems that may not even exist at the time of their matriculation. Most Otis students come from very modest family backgrounds, but their careers propel them to economic success. The average household income of students' families is approximately $45,000. Ten or more years after graduation, the average household income of Otis graduates is approximately $91,000. Otis graduates have major influence on art and design.

Pacific Northwest College of Art

http://www.pnca.edu/

A highly specialized program of study, the Bachelor of Fine Arts degree prepares students for careers in their chosen discipline or for graduate programs in fine and design arts. PNCA's curriculum features an intensive studio experience, beginning with a grounding in the basic technique, progressing through periods of innovation and critical study, and culminating in the development of an independent style. Foundation courses provide the depth of understanding necessary for critical thinking and creative expression. Liberal Arts and Science courses balance the program with cultural and historical offerings, while providing the basic requirements for the BFA degree. Pacific Northwest College of Art requires a minimum of 120 semester credits for the Bachelor of Fine Arts degree, with 42 of those credits drawn from the Liberal Arts and Science Department.

Pennsylvania State University

http://www.sva.psu.edu/svawebsite/areas.html

The School of Visual Arts helps prepare students for careers as either studio artists, designers, or as art educators through a combination of professional and liberal studies. The B.A. or B.F.A. degree can be earned in any of seven studio areas, ceramics, drawing and painting, graphic design, metals, photography, print-making, or sculpture, and the B.S. can be earned in Art Education and Graphic Design/Photography. The B.A. degree combines a comprehensive liberal education with professional studies in art. The B.F.A. is a professional degree that develops the competence necessary for a career in art or as preparation for graduate study in art. The B.S. in Art Education helps prepare art teachers for either elementary or secondary schools, for educational positions in museums, arts centers, health or custodial care centers, and similar institutions. Bachelor degree concentrations are offered in the following areas of concentration: Art Education, Ceramics, Graphic Design, Metal Arts, Photography, Printmaking, and Sculpture.

Photographic Center Northwest
http://www.pcnw.org/

The Photographic Center Northwest offers fine art photography education through: intensive ten-week courses that can be taken individually or as part of a comprehensive program; instructors who meet a high level of excellence in mastery of the art and in teaching ability a curriculum that encompasses concept, theory, aesthetics, and technical proficiency; a 53-credit Certificate Program in fine art photography culminating in a thesis; a broad-ranging curriculum and the regular creation of new courses; an open admission policy and flexible scheduling, consistent with the standards of excellence in education. The school supports the arts community and enhances public awareness of fine art photography through: gallery exhibits; workshops; lectures; collaborative projects with other arts organizations; artists-in-residence; juried exhibitions; members' programs; subsidized programs for youth, and rental darkrooms.

Pittsburgh Filmmakers, Inc.
http://www.pghfilmmakers.org/

Pittsburgh Filmmakers is one of the largest and oldest independent media arts centers in the country. Founded in 1971 to provide media-making tools to artists, Pittsburgh Filmmakers serves everyone from emerging artists to established artists to fellow non-profit organizations and students. Pittsburgh Filmmakers' artist access program provides filmmaking, photography, video and digital production and post-production equipment to artists through-out Pennsylvania at very low rates. For over 30 years Pittsburgh Filmmakers has supported independent artists in the creation of their work. Any individual wanting to use Pittsburgh Filmmakers' equipment and facilities for the production of non-commercial work is welcome to join as an Artist Member.

Pratt Institute
http://www.pratt.edu/

At the school's site, you can view the 25-acre campus, learn the history of Pratt, find out the latest news and events at Pratt today, learn about the schools and programs, and even apply to the school on-line.

Purchase College, State University of New York
http://www.purchase.edu/

Purchase College, part of the State University of New York's (SUNY) network of 64 universities and colleges, was founded in 1967 by Governor Nelson Rockefeller who envisioned a major publicly funded university system. Today with its strong conservatory programs in Theater Arts & Film, Music, Dance, its School of Art + Design encompassing the full range of visual arts, and its accomplished faculty in Humanities, Social Science and Natural Sciences, Purchase College is distinctive among other colleges in the country.

Ringling School of Art and Design
http://www.ringling.edu/

Ringling School of Art and Design recognizes that artists and designers play a significant role in society. The School's primary mission is to provide programs leading to a Bachelor of Fine Arts degree. Ringling faculty consists of professionally active and teaching-oriented artists, designers and scholars. Ringling School of Art and Design strives to enroll both full and part-time students from diverse backgrounds who intend to become professionals in the visual arts.

Academic programs and advising, career services, and an extensive co-curricular student life program prepare students for an art or design profession, or when appropriate, for continued studies on the graduate level. In addition to its degree program, Ringling School offers courses, lectures, exhibitions and other art-related services to the local and regional community through its gallery, library, continuing education and community service programs.

Roberts Wesleyan College

http://www.roberts.edu/

With an enrollment of more than 1,800 students, Roberts Wesleyan College is a leader among American liberal arts colleges with a Christian worldview. They offer over 40 undergraduate specialization programs, ranging from the liberal arts to nursing. The graduate programs include degrees in Education, Social Work or Master of Science in Management. They have national professional accreditation by the National Association of Schools of Music, the National Association of Schools of Art and Design, the National League of Nursing, the Council for Social Work Education, and the Association of Collegiate Business Schools and Programs.

Saint Louis Community College at Florissant Valley

http://www.stlcc.cc.mo.us/fv/art

The Arts and Humanities Department is a learning centered department presenting a variety of Art, Humanities, and Philosophy course offerings and programs of study. Staffed by well-trained, dedicated and professional, full-time and adjunct faculty, the department strives to create a learning environment focused on student success.

Saint Louis Community College at Meramec

http://www.stlcc.cc.mo.us/mc/dept/art/index.html

In the St. Louis Community College at Meramec Art Department, students will learn from professors who are renowned artists and teachers. The works of studio art faculty have appeared in prominent museums and galleries locally and nationally and figure in distinguished private collections. These include the Saint Louis Art Museum, the Art Institute of Chicago, the San Francisco Museum of Modern Art, the Dallas Museum of Fine Arts, the Australian National Gallery and the International Museum of Photography, George Eastman House. The St. Louis Community College at Meramec Art Department offers exceptional educational opportunities in many different disciplines. The Fine Art programs include drawing, painting, sculpture, printmaking, ceramics and photography. The Graphic Communications program is a respected vocational program with courses in illustration, graphic design, typography, computer graphics and production. Through the Meramec Art Department, you may also choose studies in architecture, interior design, art history and more.

Saint Mary's College

http://www.saintmarys.edu/

Saint Mary's has been a leader in the education of women for more than 150 years. Founded and continually sponsored by the Sisters of the Holy Cross, Saint Mary's is a close-knit community built on a recognized tradition of academic excellence and commitment to developing the spirit as well as the mind. Saint Mary's consistently ranks at the top of its category in the U.S. News and World Report's annual survey of American college's and universities. On this page under "Quick Facts" students will find a link to the 2001-2002 rankings in which Saint

Mary's ranks #1 in the "Midwest Comprehensive Colleges—Bachelor's" category. Saint Mary's pays particular attention to the rights and responsibilities of women in the worlds of work, church, and community.

Salem State College

http://www.salemstate.edu/

Salem State College is a comprehensive, publicly supported institution of higher learning located 21 miles north of Boston. Because Salem State seeks to build a community that includes all ages, races, and socioeconomic backgrounds, it offers baccalaureate and graduate degree programs responsive to the needs of a wide spectrum of individuals as well as to the needs of the Commonwealth of Massachusetts. These programs are offered throughout the year and include day, evening, and weekend classes.

San Francisco Art Institute

http://www.sfai.edu/

The Art Institute believes in a strong, comprehensive education that encompasses the fine arts, art history, and letters and science courses. The curriculum is developed to provide students with the skills and information necessary to develop their ideas and pursue work in their primary area of study.

San Francisco State University

http://www.sfsu.edu/

SFSU is part of the largest system of higher education in the country granting Bachelor's and master's degrees, the California State University (CSU). The 23 campuses served 407,000 students in fall 2002. SFSU is accredited by the Accrediting Commission for Senior Colleges and Universities of the Western Association of Schools and Colleges.

San Jose State University

http://www.sjsu.edu/

San José State University is a major, comprehensive public university located in the center of San José and in the heart of Silicon Valley. SJSU is the oldest state university in California. SJSU takes pride in and is firmly committed to teaching and learning, with a faculty that is active in scholarship, research, technological innovation, community service, and the arts.

School of the Art Institute of Chicago

http://www.artic.edu/saic

The School of the Art Institute of Chicago offers a comprehensive college education centered in the visual and related arts. The School of the Art Institute of Chicago's primary purpose is to foster the conceptual and technical education of the artist in a highly professional and studio-oriented environment. The teaching of studio art, the complementary programs in art history, theory, and criticism and liberal arts, the visiting artists, and the collections and exhibitions of one of the world's finest museums all contribute to the variety, the challenge, and the resonance of the educational experience. The museum galleries, the graduate studios and seminar rooms, the libraries, undergraduate studios, school galleries, and classrooms create an environment that facilitates the exchange of ideas among students at all levels.

School of the Museum of Fine Arts, Boston

http://www.smfa.edu/

In an effort to educate individuals who will become working artists of significance in the local and global culture, the Museum School commits itself to embracing a wide range of media and perspectives in the production of artwork. The School makes available numerous programs that accommodate the varied backgrounds and experiences of individuals interested in attending the Museum School. The Museum School allows students to choose the programs that best suit their individual needs and goals. These range from the Diploma, Fifth-Year, and Post-Baccalaureate programs to undergraduate and graduate degree programs offered in affiliation with Tufts University.

School of Visual Arts

http://www.schoolofvisualarts.edu/

The School of Visual Arts has been authorized by the New York State Board of Regents to confer the degree of Bachelor of Fine Arts on graduates of four-year programs in Advertising and Graphic Design; Art Education; Computer Art; Film, Video and Animation; Fine Arts; Illustration and Cartooning; Interior Design; Photography; and to confer the degree of Master of Fine Arts on graduates of two-year programs in Computer Art; Design; Fine Arts; Illustration as Visual Essay; and Photography and Related Media; and to confer the degree of Master of Professional Studies on graduates of the two-year program in Art Therapy.

Siena Heights University

http://www.sienahts.edu/

A Catholic university founded and sponsored by the Adrian Dominican Sisters, Siena Heights is a coeducational North Central accredited institution founded in the liberal arts tradition, offering associate's, Bachelor's and master's degrees. The university is headquartered in Adrian, Michigan with degree completion centers in Southfield, Monroe, Jackson, Battle Creek, Lansing, Benton Harbor, and Port Huron. Siena Heights is a Catholic university in Adrian, Michigan, with degree completion programs at off-campus centers across the state. Founded

in the liberal arts tradition in 1919 by the Adrian Dominican Sisters, Siena Heights enrolls a diverse community of traditional-age and working adult students in academic programs leading to associate, Bachelor's, and master's degrees.

Skidmore College

http://www.skidmore.edu/

Skidmore College is an independent, coeducational, liberal arts college located in Saratoga Springs, N.Y. The College is committed to providing its 2,200 students with a superior education in the humanities, sciences, and social sciences, as well as career preparation in fields such as business, education, social work, and the fine and performing arts. Skidmore is an independent, coeducational, liberal arts college with an enrollment of 2,200 men and women and a student-faculty ratio of 11:1. The College's 850-acre campus is located near the foothills of the Adirondack Mountains. Skidmore offers more than 60 majors in the liberal arts and pre-professional areas. The College grants the B.A., B.S., and M.A. in Liberal Studies degrees.

Sonoma State University

http://www.sonoma.edu/art

Art majors pursue studies leading to the Bachelor of arts degree with concentrations in art history, film history, or art studio. Within the art studio concentration emphases are available in painting, printmaking, photography, drawing, sculpture, and ceramics. Minors in art history, film studies, studio art, and arts management are also available. A program for students working toward a teaching credential is included within the curriculum and available through the education department. Several art and film history courses meet general education requirements. Designed specifically for the pursuit of art practices and the study of art history, film history and arts management, the department facilities are located in one of the best equipped physical plants in the country. The Art history curriculum provides a broad overview of traditional European contributions, an introduction to the arts outside the European tradition, familiarity with historical methodology and research, including online and electronic sources, and critical thinking. The film emphasis in art history situates film studies within the art historical discipline. The art studio curriculum is designed to develop the ability to create, analyze, interpret and evaluate art. Students learn to express their thoughts, feelings and values in a variety of visual forms.

Southern Illinois University, Carbondale
http://www.siu.edu/~apartphp

The College of Applied Sciences and Arts Department of Architecture & Interior Design consists of two program offerings, each leading to the Bachelor of Science degree. The programs offered include: Bachelor of Science in Architectural Studies and Bachelor of Science in Interior Design.

State University of New York, New Paltz
http://www.newpaltz.edu/

SUNY New Paltz offers undergraduate and graduate programs in the liberal arts and sciences which serve as a core for professional programs in the fine and performing arts, education, health care, business, and engineering. The location in the scenic Hudson Valley midway between the State Capital of Albany and metropolitan New York City provides unique opportunities for enriching the academic programs.

State University of West Georgia
http://www.westga.edu/~artdept

The Department of Art at the State University of West Georgia maintains high-quality undergraduate and graduate programs that impart broad-based and/or in-depth knowledge while fostering creative and intellectual growth, critical thinking abilities, and personal and social responsibility. The department maintains up-to-date studios, classrooms, and equipment that comply with national health and safety standards. The Department of Art also provides yearly opportunities for travel to various cities, both domestic and international for the purpose of viewing works of art and architecture in their context. The Study Abroad Program in Bayeux and Paris provides an introduction to another culture as well.

Stephen F. Austin State University
http://www.art.sfasu.edu/

The school encourages students to experience the arts in a variety of different ways. By encouraging students to talk and write about art, they promote the development of analytical and expressive skills. They also encourage the study of history and the recognition of the common ground of human experience. At SFA, they are committed to instruction that helps students obtain understanding and skill in the application of the fundamentals of art production. They offer many programs that aim to fulfill these goals.

Studio Art Centers International (Florence)
http://www.saci-florence.org/

The mission of Studio Art Centers International is to provide a focused studio art studies program of depth and seriousness of challenge at undergraduate and graduate U.S. university levels. The studio disciplines are complemented by courses in the humanities since Studio Art Centers International is convinced that undertaking courses in both areas is essential in the formation of the artist. SACI's goals are to make the overseas study experience pertinent by ensuring that the highest level of instruction in all areas is made available and providing in optimal settings creative intellectual and aesthetic opportunities for the formative artist. Studio Art Centers International (SACI) is a program administered through the Institute of International Education (IIE, www.iie.org). IIE is the world's most experienced, nonprofit global higher education and professional exchange agency.

Syracuse University
http://www.syr.edu/schools/soad/soad.html

Syracuse University's vision of being the leading student-centered research university is a central theme in all areas of undergraduate education. Class sizes are generally small. 84% of undergraduate classes have fewer than 30 students in them. The full-time undergraduate student/ faculty ratio is 12/1. SU has excellent computer resources to which all undergraduates have access. Syracuse has a networked client/server computing environment that give students access to more than 1,400 computers. Other computer facilities and services include online registration for both undergraduates and graduates, computer purchase consulting and several hundred computers located within cyber cafés on campus. Syracuse also has numerous special programs that offer co-curricular learning opportunities.

Texas Tech University
http://www.art.ttu.edu/

The Texas Tech University School of Art supervises degree programs leading to the Bachelor of Fine Arts in Visual Studies (leading to teacher certification), Design Communication and Studio Art; Bachelor of Arts in Art History; Master of Art Education and Master of Fine Arts; and the Doctor of Philosophy

degree in Fine Arts with an option in Visual Arts. Degree programs within the school combine professional development in the visual arts with a strong liberal education. Computer technology is an important consideration in Art, Design Communication, and Studio Art programs. The art department offers students the opportunity to minor in art history, studio art, or fine art photography.

Tyler School of Art
http://www.temple.edu/tyler

For over sixty-five years, Tyler School of Art has offered students the opportunity to pursue study of the arts within small learning communities while also providing the advantages afforded by a large comprehensive research institution. The Tyler curriculum encompasses programs in the fine arts, crafts, design, art history, art education, and architecture. From advanced technology to the most traditional methods, Tyler School of Art is dedicated to providing education in the arts the aspiring artists of today.

Union University
http://www.uu.edu/

Union University is located in Jackson, Tennessee, a city of 55,000, located 80 miles east of Memphis and 120 miles west of Nashville. It's a private, four-year, coeducational liberal arts university, founded in 1823. Degree programs include: Bachelor of Arts, Bachelor of Science, Bachelor of Music, Bachelor of Science in Business Administration, Bachelor of Science in Nursing, Bachelor of Science in Medical Technology, Master of Business Administration, Master of Education, Master of Arts in Education, Master of Science in Nursing, Doctor of Education, Bachelor of Science in Organizational Leadership, Diploma in Christian Ministry, Associate of Divinity. Academic facilities include the 225,000 square-foot

Penick Academic Complex and the 30,000 square-foot Blasingame Academic Complex. Residential/student facilities include men's and women's apartment villages, commons buildings, and a 52,000 square-foot student union building. Athletic facilities include a 2,200-seat field house, baseball and softball parks, Olympic swimming pool, and tennis courts.

University at Buffalo, The State University of New York
http://www.art.buffalo.edu/

The Department of Art evolved from the Albright Art School, which joined the University at Buffalo in 1954. The Fine Art programs at UB are some of the most comprehensive programs available in the State University of New York system. Housed in the Center for the Arts, the Department of Art shares the facility with the Departments of Media Study and Theatre & Dance, with the Department of Music in adjacent Slee Hall. The proximity of the departments offers challenging opportunities for collaboration: art students work on theater sets or costumes; a sculptor's work is on stage for a saxophone concert. The faculty, a distinguished group of artists and designers, encourage excellence and diversity in an atmosphere of intellectual inquiry and professional practice. Students choose a concentration in computer art, communication design, painting, photography, printmaking, or sculpture. A series of exhibitions and visiting speakers complements the program.

University of the Arts
http://www.uarts.edu/

The University of the Arts rejoices in a 125-year tradition. The University has evolved from two century-old institutions: the Philadelphia College of Art and the Philadelphia College of Performing Arts.

The Philadelphia College of Art (PCA) was formed in 1876 along with the Philadelphia Museum of Art. Initially known as the Pennsylvania Museum and School of Industrial Art, the institutions were established in response to the interest in art and art education that was stimulated by the country's Centennial Exposition. In 1997 the University added a new College of Media and Communication, offering degrees in communication, writing for film and television, and multimedia.

University of Akron
http://www.uakron.edu/faa/schools/art

The University of Akron has 24,101 students representing 35 U.S. states and 102 foreign countries. The student body is a culturally diverse group that comes from a broad economic spectrum. Three-fifths are under 26 years old. About 68 percent of them are enrolled to earn a Bachelor's degree. The main campus, in the heart of Akron, Ohio, has 80 buildings on 180 acres. Landmarks include the high-tech Goodyear Polymer Center, the renowned E.J. Thomas Performing Arts Hall and the stately Buchtel Hall. There are about 200 student groups, including seven sororities, 14 fraternities and 28 honorary societies. They have two 15-week semesters, the first beginning in August and the second in January. There also is an optional 15-week summer session.

University of Arizona
http://www.arts.arizona.edu/

The College of Fine Arts at the University of Arizona has a world-class reputation. The faculty and alumni contribute to the identity as a distinguished student-centered place of learning and creative inquiry. The College of Fine Arts offers undergraduate and graduate degree programs through the School of Art, the School of Music and Dance, the School of Theatre Arts, and the Department of Media Arts. The College is also home to the Peter Treistman Fine Arts Center for New Media and the Wells Fargo Digital Imaging Laboratory, two of the Digital Arts research and learning facilities. More traditional arts spaces within the College include the Marroney Theatre, Laboratory Theatre, Crowder Hall, Holsclaw Hall, Ina Gittings Dance Theatre, and the Joseph Gross and Lionel Rombach galleries.

University of Bridgeport

http://www.bridgeport.edu/design

The UB Design programs are built to emphasize the importance of practical, theoretical, and professional activities and practices in the various design fields. UB Design facilities include studio spaces, computer labs, and libraries. Each student has a space for in-class assignments with an adjacent computer design studio, a clean room for large-scale mock-ups, and a well-equipped model shop and a photography studio. In addition to the full time faculty, practicing professional designers are invited to teach studio courses ensuring that the student receives a practical and current education. They have a strong Computer Aided Design (CAD) emphasis balanced by traditional skill development. They use programs that include Vellum 3D, form·Z, Photoshop, Illustrator, IronCAD, Alias Studio, Maya, Final Cut Pro, Premiere, Flash, and Solidworks.

University of Central Arkansas

http://www.uca.edu/

The University of Central Arkansas offers a variety of undergraduate and graduate programs in the liberal and fine arts, in the basic sciences, and in technical and professional fields in addition to its historical emphasis in the field of education.

University of Cincinnati

http://www.daap.uc.edu/

DAAP offers undergraduate degrees in eleven creative fields. Graduate degrees include: Master of Arts and Fine Arts, Master of Design, Master of Community Planning, and Master of Science in Architecture. Internally, they weave their four Schools together through interdisciplinary projects.

University of Denver

http://www.du.edu/art

A degree in studio art prepares the student for a wide variety of careers and positions, including work in an art gallery, auction house or museum; a profession as an artist or photographer; art editing, framing, teaching, grant writing, and other work for non-profit organizations. An undergraduate degree in studio art may also lead to graduate school and careers in art law, art therapy, arts administration, art education, public policy, public relations and fund raising. Students with multiple interests who want a liberal arts education with a major in art and a second major or minor in a field other than art should complete the program for a Bachelor of arts (BA) degree. Students who intend to become professional artists, to excel as art teachers, or who simply want a more thorough art training should apply for one of the programs for a Bachelor of fine arts (BFA) degree.

University of Florida

http://www.arts.ufl.edu/art

At the University of Florida, the programs provide broad-based instruction in visual arts disciplines, through a strong curriculum as well as through professional experiences such as exhibitions and internships. The University of Florida School of Art and Art History has the size (more than 40 faculty and 500 art majors), the diversity of programs and degree offerings, and the facilities which constitute a fully configured art school within the largest university in the Southeast. The curriculum provides excellent instruction in the areas of studio art, design, art education and art history, and also prepares students for advanced study or potential employment in art related fields as diverse as museum operations, advertising, information graphics and production, and arts management.

University of Georgia

http://www.visart.uga.edu/

The School of Art has a large and diverse faculty of artists, designers, educators and scholars with over 1,000 undergraduate art majors and 100 graduate art students. Located in Athens, Georgia, one hour from Atlanta, The University has over 30,000 students and is an active arts community that includes the Georgia Museum of Art. The School of Art also maintains a year-round Studies Abroad Program in Cortona, Italy. The undergraduate and graduate degree programs include: Art Education, Art History, Ceramics, Drawing & Painting, Digital Media, Fabric Design, Graphic Design, Interior Design, Jewelry and Metalwork, Photography, Printmaking, Scientific Illustration, and Sculpture.

University of Idaho

http://www.uidaho.edu/art

The Department of Art and Design allows students to experience a broad range of media and perspectives on the visual arts. Students are required to complete a core of courses designed to ensure an understanding of the historical and theoretical bases of Art and Design, while developing general competency in various media and practices. The BFA degree is designed for those students who wish to develop professional careers in art. Requirements

for the degree are stringent, and include intense involvement in studio work in the senior year, closely monitored by all faculty members, culminating in the development of a portfolio and written statement in support of a professional exhibition. The BS Art Ed is a rigorous degree specializing in studio art. The B.A. degree with a major in art is designed to ensure a broad, liberal education with an emphasis in art. The Master of Fine Arts degree is a 60-credit degree designed for students wishing to prepare themselves for a career as a professional artist, designer or teacher at the college or university level. The Master of Arts in Teaching degree is a 30-credit degree designed for those students who are certified teachers wishing to strengthen their experience in studio art and pedagogy in education. The Master of Arts in Teaching (Art) online degree program allows students to complete all degree requirements online.

University of Illinois, Chicago

http://www.uic.edu/

With 25,000 students, the University of Illinois at Chicago (UIC) is the largest university in the Chicago area and is located just west of Chicago's Loop. According to U.S. News & World Report, UIC is one of the most diverse and affordable universities in the nation. UIC is a "best buy," according to Barron's Best Buys in College Education. Degrees Offered: 88 Bachelor's academic areas; 86 master's disciplines; 58 doctorate specializations.

University of Massachusetts, Dartmouth

http://www.umassd.edu/

UMass Dartmouth provides educational programs, research, and continuing education services in the liberal and creative arts and sciences and in the professions. It offers a broad range of baccalaureate and graduate degrees.

In 1991 a new University of Massachusetts structure combined the Amherst, Boston, and Worcester campuses with Southeastern Massachusetts University and the University of Lowell. Thus Southeastern Massachusetts University became the University of Massachusetts Dartmouth. In 1997 construction was completed of the School for Marine Science and Technology, located on 2.6 acres in New Bedford near Buzzards Bay. A full program of research and development is now supported in this new facility. In 2001, the university opened new visual arts studios, classrooms and the University Art Gallery at the Star Store Campus in New Bedford, a structure transformed from a landmark department store into a vibrant arts center located in the city's National Historic Waterfront Park.

University of Massachusetts, Lowell
http://www.uml.edu/

UMass Lowell, one of five campuses of the University of Massachusetts, overlooks the Merrimack River in the historic industrial city of Lowell, just 25 miles northwest of Boston. With roots more than 100 years old, UMass Lowell offers programs in the arts, humanities, and sciences; education; engineering; health professions; and management. Some 13,000 resident and commuter students of all backgrounds pursue Bachelor's, master's, and doctoral degrees as well as professional certificates. The Lowell Normal School was founded in 1894 to prepare students to become teachers, and the Lowell Textile School was founded in 1895 to train technicians and managers for the textile industry, which dominated the region at the time. Over the next 75 years, the Lowell Normal School added degree programs in health professions, liberal arts, music, and the sciences, changing its name to Lowell State College to reflect those changes. In 1991, the campus became part of the University of Massachusetts system.

University of Memphis
http://www.memphis.edu/

The University of Memphis offers 15 Bachelor's degrees in more than 50 majors and 70 concentrations, master's degrees in 46 subjects, and doctoral degrees in 21 disciplines, in addition to the Juris Doctor (law) and a specialist degree in education. The U of M campus is located on 1,160 acres with nearly 200 buildings at more than four sites. The average age of full-time undergraduates is 23. It awards more than 3,000 degrees annually. With an enrollment of approximately 20,000 students, The University of Memphis has 25 Chairs of Excellence, more than any other Tennessee university, and five state-approved centers of excellence.

University of Montevallo
http://www.montevallo.edu/

A short drive south of Birmingham, the University of Montevallo College of Fine Arts has one of the most respected and dynamic College of Fine Arts in Alabama. The College of Fine Arts prepares students as visual artists, performers, musicians, arts educators, and communication specialists. The College provides instruction, performance opportunities, and cultural events essential to the liberal arts education.

University of Nevada, Las Vegas
http://www.unlv.edu/

The University of Nevada, Las Vegas, offers artistic, cultural, and technical resources and opportunities to the broadest possible community. It promotes research programs and creative activities by students and faculty that respond to the needs of an urban community in a desert environment.

University of New Orleans
http://www.uno.edu/

The University of New Orleans is located on the south shore of Lake Ponchartrain and only minutes from downtown New Orleans and the French Quarter. With an enrollment of over 16,000 students, UNO offers both undergraduate and graduate degrees through the doctoral level. Their six colleges offer a variety of studies in business administration, education, engineering, liberal arts, sciences, and urban and public affairs. Additional student services include six tutoring services, an on-campus pharmacy and medical office, student legal counseling, and a religious center. Students can also visit the new 8700 square foot Recreation and Fitness Center complete with swimming pool, cardiovascular room, and indoor track.

University of North Alabama
http://www.una.edu/

The University of North Alabama is a comprehensive regional state university offering undergraduate and graduate degree programs, serving residential and commuting students. Professional programs (i.e., Art, Chemistry, Music, and Social Work) within the College of Arts and Sciences are separately and nationally accredited by National Association of Schools of Art and Design (NASAD), American Chemical Society (ACS), National Association of Schools of Music (NASM), and Council of Social Work (CSW) respectively. Tuition is among the lowest found at comprehensive institutions of higher education in the State of Alabama and the nation; The campus has state-of-the-art campus automation providing access to computers, technologically enhanced instruction, and the world-wide web for all students, faculty, and other members of the campus community.

University of Northern Iowa
http://www.uni.edu/

UNI has ranked second in Midwest top public universities by U.S. News and World Report for five consecutive years. Nine out of the last 10 years UNI has been in the top 10 schools in the nation in terms of its ranking on May first-time pass rates and ranked first among Carnegie-classified master's level universities for the number of students studying abroad. It is home of Dr. Grammar website, which answers questions about grammar, usage, punctuation, spelling, documentation, or general language concerns. The Gallagher-Bluedorn Performing Arts Center is the newest Midwest performance facility to open in 20 years.

University of South Dakota
http://www.usd.edu/

Founded in 1862 by the Dakota Territorial Legislature, USD is the state's oldest university. The University offers more than 100 academic programs in its eight schools and colleges. Learning opportunities are also available through distance learning - the Rural Development Telecommunications Network. USD's Weekend University is tailored for adult learners on the weekends. The University is home to the state's only law and medical schools, and the only College of Fine Arts. The institution has a professionally accredited School of Business and the College of Arts and Sciences is a center for liberal arts education.

University of South Florida
http://www.art.usf.edu/

With almost 500 majors, 25 faculty, and 10 support staff, the University of South Florida offers degree programs in Studio Art and Art History. The School of Art and Art History provides a first class education in the visual arts. They have a variety of financial assistance packages for undergraduates and graduate students. They also offer internships as well as professional practice courses and workshops.

University of Southern Maine
http://www.usm.maine.edu/

The College of Arts and Sciences (CAS) is the largest college at the University of Southern Maine with 22 departments, and more than 45 majors. These majors encompass the range of disciplines in Fine Arts, Natural Science, Social Science, and Humanities.

University of Southern Mississippi
http://www.usm.edu/

The primary purpose of the College of The Arts is to provide its students with well-rounded preparation for professional and teaching careers in one of the many branches of art, music, dance, and theatre. The College of The Arts is organized into the School of Music, the Department of Art, and the Department of Theatre and Dance. Baccalaureate majors are available in Art, Art Education, Music, Music Education, Dance, and Theatre. Undergraduate minors are available in Art, Dance, Music, and Theatre.

University of Tennessee, Knoxville
http://www.utk.edu/

The university is a statewide higher education system that includes: The University of Tennessee-the main campus at Knoxville, the Health Science Center at Memphis, the Space Institute at Tullahoma, and the statewide institutes of agriculture and public service. The UT Knoxville campus during its history has produced some distinguished academics and statesmen, including one Nobel laureate, six Rhodes Scholars, five Pulitzer Prize winners, two National Book Award winners, nine U.S. Senators, and one U.S. Supreme Court justice.

University of Texas, Austin
http://www.utexas.edu/cofa/a_ah

The University of Texas at Austin is a major research university home to over 48,000 students, 2,700 faculty and 17,000 staff members.

University of the Pacific
http://www.uop.edu/cop/art/index.html

Pacific is an independent university offering a personalized education, small class sizes, and an extensive selection of undergraduate and graduate/professional programs. The University of the Pacific has 11 schools and colleges and more than 80 majors and programs of study. Pacific's main campus is neither a strictly liberal arts college nor a research based university. It is considered a comprehensive university by virtue of the range of its offerings. The student/faculty ratio is 15:1 and the typically small classes are taught by professors who are respected scholars, writers, artists, and researchers, but primarily teachers with a vested interest in engaging their students as thinking individuals.

University of Wisconsin, Stevens Point
http://www.uwsp.edu/art-design/

The College of Fine Arts and Communication, one of three in the University of Wisconsin System, offers the Bachelor of arts, the Bachelor of science, and the Bachelor of fine arts degrees in music, theatre, dance, communication, and visual art. and the only Bachelor of arts degree in arts management in the state. Communication majors may select from six areas of concentration as varied as public relations and advertising through broadcasting. Theatre and Dance programs have been recognized by the prestigious American College Dance and The American College Theatre festivals in Washington, D.C. The College is one of twenty nationally whose programs in the arts are certified by four national accrediting associations: the National Association of Schools of Art and Design, the National Association of Schools of Theatre, the National Association of Schools of Music and the National Association of Schools of Dance. There are over 1,000 majors in various arts and communication fields with seventy faculty and staff committed to first rate teaching at the undergraduate level. Masters programs exist in music education and in communication. The College sponsors over two hundred public events in the arts each year.

Valdosta State University

http://www.valdosta.edu/

In 1993, Valdosta State College was named a Regional University. In fall 1998, Valdosta State University adopted the semester system, along with other units of the University System of Georgia. Valdosta State University offers undergraduate work leading to the following degrees: Associate of Applied Science, the Associate of Arts, the Bachelor of Arts in 14 major programs, the Bachelor of Science in 10 major programs, the Bachelor of General Studies, the Bachelor of Science in Nursing, the Bachelor of Science in Health Fitness, the Bachelor of Science in Education in 10 major programs, the Bachelor of Business Administration in 5 major programs, the Bachelor of Fine Arts in 4 major programs, and the Bachelor of Music in 2 major programs. Graduate degrees offered include Master of Education in 11 major programs; Master of Arts with majors in English and history; Master of Science with majors in psychology, sociology, and criminal justice; Master of Public Administration; Master of Business Administration; Master of Accountancy; Master of Science in Nursing; Master of Music Education; Master of Social Work; the Education Specialist in nine major programs, and the Doctor of Education degree in three major programs.

Vincennes University

http://www.vinu.edu/

VU is a public, two-year, comprehensive, community college that features a full-service student residential environment. In 2001-2002, VU conferred some 1,250 degrees in Arts, Science, and Applied Science, plus Certificates of Graduation and Certificates of Program Completion. Situated on the banks of the Wabash River, the 100-acre VU campus includes more than 30 modern buildings featuring red-brick construction consistent with the first campus building—the 1803 home of VU's founder, William Henry Harrison. The Harrison mansion is open for tours. The campus also features red-brick walkways, abundant landscaping, and easy access to the legendary Wabash River and the George Rogers Clark National Historical Park. Vincennes is situated approximately 120 miles southwest of Indianapolis at the junction of U.S. highways 41 and 50. Vincennes campus enrollment as of October 2001 was 4,883, of which 2,911 were male and 1,972 were female.

Virginia Commonwealth University

http://www.vcu.edu/artweb

The School of the Arts is one of the nation's largest arts and design schools. The faculty's work is recognized by major museums, art and design publications, PBS television, National Public Radio, the Kennedy Center and regional theatres across the country, the National Endowment for the Arts, and important awards. The School of the Arts is ranked by U.S. News & World Report as one of the nation's top 20 arts schools.

Washburn University

http://www.washburn.edu/

Washburn has smaller classes with approximately 6,400 students. The average class size ranges from

15 to 40 students. The learning programs allow many of the students to take classes by ISDN video conferencing, CD ROMs, Web site integration or even through the on-campus public television station. Ninety-eight percent of Washburn graduates are employed six months after graduation, compared to the national average of seventy-three percent.

Watkins College of Art and Design
http://www.watkins.edu/

Watkins College of Art & Design is located in Nashville, a city with a long tradition of interest in the arts. There are more than 150 arts organizations in the city including a new art museum, a symphony, a ballet company, a fine music school, many active theatre companies, a state performing arts center, numerous art studios, and many private galleries. Within this active arts community, Watkins College is unique as the only independent art and design college in the region offering four-year, undergraduate Bachelor degrees with studio-based programs that produce practicing artists.

West Virginia University
http://www.wvu.edu/

WVU's main campus is located in Morgantown, 70 miles south of Pittsburgh, Pa., near West Virginia's northern border. WVU also has regional campuses in Parkersburg, Montgomery, Keyser, and Charleston. Through 13 colleges and schools, the University offers 169 Bachelor's, master's, doctoral, and professional degree programs.

Western Kentucky University
http://www.wku.edu/

Western Kentucky University is located in Bowling Green, Kentucky, a city with a population of 50,000, and located approximately 110 miles south of Louisville and 65 miles north of Nashville, Tennessee. Western's undergraduate division provides four-year programs leading to the Bachelor of arts, the Bachelor of fine arts, the Bachelor of general studies, the Bachelor of science, the Bachelor of science in nursing and the Bachelor of music degrees. Eighty-eight (88) academic majors and fifty-seven (57) academic minors are available. A number of professional and pre-professional curricula provide additional options. Eighteen (18) associate degree programs are offered leading to the associate of arts degree, associate of science degree, associate of applied science and associate of general studies degree. Three certificate programs are also offered. Graduate Studies offers the master of arts, master of arts in education, master of business administration, master of science, master of music, master of public service, and the master of public administration.

Western Washington University
http://www.wwu.edu./

For six years in a row, U.S. News & World Report ranked Western second among the top public, master's-granting universities in the West. In the 2003 ratings, WWU is one of only two public schools ranked in the top 20 master's-granting universities in the West, a region that stretches from Texas through California. The ranking places WWU in 11th place in its category nationally. Yahoo! named Western among the nation's 100 "most wired" universities. WWU came in at 59 in 2001, right behind Harvard University at 58. Academic reputation was the number one reason cited by entering students for choosing Western, which was the first choice of 82 percent of entering freshmen and the first or second choice of 97.5 percent.

Winthrop University
http://www.winthrop.edu/

A total of 80 undergraduate and 41 graduate degree programs and options are available at Winthrop University. Winthrop has achieved 100 percent national accreditation in all eligible academic programs. It is among only the top comprehensive teaching colleges and universities in the state to reach that level of accreditation. All classes are taught by faculty, and classroom instruction is further enriched by the expertise of distinguished visiting scholars, artists and practitioners. Eight residence halls provide a variety of living arrangements on campus. Further opportunities for service and participation are available through recreational sports and more than 100 clubs and organizations. Johnson Hall, which houses the departments of mass communication and theatre and dance, was recently expanded and renovated to include some of the finest training and performance facilities in the Southeast. Features include a 331-seat main theatre, experimental theatres, large dance studios, and modern editing labs. Rutledge Building and the Conservatory of Music, both of which serve the College of Visual and Performing Arts, were renovated to include new classrooms, gallery and performance space, studios and learning labs.

Youngstown State University
http://www.fpa.ysu.edu/

Youngstown State University's College of Fine & Performing Arts is centered in Bliss Hall and the McDonough Museum of Art. It is comprised of three departments: the Department of Art, the Dana School of Music, and the Department of Communication & Theater. The College brings over 400 events to the YSU campus and Youngstown/Warren Communities which includes dozens of art exhibits, eight major theatrical productions, and more than one hundred musical events.

Additional Schools

Alabama
Auburn University

Arizona
Scottsdale Community College

Arkansas
University of Arkansas at Little Rock

California
Allan Hancock College
A/PIX Computer Art Center
Brooks Institute of Photography
Butte Community College
California College of Arts and Crafts
California State University, Long Beach
California State University, Los Angeles
De Anza College
Diablo Valley College
Los Angeles City College
Los Angeles Valley College
Loyola Marymount University
Rancho Santiago College
San Diego City College
Solano Community College
Southwestern College
University of California at Riverside
Yuba College

Colorado
Aims Community College
Metropolitan State College of Denver

Connecticut
Middlesex Community Technical College
Wesleyan University
Quinnipiac College

Delaware
Wesley College

Florida
Jacksonville University
Orlando College
University of Miami School of Communication

Georgia
Atlanta College of Art
Augusta State University
Southern College of Technology

Hawaii
Leeward Community College

Idaho
Albertson College of Idaho
Idaho State University

Illinois
College of DuPage
North Central College
Southern Illinois University at Carbondale
Westwood College of technology

Indiana
Anderson University
University of Notre Dame
University of Southern Indiana

Iowa
Iowa State University
Mount Mercy College
University of Iowa

Kansas
Fort Hays State University
Southwestern College

Kentucky
Asbury College
University of Louisville
Western Kentucky University

Louisiana
Louisiana State University
Louisiana Tech University
Nicholls State University
Northeast Louisiana University
Xavier University of Louisiana

Maine
New England School of Broadcasting

Maryland
Frederick Community College
Goucher College
Hood College
John Hopkins University

Massachusetts
Boston University
Dean College
Fitchburg State College
Framingham State College
Greenfield Community College
Mount Wachusett Community College
School of the Museum of Fine Arts
Simmons College
Tufts University
University of Lowell
Williams College
Worcester State College

Michigan
Muskegon Community College
Northern Michigan University

Spring Arbor College

Minnesota
Hennepin Technical College
Arts of Minnesota
Minneapolis Community College
Minneapolis Technical College
School of Communication Arts in Minnesota
St. Cloud University
St. Olaf College

Missouri
Drury College
St. Louis Community College at Meramec
Washington University
Webster University

Montana
University of Montana

Nebraska
Hastings College
University of Nebraska at Kearney
University of Nebraska at Omaha

Nevada
University of Nevada at Reno

New Hampshire
Keene State College
University of New Hampshire

New Jersey
County College of Morris
Essex County College
Joe Kubert School of Cartoon and Graphic Art
Kean College of New Jersey
Mercer County Community College
Montclair State University
Rowan College of New Jersey
Seton Hall University
Trenton State College

New Mexico
New Mexico Highlands University
New Mexico State University
University of New Mexico at Gallup

New York
Adelphi University
Bard College
Borough of Manhattan Community College
Cayuga Community College
City University of New York-Hunter College
City University of New York-York College
College of Saint Rose
Genesee Community College
Hofstra University
Ithaca College
Long Island University at Brooklyn
Marist College
New School for Social Research
Saint John's University
Skidmore College
State University of New York at Binghamton
State University of New York at Oswego
State University of New York at Purchase
State University of New York at Stony Brook
Suffolk County Community College

North Carolina
Barton College
Duke University
Pembroke State University
Southwestern Community College

North Dakota
University of North Dakota

Ohio
Antioch College
Central State University
Denison University
Franklin University
Oberlin College

Xavier University

Oklahoma
Oklahoma State University
Rose State College
University of Oklahoma
University of Tulsa

Oregon
George Fox College
Lane Community College
Northwest Film Center
Oregon State University
Portland State University
Portland State University
University of Oregon

Pennsylvania
Albright College
Bucks County Community College
Community College of Beaver County
East Stroudsburg University
Gettysburg College
Indiana University of Pennsylvania
King's College
Kutztown University
Pittsburgh Filmmakers
Point Park College
University of Pittsburgh
University of Pittsburgh at Bradford
University of Pittsburgh at Johnstown
University of Scranton

Rhode Island
Roger Williams University
University of Rhode Island

South Dakota
Northern State University
University of South Dakota

Tennessee
Carson-Newman College
University of Tennessee at Chattanooga

Texas
Baylor University
Our Lady of the Lake University
Prairie View A&M University
Rice University
Southern Methodist University: Center for
    Communication Arts
Tarrant County Junior College
Texas Christian University
Texas Tech University
University of Texas at El Paso

Utah
Brigham Young University
Southern Utah University

Vermont
Bennington College
Lyndon State College
Saint Michael's College

Virginia
Hollins College
Radford University
Virginia Intermont College
Washington
Bellevue Community College
Evergreen State College
Seattle Central Community College
University of Washington

Washington DC
American University
Corcoran School of Art
Gallaudet University
University of the District of Columbia

West Virginia
Bethany College
Marshall University
West Liberty State College

Wisconsin
Beloit College
Marquette University
Milwaukee Institute of Art and Design
Saint Norbert College
University of Wisconsin at Eau Claire
University of Wisconsin at Green Bay
University of Wisconsin at Parkside
University of Wisconsin at Stevens Point

Index

N

O

X

Y